DAILY PRAYER 2012

Sunday Year B ✦ Weekday Year II

*A book of prayer for each
day of the liturgical year.*

Mary Catherine Craige

LTP

LITURGY
TRAINING
PUBLICATIONS

Nihil Obstat
Very Reverend Daniel A. Smilanic, JCD
Vicar for Canonical Services
Archdiocese of Chicago
May 26, 2011

Imprimatur
Reverend Monsignor
John F. Canary, STL, DMIN
Vicar General
Archdiocese of Chicago
May 26, 2011

Daily Prayer is based in part on the pattern established in *Children's Daily Prayer*, by Elizabeth McMahon Jeep.

As a publisher, LTP works toward responsible stewardship of the environment. We print the text of *Daily Prayer 2012* with ink that contains renewable linseed oil on paper that is 100% recycled and contains a minimum of 40% postconsumer waste. ✪ Although many de-inking processes use highly toxic bleach, this paper was processed using PCF (Processed Chlorine Free) technologies. The printing process used to manufacture this book is a non-heatset process that significantly reduces emission of volatile organic compounds (VOCs) into the atmosphere.

Printed in the United States of America.
ISBN 978-1-56854-962-0
DP12

For my mother, in thanksgiving for all her love and constant prayer for me, my brother, and my sister.

For don Carlo Pioppi, in gratitude for his encouragement and daily prayer for me and all his spiritual children.

For my dear friends, Caroline and Eleanor.

For all my readers. This book is for you. I have prayed for you through the writing of each page of this book and for every day of this year. May you encounter Jesus Christ in the liturgy and through his word.

Table of Contents

Introduction

Rejoice always.
Pray without ceasing.
In all circumstances give thanks,
  for this is the will of God for
  you in Christ Jesus.

1 Thessalonians 5:16–18

Welcome to *Daily Prayer 2012*, Sunday Year B and Weekday Year II! This edition of the well-loved prayer book provides a familiar order of prayer for each day of the liturgical year, from the First Sunday of Advent, November 27, 2011, to December 31, 2012. Readings from the daily Mass are provided, and the prayer texts and reflections are connected to the liturgical time, solemnities, feasts of the Lord, and the memorials of the saints. The prayers on these pages will inspire and bring you to a deeper appreciation for the word that is proclaimed and for Eucharist that is shared in the liturgical life of the Church.

The Order of Prayer

Daily Prayer 2012 follows a simple order of prayer: it begins with an opening verse with the Sign of the Cross, followed by a Psalm, a reading from the daily Mass, a brief reflection, Prayer of the Faithful, the Lord's Prayer, a closing prayer, and a closing verse with the Sign of the Cross. This order remains consistent for each day of the liturgical year, allowing its repetition to become part of your daily rhythm and routine.

Daily Prayer 2012 is organized by liturgical time, and the Psalter is located in the back of the book (pages 402–424).

Everything you need is conveniently contained in this resource. Refer to the table of contents for easy reference.

Daily Heading

Daily Prayer is easy to use. A heading is provided for each day of prayer so you will always know where you are and what you should pray. The heading includes the date and the name of the liturgical observance. Typically, optional memorials are not celebrated in this edition of *Daily Prayer*; however, if celebrated, the optional memorial will be noted in the heading. The liturgical observances are those according to the norms prescribed by the Secretariat of Divine Worship.

OPENING AND CLOSING VERSICLE WITH SIGN OF THE CROSS

The order of prayer begins each day with the Sign of the Cross and a versicle, or opening verse. The versicles are taken from the refrains proper to the Responsorial Psalms from the Mass; antiphons from the Liturgy of the Hours and *The Roman Missal*; verses from the Acclamation before the Gospel (*Lectionary for Mass*), and lines from scripture, especially the Psalms.

PSALMODY

The Psalms are an important part of Catholic prayer. As poetic readings from Sacred Scripture, the Psalms reflect upon God's saving work in various ways—praise, thanksgiving, and lamentation. The Psalms in *Daily*

Prayer 2012 have been selected by their liturgical significance. Psalms for Advent implore for God's return; Psalms for Christmas shout for joy; Psalms for Lent evoke the need for God's mercy and forgiveness; Psalms for Easter give praise for his glory and salvation; and Psalms for Ordinary Time give thanks for all that is good.

READING
Each day of prayer includes a reading from the daily Mass. This enables further reflection upon the word of God proclaimed during the Eucharistic celebration (Mass)—the source and summit of our faith. On some days, excerpts, not the full text, from the scripture passage have been selected. The Gospel is used for each Sunday, solemnity, and feast of the Lord.

REFLECTION
The author for this year has provided beautiful insights for meditation and reflection. These reflections are witty, yet challenging, as they guide the reader to a deeper relationship with God, neighbor, and self.

PRAYER OF THE FAITHFUL
The Prayer of the Faithful, sometimes referred to as the General Intercessions, Bidding Prayer, or Universal Prayer, is a prayer of the baptized who, through Christ, voice their concerns to God regarding the Church, the world, the oppressed, local needs, and other concerns. Thus, the prayers in this book connect the individual and small faith groups to the universal Church and those in most need of God's love and mercy. Although specific prayers are provided in this resource, others may be added.

THE LORD'S PRAYER
Jesus taught us how to pray. It is fitting to follow the Prayer of the Faithful with the Lord's Prayer, for it encapsulates the humility and reverence we give to our God—and neighbor—while asking for his mercy and forgiveness.

CLOSING PRAYER
The closing prayer follows the form of the traditional Collect. The prayers are "addressed to God the father, through Christ, in the Holy Spirit" (*General Instruction of the Roman Missal*, 54). Essentially, this prayer "collects" our daily prayer, the prayers found in this book, and those of our hearts and minds, those as individuals or groups, into one Trinitarian prayer, concluding with our assent of faith in the response "Amen."

USING THE BOOK
This resource may be used by individuals, families, or prayer groups; on retreats; to begin meetings or catechetical sessions, formational and youth ministry events; or as prayer with the aged, sick, and homebound. The prayers may be used at any time during the day, and, given this book's convenient size, it is easily transported to meet various prayer needs and situations.

The order of prayer may be prayed silently, or, especially for group prayer, prayed out loud. If used for prayer gatherings, it might be helpful to designate someone to open the prayer, lead the Prayer of the Faithful, begin the Lord's Prayer, and to conclude the prayer. Select an additional volunteer to proclaim the reading. Allow the faithful to read the Psalm together either as an entire group or divide the stanzas among the faithful with alternating recitation.

Feel free to adapt these prayers for specific needs—intercessions (or petitions) may be added, music may begin and conclude the service, and the Psalm, response to the Prayer of the Faithful, and the Lord's Prayer may be chanted and sung.

Other Uses for Daily Prayer

Daily Prayer 2012 may also be used in other situations or for various needs.

• Use the Prayer of the Faithful during the Mass. The prayers have been written in accordance with the *General Instruction of the Roman Missal*, 69 and 70. Since this book contains prayers for each day of the liturgical year, you may use the intercessions for every day of the year for Mass.

• Use the included reflections as homily sparkers and catechetical tools.

Customer Feedback

Daily Prayer 2012 is the eleventh edition of an annual publication; *Daily Prayer 2013* is already being prepared. Because it is an annual, it can be changed from year to year to become a better tool for your daily prayer. As you use this book and adapt it for yourself, you may have ideas about how it can be made more useful for your prayer. Feel free to e-mail us at DailyPrayer@LTP.org.

About the Author

Mary Catherine Craige is a graduate of Franciscan University of Steubenville where she received a BA in both theology and catechetics. She continued her studies at the Pontifical Institute of the Holy Cross in Rome, Italy. While in Rome, she also completed her training in Catechesis of the Good Shepherd at the Center for Montessori Catechesis. She is currently pursuing her MA in Montessori education.

✟ Lord, make us turn to you; let us see your face and we shall be saved.

Psalm 85 *page 411*

Reading *Mark 13:33–37*

Jesus said to his disciples: "Be watchful! Be alert! You do not know when the time will come. It is like a man traveling abroad. He leaves home and places his servants in charge, each with his own work, and orders the gatekeeper to be on the watch. Watch, therefore; you do not know when the Lord of the house is coming, whether in the evening, or at midnight, or at cockcrow, or in the morning. May he not come suddenly and find you sleeping. What I say to you, I say to all: 'Watch!' "

Reflection *Graziano Marcheschi*

We often fail to take the words seriously. "Watch," says Jesus. Watch for what? The tone is ominous. But our tendency is to dismiss the fearful. After all, tomorrow always comes; what seems dire at night always looks better in the morning. But Jesus is serious and the Church takes his message seriously. Advent is a time for preparing to celebrate the birth of Jesus and a time to contemplate his return and assess what we must do to be ready for it. The season requires that we factor it into the mix of demands we juggle daily. Tomorrow will likely come, but someday it won't. There is not an infinite number of tomorrows for anyone. Don't let him find you sleeping. "Watch!"

Prayers *others may be added*

As we prepare for the coming of Christ, we pray:

◆ Come, Lord Jesus, hear our prayer.

For Holy Mother Church, that during this time of Advent we may wait in vigilant expectation of the coming of Jesus Christ, we pray: ◆ For all public officials, that their work may aid the conversion of all nations, we pray: ◆ For the sick and suffering, that they may be strengthened in hope as they await Jesus Christ, who comes to bring peace and healing, we pray: ◆ For all families of our parish community, we pray: ◆ For all peoples, that, renewed by the time of Advent, we may be radiant with joy as we look to the coming of our Savior, we pray: ◆

Our Father . . .

Heavenly Father,
bless us with every abundance
as we begin this new year
in this time of Advent
in preparation for the
coming of your Son, Jesus Christ,
who lives and reigns with you in the unity
of the Holy Spirit,
one God, forever and ever.
Amen.

✟ Lord, make us turn to you; let us see your face and we shall be saved.

✝ Let us go rejoicing to the house of the Lord.

Psalm 85   *page 411*

Reading   *Matthew 8:5–11*

When Jesus entered Capernaum, a centurion approached him and appealed to him, saying, "Lord, my servant is lying at home paralyzed, suffering dreadfully." He said to him, "I will come and cure him." The centurion said in reply, "Lord, I am not worthy to have you enter under my roof; only say the word and my servant will be healed. For I too am a man subject to authority, with soldiers subject to me. And I say to one, 'Go,' and he goes; and to another, 'Come here,' and he comes; and to my slave, 'Do this,' and he does it." When Jesus heard this, he was amazed and said to those following him, "Amen, I say to you, in no one in Israel have I found such faith. I say to you, many will come from the east and the west, and will recline with Abraham, Isaac, and Jacob at the banquet in the Kingdom of heaven."

Reflection

Today in the Gospel the centurion demonstrates great faith in asking Jesus to heal his servant. He recognizes the authority of Jesus and knows that his petition will be granted if he only receives the word from Jesus. So great was his faith, that this response is more clearly evident in the revised translation of the prayers we say at Mass before receiving the Body and Blood of Christ in Holy Communion. May we imitate the centurion by coming to the Lord in faith, confident that he will hear and grant all our petitions.

Prayers   *others may be added*

With faith in your divine authority, we pray:

◆ Lord, hear our prayer and come to our aid.

For the Holy Father, that as the Vicar of Christ, he may guide all to the kingdom of God, we pray: ◆ For public officials, that they may exercise their authority well as they lead others toward truth and justice, we pray: ◆ For the sick, the poor and the suffering, that they may have faith in Jesus Christ who provides for all our needs, we pray: ◆ That each of us may be the face of Christ and help those in need and in difficult situations, we pray: ◆

Our Father . . .

Heavenly Father,
confident in your most holy
    and perfect will,
accomplished in your Son, Jesus Christ,
pour your healing upon us
and strengthen your Church.
We ask this through our Lord Jesus
    Christ, your Son,
who lives and reigns with you in the unity
    of the Holy Spirit,
one God, forever and ever.
Amen.

✝ Let us go rejoicing to the house of the Lord.

✝ Justice shall flourish in his time, and fullness of peace for ever.

Psalm 85 *page 411*

Reading *Luke 10:21–24*

Jesus rejoiced in the Holy Spirit and said, "I give you praise, Father, Lord of heaven and earth, for although you have hidden these things from the wise and the learned you have revealed them to the childlike. Yes, Father, such has been your gracious will. All things have been handed over to me by my Father. No one knows who the Son is except the Father, and who the Father is except the Son and anyone to whom the Son wishes to reveal him."

Turning to the disciples in private he said, "Blessed are the eyes that see what you see. For I say to you, many prophets and kings desired to see what you see, but did not see it, and to hear what you hear, but did not hear it."

Reflection

Today, Jesus calls us blessed for the things that we have seen and heard. Most specifically, we are blessed because we have seen and heard the Father through our Lord, Jesus Christ. Let us imitate Jesus in rejoicing in the Holy Spirit while giving praise to our heavenly Father for his greatness and all his abounding blessings. May our littleness and weaknesses never be an obstacle for us, but rather a means in which we turn even more humbly to the Lord as a child of God, our Father.

Prayers *others may be added*

Father, you have revealed your mysteries to the childlike; in humble confidence, we pray:

◆ **Heavenly Father, heed the voice of your children.**

For the Church, that she may be strengthened in her union with Jesus Christ and bring all our needs to the Father by the power of the Holy Spirit, we pray: ◆ For all nations suffering from war and division, that Jesus may come and bring peace and healing, we pray: ◆ For the poor, the sick, and the marginalized, that they may recognize the tender love and compassion of Christ, we pray: ◆ For all children, that they may be protected and continue to bring light and joy to their families and the whole world as they teach us the way to the Father, we pray: ◆

Our Father . . .

Heavenly Father,
rejoicing in the gift of life in the
    Holy Spirit,
we give you thanks for your goodness
and all your abundant blessings.
Continue to bless and strengthen us
as we wait for the coming of your Son,
    Jesus Christ,
who lives and reigns with you in the unity
    of the Holy Spirit,
one God, forever and ever.
Amen.

✝ Justice shall flourish in his time, and fullness of peace for ever.

Wednesday, November 30, 2011
Feast of Saint Andrew, Apostle

✝ Behold, our Lord shall come with power; he will enlighten the eyes of his servants.

Psalm 85
page 411

Reading
Matthew 4:18–22

As Jesus was walking by the Sea of Galilee, he saw two brothers, Simon who is called Peter, and his brother Andrew, casting a net into the sea; they were fishermen. He said to them, "Come after me, and I will make you fishers of men." At once they left their nets and followed him. He walked along from there and saw two older brothers, James, the son of Zebedee, and his brother John. They were in a boat, with their father Zebedee, mending their nets. He called them, and immediately they left their boat and their father and followed him.

Reflection

Andrew was a follower of John the Baptist, as he waited with anticipation for the coming of the Messiah. When Jesus called Andrew, he recognized him as the Messiah and immediately followed. May we imitate Andrew's vigilant anticipation for the coming of the Messiah during this Advent, and may we have the courage to follow Christ with the same abandon as Saint Andrew.

Prayers
others may be added

In anticipation of your coming, we pray:

◆ Lord, prepare our hearts.

For all the Church to imitate the lives of all the Apostles, we pray: ◆ For leaders of nations, that they may seek Jesus Christ, we pray: ◆ For those who are persecuted for their faith, that the witness of the martyrs may give them courage, we pray: ◆ That we may say yes to the call of Christ, following him in our unique paths to sanctity, we pray: ◆

Our Father . . .

Heavenly Father,
you give us the witness
of the martyr and apostle, Saint Andrew.
By the help of his prayers,
may we have the courage to do your will
as we follow the call of Jesus Christ,
through whom we ask this prayer.
Amen.

✝ Behold, our Lord shall come with power; he will enlighten the eyes of his servants.

✝ Blessed is he who comes in the name of the Lord.

Psalm 85 *page 411*

Reading *Matthew 7:21, 24–27*

Jesus said to his disciples: "Not everyone who says to me, 'Lord, Lord,' will enter the Kingdom of heaven, but only the one who does the will of my Father in heaven.

"Everyone who listens to these words of mine and acts on them will be like a wise man who built his house on rock. The rain fell, the floods came, and the winds blew and buffeted the house. But it did not collapse; it had been set solidly on rock. And everyone who listens to these words of mine but does not act on them will be like a fool who built his house on sand. The rains fell, the floods came, and the winds blew and buffeted the house. And it collapsed and was completely ruined."

Reflection

Today, Jesus tells us that it is most important to do the will of God. Our heavenly Father, in his loving providential care, has a plan of love and life for each of us. Following the will of God is our path to true joy. Jesus explains that those who listen to his words and put them into practice will not be foolish as others, but will possess true wisdom and will remain firm in strength.

Prayers *others may be added*

Listening to God's word, we pray:

♦ Your will be done, O Lord.

For Holy Mother Church, that she may forever listen to the voice of her Bridegroom, Jesus, and so stand firm against the attacks of the world, we pray: ♦ For all politicians, that they may grow in wisdom, we pray: ♦ For all those who suffer from natural disasters, we pray: ♦ That the grace of the Holy Spirit may open all hearts to hear the word of God and put it into practice, we pray: ♦ For all who suffer illness, hunger, and poverty, that they may receive the help and care they need, we pray: ♦ For the grace to surrender to the loving and providential care of the Father, we pray: ♦

Our Father . . .

Heavenly Father,
you call us to seek
your will in all things.
Send your Holy Spirit upon us
to open our hearts, and to hear your word
    and put it into practice.
We ask this through our Lord Jesus
    Christ, your Son,
who lives and reigns with you in the unity
    of the Holy Spirit,
one God, forever and ever.
Amen.

✝ Blessed is he who comes in the name of the Lord.

✝ The Lord is my light and salvation.

Psalm 85 *page 411*

Reading *Matthew 9:27–31*

As Jesus passed by, two blind men followed him, crying out, "Son of David, have pity on us!" When he entered the house, the blind men approached him and Jesus said to them, "Do you believe that I can do this?" "Yes, Lord," they said to him. Then he touched their eyes and said, "Let it be done for you according to your faith." And their eyes were opened. Jesus warned them sternly, "See that no one knows about this." But they went out and spread word of him through all that land.

Reflection

Jesus is passing by. Do we have faith enough to cry out to him to heal us? Today the two blind men in the Gospel are not ashamed to call to Jesus and ask him to show them his mercy. Through their faith, Jesus heals their blindness and they go out to proclaim what Jesus has done for them. As we await the coming of his Light this Advent, may we beg Jesus to give us the grace to see with eyes of faith.

Prayers *others may be added*

With faith in Jesus Christ, we pray:

◆ Open our eyes to see your Light.

For the Holy Father, that he may be given clear vision as he leads and guides the Church, we pray: ◆ For all war-torn countries, that their leaders may be given insight to facilitate peace between the nations, we pray: ◆ For all those who suffer from blindness and other illnesses, that Jesus Christ may touch them with grace and healing, we pray: ◆ For all the sick, the poor, and the lonely, that they may be comforted in their affliction, we pray: ◆ That Christ may shine upon all families and give them the grace of charity toward one another, we pray: ◆ For all the faithful departed, that they may be brought into the eternal radiance and joy of heaven, we pray: ◆

Our Father . . .

Jesus, our Messiah,
you heal the sick
and restore sight to the blind.
Shine your light upon us
and dispel the darkness of our lives,
that we may truly see you as you are,
who lives and reigns with the Father,
in the unity of the Holy Spirit,
one God, forever and ever.
Amen.

✝ The Lord is my light and salvation.

✝ A light for revelation to the Gentiles, and glory for your people Israel.

Psalm 85 *page 411*

Reading *Matthew 9:35—10:1, 5a, 6–8*

Jesus went around to all the towns and villages, teaching in their synagogues, proclaiming the Gospel of the Kingdom, and curing every disease and illness. At the sight of the crowds, his heart was moved with pity for them because they were troubled and abandoned, like sheep without a shepherd. Then he said to his disciples, "The harvest is abundant but the laborers are few; so ask the master of the harvest to send out laborers for his harvest."

Then he summoned his Twelve disciples and gave them authority over unclean spirits to drive them out and to cure every disease and every illness.

Jesus sent out these twelve after instructing them thus, "Go to the lost sheep of the house of Israel. As you go, make this proclamation: 'The Kingdom of heaven is at hand.' Cure the sick, raise the dead, cleanse lepers, drive out demons. Without cost you have received; without cost you are to give."

Reflection

Today we celebrate the feast of Saint Francis Xavier, Jesuit priest and missionary. Like Jesus in the Gospel, Saint Francis proclaimed the kingdom of God to hundreds of people. Today we honor him for the witness of his apostolic work and his zeal for souls. May we imitate Jesus and this great missionary saint to work for the kingdom by generously tending the harvest with charity and apostolic zeal.

Prayers *others may be added*

Heeding the words of the Gospel, we pray:

◆ **Master, send laborers for the harvest.**

For the Holy Father, that he may be strengthened to fulfill his duty to care for the sheep of his flock, we pray: ◆ For all bishops, priests, and deacons, that they may be given the grace to tend to the needs of all who are under their care, we pray: ◆ For all the marginalized, the poor, and the outcast, that those around them may generously offer help for their needs, we pray: ◆ For the sick, that they may offer their prayers and sufferings for the fruitfulness of missionaries and all peoples, we pray: ◆ That the Gospel of Jesus may be proclaimed to all peoples of every nation, we pray: ◆

Our Father . . .

Heavenly Father,
you called Saint Francis Xavier
to proclaim the Gospel to the lands
    of the East.
Inspired by his witness of charity and
    apostolic zeal,
may we generously work for the reign of
    your kingdom among our families
    and friends and throughout the world.
Grant this through Christ our Lord.
Amen.

✝ A light for revelation to the Gentiles, and glory for your people Israel.

✝ Prepare the way of the Lord, make straight his paths.

Psalm 85 *page 411*

Reading *Mark 1:1–5, 7–8*

The beginning of the gospel of Jesus Christ the Son of God.

As it is written in Isaiah the prophet: / *Behold, I am sending my messenger ahead of you; / he will prepare your way. / A voice of one crying out in the desert: / "Prepare the way of the Lord, / make straight his paths."* / John the Baptist appeared in the desert proclaiming a baptism of repentance for the forgiveness of sins. People of the whole Judean countryside and all the inhabitants of Jerusalem were going out to him and were being baptized by him in the Jordan River as they acknowledged their sins. . . . And this is what he proclaimed: "One mightier than I is coming after me. I am not worthy to stoop and loosen the thongs of his sandals. I have baptized you with water; he will baptize you with the Holy Spirit."

Reflection

Today we hear about the prophet John the Baptist. John fulfilled the prophecy of Isaiah as he prepared the way of the Lord by preaching conversion and repentance. Let us imitate the prophet John as we prepare the way of the Lord by pointing others to Jesus Christ, the Way, the Truth, and the Life.

Prayers *others may be added*

Turning to Christ, we pray:

◆ Come, Lord Jesus, and hear our prayer.

For the Church, that she may be strengthened in her work to lead all peoples to Christ, we pray: ◆ For the strength and protection of the Holy Father and all bishops, priests, and deacons as they prepare the way of the Lord, we pray: ◆ For leaders of all nations, that they may serve others in humility for the sake of Christ, we pray: ◆ For those weighed down by poverty or illness, that they may feel the nearness of Christ in their suffering, we pray: ◆ For all believers everywhere, that they may accomplish their duty to prepare the way of the Lord through their daily life, we pray: ◆ For all who have fallen asleep in Christ, that they may enjoy the eternal rest of heaven, we pray: ◆

Our Father . . .

Heavenly Father,
we worship you and give you praise
for sending us your Son, Jesus Christ.
Through our Advent preparations,
may you unite us ever more closely
    to you,
who lives and reigns with our Lord
    Jesus Christ,
in the unity of the Holy Spirit,
one God, forever and ever.
Amen.

✝ Prepare the way of the Lord, make straight his paths.

✝ Our God will come to save us!

Psalm 85   *page 411*

Reading   *Luke 5:17–26*

One day as Jesus was teaching, Pharisees and teachers of the law, who had come from every village of Galilee and Judea and Jerusalem, were sitting there, and the power of the Lord was with him for healing. And some men brought on a stretcher a man who was paralyzed; they were trying to bring him in and set him in his presence. But not finding a way to bring him in because of the crowd, they went up on the roof and lowered him on the stretcher through the tiles into the middle in front of Jesus. When Jesus saw their faith, he said, "As for you, your sins are forgiven."

Reflection

Today we read in the Gospel how the people glorified God for the incredible things they had seen. Jesus reveals himself to the people as the divine Messiah who heals the sick and the lame. But he teaches that the most important healing is the healing of our souls through the forgiveness of sins. Let us rejoice in the great miracles and blessings that God continues to work among us even today.

Prayers   *others may be added*

Rejoicing in God's healing power, let us pray:

◆ Lord, save your people.

That the Church, the Mystical Body of Christ, be ever more a wellspring of healing for all peoples, we pray: ◆ For those who work for justice and peace, that the power of the Lord may be with them, we pray: ◆ For all those who suffer illness and disease, that Christ's healing power may free them from sickness and give them courage to bear their hardships with hope, we pray: ◆ For all unbelievers, that Christ's life still at work among us may turn their minds and hearts to true life and peace, we pray: ◆ For all the faithful departed, that they may be brought into the eternal presence of the Holy Trinity, we pray: ◆

Our Father . . .

Heavenly Father,
you pour your gifts of healing and
    forgiveness
upon all peoples through your Son,
    Jesus Christ.
By the power of the Holy Spirit,
may all be brought to worship and
    praise you
forever and ever in life everlasting.
We ask this through Christ our Lord.
Amen.

✝ Our God will come to save us!

Tuesday, December 6, 2011
Advent Weekday

✝ Let the heavens be glad and the earth rejoice.

Psalm 85 *page 411*

Reading *Matthew 18:12–14*

Jesus said to his disciples: "What is your opinion? If a man has a hundred sheep and one of them goes astray, will he not leave the ninety-nine in the hills and go in search of the stray? And if he finds it, amen, I say to you, he rejoices more over it than over the ninety-nine that did not stray. In just the same way, it is not the will of your heavenly Father that one of these little ones be lost."

Reflection

Our heavenly Father desires that each one of us be united to him. Today in the Gospel, Jesus teaches us about the Father's love for us. It is the Father's will that none of his little ones be lost. His love for us is so great that it is described as a shepherd who would leave ninety-nine other sheep merely to find the one who was lost. Let us rejoice in the love of God who seeks to be with each and every sheep of his flock whether near or far.

Prayers *others may be added*

With confidence in our Father's love for us, let us pray:

◆ Good Shepherd, bring us back.

For the Holy Father, that he may shepherd the Church with paternal love and care for all peoples, we pray: ◆ For all bishops, priests, and deacons, that they may always be a good example to shepherd those entrusted to them, we pray: ◆ For all those who have wandered astray through sin, that Jesus Christ may lead them to true life and love, we pray: ◆ For all peoples, that they may rededicate themselves to seeking out those in need through works of charity and generosity, we pray: ◆ For all who have died and for those who grieve their loss, we pray: ◆

Our Father . . .

Heavenly Father,
in Jesus Christ you reveal your fatherly care for us.
Strengthen us in faith and courage
and open our hearts to receive your love.
We ask this through our Lord Jesus Christ, your Son,
who lives and reigns with you in the unity of the Holy Spirit,
one God, forever and ever.
Amen.

✝ Let the heavens be glad and the earth rejoice.

✝ O bless the Lord, my soul!

Psalm 85
page 411

Reading
Matthew 11:28–30

Jesus said to the crowds: "Come to me, all you who labor and are burdened, and I will give you rest. Take my yoke upon you and learn from me, for I am meek and humble of heart; and you will find rest for yourselves. For my yoke is easy, and my burden light."

Reflection

Today, Jesus invites us to come to him. During this time of Advent, we are preparing for Christ's coming; however, as he comes to us, he also invites us to come to him. The Gospel reminds us that only in Jesus Christ will we find true rest and true peace. In the midst of our work and our family life, let us constantly seek God's presence. May we have hope in him who renews our strength.

Prayers
others may be added

With hope in him who gives us rest, let us pray:

◆ Lord Jesus, hear our prayer.

For the Church, that united to Jesus Christ, she may forever be a refuge for the weary and a source of strength for the weak, we pray: ◆ For the Holy Father, for all bishops, priests, and consecrated ones who labor for the good of others; may they be fortified in all their good works, we pray: ◆ For the poor, the lonely, and the suffering, that they may experience the peace that Christ gives to those who suffer and struggle, we pray: ◆ For all people who work throughout the world, that their efforts may bear fruit, we pray: ◆ For all peoples, that they may turn to Jesus Christ and learn from his example, we pray: ◆ For all the faithful departed that they may be brought into the eternal rest and joys of God's heavenly kingdom, we pray: ◆

Our Father . . .

God, our Father,
you choose the weak and make
    them strong.
United to Jesus Christ,
the source of our strength and our hope,
may our labors prove fruitful
to the glory of your name,
that we may enter into your blessed rest
    by the power of the Holy Spirit,
who lives and reigns in union with you
and your Son, forever and ever.
Amen.

✝ O bless the Lord, my soul!

Thursday, December 8, 2011
Solemnity of the Immaculate Conception
of the Blessed Virgin Mary

✝ Sing to the Lord a new song, for he has done marvelous deeds.

Psalm 85 *page 411*

Reading *Luke 1:38*

Mary said, "Behold, I am the handmaid of the Lord. May it be done to me according to your word."

Reflection *Graziano Marcheschi*

Such a simple sentence . . . and yet it changed human history. Words like these don't just spontaneously issue from a person's mouth. It takes a lifetime to build a character that can recognize the source of a request and that can make so complete and generous a response. Mary does not become the "handmaid of the Lord" on this day. She is naming who she is, not who she's going to be. Without knowing it, Mary has prepared for this moment during all the days of her short life. Love of God and God's will doesn't come all at once. It takes years to build and it happens one small decision at a time. Only such a history could enable this young woman to risk the words "May it be done to me . . . " Mary is making her whole life available to God, not just her womb. Young as she is, she can't be unaware of the daggers that will be aimed at her if she says "yes." If we need a model for courage, here's the place to look.

Prayers *others may be added*

Aided by the intercession of our Mother Mary, we pray:

◆ Jesus, Son of Mary, hear our prayer.

For Holy Mother Church, that through the prayers of the Immaculate Virgin Mary, the Church may remain pure and spotless, we pray: ◆ For the Holy Father and all the bishops, priests, and deacons, that they may have health and fortitude to carry out their mission through the maternal protection of Our Lady, we pray: ◆ That all nations may experience true peace through the prayers and intercession of Our Lady, we pray: ◆ For the weak, the suffering, the sick, and the homeless, that Our Lady may be a refuge for all who seek comfort, we pray: ◆ That we may all follow Mary's lead of discipleship, we pray: ◆ For respect for the sanctity of life at all stages of development, we pray: ◆

Our Father . . .

Heavenly Father,
you sanctified the Blessed Virgin Mary
in the womb of Saint Anne,
creating her to be a pure and spotless
    dwelling place to bear your Son.
United to her prayers, and inspired by her
    virtuous example,
may we be led to the heavenly glory of
    your Son, Jesus,
who lives and reigns with you in the unity
    of the Holy Spirit,
one God, forever and ever.
Amen.

✝ Sing to the Lord a new song, for he has done marvelous deeds.

Friday, December 9, 2011

Advent Weekday

✝ Those who follow you, Lord, will have the light of life.

Psalm 85 *page 411*

Reading *Matthew 11:16–19*

Jesus said to the crowds: "To what shall I compare this generation? It is like children who sit in marketplaces and call to one another, 'We played the flute for you, but you did not dance, we sang a dirge but you did not mourn.' For John came neither eating nor drinking, and they said, 'He is possessed by a demon.' The Son of Man came eating and drinking and they said, 'Look, he is a glutton and a drunkard, a friend of tax collectors and sinners.' But wisdom is vindicated by her works."

Reflection

We can never please everyone. In scripture, we hear that the crowds criticized John the Baptist for fasting, but then they criticized Jesus for eating and drinking with sinners and tax collectors. Our current generation is the same as in Jesus' time. Today, Jesus calls us to reject the temptations of being lukewarm. Jesus speaks to the crowds to wake them from their stupor of complacency. Regardless of what others may say, the works of Jesus Christ reveal the truth of God made manifest in our lives. And those who follow his wisdom are blessed with prosperity and fruitfulness.

Prayers *others may be added*

With faith in the truth of Jesus Christ, we pray:

◆ O Incarnate Wisdom, hear our prayer.

For Holy Mother Church, our mother and teacher, that she may remain fruitful and prosperous as she remains united to God's Law in Jesus Christ, we pray: ◆ For the Holy Father, that he may continue to guide the Church in imitation of Christ, we pray: ◆ For all nations throughout the generations, that they may turn to the truth of Jesus Christ, we pray: ◆ For all those who are uncertain, doubting, lukewarm, or indifferent to matters of faith, that the works of God may reveal the truth to those who are seeking, we pray: ◆ For all those who have died and their family members who mourn for them, we pray: ◆

Our Father . . .

Father of all wisdom,
you sent your Son, Jesus Christ,
teacher and instructor of all things good,
to show us the way to heaven.
Through the power of the Holy Spirit,
stir up within us the desire
to follow you more closely
with renewed dedication and
   perseverance.
We ask this through Christ our Lord.
Amen.

✝ Those who follow you, Lord, will have the light of life.

✝ Lord, make us turn to you; let us see your face and we shall be saved.

Psalm 85 *page 411*

Reading *Matthew 17:9a, 10–13*

As they were coming down from the mountain, the disciples asked Jesus, "Why do the scribes say that Elijah must come first?" He said in reply, "Elijah will indeed come and restore all things; but I tell you that Elijah has already come, and they did not recognize him but did to him whatever they pleased. So also will the Son of Man suffer at their hands." Then the disciples understood that he was speaking to them of John the Baptist.

Reflection

Today in the Gospel the apostles ask Jesus about the fulfillment of the messianic prophecy of the coming of Elijah. These prophecies are fulfilled in John the Baptist, who came in the spirit of Elijah to prepare the people for the Messiah's coming. Jesus begins to prepare the apostles for his suffering and death as he explains that the people did not recognize the prophet John the Baptist and likewise do not recognize the presence of the Messiah.

Prayers *others may be added*

As we await the coming of the Lord, in prayer and penance we call upon the Lord:

◆ Come, Lord Jesus, hear our prayer.

For the Church throughout the world, that she may be renewed in her task to prepare the way of the Lord for all peoples, we pray: ◆ For leaders of all nations, that they may guide their people in peace and solidarity, being ever mindful of the poor and needy, we pray: ◆ That Christians everywhere may be stirred on to prepare the way of the Lord by reaching out in charity to the poor, the lonely, the sick and suffering, and to those who have no one to care for them, we pray: ◆ For all the dying, that, strengthened by the prayers of the Church, they may be prepared to enter into union with the Holy Trinity, we pray: ◆

Our Father . . .

O God,
our Father almighty,
you send us your Son, Jesus Christ,
our Priest, Prophet, and King to teach us
   your truth,
and to bring us into communion with you.
Open our hearts by the gift of your Spirit,
to recognize the coming presence of
   your Son.
Make us faithful witnesses of your love.
We ask this through Jesus Christ,
   Our Lord,
Amen.

✝ Lord, make us turn to you; let us see your face and we shall be saved.

✝ My soul proclaims the greatness of the Lord.

Psalm 85   *page 411*

Reading   *John 1:6–8, 19–23*

A man named John was sent from God. He came for testimony, to testify to the light, so that all might believe through him. He was not the light, but came to testify to the light.

And this is the testimony of John. When the Jews from Jerusalem sent priests and Levites to him to ask him, "Who are you?" he admitted and did not deny it, but admitted, "I am not the Christ." So they asked him, "What are you then? Are you Elijah?" And he said, "I am not." "Are you the Prophet?" He answered, "No."

So they said to him, "Who are you, so we can give an answer to those who sent us? What do you have to say for yourself?" He said: / "I am *the voice of one crying out in the desert, / make straight the way of the Lord." /*

Reflection

Today we are filled with joy as we rejoice with the whole Church in preparation for Christ who is both coming *again* and is *already* here among us. For generations and generations, God prepared his Chosen People for the coming of the Messiah. John the Baptist identifies Jesus as the Messiah, the one anointed by the Spirit, who brings glad tidings to the poor, heals the broken-hearted, and brings liberty to captives. Let us rejoice, for the Lord is near!

Prayers   *others may be added*

In expectation for the coming of Christ, we pray:

◆ Come, Lord Jesus, hear our prayer.

For Holy Mother Church, that she may be filled with renewed joy and hope as she awaits the coming of her Savior, we pray: ◆ For war-torn countries, that government officials may seek means of dialogue in order to bring peace to all nations, we pray: ◆ For all the sick and suffering, that they may have patience in their trials, we pray: ◆ For those who have died, that they may rejoice forever in the light and life of the Trinity, we pray: ◆ That Our Lady of Guadalupe may wrap all nations in her maternal mantle to bring them closer to her Son, we pray: ◆ For all young people, that they may turn from the temptations of pessimism and be filled with the life of Jesus Christ, we pray: ◆

Our Father . . .

Heavenly Father,
you prepared the generations for the
    coming of your Son.
Inspired by the words and witness of
    the prophets,
grant that we may seek him who comes to
    heal us and set us free.
Pour your Holy Spirit upon us,
that even in the midst of great difficulties
and trials we may persevere in joy.
We ask this through Christ our Lord.
Amen.

✝ My soul proclaims the greatness of the Lord.

Monday, December 12, 2011
Feast of Our Lady of Guadalupe

✝ My soul rejoices in my God.

Psalm 85 *page 411*

Reading *Luke 1:46–47*

And Mary said:
"My soul proclaims the greatness of the Lord; / my spirit rejoices in God my savior."

Reflection *Graziano Marcheschi*

This joyful feast has been a gift to all the peoples of the Americas. Blessed Pope John Paul II designated Our Lady of Guadalupe as patroness of the Americas. Especially venerated by the people of Mexico, La Guadalupana is recognized as mother of us all. What she said to Juan Diego, she proclaims to all: "Hear me and understand well, my son the least, that nothing should frighten or grieve you. Let not your heart be disturbed." Mary's journey to her exalted role as heaven's queen and universal mother began on the day she uttered the words in today's Gospel. Invited to lend her flesh to the son of God, to birth and rear him, and endure the trials that would inevitably come, she responds with words of praise. Her very being proclaims the glory of God: her essence expresses the joy she finds in her relationship with God. That's key to understanding Mary. The Annunciation is no singular moment in her life. It is the culmination of intimate moments with God. How could she proclaim the greatness of a God she does not know? How could she rejoice if she didn't already know God as Savior, friend, and Lord?

Prayers *others may be added*

In expectation for the coming of Christ, we pray:

◆ Holy Spirit, fill us with joy and gladness.

For the Church, that she may be guided by the intercession and maternal protection of Mary immaculate, we pray: ◆
For war-torn countries, that government officials may seek means of dialogue in order to bring peace to all nations, we pray: ◆ For all the unborn, and for the end of all anti-life practices, we pray: ◆
For all the sick and suffering, that they may have patience in their trials, as they experience the maternal presence of Our Lady, who holds them in the crossing of her arms, we pray: ◆ For those who have died, we pray: ◆

Our Father . . .

Heavenly Father,
you prepared the generations for the
    coming of your Son.
By the prayers of Our Lady of Guadalupe,
convert our hearts and bring us to
    deeper union
with your Son, our Lord Jesus Christ,
who lives and reigns with you in the unity
    of the Holy Spirit,
one God, forever and ever.
Amen.

✝ My soul rejoices in my God.

† The Lord hears the cry of the poor.

Psalm 85 *page 411*

Reading *Matthew 21:28–31*

"What is your opinion? A man had two sons. He came to the first and said, 'Son, go out and work in the vineyard today.' He said in reply, 'I will not,' but afterwards changed his mind and went. The man came to the other son and gave the same order. He said in reply, 'Yes, sir,' but did not go. Which of the two did his father's will?" They answered, "The first." Jesus said to them, "Amen, I say to you, tax collectors and prostitutes are entering the Kingdom of God before you."

Reflection

Sometimes it is easy for us to become lazy and complacent in our spiritual lives. However, today Jesus speaks strongly as he says that sinners and prostitutes are entering heaven before those who are considered holy and righteous. May we respond to God's call to live a life of obedience and asceticism, persevering in prayer.

Prayers *others may be added*

Asking for the grace to live out God's call for our lives, we pray:

◆ Help us do your will, O Lord.

For the Holy Father in his guidance of the Church; may his work in the vineyard bear fruit throughout the world, we pray: ◆ For leaders of nations, that, inspired by the prompting of the Holy Spirit, they may follow in the way of righteousness to bring solidarity among countries, we pray: ◆ For those who are sick, suffering, lonely, or depressed, that they may persevere in their suffering, confident that the Lord is close to the brokenhearted, we pray: ◆ For all sinners and those far away from God, that the prayers and lived example of Christians may help them to realize the joy that comes from faithfully following Christ, we pray: ◆ For the dying, that they may turn to the Lord and seek his face, so as to behold the eternal radiance of his countenance in heaven, we pray: ◆

Our Father . . .

Heavenly Father,
you are the vine master who calls us
and sends us to labor in your vineyard.
May we turn to you in loving obedience
to fulfill your will with perseverance
    and joy.
We ask this through Jesus Christ,
    our Lord,
who lives and reigns with you in the unity
    of the Holy Spirit,
one God, forever and ever.
Amen.

† The Lord hears the cry of the poor.

Wednesday, December 14, 2011
Memorial of Saint John of the Cross,
Priest and Doctor of the Church

✝ Let the clouds rain down the Just
One, and the earth bring forth
a Savior.

Psalm 85 page 411

Reading Luke 7:18b–23

At that time, John summoned two of his
disciples and sent them to the Lord to
ask, "Are you the one who is to come,
or should we look for another?" When
the men came to the Lord, they said,
"John the Baptist has sent us to you to
ask, 'Are you the one who is to come,
or should we look for another?'" At that
time Jesus cured many of their diseases,
sufferings, and evil spirits; he also
granted sight to many who were blind.
And Jesus said to them in reply, "Go
and tell John what you have seen and
heard: the blind regain their sight, the
lame walk, lepers are cleansed, the deaf
hear, the dead are raised, the poor have
the good news proclaimed to them. And
blessed is the one who takes no offense
at me."

Reflection

The Lord does not always answer our
questions in the way in which we would
hope. In the Gospel, Jesus does not
immediately answer John's question of
whether he is the Messiah. Instead,
Jesus tells the disciples to tell John of
healings and wonders that he has
worked among the people. These works
and wonders of Jesus are fulfillment of
the messianic prophecies of the Old
Testament, offering proof that Jesus is
truly the Messiah.

Prayers others may be added

Confident in the providence of our
Triune God, as we pray:

◆ Jesus, our Messiah, come save us.

For the Church, that, united to Jesus
Christ, she may continue to be the source
and font of life for the world, we pray: ◆
For the leaders of nations, that they may
seek justice and peace for the common
good of all people, we pray: ◆ For those
who are suffering the effects of war,
natural disasters, and political strife,
we pray: ◆ For married couples and those
preparing for marriage, we pray: ◆
For mothers and fathers expecting the
birth of a child, we pray: ◆

Our Father . . .

Most heavenly Father,
you know our needs
even before we speak them.
Pour your blessings upon us
as we listen and follow
your Son Jesus, our Messiah and Lord.
Inspire us with your Holy Spirit,
the consoler who guides us
to all understanding and truth.
Confident that you always hear us,
we ask that you answer our petitions
through Christ our Lord,
who lives and reigns with you in the unity
of the Holy Spirit,
one God, forever and ever.
Amen.

✝ Let the clouds rain down the Just
One, and the earth bring forth
a Savior.

Thursday, December 15, 2011
Advent Weekday

✝ I will praise you, Lord, for you have rescued me.

Psalm 85 *page 411*

Reading *Luke 7:24–27*

When the messengers of John the Baptist had left, Jesus began to speak to the crowds about John. "What did you go out to the desert to see—a reed swayed by the wind? Then what did you go out to see? Someone dressed in fine garments? Those who dress luxuriously and live sumptuously are found in royal palaces. Then what did you go out to see? A prophet? Yes, I tell you, and more than a prophet. This is the one about whom scripture says: / *Behold, I am sending my messenger ahead of you, / he will prepare your way before you.*" /

Reflection *Graziano Marcheschi*

As cousins, John and Jesus share a bloodline and so much more. Each is in the grip of the living God; each has surrendered fully to God's will, and each will pay dearly for the privilege. Jesus speaks of no one else as highly as he speaks of John. But the praise didn't save John's head. John knew what he was here for and he walked straight toward his destiny. The questions Jesus poses about John could as easily be asked of himself. And as easily as they were posed to the crowd, they could be posed to us. What would have drawn us to Jesus: his miracles and healings, his teaching and authority, his willingness to thumb his nose at the authorities? What would we have gone out to see?

No answer would be sufficient. And so in John there was much more than the people could detect. The same was true of Jesus. What mercy and what wondrous love that God has given us eyes to see and hearts that understand, that recognize the Lamb of God and the messenger who went before him.

Prayers *others may be added*

As little children, we turn to our heavenly Father to present our prayers and petitions, as we pray:

◆ Hear, O Lord, and have mercy on us.

For the Church, especially in those parts that suffer religious persecution, we pray: ◆ That leaders may use their authority and power to guide others to the truth, we pray: ◆ For those who are sick, that God may bless them in their weakness and bestow upon them the crown of greatness, we pray: ◆ For our parish community, that it may grow closer in unity and be zealous, we pray: ◆

Our Father . . .

Heavenly Father,
in our daily trials and sufferings,
increase our faith,
that the seed of the word of God
may grow in our hearts
and blossom with the virtues of charity
and generosity for others.
May your Holy Spirit breathe his peace
    upon us.
We ask this through Christ our Lord.
Amen.

✝ I will praise you, Lord, for you have rescued me.

✝ Justice shall flourish in his time, and fullness of peace for ever.

Psalm 85
page 411

Reading
John 5:33–36

Jesus said to the Jews: "You sent emissaries to John, and he testified to the truth. I do not accept testimony from a human being, but I say this so that you may be saved. John was a burning and shining lamp, and for a while you were content to rejoice in his light. But I have testimony greater than John's. The works that the Father gave me to accomplish, these works that I perform testify on my behalf that the Father has sent me."

Reflection

God the Father has sent his Son to shine his light and life among us! That is the mystery we celebrate today! God has assumed human flesh and has been born of a woman. This is not an event of the past, but rather, Jesus lives among us today. Jesus Christ, the God-man, has a human face and he is born among us. Let us seek his face so that we may be brought into the light of his divine life with the Father.

Prayers
others may be added

As we wait and prepare during Advent, we pray:

◆ O wisdom of God, come and teach us your ways.

For the Holy Father, that he may be blessed with strength and health to continue his work as the spiritual father of all souls, we pray: ◆ For leaders of nations and public officials, that, inspired by the Holy Spirit, they may be guided to make right decisions to ensure unity and justice, we pray: ◆ For all the poor, that Christians throughout the world may reach out in charity and generosity for all those in need, we pray: ◆ For those who have died and those who are grieving the loss of a child, relative, or friend, that the Blessed Mother may comfort them in their sorrow, we pray: ◆ For all fathers, that they may be blessed in all their work and sacrifice, and that they may never tire in offering good example to their children through the witness of their lives, we pray: ◆

Our Father . . .

God our Father,
as we await the celebration
of the birth of your Son,
fill us with renewed joy
in the anticipation of his coming.
May your living Spirit
come upon us to convert our hearts
and make us ready to welcome your Son.
We ask this in Jesus' name.
Amen.

✝ Justice shall flourish in his time, and fullness of peace for ever.

✟ Justice shall flourish in his time, and fullness of peace for ever.

Psalm 85
page 411

Reading
Matthew 1:17

Thus the total number of generations from Abraham to David is fourteen generations; from David to the Babylonian exile, fourteen generations; from the Babylonian exile to the Christ, fourteen generations.

Reflection

God has become man! That is the mystery we celebrate today. In today's Gospel we hear of the genealogy of Jesus Christ. God has assumed human flesh and has been born of a woman. This is not an event of the past, but rather, Jesus lives among us today. Jesus Christ, the God-man, has a human face and he is born among us. Let us seek his face so that we may be brought into his divine life.

Prayers
others may be added

As we wait and prepare during Advent, we pray:

◆ O wisdom of God, come and teach us your ways.

For the Holy Father, that he may be blessed with strength and health to continue his work as the spiritual father of all peoples, we pray: ◆ For leaders of nations and all public officials, that, inspired by the Holy Spirit, they may be guided to make right decisions to ensure unity, peace, and justice, we pray: ◆ For all the poor, that Christians throughout the world may reach out in charity and generosity for all those in need, we pray: ◆ For those who have died and those who are grieving the loss of a child, relative, or friend, that the Blessed Mother may comfort them in their sorrow, we pray: ◆ For all fathers, that they may be blessed in all their work and sacrifice, and that they may never tire in offering good example to their children through the witness of their lives, we pray: ◆

Our Father . . .

God our Father,
as we await the celebration
of the birth of your Son,
fill us with renewed joy
in the anticipation of his coming.
May your living Spirit
come upon us to convert our hearts
and make us ready to welcome your Son.
We ask this through Christ our Lord.
Amen.

✟ Justice shall flourish in his time, and fullness of peace for ever.

✝ For ever I will sing the goodness
of the Lord.

Psalm 85 *page 411*

Reading *Luke 1:38*

[Mary said,] "Behold, I am the handmaid of the Lord. May it be done to me
according to your word."

Reflection

We now begin the last week of Advent.
We are ready for Christmas! We have
been waiting and preparing for weeks
for this great celebration. In these last
days, let us remember to take time to be
silent and rejoice in the great mystery
that we are celebrating: God comes to
us as human and makes his dwelling
among us. God has made his home among
us so that, united to him, he may bring
us to our true home with the Father,
Son, and Holy Spirit.

Prayers *others may be added*

Waiting in preparation for the coming
of the Lord, we pray:

◆ *Marana tha*; Come, Lord Jesus!

For the Holy Father, that he may be given
strength and health during this time of
preparation for the Christmas celebrations,
we pray: ◆ For the Church throughout
the world, that she may not become
distracted by materialism and commer-
cialism, but rather, fix her eyes upon
Jesus Christ, we pray: ◆ For all countries
throughout the world experiencing war or
strife, that leaders of these nations may
work to bring about resolutions of justice,
peace, and unity, we pray: ◆ For the
homeless, the poor, and the lonely; for
those who have no home and no family
to welcome them during this Christmas
Time, we pray: ◆ For all those who have
died, that God may have mercy upon
them and bring them safely to their heavenly home, we pray: ◆ For lapsed Catholics, that this time of grace may invite
them to return to the Church, we pray: ◆
For all of us gathered today, that these
last days of Advent may not be a time
of stress and anxiety, but rather a time of
peace and joy as we look to the birth of
Christ, the one who comes to save us,
we pray: ◆

Our Father . . .

Heavenly Father,
you have sent your Son to dwell
   among us.
Through the prayers of the Virgin Mary,
fill our hearts with your Holy Spirit,
that our hearts may overflow with the joy
   and peace
that comes from union with your Son,
   Jesus Christ,
who lives and reigns with you in the unity
   of the Holy Spirit,
one God, forever and ever.
Amen.

✝ For ever I will sing the goodness
of the Lord.

✝ Let the Lord enter; he is the king of glory.

Psalm 85   *page 411*

Reading   *Luke 1:13–17*

But the angel said to [Zechariah], "Do not be afraid, Zechariah, because your prayer has been heard. Your wife Elizabeth will bear you a son, and you shall name him John. And you will have joy and gladness, and many will rejoice at his birth, for he will be great in the sight of the Lord. He will drink neither wine nor strong drink. He will be filled with the Holy Spirit even from his mother's womb, and he will turn many of the children of Israel to the Lord their God. He will go before him in the spirit and power of Elijah to turn the hearts of fathers toward children and the disobedient to the understanding of the righteous, to prepare a people fit for the Lord."

Reflection   *Graziano Marcheschi*

In the business and rush of the waning days until Christmas can you hear the echo of the Angel's words to Mary: "For nothing will be impossible for God." If those words don't apply to you as much as Mary, then God's a liar. God doesn't lie. Nothing is impossible in Mary's life and ours. Mary had the faith to believe. Do we? How dare we prepare to celebrate the impossible—God becoming human—if we don't believe that miracles can happen also in our lives . . . at Christmas and every other day.

Prayers   *others may be added*

As we continue to await and prepare for Christ's coming, we present our prayers and petitions, as we pray:

◆ O Key of David, come and free us!

For the Holy Father, we pray: ◆ For all governmental officials and leaders of all nations, we pray: ◆ For those who are lonely, we pray: ◆ For all peoples throughout the world, we pray: ◆ For all in need, we pray: ◆

Our Father . . .

Most loving Father,
we come to you as children,
confident that you know our every need.
Hear our prayer and grant us rest
in your fatherly embrace.
We ask this through Christ our Lord.
Amen.

✝ Let the Lord enter; he is the king of glory.

✝ Let the Lord enter; he is the king
of glory.

Psalm 85
page 411

Reading
Luke 1:34–38

But Mary said to the angel [Gabriel], "How can this be, since I have no relations with a man?" And the angel said to her in reply, "The Holy Spirit will come upon you, and the power of the Most High will overshadow you. Therefore the child to be born will be called holy, the Son of God. And behold, Elizabeth, your relative, has also conceived a son in her old age, and this is the sixth month for her who was called barren; for nothing will be impossible for God."

Mary said, "Behold, I am the handmaid of the Lord. May it be done to me according to your word."

Reflection
Graziano Marcheschi

Mary doesn't ask "if" but "how"; not whether God will be able to work this miracle, but in what way God will make the impossible occur. Her faith is already present. Mary knows God has no limits; it's her limits she recognizes. She's asking how God will surmount them, and the answer is the Holy Spirit. It was the Spirit who led Jesus into the desert and hovered above at his baptism. God gives us his Spirit, too. God never does things only once: he saved Israel from slavery and continues to save us from the enslavement we bring upon ourselves; God became human in Christ and now works through us who are Christ's body.

Prayers
others may be added

As we continue to wait and prepare for Christ's coming, we present our prayers and petitions, as we pray:

◆ O Key of David, come and free us!

For the Holy Father, that he may be filled with every blessing as he leads all peoples to the love of the Christ child, we pray: ◆ For all governmental officials and leaders of nations, that they may be led to make just laws out of the good of all whom they serve, we pray: ◆ For those who are lonely, for the mentally ill, and all those who care for them, that their suffering may be a fruitful and joyful offering to the Lord, we pray: ◆ For all who work long hours during these busy days before Christmas, that they may fulfill their daily tasks with patience, we pray: ◆ For all the intentions of our community, most especially those within the silence of our hearts, that God may come to our aid and hear our prayer, we pray: ◆

Our Father . . .

Most loving Father,
we come to you as children,
confident that you know our every need.
Hear our prayers,
and grant us rest in your fatherly embrace,
where you live and reign with your Son,
   our Lord, Jesus Christ,
in the unity of the Holy Spirit,
one God, forever and ever.
Amen.

✝ Let the Lord enter; he is the king
of glory.

✝ Arise, my beloved, my beautiful one, and come! *(Song of Songs 2:10)*

Psalm 85   *page 411*

Reading   *Luke 1:39–45*

Mary set out in those days and traveled to the hill country in haste to a town of Judah, where she entered the house of Zechariah and greeted Elizabeth. When Elizabeth heard Mary's greeting, the infant leaped in her womb, and Elizabeth, filled with the Holy Spirit, cried out in a loud voice and said, "Most blessed are you among women, and blessed is the fruit of your womb. And how does this happen to me, that the mother of my Lord should come to me? For at the moment the sound of your greeting reached my ears, the infant in my womb leaped for joy. Blessed are you who believed that what was spoken to you by the Lord would be fulfilled."

Reflection

Truly rare is the kind of vision demonstrated by Elizabeth and the child within her womb. This is her cousin, after all; how could Elizabeth recognize in this young relative the "most blessed" of women? How could a child still growing in the womb sense the fullness of grace and the presence of divinity? Luke's answer is the Holy Spirit. God's Spirit is not just a Pentecost phenomenon but a reality that pervades the Christian life. Christmas is nearly upon us, but we must sense the Spirit's radi-ance around the manger and invite him into every aspect of our lives.

Prayers   *others may be added*

With joy, let us call upon Christ who comes to bring us life, we pray:

◆ **O Emmanuel, come and save us, Lord our God!**

For Holy Mother Church, that through the intercession of the Blessed Virgin Mary, she may increase in faith, hope, and love in the promise of Jesus Christ, we pray: ◆ For all nations of the world, that they may be one in solidarity, we pray: ◆ For the outcast, the downtrodden, the lonely, and abandoned, that the mercy of God may come upon them to give them help and strength, we pray: ◆ For the graces of this holy time to turn our hearts away from selfish pride and vanity and seek the face of the Christ child, we pray: ◆ For the mystery of the Incarnation to unite us ever more in fraternal charity, we pray: ◆

Our Father . . .

Hear, O Lord,
the prayers of your children gathered here
    before you,
awaiting the coming of your Son Jesus.
Give us the grace to find joy even in
    moments of agitation.
Bring us to lasting peace in eternal glory
    with your Son Jesus,
who lives and reigns with you in the unity
    of the Holy Spirit,
one God, forever and ever.
Amen.

✝ Arise, my beloved, my beautiful one, and come!

Thursday, December 22, 2011
Advent Weekday

✝ My heart exults in the LORD.

Psalm 85 *page 411*

Reading *Luke 1:46–56*

"My soul proclaims the greatness of the Lord; / my spirit rejoices in God my savior, / for he has looked upon his lowly servant. / From this day all generations will call me blessed: / the Almighty has done great things for me, / and holy is his Name. / He has mercy on those who fear him / in every generation. / He has shown the strength of his arm, / and has scattered the proud in their conceit. / He has cast down the mighty from their thrones / and has lifted up the lowly. / He has filled the hungry with good things, / and the rich he has sent away empty. / He has come to the help of his servant Israel / for he remembered his promise of mercy, / the promise he made to our fathers, / to Abraham and his children for ever." /

Mary remained with Elizabeth about three months and then returned to her home.

Reflection

Today in the Gospel we hear Mary's song of praise as she visits her cousin Elizabeth. She proclaims God's greatness and exclaims, "The Almighty has done great things for me!" How many good things the Lord has done for us as well. Let us thank the Father, the giver of all good gifts, especially for the most precious gift of his Son, Jesus.

Prayers *others may be added*

With thanksgiving to Jesus Christ who has become man for us, we pray:

◆ O King of Nations, come and save us!

For the Holy Father, and all priests, bishops, deacons, religious, and the laity, that they may never cease to proclaim the greatness of the Lord, we pray: ◆ For our nation's president, that he may be led by the Holy Spirit to make just decisions to lead our country to true freedom, we pray: ◆ For all families, that, inspired by Mary's charity to her cousin Elizabeth, they may be ever willing to serve one another in generosity, patience, and love, we pray: ◆ For the poor, the sick, and the suffering, that the Lord will fulfill his promise to raise up the lowly to his glory forever, we pray: ◆ For the members of our Church and community, that the mystery of Christ's Incarnation may stir deeper conversion in the hearts of all, we pray: ◆

Our Father . . .

O King of the Universe
and Desire of all Nations,
all peoples seek your face.
Grant that during Advent,
God may convert our hearts
and draw us deeper into
the mystery of his love.
You live and reign forever.
Amen.

✝ My heart exults in the LORD.

✝ Raise your heads because your redemption is at hand.

Psalm 85   *page 411*

Reading   *Luke 1:57–63*

When the time arrived for Elizabeth to have her child she gave birth to a son. Her neighbors and relatives heard that the Lord had shown his great mercy toward her, and they rejoiced with her. When they came on the eighth day to circumcise the child, they were going to call him Zechariah after his father, but his mother said in reply, "No. He will be called John." But they answered her, "There is no one among your relatives who has this name." So they made signs, asking his father what he wished him to be called. He asked for a tablet and wrote, "John is his name," and all were amazed.

Reflection   *Graziano Marcheschi*

Traditions fall by the wayside at the naming of John, who is given neither his father's nor, more typically, his grandfather's name. Instead, he receives the name the angel had assigned to him when he prophesied the child's birth to Zechariah. God is doing something entirely new but he works through his chosen people to achieve it. Circumcision incorporates John, and later Jesus, into the people of Israel. Luke presents both John and Jesus as good sons of Israel. And out of the ground of that tradition and ancient covenant, God fashions a new covenant that will embrace all the peoples of the earth.

Prayers   *others may be added*

In hope we pray to the Father, who, in his great mercy, sends us his Son to save us from our sins:

◆ **O Emmanuel, come and save us!**

For the Church, that she may be joyful in the expectation of the coming of the Savior, we pray: ◆ For all nations and their leaders, that the desire for Jesus Christ may be realized in a deep and personal encounter with him, we pray: ◆ For American citizens, that they may recognize the dignity and respect for life from conception until natural death, we pray: ◆ For the poor, the sick, and the suffering, that they may be witnesses to the joy of Christ's goodness even in difficult trials, we pray: ◆ For preparing for the great celebration of Christmas, that their work may be blessed, and that it may give glory to God, we pray: ◆

Our Father . . .

Heavenly Father,
you look upon us, your children,
in our weakness and sinfulness.
Not wanting even one of your children to
    be lost,
you send us your only begotten Son,
    Jesus Christ,
to free us and bring us into union
    with you.
Pour your Holy Spirit upon us
to convert our hearts,
and bring us more deeply into union with
    your love.
We ask this through Christ our Lord.
Amen.

✝ Raise your heads because your redemption is at hand.

✝ For ever I will sing the goodness of the Lord.

Psalm 85
page 411

Reading
Luke 1:67, 73–79

Zechariah his father, filled with the Holy Spirit, prophesied, saying: . . . / "This was the oath he swore to our father Abraham: / to set us free from the hand of our enemies, / free to worship him without fear, / holy and righteous in his sight all the days of our life. / You, my child, shall be called the prophet of the Most High, / for you will go before the Lord to prepare his way, / to give his people knowledge of salvation / by the forgiveness of their sins. / In the tender compassion of our God / the dawn from on high shall break upon us, / to shine on those who dwell in darkness and the shadow of death, / and to guide our feet into the way of peace."

Reflection
Graziano Marcheschi

Before Zechariah sings his canticle, the neighbors wonder, "What, then, will this child be?" Zechariah provides a Spirit-guided answer. Through this child the longings of the people will be answered and the promises made to ancestors fulfilled. Zechariah sees a man of God who will bring "knowledge of salvation." Many parents long to look into the future. Had Zechariah seen that John would pay with his head for the privilege of prophecy, he'd likely not have changed his song, for when God gives the vision, he also gives courage and hope.

Prayers
others may be added

◆ *Marana tha;* Come, Lord Jesus!

For the Holy Father, that he may be blessed with strength and health and every spiritual blessing in the approaching Christmas Time, we pray: ◆ For peace among all nations, that leaders of countries may discover solutions in areas of difficulty and discord, we pray: ◆ For all the sick, the suffering, the lonely, and the poor, that they may be comforted by the Christ child who comes to earth in poverty and weakness, we pray: ◆ For all those who have died, especially for those who have died within this past year, that their families and friends may be comforted, and that they may enjoy eternal life with the Triune God, we pray: ◆ For our local community, that each one of us may take the opportunity to enjoy the peace and stillness of the great mystery of Christ's Incarnation, even in the midst of the busyness of Christmas preparations, we pray: ◆

Our Father . . .

O Radiant Dawn,
O Sun of Justice,
you are the great Morning Star that rises
to shine your light among
all the peoples who walk in darkness.
Penetrate our hearts with your light,
that, illuminated by your glory,
we may see you, who lead us
and guide us along the path of life.
You live and reign forever.
Amen.

✝ For ever I will sing the goodness of the Lord.

✝ The people who walked in darkness have seen a great light. (*Isaiah 9:1*)

Psalm 98   *page 413*

Reading   *John 1:14*

And the Word became flesh / and made his dwelling among us, / and we saw his glory, / the glory as of the Father's only Son, / full of grace and truth.

Reflection

Today our God is born among us. At times in our daily lives, it can be difficult to understand the mystery of this great event. However, the angel tells *us*: Do not be afraid, for Jesus' birth is a message of great joy! Today Jesus comes to us, banishing all fear and worry. We are no longer alone, no longer lost, and trapped in our sin. But rather, in the mystery of Jesus Christ born in Bethlehem, God brings us freedom by the power of his love. Let us have faith and hope in the greatness of the mystery we celebrate today.

Prayers   *others may be added*

Heavenly Father, you send us your Son to free us from our sins and bring us into the union of your love, with joyful hearts, we cry:

◆ Shine on us the light of your glory!

For the Holy Father and Holy Mother Church, that this day may be a day of true conversion for all peoples as they come to know the love of the Christ child, we pray: ◆ For the end of violence, abuse, and war throughout the world, that Jesus' light may shine upon all peoples to bring true and lasting peace, we pray: ◆ For all military personnel and those who serve our country abroad, that they may realize and experience the spiritual closeness with their loved ones in the Eucharist, we pray: ◆ For the sick and suffering, for the mentally ill, and especially for those who are lonely, that the nearness of Christ may break through their loneliness and pain to bring true union with God who is always with us, we pray: ◆ For all families, that, inspired by the love of the Holy Family, they may be brought together in unity, we pray: ◆ For all who have died and for those who grieve their losses this Christmas Time, that they may be comforted by the prayers and intercession of our most holy Mother Mary, we pray: ◆

Our Father . . .

Good and gracious Father,
every good and gracious gift comes
   from you.
Today you send us the gift of your Son,
   Jesus Christ,
the Word Incarnate, the true Light of
   the World,
to bring us back into unity with you.
Through the power of the Holy Spirit,
pour your blessings upon us,
that we may be able to share
the joy of the Good News of Christ's birth
through the witness of our daily lives.
We ask this through your Son, Jesus
   Christ, our Lord,
who lives and reigns with you in the unity
   of the Holy Spirit,
one God, forever and ever.
Amen.

✝ The people who walked in darkness have seen a great light.

✝ Into your hands, O Lord, I commend my spirit.

Psalm 98 *page 413*

Reading *Matthew 10:17–22*

Jesus said to his disciples, "Beware of men, for they will hand you over to the courts and scourge you in their synagogues, and you will be led before governors and kings for my sake as a witness before them and the pagans. When they hand you over, do not worry about how you are to speak or what you are to say. You will be given at that moment what you are to say. For it will not be you who speak but the Spirit of your Father speaking through you. Brother will hand over brother to death, and the father his child; children will rise up against parents and have them put to death. You will be hated by all because of my name, but whoever endures to the end will be saved."

Reflection

Today we celebrate the feast of Saint Steven, the first Christian martyr. On this second day of Christmas, this feast calls us to witness to the truth of the life of Jesus Christ present among us. Jesus tells us not to worry if others persecute us for our faith, but rather, that the Holy Spirit will give us the words we need at the proper time. Let us ask the intercession of Saint Stephen, so that we may persevere in witnessing to the truth of Jesus Christ through our word and example.

Prayers *others may be added*

Jesus Christ, all the martyrs give witness to your holy name; hear our prayers that we place before you today, as we pray:

◆ King of Glory, hear our prayer.

For the Holy Father, that he may be renewed in carrying out his task to witness to the truth of Jesus Christ, we pray: ◆ For leaders of nations, that they may be filled with the Holy Spirit to speak the words of truth that will bring about solidarity among all cultures, we pray: ◆ For all those who are physically, mentally, or emotionally unwell, that Jesus Christ may be their strength and their refuge, we pray: ◆ For the individual needs of our community, we pray: ◆

Our Father . . .

Most Holy Trinity,
we worship you as Father, Son, and
    Holy Spirit,
We bless you for your goodness
and we praise the glory of your name.
Through the prayers of Saint Stephen,
    the first martyr,
may we be encouraged to witness
    to your goodness
through the great and small trials
and persecutions of each day.
May our lives be a living testimony
to your light and to your truth.
We ask this through Christ our Lord.
Amen.

✝ Into your hands, O Lord, I commend my spirit.

✝ Rejoice in the Lord, you just!

Psalm 98
page 413

Reading
John 20:1–8

On the first day of the week, Mary of Magdala came to the tomb early in the morning, while it was still dark, and saw the stone removed from the tomb. So she ran and went to Simon Peter and to the other disciple whom Jesus loved, and told them, "They have taken the Lord from the tomb, and we don't know where they put him." So Peter and the other disciple went out and came to the tomb. They both ran, but the other disciple ran faster than Peter and arrived at the tomb first; he bent down and saw the burial cloths there, but did not go in. When Simon Peter arrived after him, he went into the tomb and saw the burial cloths there, and the cloth that had covered his head, not with the burial cloths but rolled up in a separate place. Then the other disciple also went in, the one who had arrived at the tomb first, and he saw and believed.

Reflection

In the Gospel account we hear that John "saw and believed" (John 20:8) in Christ's Resurrection after running with Peter to the empty tomb. The life of Jesus Christ is what we proclaim even during this Christmas Time. Because the Word has been made flesh, we have seen and heard and touched this Word of Life. By the Incarnation, God is made visible, and we testify to this Christmas joy.

Prayers
others may be added

We pray to our heavenly Father:

◆ Lord, hear our prayer.

For the Church, that she may continue to give witness to the truth of Jesus Christ throughout the world, we pray: ◆ For all nations, that the love of Christ may touch each culture and land, that all peoples may see and know the Word of Life, we pray: ◆ For the poor, the lonely, and the marginalized, that others may recognize their needs and be stirred to reach out in service, we pray: ◆ For all young people, that they may not fear to follow Christ, who is the source of true happiness and joy, we pray: ◆ For the needs of our community family, that the love of God may be poured out into our hearts so that all may know they are beloved by the Lord, we pray: ◆

Our Father . . .

Heavenly Father,
you have become visible to us
through your Son Jesus Christ,
born of a sinless virgin,
that we may come to fellowship with you.
Through the prayers and intercession
of the apostle and evangelist John,
may we be strengthened to testify
to the light of Jesus Christ,
who dispels the darkness and brings
   eternal life.
We ask this through Christ our Lord.
Amen.

✝ Rejoice in the Lord, you just!

✝ Our soul has been rescued like a bird from the fowler's snare.

Psalm 98 *page 413*

Reading *Matthew 2:13–15*

When the magi had departed, behold, the angel of the Lord appeared to Joseph in a dream and said, "Rise, take the child and his mother, flee to Egypt, and stay there until I tell you. Herod is going to search for the child to destroy him." Joseph rose and took the child and his mother by night and departed for Egypt. He stayed there until the death of Herod, that what the Lord had said through the prophet might be fulfilled, / *Out of Egypt I called my son.*

Reflection *Graziano Marcheschi*

Joseph, spouse of Mary and guardian of the Holy Family, doesn't hesitate to respond to his portentous dream. What's significant is not that Joseph put such stock in a dream, something we'd be unlikely to do today. What matters is that he believed God would guide him and give him the right instincts to carry out the grave responsibility entrusted to him. The Christian life holds little attraction if we think we're all on our own, left to travel a road without a map. But God is always communicating with us and guiding us. Joseph knew that and when the message came, he recognized it. Are we prepared to hear God when he speaks, whether it's through a friend, his Word, or even a dream?

Prayers *others may be added*

Heavenly Father, you are near to us in both our sufferings and our joys; with faith, we present to you our petitions, as we pray:

◆ Have mercy on your people, Lord.

For the Holy Father, that he may continue to lead and guide the Church in truth, we pray: ◆ For the leaders of all nations, that they may make just laws, we pray: ◆ For all who have suffered the effects of abortion, that God's merciful love will bring healing, we pray: ◆ For children who are sick and suffering, that others may generously open their hearts to them, we pray: ◆ For all families who grieve the loss of a child, we pray: ◆ For the personal, material, and spiritual needs of our community, we pray: ◆

Our Father . . .

Heavenly Father,
in your great mystery
you send us your Son, Jesus Christ
to come to us as a little child.
Help us to understand and know
the importance of spiritual childhood
as we seek to do your will
and receive your love.
Through the intercession and prayers
of all the Holy Innocents,
may all peoples come to understand
the beauty and gift of human life.
We ask this through Christ our Lord.
Amen.

✝ Our soul has been rescued like a bird from the fowler's snare.

✝ Announce his salvation, day after day.

Psalm 98
page 413

Reading
Luke 2:25–35

Now there was a man in Jerusalem whose name was Simeon. This man was righteous and devout, awaiting the consolation of Israel, and the Holy Spirit was upon him. It had been revealed to him by the Holy Spirit that he should not see death before he had seen the Christ of the Lord. He came in the Spirit into the temple; and when the parents brought in the child Jesus to perform the custom of the law in regard to him, he took him into his arms and blessed God, saying: / "Lord, now you let your servant go in peace; / your word has been fulfilled: / my own eyes have seen the salvation / which you have prepared in the sight of every people, / a light to reveal you to the nations / and the glory of his people Israel."

Reflection
Graziano Marcheschi

An old man's dream is realized and God's promise fulfilled. Another one of those things that only happen in the Bible. Would that *we* could experience what Simeon did! But what good are events that only happen in the Bible? If the stories of scripture are not also our stories, they have little value and even less influence on our lives. Think about it, and you'll see that some of your dreams have come true and some your life stories are too good to be true. And then give thanks, like Simeon did.

Prayers
others may be added

Father, hear the prayers that we present before you now, as we pray:

◆ Lord, hear our prayer.

For the Church, that she may be renewed in joy as she celebrates the birth of Jesus Christ, we pray: ◆ For the leaders of nations, and for all countries far away from God's word, that the Light of the World may illuminate the darkness to bring truth to all peoples, we pray: ◆ For the sick and the suffering, especially those who suffer from loneliness, that God's mercy may fulfill their spiritual and material needs through the help and generosity of others, we pray: ◆ For all who have died, that they may be received into the union of the Holy Trinity, we pray: ◆ For all Christians, that they may be countercultural in continuing to celebrate this Christmas Time with great joy, we pray: ◆

Our Father . . .

Good and gracious Father,
you call us to love through your Son and
the Holy Spirit,
Pour your love into our hearts,
that, filled with your love,
we may listen and obey your
commandments.
Give us the grace to sing forever
the goodness of your name,
announcing to all the nations your praises.
Open our hearts to receive your grace.
We ask this through Christ our Lord.
Amen.

✝ Announce his salvation, day after day.

✝ A light for revelation to the Gentiles, and glory for your people Israel.

Psalm 98 page 413

Reading Luke 2:22,39–40

When the days were completed for their purification according to the law of Moses, they took [Jesus] up to Jerusalem to present him to the Lord.

When they had fulfilled all the prescriptions of the law of the Lord, they returned to Galilee, to their own town of Nazareth. The child grew and became strong, filled with wisdom; and the favor of God was upon him.

Reflection

God really became human. And not just to teach us how to live a human life, not just to save us from our sins, but because human life is good. God made it. It must be good. If we need persuading, we need only ponder the fact that for thirty years Jesus lived a "normal" life apparently unremarkable and completely undocumented. He was a good son to his parents and he grew up. That was all. And that was enough.

Prayers others may be added

Holy God, is it you under whom every family is named. Be gracious to us and hear our prayers, as we pray:

◆ Draw us into the love of the Holy Family.

For the Church, that all people may feel welcome to call her their home and spiritual family, we pray: ◆ For the Holy Father, that God may bless his work and vocation as Father for all peoples, we pray: ◆ For public officials, that they protect and respect the rights and dignity of the family, we pray: ◆ For all married couples, that fathers may look to the example of Saint Joseph, that mothers may look to the example of the Blessed Virgin, and that all families may strive to be united in holiness, we pray: ◆ For all children who suffer the effects of divorce, that they may know the love of God their Father, who heals all wounds, we pray: ◆ For those who have died, especially family members and friends, we pray: ◆ In thanksgiving for the gift of life and for the gift of our own families, we pray: ◆

Our Father . . .

Heavenly Father,
you have created every family
as an image of your Trinitarian love
with the Son and Holy Spirit.
By your grace, renew and heal
 the wounds
of all peoples throughout the world.
Illuminate our hearts,
to understand the beauty and dignity of
 family life,
that, united more deeply to one another,
we may become ever more united to you
in the eternal love of the Holy Trinity.
We ask this through Christ our Lord.
Amen.

✝ A light for revelation to the Gentiles, and glory for your people Israel.

✝ The Word became flesh and made his dwelling among us.

Psalm 98 *page 413*

Reading *John 1:10–14*

He was in the world, / and the world came to be through him, / but the world did not know him. / He came to what was his own, / but his own people did not accept him.

But to those who did accept him / he gave power to become children of God, / to those who believe in his name, / who were born not by natural generation / nor by human choice nor by a man's decision / but of God.

And the Word became flesh / and made his dwelling among us, / and we saw his glory, / the glory as of the Father's only-begotten Son, / full of grace and truth.

Reflection *Graziano Marcheschi*

Good parents learn to let go of their children. Mary had little choice. Jesus was single-minded about his mission. But still, you have to wonder if it hurt to have perfect strangers called "my mother and my brothers." In so many ways, Mary models ideal discipleship and here is one more example. Though she carried him in her womb and nursed him at her breast, she willingly shares her son with all the world. She could only do that because she saw clearly enough to understand who he really was. If we truly understand Jesus, we, too, will have no choice but to love him . . . and to give him away.

Prayers *others may be added*

Father in heaven, all glory belongs to you, accept our petitions as we pray:

◆ Light of the World, hear our prayer.

For the Church, that she may be a beacon of light to all peoples, forever illuminating the darkness of sin and error with the truth of Jesus Christ, we pray: ◆ For government officials and leaders of nations, that they may work to better society and the common good of all peoples, we pray: ◆ For all of the poor, the sick, and the homeless, that their suffering may be a means to give glory to God, we pray: ◆ For all who have died, that the mercy of God may shine upon them so they may forever enjoy eternal life with all the saints, we pray: ◆ For all who travel, that they may be protected from all harm, we pray: ◆ For our local community and for all peoples, we pray: ◆

Our Father . . .

Jesus Christ,
true Light of the World,
you were sent by the Father
to dispel the darkness of sin.
You are the Word made Flesh
who dwells among us.
Send your Holy Spirit upon us
to illuminate our hearts and minds
with the light of your truth,
so that through you we may become
children of God to give you glory
and praise forever and ever.
You live and reign forever.
Amen.

✝ The Word became flesh and made his dwelling among us.

Sunday, January 1, 2012
The Octave Day of the Nativity of the Lord/
Solemnity of Mary, the Holy Mother of God

✝ Blessed are you among women, and blessed is the fruit of your womb.

Psalm 72 *page 411*

Reading *Luke 2:16–20*

The shepherds went in haste to Bethlehem and found Mary and Joseph, and the infant lying in the manger. When they saw this, they made known the message that had been told them about this child. All who heard it were amazed by what had been told them by the shepherds. And Mary kept all these things, reflecting on them in her heart. Then the shepherds returned, glorifying and praising God for all they had heard and seen, just as it had been told to them.

Reflection

Today, on this first day of the new year, we celebrate the solemnity of Mary, the Holy Mother of God. At the Council of Ephesus, Mary was proclaimed the *Theotokos*, the Mother of God or Godbearer, to affirm Mary's motherhood of Jesus Christ who is true God and true man. As the Mother of God, Mary is also our mother, and we honor her today for her maternal help and intercession. As we begin this new year, Mary is a model for us as she teaches us how to live our lives united to God.

Prayers *others may be added*

Father, hear the prayers that we present before you today, as we say:

◆ Renew us in your love, O Lord.

For the Church throughout the world, that through the prayers of Mary, the Church may be strengthened to remain mother and teacher of all peoples, we pray: ◆ For all nations, that this new year may be a time of active efforts for peace and justice throughout all the world, we pray: ◆ For the poor, the lonely, the sick and suffering, that, through the intercession of the prayers of the Mother of God, they may receive consolation and relief, we pray: ◆ For all mothers, that they may fulfill their daily duties with joy and cheerfulness out of love for God and service to their families, we pray: ◆ For the repose of the souls of all the faithful departed, we pray: ◆ For our personal intentions and the needs of our community, that we may become more devoted to Mary, the Holy Mother of God and our mother, we pray: ◆

Our Father . . .

Heavenly Father,
you send us your Son, Jesus Christ,
born of a woman, by the power of
    the Spirit.
By the prayers of Mary, the Holy Mother
    of God,
may we come to share in your glory
for all the years to come.
We ask this through Christ our Lord.
Amen.

✝ Blessed are you among women, and blessed is the fruit of your womb.

Monday, January 2, 2012
Memorial of Saints Basil the Great and Gregory Nazianzen, Bishops and Doctors of the Church

✝ Children, remain in him.

Psalm 72 page 411

Reading John 1:19–23

This is the testimony of John. When the Jews from Jerusalem sent priests and Levites to him to ask him, "Who are you?" he admitted and did not deny it, but admitted, "I am not the Christ." So they asked him, "What are you, then? Are you Elijah?" And he said, "I am not." "Are you the Prophet?" He answered, "No." So they said to him, "Who are you, so we can give an answer to those who sent us? What do you have to say for yourself?" He said: "I am *the voice of one crying out in the desert, / 'Make straight the way of the Lord,'* as Isaiah the prophet said."

Reflection

Are we able to see Christ in daily events? Or is he hard to recognize? Today in the Gospel, John the Baptist testifies to Jesus and tells the people that there is one among them whom they do not recognize. The same is true for today. Jesus has made his dwelling among us. We, likewise, must open our eyes to recognize him in our everyday work, because it is Jesus who comes to meet us in the ordinary circumstances of life.

Prayers others may be added

Good and loving Father, hear our prayers that we present to you today, as we pray:

◆ Anoint us with your Spirit.

For the Church throughout the world, that she may be filled with grace to welcome all peoples into her loving embrace, we pray: ◆ For the Pope, bishops, and clergy, that they may be a "voice crying in the desert" as they tirelessly testify to Jesus Christ, we pray: ◆ For all rulers and leaders of nations, that they may humbly fulfill their duties of service to their people with responsibility and diligence, we pray: ◆ For the poor, the lonely, and for all those who suffer, that their trials may be a testimony to the cross of Christ in which they share, we pray: ◆ For all those who have died and for their family and friends who grieve their loss, we pray: ◆ For our own personal needs and those of our community, that the Holy Spirit may open our eyes to recognize Jesus Christ present among us, we pray: ◆

Our Father . . .

Good and gracious God,
you have come among us
to bring us into union with you.
By the anointing of your Spirit,
you have poured your life into our hearts
and you remain with us always.
We seek your face;
teach us to see you in the daily events
    of our lives.
We ask this through Christ our Lord.
Amen.

✝ Children, remain in him.

Tuesday, January 3, 2012
Christmas Weekday

✝ All the ends of the earth have seen the saving power of God.

Psalm 72
page 411

Reading
John 1:29–34

John the Baptist saw Jesus coming toward him and said, "Behold, the Lamb of God, who takes away the sin of the world. He is the one of whom I said, 'A man is coming after me who ranks ahead of me because he existed before me.' I did not know him, but the reason why I came baptizing with water was that he might be made known to Israel." John testified further, saying, "I saw the Spirit come down like a dove from heaven and remain upon him. I did not know him, but the one who sent me to baptize with water told me, 'On whomever you see the Spirit come down and remain, he is the one who will baptize with the Holy Spirit.' Now I have seen and testified that he is the Son of God."

Reflection

In the time of Jesus, some of the people questioned the unusual actions of John the Baptist. However, John remained certain of his purpose and his work that he must do. He courageously points out Jesus as the Messiah and the Lamb of God. John's purpose is clear: "I came baptizing with water that he might be made known to Israel." Is it also clear that we too must make Jesus known in our daily lives?

Prayers
others may be added

Turn your merciful gaze upon us, God our Father, as we pray:

◆ Draw us deeper in your love, O Lord.

For the Church, that through the outpouring of the Holy Spirit, she may be given the fortitude to point out the Lamb of God to all the nations, we pray: ◆ For all war-torn countries and for all public officials, that they may faithfully serve their people to bring peace to all nations, we pray: ◆ For all young people, that they may not fear to proclaim Jesus Christ who is alive and present in our daily lives, we pray: ◆ For the sick and suffering, for those in hospitals, and for those who have no one to care for them, that the grace of God may bring them comfort and healing, we pray: ◆ For the souls of the faithful departed, that they may swiftly behold the face of God in the eternal bliss of heaven, we pray: ◆ For the needs of our community, that the graces of this holy time may renew us in charity for one another, we pray: ◆

Our Father . . .

God, our Father,
you have called us to be your children,
    and so we are.
Through the prayers of the Blessed
    Virgin Mary,
may we remain forever united to you
by staying close to your Son, Jesus Christ,
    the Word of Life,
through whom we ask this prayer.
Amen.

✝ All the ends of the earth have seen the saving power of God.

Wednesday, January 4, 2012
Memorial of Saint Elizabeth Ann Seton, Religious

✟ Behold, the Lamb of God.

Psalm 72   *page 411*

Reading   *John 1:35–42*

John was standing with two of his disciples, and as he watched Jesus walk by, he said, "Behold, the Lamb of God." The two disciples heard what he said and followed Jesus. Jesus turned and saw them following him and said to them, "What are you looking for?" They said to him, "Rabbi" (which translated means Teacher), "where are you staying?" He said to them, "Come, and you will see." So they went and saw where he was staying, and they stayed with him that day. It was about four in the afternoon. Andrew, the brother of Simon Peter, was one of the two who heard John and followed Jesus. He first found his own brother Simon and told him, "We have found the Messiah," (which is translated Christ). Then he brought him to Jesus. Jesus looked at him and said, "You are Simon the son of John; you will be called Cephas," which is translated Peter.

Reflection

Like the apostles in the Gospel, we too have heard John proclaim, "Behold, the Lamb of God," and we too have followed Jesus. Jesus likewise asks us today, "What are you looking for?" Saint Elizabeth Ann Seton, whose memorial we celebrate, is a U.S.-born saint who also sought and followed the Lord. She converted to the Catholic faith and dedicated her life to education by starting schools and convents in the United States. Her example and intercession encourage us to continue to seek Jesus Christ and lead others to where he can be found.

Prayers   *others may be added*

Loving God, graciously hear us as we pray:

◆ Stay with us, Lord.

For our Holy Mother Church, that she may become ever more radiant with the light of Jesus Christ, we pray: ◆ For the United States, that through the witness of its saints, it may become ever more a beacon of the light and truth of Jesus Christ, we pray: ◆ For all nurses, doctors, and families who care for those who are ill, that the Lord may bless their work and bring healing and fortitude to all the sick and suffering, we pray: ◆ For all teachers and catechists, that their work may bring many souls to the knowledge of the truth, we pray: ◆ For our local schools, that they may lead their students to the truth that they seek, and that students may use their knowledge in service to all people, we pray: ◆

Our Father . . .

Lord Jesus Christ,
you give us the example of the saints
to encourage us on our pilgrimage of life.
By the power of your Spirit,
give us the grace to continue to seek you
and to proclaim your name to all peoples.
You live and reign forever.
Amen.

✟ Behold, the Lamb of God.

✝ Let all the earth cry out to God
with joy.

Psalm 72   *page 411*

Reading   *John 1:48–51*

Nathanael said to [Jesus], "How do you
know me?" Jesus answered and said to
him, "Before Philip called you, I saw
you under the fig tree." Nathanael
answered him, "Rabbi, you are the Son
of God; you are the King of Israel."
Jesus answered and said to him, "Do
you believe because I told you that I saw
you under the fig tree? You will see
greater things than this." And he said
to him, "Amen, amen, I say to you, you
will see the sky opened and the angels
of God ascending and descending on
the Son of Man."

Reflection   *S. Anne Elizabeth Sweet, CSO*

A beautiful model for believers is found
in the example of Andrew, and today,
Philip, who, after they have found Jesus,
now bring others to him. Nathanael is
not to be deceived. How do you know
Jesus is the one promised in the law and
the prophets? Nathanael needs a sign,
and he gets one from Jesus. Immediately he confesses faith in Jesus, who
assures him that there will be even more
signs.

Prayers   *others may be added*

Calling upon our Father, the Lord and
giver of life, we pray:

◆ Strengthen us in service, Lord.

For the Holy Father, that he may be
renewed to fulfill his mission as priest,
prophet, and king, as successor of the
apostles, we pray: ◆ For all countries
afflicted by war and violence, that their
leaders may work together to bring peace
and solidarity, we pray: ◆ For the poor,
the lonely, and the sick and suffering, that
they may know the presence of Christ in
all of their trials, we pray: ◆ For the
missions throughout the world, that men
and women may have the courage to
continue to bring the joy of Jesus Christ
to all the world, we pray: ◆ For the souls
of the faithful departed, we pray: ◆
For our families and friends, that we may
witness to one another through our example
of friendship and Christian charity,
we pray: ◆

Our Father . . .

Heavenly Father,
you send your servants into the vineyard
to reap a bountiful harvest.
By the power of your Holy Spirit,
unite us ever more deeply to your Son,
that our work may become ever more
    fruitful for others.
Fill us with your grace of fortitude,
so that we may be able to boldly proclaim
your glory through the example of
    our lives.
We ask through Christ our Lord.
Amen.

✝ Let all the earth cry out to God
with joy.

✝ Praise the Lord, Jerusalem.

Psalm 72 *page 411*

Reading *Mark 1:7–11*

This is what John the Baptist proclaimed: "One mightier than I is coming after me. I am not worthy to stoop and loosen the thongs of his sandals. I have baptized you with water; he will baptize you with the Holy Spirit."

It happened in those days that Jesus came from Nazareth of Galilee and was baptized in the Jordan by John. On coming up out of the water he saw the heavens being torn open and the Spirit, like a dove, descending upon him. And a voice came from the heavens, "You are my beloved Son; with you I am well pleased."

Reflection

Traditionally, today celebrates the solemnity of the Epiphany of the Lord; however, in the United States of America it is transferred to Sunday. The word *epiphany* means "manifestation." The solemnity of the Epiphany celebrates Jesus' manifestation as the Messiah, the Son of God and Savior of the world. This great solemnity is made up of three events in which Jesus is manifested as Son of God: the adoration of the Magi, the wedding feast at Cana, and the baptism in the Jordan. In these next days let us listen to the Word of God as Jesus reveals and manifests himself to us.

Prayers *others may be added*

Heavenly Father, grant the prayers we humbly ask of you, as we pray:

◆ Lord, send us your Spirit.

For the Holy Father, for his health and his intentions, that, inspired by the Holy Spirit, he may lead the Church ever more deeply to an encounter with Christ through our pilgrimage of life, we pray: ◆ For government officials and leaders of all countries, that they may seek dialogue with one another in order to build up nations founded on Gospel values, we pray: ◆ For the poor, the weak, and the suffering, that they may know and hear the voice of the Father, who calls them his beloved, we pray: ◆ For all who have died and for those in Purgatory who await the glory of heaven, that they may be swiftly taken into the eternal union with God, the Lord and giver of life, we pray: ◆ That all people may know the personal love of God the Father, who calls us to be his children through the power of the Holy Spirit, we pray: ◆

Our Father . . .

Lord Jesus Christ,
through the Incarnation
you have revealed to us
the glory of the Father.
You have sent the Holy Spirit upon us
as testimony to the glory of your name.
In you, we are given eternal life.
May we always remain united to you,
the source and fountain of life and light.
You live and reign forever.
Amen.

✝ Praise the Lord, Jerusalem.

Saturday, January 7, 2012
Christmas Weekday

✝ The Lord takes delight in his people.

Psalm 72
page 411

Reading
John 2:1–5

There was a wedding at Cana in Galilee, and the mother of Jesus was there. Jesus and his disciples were also invited to the wedding. When the wine ran short, the mother of Jesus said to him, "They have no wine." And Jesus said to her, "Woman, how does your concern affect me? My hour has not yet come." His mother said to the servers, "Do whatever he tells you."

Reflection

Today we hear in the Gospel about the wedding feast at Cana where Jesus begins his public ministry. Out of obedience to his mother Mary, Jesus performs his first public miracle and turns the water into wine. This miracle is a manifestation of Jesus' glory, and because of this sign, many people come to believe in him. This event is an "epiphany" in which Jesus is revealed as the Son of God. His mother, Mary, tells the servants very simple words that we should practice today, "Do whatever he tells you" (John 2:5).

Prayers
others may be added

With confidence in the Father, we pray:

◆ Reveal yourself to us, O Lord.

For the Church, that she may remain the spotless bride of Christ, we pray: ◆
For all countries, especially those that suffer from war, violence, and political unrest, that leaders and politicians may work in harmony to bring about solutions for world peace, we pray: ◆ For those who suffer from hopelessness and despair, that Jesus may reveal his power and mercy to all who are in need, we pray: ◆ For all married couples, and especially for those who are undergoing difficulty within their marriage, that Christ may transform their suffering into renewed love for one another, we pray: ◆ For the needs and petitions of our local Church family, that they may be brought closer into fraternal charity with one another, we pray: ◆

Our Father . . .

Lord Jesus Christ,
you reveal your glory to your people
through the miracle of the water and
    the wine.
In the events of our daily lives,
reveal yourself ever more deeply to us,
that we may always come to know
    you more,
you, who are King, Messiah, and Lord.
Open our ears to listen to your word,
and to do your will with joyful obedience.
You live and reign forever.
Amen.

✝ The Lord takes delight in his people.

Sunday, January 8, 2012
Solemnity of the Epiphany of the Lord

✝ Lord, every nation on earth will adore you.

Psalm 72
page 411

Reading
Matthew 2:1–2, 9–11

When Jesus was born in Bethlehem of Judea, in the days of King Herod, behold, magi from the east arrived in Jerusalem, saying, "Where is the newborn king of the Jews? We saw his star at its rising and have come to do him homage." . . . After their audience with the king they set out. And behold, the star that they had seen at its rising preceded them, until it came and stopped over the place where the child was. They were overjoyed at seeing the star, and on entering the house they saw the child with Mary his mother. They prostrated themselves and did him homage. Then they opened their treasures and offered him gifts of gold, frankincense, and myrrh.

Reflection

The star has risen in the east. The wise men journey to seek the Christ child. Finding him with his mother, they worship him and offer him costly treasures. Christ's light has shone upon all the nations. All peoples are invited to come and worship the Christ child. He has become human for everyone: the poor and the rich, the simple and the learned, the powerful and the weak. All are invited to seek and to find the child of Bethlehem who awaits our gift of love.

Prayers
others may be added

By the light of the star, the wise men sought the Christ child. Hear the prayers that we offer you today, as we pray:

◆ **Light of hope, shine in our hearts.**

For the Church, that, guided by the light of Christ, she may remain faithful in her pilgrim journey until the attainment of the heavenly glory, we pray: ◆ For all nations throughout the world, that, guided by their leaders, they may seek the light of truth and come to worship the one true God, we pray: ◆ For all the sick and suffering, the poor, the lonely, and the homeless, that they may hear the Good News that Jesus has come to make his dwelling among the poor and the weak, we pray: ◆ For all scientists, all students, and for all the learned, that they may use their knowledge for the good of all peoples as they work to seek the truth, we pray: ◆

Our Father . . .

Jesus Christ, our King and Lord,
today in the humble city of Bethlehem
you manifest yourself to all peoples
as our God and Savior and King.
Led by a star in the sky,
the wise men sought your presence.
By the help and prayers
of the Blessed Virgin Mary,
may we be given the help we need
to travel along the journey of life
until we attain eternal glory.
You live and reign forever.
Amen.

✝ Lord, every nation on earth will adore you.

✝ You will draw water joyfully from the springs of salvation.

Psalm 72   *page 411*

Reading   *Mark 1:7–11*

This is what [John the Baptist] proclaimed: "One mightier than I is coming after me. I am not worthy to stoop and loosen the thongs of his sandals. I have baptized you with water; he will baptize you with the Holy Spirit."

It happened in those days that Jesus came from Nazareth of Galilee and was baptized in the Jordan by John. On coming up out of the water he saw the heavens being torn open and the Spirit, like a dove, descending upon him. And a voice came from the heavens, "You are my beloved Son; with you I am well pleased."

Reflection

Today we hear the beautiful manifestation of the Trinity. Jesus is baptized in the Jordan; the Holy Spirit descends upon him as a dove; the Father's voice speaks from the heavens. God the Father has sent his Son into the world to bring us freedom and life. In total obedience, the Son fulfills the loving will of the Father. By the outpouring of his life, the Son sends us his Holy Spirit. Through this most holy baptism of the Lord, God reveals to us his glory.

Prayers   *others may be added*

To you who are Father, Son, and Holy Spirit, we offer our petitions as we pray:

◆ Lord, hear our prayer.

For Holy Mother Church, that, united to Jesus Christ, and led by the Holy Spirit, she may fulfill the will of the Father, we pray: ◆ For all those who are preparing for Baptism and for the newly baptized, that by God's grace they may be faithful Christians, constantly growing in maturity and faithfulness in their vocation to holiness, we pray: ◆ For all the poor and the suffering, that they may come to freely receive from the waters of life, we pray: ◆ For all baptized Christians, by the grace of the sacrament of Baptism, that the Holy Trinity may dwell ever more perfectly in our hearts and souls, we pray: ◆ For all the faithful departed, through their Baptism they died to sin; may they rise to the eternal new life in the heavenly glory, we pray:

Our Father . . .

Father God,
in the baptism of the Jordan,
you manifest to us your Son's glory.
By the outpouring of your Holy Spirit,
you anoint Jesus as Messiah and Lord.
Through the grace of the sacraments,
unite us more deeply into union with you,
who lives and reigns with our Lord Jesus
    Christ, your Son,
in the unity of the Holy Spirit,
one God, forever and ever.
Amen.

✝ You will draw water joyfully from the springs of salvation.

Tuesday, January 10, 2012
Weekday
First Week in Ordinary Time

✝ I will offer a sacrifice of thanksgiving and call on the name of the LORD. *(Psalm 116:17)*

Psalm 19   ▸ *page 403*

Reading   *Mark 1:14–20*

After John had been arrested, Jesus came to Galilee proclaiming the gospel of God: "This is the time of fulfillment. The Kingdom of God is at hand. Repent, and believe in the Gospel."

As he passed by the Sea of Galilee, he saw Simon and his brother Andrew casting their nets into the sea; they were fishermen. Jesus said to them, "Come after me, and I will make you fishers of men." Then they abandoned their nets and followed him. He walked along a little farther and saw James, the son of Zebedee, and his brother John. They too were in a boat mending their nets. Then he called them. So they left their father Zebedee in the boat along with the hired men and followed him.

Reflection

Jesus comes to meet us in the events of our everyday life. Look how in today's Gospel Jesus simply calls the brothers. Simon and Andrew were busy fishing, casting their nets into the sea. Jesus calls, and they leave their nets to follow after him. Then he calls James and his brother John. Immediately, they leave their nets, and their father, too, and follow Jesus. How is the Lord calling us to follow him in our own daily life and work?

Prayers   *others may be added*

Lord Jesus, you call the hearts of all peoples to work for your kingdom. With hope, we pray:

◆ Send laborers into your vineyard, Lord.

For the Holy Father, in thanksgiving for his "yes" to Christ, and being faithful to serving his spiritual sons and daughters throughout the world, we pray: ◆ For all the sick, the poor, and the lonely, that they may answer Jesus' call to follow him along the Way of the Cross as they strive to endure their suffering with patience and joy, we pray: ◆ For all women who suffer the grief of being unable to conceive, that the Lord will bring them healing and make them fruitful with biological children as well as numerous spiritual children, we pray: ◆

Our Father . . .

God our Father,
you are the vine dresser
who calls each of us
to work in your vineyard.
To each you give a different
and unique task to fulfill.
Keep us faithful to your call,
and may we always persevere
to love you with our whole
heart and with our whole soul.
We ask this through Christ our Lord.
Amen.

✝ I will offer a sacrifice of thanksgiving and call on the name of the LORD.

Wednesday, January 11, 2012
Weekday

✝ Here I am, Lord, I come to do your will.

Psalm 34 — page 406

Reading — Mark 1:29–39

On leaving the synagogue Jesus entered the house of Simon and Andrew with James and John. Simon's mother-in-law lay sick with a fever. They immediately told him about her. He approached, grasped her hand, and helped her up. Then the fever left her and she waited on them.

When it was evening, after sunset, they brought to him all who were ill or possessed by demons. The whole town was gathered at the door. He cured many who were sick with various diseases, and he drove out many demons, not permitting them to speak because they knew him.

Rising very early before dawn, he left and went off to a deserted place, where he prayed. Simon and those who were with him pursued him and on finding him said, "Everyone is looking for you." He told them, "Let us go on to the nearby villages that I may preach there also. For this purpose have I come." So he went into their synagogues, preaching and driving out demons throughout the whole of Galilee.

Reflection

Jesus' work never ceases. Immediately after preaching in the synagogue, Jesus enters the house of his friends, and later the whole town comes to him so that he may heal the sick and the possessed. Jesus wakes very early to go off and pray, but everyone is looking for him. He goes to the nearby villages and continues to preach and drive out demons. Jesus reminds his disciples that his purpose is to teach and to heal.

Prayers — others may be added

Lifting our prayers to God, we say:

◆ Speak, Lord, your servant is listening.

For all the ordained, that, united to the prophetic ministry of Jesus Christ, they may proclaim God's mystery by their apostolic ministry, we pray: ◆ That all governmental officials and political leaders may imitate the ministry of Jesus Christ who has come to serve, we pray: ◆ For all who suffer in spirit, mind, or body, that they may turn to God in faith, we pray: ◆ For all Christians, that they may give thanks for the wonders the Lord has worked for them, by going out in turn to serve others, we pray: ◆

Our Father . . .

Lord, our God,
you call us out of ourselves
to do your work and serve your people.
Grant us the grace of a humble heart.
we ask this through Christ our Lord.
Amen.

✝ Here I am, Lord, I come to do your will.

✝ Rise up, help us! Redeem us as your love demands. (*Psalm 44:27*)

Psalm 63
page 410

Reading
Mark 1:40–45

A leper came to [Jesus] and kneeling down begged him and said, "If you wish, you can make me clean." Moved with pity, he stretched out his hand, touched him, and said to him, "I do will it. Be made clean." The leprosy left him immediately, and he was made clean. Then, warning him sternly, he dismissed him at once. Then he said to him, "See that you tell no one anything, but go, show yourself to the priest and offer for your cleansing what Moses prescribed; that will be proof for them." The man went away and began to publicize the whole matter. He spread the report abroad so that it was impossible for Jesus to enter a town openly. He remained outside in deserted places, and people kept coming to him from everywhere.

Reflection
If we listen closely to the Gospel, we can begin to know more the person of Jesus. He preaches in the synagogues with authority unlike any other teacher, he has the power to heal every kind of serious ailment and sickness, he has compassion on all who suffer, and his fame spreads throughout all the peoples. But this man is not only man, but also God. Jesus Christ, true God and true man, invites us to enter into his mystery.

Prayers
others may be added

God our Father has sent us his Son to save us from our sins and heal us from all our ills. Let us pray:

◆ Cleanse us, O Lord.

For the Church, that she may be a font of healing and a refuge for all peoples who are seeking the truth, we pray: ◆ For leaders of nations, that they may implement policies to care for the beauty and goodness of God's creation, we pray: ◆ For all the sick and suffering, and for those who suffer from serious diseases, that they may be assured of Jesus' healing love, which brings life out of suffering and pain, we pray: ◆ For all peoples, that they may have the courage to fight and defend the truth, we pray: ◆ That all Catholics may turn to the healing sacraments of Reconciliation and the Holy Eucharist to receive forgiveness and unity with God, we pray: ◆

Our Father . . .

God of mercy and healing,
turn your loving gaze
upon your children who struggle
to serve you through the difficulties
and sufferings of this present life.
We beg of you to heal us
by the power of your Holy Spirit,
according to your most perfect and
    merciful will.
We ask this through Christ our Lord.
Amen.

✝ Rise up, help us! Redeem us as your love demands.

✝ For ever I will sing the goodness of the Lord.

Psalm 95 — page 413

Reading — Mark 2:1–12

When Jesus returned to Capernaum after some days, it became known that he was at home. Many gathered together so that there was no longer room for them, not even around the door, and he preached the word to them. They came bringing to him a paralytic carried by four men. Unable to get near Jesus because of the crowd, they opened up the roof above him. After they had broken through, they let down the mat on which the paralytic was lying. When Jesus saw their faith, he said to the paralytic, "Child, your sins are forgiven." Now some of the scribes were sitting there asking themselves, "Why does this man speak that way? He is blaspheming. Who but God alone can forgive sins?" Jesus immediately knew in his mind what they were thinking to themselves, so he said, "Why are you thinking such things in your hearts? Which is easier, to say to the paralytic, 'Your sins are forgiven,' or to say, 'Rise, pick up your mat and walk'? But that you may know that the Son of Man has authority to forgive sins on earth"—he said to the paralytic, "I say to you, rise, pick up your mat, and go home." He rose, picked up his mat at once, and went away in the sight of everyone. They were all astounded and glorified God, saying, "We have never seen anything like this."

Reflection

Before healing the man's physical ailment, Jesus first heals him internally by forgiving him of his sins. The people are scandalized, because only God can forgive sins. However, in doing so, Jesus reveals himself as the Son of God, by being able to heal the man both spiritually and physically. The people who witness this event remain in awe of his power and might.

Prayers — *others may be added*

With confidence we pray:

◆ Heal us, Lord.

For the Holy Father, that he may persevere in Christ's ministry as Priest, Prophet, and King, we pray: ◆ For nations that suffer from hunger and violence, we pray: ◆ For all who are ill, that they may receive healing and strength, we pray: ◆ For all who have died, that the death and Resurrection of Jesus Christ may bring new life to their souls and bodies, we pray: ◆ That all Christians may have the courage to boldly live a Christian witness, we pray: ◆

Our Father . . .

Jesus Christ, our King,
have mercy on us for our offenses.
May we never reject or offend you,
for you are the King of our hearts.
Reign over us in your goodness and power.
In your name, we pray.
Amen.

✝ For ever I will sing the goodness of the Lord.

✝ Let all the earth cry out to God with joy.

Psalm 95 *page 413*

Reading *Mark 2:13–17*

Jesus went out along the sea. All the crowd came to him and he taught them. As he passed by, he saw Levi, son of Alphaeus, sitting at the customs post. Jesus said to him, "Follow me." And he got up and followed Jesus. While he was at table in his house, many tax collectors and sinners sat with Jesus and his disciples; for there were many who followed him. Some scribes who were Pharisees saw that Jesus was eating with sinners and tax collectors and said to his disciples, "Why does he eat with tax collectors and sinners?" Jesus heard this and said to them, "Those who are well do not need a physician, but the sick do. I did not come to call the righteous but sinners."

Reflection

We live in a society where strength and success are valued as the most important qualities a person can possess. However, today in the Gospel, we learn that Jesus calls the weak and the sinful. This is the reason why he has come to dwell among us. Those who are sick need a physician, and we who are sinful and weak are in need of Jesus Christ who brings us salvation and life.

Prayers *others may be added*

With confidence, we pray:

◆ Heal us, O Lord, in your mercy.

For the Church, that she may be the source of salvation for all sinners, we pray: ◆ For all nations, especially those that suffer from war, violence, and sorrow, we pray: ◆ For all who are sick and dying, for those who suffer physically, mentally, or emotionally, that they may receive the help they need to receive healing and peace, we pray: ◆ For the needs of our local community, that all may be renewed in faith to offer a generous "yes" to follow the Lord when he calls, we pray: ◆

Our Father . . .

Merciful Father,
You sent your Son as our strength
    and health.
He is the divine physician
who heals all our physical and
    spiritual ills.
Breathe your Spirit upon us,
that, strengthened by your life,
we may follow you with renewed
perseverance and devotion.
We ask this through Christ our Lord.
Amen.

✝ Let all the earth cry out to God with joy.

✝ I come to do your will.

Psalm 100 *page 414*

Reading *John 1:35–42*

John was standing with two of his disciples, and as he watched Jesus walk by, he said, "Behold, the Lamb of God." The two disciples heard what he said and followed Jesus. Jesus turned and saw them following him and said to them, "What are you looking for?" They said to him, "Rabbi"—which translated means Teacher—, "where are you staying?" He said to them, "Come, and you will see." So they went and saw where he was staying, and they stayed with him that day. It was about four in the afternoon. Andrew, the brother of Simon Peter, was one of the two who heard John and followed Jesus. He first found his own brother Simon and told him, "We have found the Messiah"—which is translated Christ. Then he brought him to Jesus. Jesus looked at him and said, "You are Simon the son of John; you will be called Cephas"—which is translated Peter.

Reflection

Where can we find Jesus Christ, our Teacher? Where is he staying? Jesus has given us his Body and Blood in the most holy sacrament of the Eucharist, and he remains waiting for us to come and to stay with him. He is the sacrificial lamb, the Lamb of God, who takes away the sins of the world through the mystery of his Passion, death, and Resurrection.

Prayers *others may be added*

You do not desire that we be left orphans, but rather you give us your true Body and Blood in the Eucharist. Let us pray:

◆ Stay with us, O Lord.

For the Holy Father, bishops, priests, and deacons, that they may faithfully serve the Mystical Body of Christ through the daily sacrifice of the Eucharist, we pray: ◆ For all political leaders who work for justice among nations, that their work may be a means by which all people encounter the Gospel values of Jesus Christ, we pray: ◆ For the sick, that their physical and mental sufferings may gain for them a lasting crown in heaven, we pray: ◆ That all Catholics may grow in their love for Christ present in the Eucharist, we pray: ◆

Our Father . . .

Jesus Christ, our teacher, we seek you
and we desire to be with you.
Reveal to us your presence in
　Holy Eucharist.
Increase our faith,
that we may know with full conviction
that it is truly you
who is present, body, blood, soul,
　and divinity
under the appearances of the bread
　and wine.
Reveal to us that you are our Messiah,
the Lamb of God who comes to save us.
Stay with us, Lord. We seek your face.
You live and reign forever.
Amen.

✝ I come to do your will.

Monday, January 16, 2012
Weekday

✝ Before I formed you in the womb,
I knew you.

Psalm 103 *page 415*

Reading *Mark 2:18–22*

The disciples of John and of the Pharisees were accustomed to fast. People came to him and objected, "Why do the disciples of John and the disciples of the Pharisees fast, but your disciples do not fast?" Jesus answered them, "Can the wedding guests fast while the bridegroom is with them? As long as they have the bridegroom with them they cannot fast. But the days will come when the bridegroom is taken away from them, and then they will fast on that day. No one sews a piece of unshrunken cloth on an old cloak. If he does, its fullness pulls away, the new from the old, and the tear gets worse. Likewise, no one pours new wine into old wineskins. Otherwise, the wine will burst the skins, and both the wine and the skins are ruined. Rather, new wine is poured into fresh wineskins."

Reflection

Since the time of the disciples, the followers of Christ have been criticized. To be a Christian means to be different, to go against the grain, to be radical. Today in the Gospel, the Pharisees are scandalized that Jesus' followers do not fast. Let us not be afraid of criticism or rejection, and let us clarify the misconceptions others have toward Christianity and its morals.

Prayers *others may be added*

Father, the giver of life, with confidence in your paternal love, hear our prayer:

◆ Give us life, O Lord.

For the Holy Father, that he may always lead and guide the Church to protect the life of all peoples, boldly clarifying the truth with fortitude and charity, we pray: ◆ That all governmental officials may implement laws to respect life from conception until natural death, we pray: ◆ For all women, men, families, and children who suffer the effects of the evil of abortion and all anti-life practices, we pray: ◆ For all who work to uphold the dignity and respect for life, that they may bear fruit by their prayers and good works, we pray: ◆ In thanksgiving for the gift of life and the lives of our family and friends, we pray: ◆

Our Father . . .

Heavenly Father,
you are the Lord, the giver of life.
You have created us in your image
    and likeness,
and you have made our bodies good
    and holy
to give you glory and fulfill your
    perfect will.
Protect and preserve all life, so that
all may enjoy the fullness of your love.
We ask this in the name of your Son,
    Jesus Christ.
Amen.

✝ Before I formed you in the womb,
I knew you.

✝ The Lord looks into the heart.

Psalm 145   *page 422*

Reading   *Mark 2:23–28*

As Jesus was passing through a field of grain on the sabbath, his disciples began to make a path while picking the heads of grain. At this the Pharisees said to him, "Look, why are they doing what is unlawful on the sabbath?" He said to them, "Have you never read what David did when he was in need and he and his companions were hungry? How he went into the house of God when Abiathar was high priest and ate the bread of offering that only the priests could lawfully eat, and shared it with his companions?" Then he said to them, "The sabbath was made for man, not man for the sabbath. That is why the Son of Man is lord even of the sabbath."

Reflection

The Pharisees continue to search for ways in which they can find fault with Jesus and his disciples. Today in the Gospel, they criticize their actions on the sabbath day, but Jesus clarifies their misunderstandings. The sabbath and all the prescriptions of the law are not ends in themselves, but rather, means by which man is united to God. Jesus reveals himself as the Messiah as he asserts his authority even over the sabbath day.

Prayers   *others may be added*

With confidence, we pray:

◆ Purify our hearts, Lord.

For all ministers of the Church, that their work will bring about the kingdom in justice and truth, we pray: ◆ For nations that hunger for the truth of the Gospel, that they may be fed with the bread of the living Word of God, we pray: ◆ For countries torn by violence, hunger, and discrimination, that the Lord may send out leaders to bring about justice, we pray: ◆ For the sick, the anxious, the oppressed, and the poor, that they may offer their sufferings as a spiritual sacrifice pleasing to the Lord, we pray: ◆ For all who have died, that angels may lead them safely to the arms of their Father, we pray: ◆ For our local community, that we may see the beauty of each person as a gift created by God, we pray: ◆

Our Father . . .

God, our loving Father,
you do not judge by appearance,
but, you, O Lord, look into the heart.
Purify us, Lord, our God,
Help us to see as you see,
to love as you love,
and to forgive as you forgive.
We ask this through Christ our Lord.
Amen.

✝ The Lord looks into the heart.

✝ Blessed be the LORD my rock . . . ;
My safeguard and my fortress, my
stronghold, my deliverer, My shield,
in whom I trust.

Psalm 27 page 405

Reading Mark 3:1–6

Jesus entered the synagogue. There was a man there who had a withered hand. They watched him closely to see if he would cure him on the sabbath so that they might accuse him. He said to the man with the withered hand, "Come up here before us." Then he said to them, "Is it lawful to do good on the sabbath rather than to do evil, to save life rather than to destroy it?" But they remained silent. Looking around at them with anger and grieved at their hardness of heart, he said to the man, "Stretch out your hand." He stretched it out and his hand was restored. The Pharisees went out and immediately took counsel with the Herodians against him to put him to death.

Reflection

The Pharisees are watching Jesus carefully. But they are not looking at him with admiration. Rather, they are watching his every action in order to find fault with him. However, Jesus does not change himself based on what other people think of him. He continues his work and heals the man's withered hand before everyone in the synagogue. May we follow Jesus' example and boldly live our Christian faith without fear from those who may criticize us.

Prayers *others may be added*

Most holy God, you are the same yesterday, today, and always. Teach us your word and heal all our ills, as we pray:

◆ Speak, Lord, your servant is listening.

That ministers of the Church may proclaim God's mystery by their apostolic service, we pray: ◆ That all governmental officials and political leaders may imitate the ministry of Jesus Christ who has come to serve, we pray: ◆ That all who suffer in spirit, mind, or body may turn to God in faith, we pray: ◆ That all doctors, nurses, and health care workers may be united to the work of Jesus, the divine physician, we pray: ◆ That all Christians may give thanks for the wonders the Lord has worked for them, we pray: ◆

Our Father . . .

Lord, our God,
you desire great things from us.
You call us out of ourselves
to do your work and serve your people.
Grant us the grace of a humble heart,
which knows how to respond
    with readiness
to the joy and glory of your word.
We ask this through Christ our Lord.
Amen.

✝ Blessed be the LORD my rock . . . ;
My safeguard and my fortress, my
stronghold, my deliverer, My shield,
in whom I trust.

✝ In God I trust; I shall not fear.

Psalm 27 *page 405*

Reading *Mark 3:7–12*

Jesus withdrew toward the sea with his disciples. A large number of people followed from Galilee and from Judea. Hearing what he was doing, a large number of people came to him also from Jerusalem, from Idumea, from beyond the Jordan, and from the neighborhood of Tyre and Sidon. He told his disciples to have a boat ready for him because of the crowd, so that they would not crush him. He had cured many and, as a result, those who had diseases were pressing upon him to touch him. And whenever unclean spirits saw him they would fall down before him and shout, "You are the Son of God." He warned them sternly not to make him known.

Reflection

In the Gospel, so many people come to Jesus, that he tells his apostles to have a boat ready so that he is not crushed by the crowds. Today, do a large number of people from many nations follow after Jesus? Do we come to him and beg him to heal our physical and spiritual illnesses? Is the knowledge and fame of Jesus Christ spreading throughout, because of the miracles he has worked in our lives?

Prayers *others may be added*

With faith, we turn to you and pray:

◆ Stir into flame the gifts of your Holy Spirit.

For the ordained, that they may guard, protect, and hand on the deposit of faith of the Church, we pray: ◆ For leaders of all nations, that they may not fear to work for justice, we pray: ◆ For all those who serve the ill, that they may bring the presence of Jesus Christ and the comfort of the word of God, we pray: ◆ For those persecuted in Jesus' name, that they may persevere in faith, and that they may continue to be a source of peace in the midst of evil, we pray: ◆ That all of us may be powerful instruments to further the kingdom of God, we pray: ◆

Our Father . . .

Almighty and everlasting Father,
by the power of your Spirit, stir into flame
the gifts that we receive through
    your sacraments.
Give us a spirit of power and of
    self-control,
and cast out all cowardice so that we may
not be ashamed to testify to your Son,
    Jesus Christ.
Give us the strength that comes from
    you alone
to bear our share of the hardship for
    the Gospel.
We ask this through Christ our Lord.
Amen.

✝ In God I trust; I shall not fear.

✝ For ever I will sing the goodness of the Lord.

Psalm 95 *page 413*

Reading *Mark 3:13–19*

Jesus went up the mountain and summoned those whom he wanted and they came to him. He appointed Twelve whom he also named Apostles that they might be with him and he might send them forth to preach and to have authority to drive out demons: He appointed the Twelve: Simon, whom he named Peter; James, son of Zebedee, and John the brother of James, whom he named Boanerges, that is, sons of thunder; Andrew, Philip, Bartholomew, Matthew, Thomas, James the son of Alphaeus; Thaddeus, Simon the Cananean, and Judas Iscariot who betrayed him.

Reflection

In today's Gospel, Jesus calls 12 persons by name to be his apostles. Jesus likewise has called us each by name to be with him and to share in his apostolic ministry. Jesus called those whom he wanted so that they might be with him. Jesus wants us. Jesus desires to be with us. By the sacraments, God has united us into his divine life and he has sent us out to continue his work. Each day may we respond to Jesus' loving invitation to be with him ever more closely and to faithfully share in his work of service and love.

Prayers *others may be added*

With confidence, we pray:

◆ Heal us, Lord, and grant us your salvation.

For the Holy Father, that he may be encouraged by the prayers of all the faithful to persevere in Christ's ministry, we pray: ◆ For all nations who suffer from hunger and violence, we pray: ◆ For all who are ill, that their trials may be a means to seek spiritual healing in virtues of patience and fortitude, we pray: ◆ That Jesus Christ may reign in the hearts of each person as Lord and King, we pray: ◆ For all who have died, that the death and Resurrection of Jesus Christ may bring new life to their souls and bodies, we pray: ◆ That all Christians may have the courage to boldly live a Christian witness, we pray: ◆

Our Father . . .

Jesus Christ, our King,
have mercy on us for our offenses.
May we never reject or offend you,
for you are the King of our hearts.
Reign over us in your goodness
    and power,
so that your kingdom may spread
throughout all the world,
that your glory may radiantly shine forth
in good works and virtue
through the witness and example of
    our lives.
We ask this through Christ our Lord.
Amen.

✝ For ever I will sing the goodness of the Lord.

Saturday, January 21, 2012
Memorial of Saint Agnes, Virgin and Martyr

✝ Let us see your face, Lord, and we shall be saved.

Psalm 95 *page 413*

Reading *Mark 3:20–21*

Jesus came with his disciples into the house. Again the crowd gathered, making it impossible for them even to eat. When his relatives heard of this they set out to seize him, for they said, "He is out of his mind."

Reflection

In today's short Gospel, we hear that even members of Jesus' family think he is crazy. Jesus has cured so many people both physically and spiritually and who press upon him, so that after Jesus calls the twelve apostles, they come back, and the crowds continue to press upon them, making it impossible for them to eat. The others criticize Jesus, thinking that he has lost his mind as he continues to heal the sick and drive out demons. If we are radically living our lives as true Christians, other people, including our families, may think that we are crazy too. Yet, like Christ, our food ought to be the will of the Father, and we must remain faithful to the humble work God has asked of us.

Prayers *others may be added*

We bring before the Lord our petitions, as we pray:

◆ Heal us, O Lord, in your mercy.

For the Church, that she may be the source of salvation for all sinners, we pray: ◆ For all the nations of the world, especially those that suffer from war, violence, and sorrow, that good Christians everywhere may work with political leaders to establish a culture of love, we pray: ◆ For all who are sick and dying, for those who suffer physically, mentally, or emotionally, that they may receive the help they need to receive healing and peace, we pray: ◆ For all missionaries, that they may preach the Gospel to all nations, announcing the Good News to all who have not yet encountered the Lord, we pray: ◆ For the needs of our local community, that all may be renewed in faith to offer a generous "yes" to follow the Lord where he calls, we pray: ◆

Our Father . . .

Merciful Lord Jesus Christ,
you were sent from the Father
as our Redeemer and Savior.
You are our strength and our health,
the divine physician who heals
all our physical and spiritual ills.
Breathe your Spirit upon us,
that, strengthened by your life,
we may follow you with renewed
perseverance and devotion.
You live and reign forever.
Amen.

✝ Let us see your face, Lord, and we shall be saved.

✝ Guide me in your truth and teach me, for you are God my savior.

Psalm 63   *page 410*

Reading   *Mark 1:14–20*

After John had been arrested, Jesus came to Galilee proclaiming the gospel of God: "This is the time of fulfillment. The kingdom of God is at hand. Repent, and believe in the gospel."

As he passed by the Sea of Galilee, he saw Simon and his brother Andrew casting their nets into the sea; they were fishermen. Jesus said to them, "Come after me, and I will make you fishers of men." Then they abandoned their nets and followed him. He walked along a little farther and saw James, the son of Zebedee, and his brother John. They too were in a boat mending their nets. Then he called them. So they left their father Zebedee in the boat along with the hired men and followed him.

Reflection

"Repent, and believe." This is the command that Jesus enjoins us with today. Turn away from sin to the truth of Jesus Christ present in his Word. Like the apostles who are called on the Sea of Galilee, Jesus also calls us to come after him. As Jesus transforms the apostles' human profession, Christ, likewise, calls us in the midst of our work and transforms our efforts for the glory of the Father.

Prayers   *others may be added*

The kingdom is at hand. O God, turn our hearts to you and give us faith, as we pray:

◆ Teach us your ways, O Lord.

For the sanctification of the Holy Father, all bishops, priests, and deacons, that they may faithfully live out their vocation to follow the Master's call in service and in love, we pray: ◆ For all political leaders, that they may be attentive to the voice of the Holy Spirit, who calls them to repent from evil and turn in faith to the truth of Jesus Christ, we pray: ◆ For all the sick and suffering, that the power of Christ's Resurrection may bring them physical and spiritual strength and healing, we pray: ◆ For all who have died, that the angels may bring them swiftly into paradise, we pray: ◆

Our Father . . .

O God,
you are our refuge and our strength,
our stronghold in the time of trouble.
Despite our weaknesses and inabilities,
you call us to serve you on our own
    unique path.
We surrender our lives into your hands.
In our weakness, Lord, be our strength.
We ask this through our Lord Jesus
    Christ, your Son,
who lives and reigns with you in the unity
    of the Holy Spirit,
one God, forever and ever.
Amen.

✝ Guide me in your truth and teach me, for you are God my savior.

✝ My loyalty and love will be with him.

Psalm 95 *page 413*

Reading *Mark 3:22–30*

The scribes who had come from Jerusalem said, "[Jesus] is possessed by Beelzebul," and "By the prince of demons he drives out demons."

Summoning them, [Jesus] began to speak to them in parables, "How can Satan drive out Satan? If a kingdom is divided against itself, that kingdom cannot stand. And if a house is divided against itself, that house will not be able to stand. And if Satan has risen up against himself and is divided, he cannot stand; that is the end of him. But no one can enter a strong man's house to plunder his property unless he first ties up the strong man. Then he can plunder his house. Amen, I say to you, all sins and all blasphemies that people utter will be forgiven them. But whoever blasphemes against the Holy Spirit will never have forgiveness, but is guilty of an everlasting sin."

Reflection

Let us turn to the Lord with undivided hearts. Jesus tells us that "a kingdom divided against itself cannot stand." We must worship the Lord above all things, and we must not separate our faith from the rest of our lives. Let us place God at the center, for he has assured us not to worry, but to "seek first the Kingdom of God" (Matthew 7:34).

Prayers *others may be added*

Almighty God, hear the prayers we place before you as we pray:

◆ Have mercy on us, Lord; free us from our sins.

That the Church may be renewed in her work of ecumenical formation and dialogue, we pray: ◆ That through the work of governmental officers and national leaders, all nations will be freed from division and discord, we pray: ◆ That those who are suffering, especially those who suffer from addiction, abuse, or spiritual attack, may be free, we pray: ◆ That our Christian community may become more united through constant personal conversion, prayer, friendship, and service to one another, we pray: ◆

Our Father . . .

God of mercy and healing,
turn your loving gaze
upon your children who struggle
to serve you through the difficulties
and sufferings of this present life.
We beg of you to heal us
by the power of your Holy Spirit,
according to your most perfect and
merciful will.
We ask this through Christ our Lord.
Amen.

✝ My loyalty and love will be with him.

Tuesday, January 24, 2012
Memorial of Saint Francis de Sales, Bishop and Doctor of the Church

✝ The LORD looks into the heart.

Psalm 145   *page 422*

Reading   *Mark 3:31–35*

The mother of Jesus and his brothers arrived. Standing outside they sent word to him and called him. A crowd seated around him told him, "Your mother and your brothers and your sisters are outside asking for you." But he said to them in reply, "Who are my mother and my brothers?" And looking around at those seated in the circle he said, "Here are my mother and my brothers. For whoever does the will of God is my brother and sister and mother."

Reflection

God desires to share deep intimacy with us. He desires to be so close with us, that even our wills are united as one. Through this union of wills, we share in God's own divine familial life. By doing the will of God we become members of God's own family. In today's Gospel, we encounter this mystery as the Lord invites us to do his will and experience the depth of joy and freedom that comes through union with him.

Prayers   *others may be added*

With faith in the love and mercy of the Father, we pray:

◆ Hear I am, Lord; I come to do your will.

For the ordained and lay ministers of the Church, that their work will bring about the kingdom in justice and truth, we pray: ◆ For the nations that hunger for the truth of the Gospel, that they may be fed with the living Word of God, we pray: ◆ For countries torn by violence, hunger, and discrimination, that the Lord may send out leaders to bring about justice, we pray: ◆ For the sick, the anxious, the oppressed, and the poor, that they may offer their sufferings as a spiritual sacrifice pleasing to the Lord, we pray: ◆ For all who have died, that angels may lead them safely to the arms of their Father, we pray: ◆

Our Father . . .

God, our loving Father,
give us strength to faithfully
fulfill your holy will.
Liberate us from our selfishness,
that we may know and understand
that a life in union with you
is a life of true freedom and joy.
We ask this through Christ our Lord.
Amen.

✝ The LORD looks into the heart.

✝ Go into the whole world and proclaim the gospel to every creature.

Psalm 19   *page 403*

Reading   *Mark 16:15–20*

Jesus appeared to the Eleven and said to them: "Go into the whole world and proclaim the Gospel to every creature. Whoever believes and is baptized will be saved; whoever does not believe will be condemned. These signs will accompany those who believe: in my name they will drive out demons, they will speak new languages. They will pick up serpents with their hands, and if they drink any deadly thing, it will not harm them. They will lay hands on the sick, and they will recover."

Reflection

Today we celebrate the great feast of the conversion of Saint Paul, the apostle, to the Gentiles, who, prior to his conversion, had persecuted numerous Christians, but then through the grace of God, went out to proclaim the Good News of Jesus Christ to the nations. May Saint Paul help us to be faithful apostles and disciples of Jesus Christ.

Prayers   *others may be added*

Your word, O Lord, is spirit and truth. Hear the prayers we present before you. We pray:

◆ Lord, send us your Spirit.

For the Church, that she may be renewed in her work of evangelization, that all the nations may come to know the Good News, we pray: ◆ For all nations, especially for those that are farthest away from Christ, that good and holy political leaders may rise up to encourage Gospel values among all cultures, we pray: ◆ For all the sick and the suffering, that they may receive strength from the Lord in their weakness, we pray: ◆ For those who are persecuted for the faith, that they may be strengthened in their love for God, we pray: ◆ For all evangelists, catechists, and teachers, and for all those who form and instruct those in the faith, we pray: ◆

Our Father . . .

God our Father,
you grant us a share in the mission
of your Son Jesus Christ, to go forth
and to proclaim your glory to all nations.
Anoint us with your same Spirit,
that, inflamed with love for all the world
     and for all peoples,
we may be spurred on to magnify the
     goodness of your Son's name.
We ask this through Christ our Lord.
Amen.

✝ Go into the whole world and proclaim the gospel to every creature.

Thursday, January 26, 2012
Memorial of Saints Timothy and Titus, Bishops

✝ Bear your share of hardship for the Gospel with the strength that comes from God.

Psalm 27
page 405

Reading
Mark 4:21–25

Jesus said to his disciples, "Is a lamp brought in to be placed under a bushel basket or under a bed, and not to be placed on a lampstand? For there is nothing hidden except to be made visible; nothing is secret except to come to light. Anyone who has ears to hear ought to hear." He also told them, "Take care what you hear. The measure with which you measure will be measured out to you, and still more will be given to you. To the one who has, more will be given; from the one who has not, even what he has will be taken away."

Reflection

Jesus sends us out as salt and light for the world. He desires that the uniqueness of our Christian lives offer abundant richness and flavor to the world. United to him, our lives must shine out as radiant light, so that others may see the joy and beauty of being a Christian— that all peoples may glorify God and share in the goodness of his life.

Prayers
others may be added

With faith, we turn to you and pray:

◆ Lord, hear our prayer.

For the Holy Father, that he may guard, protect, and hand on the deposit of faith of the Church, we pray: ◆ For leaders of all nations, that they may not fear to work for justice by establishing better methods of communication and dialogue, we pray: ◆ For those who serve the ill, that they may bring the presence of Jesus Christ and the comfort of his Word, we pray: ◆ That all peoples may be powerful instruments to further the kingdom of God, we pray: ◆

Our Father . . .

Almighty and everlasting Father,
you strengthen us by the witness of Saints
    Timothy and Titus,
who fulfilled your will as holy bishops
    in the service of your Word.
By the power of your Spirit, stir
    into flame
the gifts that we receive through
    your sacraments.
Give us a spirit of power and of
    self-control
and cast out all cowardice so that we may
not be ashamed to testify to your Son,
    Jesus Christ.
Give us the strength that comes from
    you alone
to bear our share of the hardship for
    the Gospel.
We ask this through Christ our Lord.
Amen.

✝ Bear your share of hardship for the Gospel with the strength that comes from God.

✝ Let your love for one another be intense. (*1 Peter 4:8*)

Psalm 34 *page 406*

Reading *Mark 4:30–34*

[Jesus said to the crowds:] "To what shall we compare the Kingdom of God, or what parable can we use for it? It is like a mustard seed that, when it is sown in the ground, is the smallest of all the seeds on the earth. But once it is sown, it springs up and becomes the largest of plants and puts forth large branches, so that the birds of the sky can dwell in its shade." With many such parables he spoke the word to them as they were able to understand it. Without parables he did not speak to them, but to his own disciples he explained everything in private.

Reflection

The kingdom of God is a great mystery. It is like the sown seed that grows quietly and gradually, which the farmer does not understand how. The kingdom is also like the tiny mustard seed hidden in the soil that eventually grows to be a large tree that gives shade and rest. Through prayer and meditation of the word of God, Jesus personally reveals himself and the mystery of his kingdom to us as he did for his disciples.

Prayers *others may be added*

In faith, let us pray:

◆ May your word grow in our hearts.

For the Church, that united to the work of Jesus Christ, she may sow the word of truth throughout all the world, we pray: ◆ For public officials, that they may always seek truth as they work to cultivate political relations based on the mutual search for the good of the human person and society, we pray: ◆ For all children, young people, the underprivileged, and the weak, that they may be assured that God does great things through our human weakness and insufficiencies, we pray: ◆ For our local community, that it may be stirred to contemplate the great mystery of God and his kingdom through faithful prayer, we pray: ◆

Our Father . . .

Almighty Father,
in your Son, Jesus Christ,
you teach us the mysteries of
    your kingdom.
You call the weak and make them strong,
that we can boast only of your grace.
Send your Spirit upon us,
that the word of God, sown in our hearts,
may grow in fruitfulness;
all for your glory of you and the good of
    your Church.
We ask this through Christ our Lord.
Amen.

✝ Let your love for one another be intense.

✝ A clean heart create for me, God.
(*Psalm 51:12*)

Psalm 19   *page 403*

Reading   *Mark 4:35–41*

On that day, as evening drew on, Jesus said to them, "Let us cross to the other side." Leaving the crowd, they took him with them in the boat just as he was. And other boats were with him. A violent squall came up and waves were breaking over the boat, so that it was already filling up. Jesus was in the stern, asleep on a cushion. They woke him and said to him, "Teacher, do you not care that we are perishing?" He woke up, rebuked the wind, and said to the sea, "Quiet! Be still!" The wind ceased and there was great calm. Then he asked them, "Why are you terrified? Do you not yet have faith?" They were filled with great awe and said to one another, "Who then is this whom even wind and sea obey?"

Reflection

Is it not enough for Jesus to simply be with us? Or do we want him to be constantly working miracles? Our God is a god whom even the wind and the seas obey, who has power over all things. This knowledge ought to give us courage and deep peace to remain calm even in the midst of great difficulties. Let us pray for a deep faith, so that we may have confidence in God, who is present among us, and who is the source of our peace and calm.

Prayers   *others may be added*

God our Father, you call us to a life of peace and freedom. By the merits and prayers of your Son, increase your faith in us, as we pray:

◆ Lord, I believe, help my unbelief.

That the Church, as the bark of Peter, may continue to be a refuge of peace and calm for all peoples amid the storms and difficulties of life, we pray: ◆ For all world leaders, that they may have the faith to call upon God's grace in order to resolve conflict, we pray: ◆ For all who suffer from the darkness of depression or mental illness, that Jesus Christ may awaken their hearts and calm the anxieties of their minds, we pray: ◆ For our local community, that united together as God's faithful, we may have the courage to always turn to the Lord in time of need, we pray: ◆

Our Father . . .

Lord Jesus Christ,
only Son of the Father,
you are wisdom incarnate.
You are the truth for which
our body and spirit yearn.
We turn our gaze to you
to contemplate your majesty.
Send your Spirit upon us,
that we may know and love you
and always walk in the light of your truth.
You live and reign forever.
Amen.

✝ A clean heart create for me, God.

✝ If today you hear his voice, harden not your hearts.

Psalm 27 *page 405*

Reading *Mark 1:21–28*

Then they came to Capernaum, and on the sabbath Jesus entered the synagogue and taught. The people were astonished at his teaching, for he taught them as one having authority and not as the scribes. In their synagogue was a man with an unclean spirit; he cried out, "What have you to do with us, Jesus of Nazareth? Have you come to destroy us? I know who you are—the Holy One of God!" Jesus rebuked him and said, "Quiet! Come out of him!" The unclean spirit convulsed him and with a loud cry came out of him. All were amazed and asked one another, "What is this? A new teaching with authority. He commands even the unclean spirits and they obey him." His fame spread everywhere throughout the whole region of Galilee.

Reflection

Jesus' power and authority extend over all things. In the Gospel the people marvel that even the unclean spirits obey him. Even today, Jesus' divine word possesses the same strength and authority. Jesus is the prophet and teacher who speaks the word of the Father on the breath of the Spirit. Let us open our hearts to hear his voice.

Prayers *others may be added*

God of goodness, all power belongs to you. Confident in your faithfulness, we pray:

◆ Open our hearts, to your word.

For the Holy Father, that he may continue to lead the Church on the path of holiness until we attain the glory of our heavenly rest, we pray: ◆ For civil leaders, that they may responsibly seek the common good for all peoples, we pray: ◆ For all those who are ill, that the word of God may be a source of comfort for all who suffer in any way, we pray: ◆ For all religious, consecrated, married couples, and single people, that they may live the virtue of chastity according to their state of life, we pray: ◆ For our faith community, that, through prayer and the sacraments, Jesus Christ may quiet our hearts to give us lasting peace, we pray: ◆ For the grace this week to be free of anxiety and to seek the way of the Lord without distraction, we pray: ◆

Our Father . . .

Good and loving Father,
open our hearts to hear your voice
and to fulfill your holy will
as we strive to remain always
united in communion with you.
Grant us the daily grace, Lord,
to live in your Triune life
in the glory of the Resurrection.
We ask this through Christ our Lord.
Amen.

✝ If today you hear his voice, harden not your hearts.

✝ My loyalty and love will be with him. (*Psalm 89:25*)

Psalm 95 *page 413*

Reading *Mark 5:15–20*

As [the people] approached Jesus, they caught sight of the man who had been possessed by Legion, sitting there clothed and in his right mind. And they were seized with fear. Those who witnessed the incident explained to them what had happened to the possessed man and to the swine. Then they began to beg him to leave their district. As [Jesus] was getting into the boat, the man who had been possessed pleaded to remain with him. But Jesus would not permit him but told him instead, "Go home to your family and announce to them all that the Lord in his pity has done for you." Then the man went off and began to proclaim in the Decapolis what Jesus had done for him; and all were amazed.

Reflection

Today in the Gospel, the man with leprosy pleads with Jesus to stay with him. Instead, Jesus sends him away to spread the news about what he has done. God heals us and gives us the grace to go forth and do his will.

Prayers *others may be added*

Almighty God, you alone have the power to forgive us our sins and to heal us in body and spirit. Hear the prayers we place before you, as we pray:

◆ Have mercy on us, Lord; free us from our sins.

For the Church, that she may unite all her members into the truth of Jesus Christ, we pray: ◆ That through the work of governmental officers and the national leaders, all nations will be freed from division and discord, and that they may come together to heal the wounds caused by sin and separation, we pray: ◆ For those who are suffering, especially those who suffer from addiction, abuse, or spiritual attack, that by God's most powerful grace they may be free, we pray: ◆ For all of us, that our Christian community may become more united through constant personal conversion, prayer, friendship, and service to one another, we pray: ◆

Our Father . . .

God, our loving Father,
give us strength to faithfully
fulfill your holy will.
Liberate us from our selfishness,
that we may know and understand
that a life in union with you
is a life of true freedom and joy.
We ask this through Christ our Lord.
Amen.

✝ My loyalty and love will be with him.

Tuesday, January 31, 2012
Memorial of Saint John Bosco, Priest

✝ Bless the LORD, my soul!
 (Psalm 103:1)

Psalm 95 — page 413

Reading — Matthew 18:1–3

The disciples approached Jesus and said, "Who is the greatest in the Kingdom of heaven?" He called a child over, placed it in their midst, and said, "Amen, I say to you, unless you turn and become like children, you will not enter the Kingdom of heaven."

Reflection

Jesus tells us in today's Gospel that whoever does the will of God is received into the family of God. Mary is our model for following the will of God, for throughout her whole life she most perfectly fulfilled the will of God. Let us not seek our own selfish wants; rather, let us seek the perfect good that our all-loving God desires for us.

Prayers — *others may be added*

Through the prayers of Saint John Bosco, we pray:

◆ Be it done unto us, according to your will.

For the Church, that she may be ever renewed in grace and charity to proclaim the goodness of God's word to all the nations, we pray: ◆ For all nations that suffer violence, war, and tyranny, that the work of civil leaders and all Christians may help to bring justice and peace, we pray: ◆ For the poor, the lonely, the sick, and all who suffer, that they may receive the help they need from the generosity and service of good Christians everywhere, we pray: ◆ For teachers, catechists, and youth ministers, and for all who work for the care of children and youth, we pray: ◆ For our personal community, that we may become more docile to surrender to the most holy and perfect will of God, we pray: ◆

Our Father . . .

O God of peace,
with joyful hearts
we come to give you praise.
Cast out all anxiety, O Lord,
and free us all from our worries,
for in your most holy and perfect will,
there is our true happiness and peace.
Through the prayers of Saint John Bosco,
teach us to spread your word with joy
and love to the little ones of your
    kingdom.
We ask this through Christ, our Lord.
    Amen.

✝ Bless the LORD, my soul!

✝ Lord, forgive the wrong I have done.

Psalm 95   *page 413*

Reading   *Mark 6:1–6*

Jesus departed from there and came to his native place, accompanied by his disciples. When the sabbath came he began to teach in the synagogue, and many who heard him were astonished. They said, "Where did this man get all this? What kind of wisdom has been given him? What mighty deeds are wrought by his hands! Is he not the carpenter, the son of Mary, and the brother of James and Joseph and Judas and Simon? And are not his sisters here with us?" And they took offense at him. Jesus said to them, "A prophet is not without honor except in his native place and among his own kin and in his own house." So he was not able to perform any mighty deed there, apart from curing a few sick people by laying his hands on them. He was amazed at their lack of faith.

Reflection

If we are resistant to God's grace, he will not be able to do his work in our lives. Today's Gospel recounts that the people of Jesus' own homeland criticize him, assuming that they know him because they know his relatives and friends. May we remain open to the work of God in our lives, even if it may be different from our expectations or ideas of who Jesus is and what we think he ought to do.

Prayers   *others may be added*

Every day is an opportunity to encounter the Lord more profoundly. With open hearts, we pray:

◆ Renew our faith in you, O Lord.

For the Church, especially in times of persecution, that the Pope and all the bishops may remain faithful to the service of the truth, we pray: ◆ For all who work for the good of their country, we pray: ◆ For all families, that the home may be a place of mutual love and sacrifice, we pray: ◆ For those who suffer from illness or disease, that they may be renewed in faith as they await healing and consolation of Jesus Christ, we pray: ◆ For our local community, that we may receive the grace to live a virtuous life despite what others may think of us, we pray: ◆

Our Father . . .

Father in heaven,
you sent us Jesus Christ
to heal our physical infirmities
and to free us from our sins.
Open our hearts to receive your grace.
Increase in us the gift of faith
through the power of the Holy Spirit
sent forth for the forgiveness of sins.
We ask this through our Lord Jesus
    Christ, your Son,
who lives and reigns with you in the unity
    of the Holy Spirit,
one God, forever and ever.
Amen.

✝ Lord, forgive the wrong I have done.

✝ Who is this king of glory? It is the Lord!

Psalm 103   page 415

Reading   Luke 2:25–32

Now there was a man in Jerusalem whose name was Simeon. This man was righteous and devout, awaiting the consolation of Israel, and the Holy Spirit was upon him. It had been revealed to him by the Holy Spirit that he should not see death before he had seen the Christ of the Lord. He came in the Spirit into the temple; and when the parents brought in the child Jesus to perform the custom of the law in regard to him, he took him into his arms and blessed God, saying: / "Now, Master, you may let your servant go / in peace, according to your word, / for my eyes have seen your salvation, / which you prepared in sight of all the peoples: / a light for revelation to the Gentiles, / and glory for your people Israel."

Reflection

Simeon was "righteous and devout" and so were Mary and Joseph. Because each followed the law and did the unremarkable things they were supposed to do, they received great blessings. Simeon lives on in Christian faith simply for being faithful. When God spoke to him, he recognized it as God's word. Mary and Joseph simply followed the "custom of the law" and thus heard this man of God speak comforting words. Great blessings can come from remaining faithful and simply doing our duty.

Prayers   others may be added

Our God is like a refiner's fire who refines and purifies our hearts. With openness to his work in our lives, let us pray:

◆ Purify our hearts, O God.

For the Church, as she awaits the Second Coming of Jesus, that Christ may strengthen his bride with patience and perseverance, we pray: ◆ That Jesus Christ, the light of nations, may guide and illuminate the minds and hearts of all civil leaders and all those who work for peace and justice, we pray: ◆ For all who suffer and seek consolation, that they may receive comfort in Christ, we pray: ◆ For all widows and widowers, that they may be renewed in worship, prayer, and thanksgiving, we pray: ◆ For all who will die today, that they may enter the heavenly kingdom in peace and new life, we pray: ◆

Our Father . . .

God our Father,
through all the ages you prepare
your people for the coming of the Messiah.
In the fullness of time you sent us
   your Son.
Grant us the grace of your Spirit,
that, united to him, we may always walk
   in the light
of Jesus Christ,
as we seek the glory of his face.
We ask this through Christ our Lord.
Amen.

✝ Who is this king of glory? It is the Lord!

Friday, February 3, 2012
Weekday
Optional memorial of Saint Blaise, Bishop and Martyr

✝ Blessed be God my salvation!

Psalm 145   *page 422*

Reading   *Mark 6:21b–24*

Herod, on his birthday, gave a banquet for his courtiers, his military officers, and the leading men of Galilee. His own daughter came in and performed a dance that delighted Herod and his guests. The king said to the girl, "Ask of me whatever you wish and I will grant it to you." He even swore many things to her, "I will grant you whatever you ask of me, even to half of my kingdom." She went out and said to her mother, "What shall I ask for?" Her mother replied, "The head of John the Baptist." The girl hurried back to the king's presence and made her request, "I want you to give me at once on a platter the head of John the Baptist."

Reflection

Today we celebrate the optional memorial of Saint Blaise, who was a physician from Armenia during the fourth century. He later became a Bishop and is primarily known for having miraculously healed a child who had a fish bone caught in his throat. He is the patron of illnesses, especially those relating to the throat. At Mass on this day, it is tradition to receive the blessing of the throat to pray for healing and his protection against illness.

Prayers   *others may be added*

God the Father has sent us his Son to reveal to us the mystery of his kingdom. In faith, let us pray:

◆ May your word grow in our hearts.

For the Church, that, united to the work of Jesus Christ, she may sow the word of truth throughout all the world, we pray: ◆ For public officials, that they may always seek truth as they work to cultivate political relations based on the mutual search for the good of the human person and society, we pray: ◆ For all who suffer illnesses of the throat or any other kind of illness, that through the intercession of Saint Blaise they may be healed, we pray: ◆ For all children, young people, the underprivileged, and the weak, that they may be assured that God does great things through our human weakness and insufficiencies, we pray: ◆ For our local community, that it may be stirred to contemplate the great mystery of God and his kingdom through faithful prayer, we pray: ◆

Our Father . . .

Almighty Father,
in your Son, Jesus Christ,
you teach us to be faithful witnesses
to your most holy word.
Through the intercession of Saint Blaise,
    Bishop and Martyr,
deliver us from every disease of the throat
and every other illness.
We ask this through Christ our Lord.
Amen.

✝ Blessed be God my salvation!

Saturday, February 4, 2012
Weekday

✝ Lord, teach me your statutes.

Psalm 19 *page 403*

Reading *Mark 6:30–34*

The Apostles gathered together with Jesus and reported all they had done and taught. He said to them, "Come away by yourselves to a deserted place and rest a while." People were coming and going in great numbers, and they had no opportunity even to eat. So they went off in the boat by themselves to a deserted place. People saw them leaving and many came to know about it. They hastened there on foot from all the towns and arrived at the place before them.

When Jesus disembarked and saw the vast crowd, his heart was moved with pity for them, for they were like sheep without a shepherd; and he began to teach them many things.

Reflection

Jesus recognizes both our physical and spiritual needs. He calls to us, saying, "Come away by yourselves to a deserted place and rest awhile." In the busyness and difficulties of the responsibilities of our work, study, or family life, we need time to get away and to rest a little. However, quiet time is not only important for us physically, but essential for our spiritual life. Jesus teaches us the secret of prayer and reflection: to come away and to be still and quiet as we listen to him.

Prayers *others may be added*

God our Father, you call us to a life of peace and freedom. By the merits and prayers of your Son, we ask you to increase your faith in us, as we pray:

◆ Lord I believe; help my unbelief.

That the Church, as the bark of Peter, may continue to be a refuge of peace and calm for all peoples amid the storms and difficulties of life, we pray: ◆ For world leaders, that they may have the faith to call upon God's grace in order to resolve conflict, we pray: ◆ For all who suffer from the darkness of depression or mental illness, that Jesus Christ may awaken their hearts and calm the anxieties of their minds, we pray: ◆ For our local community, that, united together as God's faithful, we may have the courage to always turn to the Lord in time of need, we pray: ◆

Our Father . . .

Lord Jesus Christ,
only Son of the Father,
you are wisdom incarnate.
You are the truth for which
our body and spirit yearns.
We turn our gaze to you
to contemplate your majesty.
Send your Spirit upon us,
so that we may know and love you
and always walk in the light of your truth.
You live and reign forever.
Amen.

✝ Lord, teach me your statutes.

✞ Praise the Lord, who heals the brokenhearted.

Psalm 27
page 405

Reading
Mark 1:29–32

On leaving the synagogue Jesus entered the house of Simon and Andrew with James and John. Simon's mother-in-law lay sick with a fever. They immediately told him about her. He approached, grasped her hand, and helped her up. Then the fever left her and she waited on them.

When it was evening, after sunset, they brought to him all who were ill or possessed by demons.

Reflection

Jesus' power and authority extend over all things. In the Gospel, Jesus cures the sick, and he drives out evil spirits. Even today, Jesus' divine word possesses the same strength and authority. Jesus is the prophet and teacher who speaks the word of the Father on the breath of the Spirit. Let us open our hearts to hear his voice and receive his healing power.

Prayers
others may be added

God of goodness, all power belongs to you. Confident in your faithfulness, we present our petitions:

◆ Open our hearts, to your word.

For the Holy Father, that he may use the authority given to him by Christ and handed on by the apostles, to continue to lead the Church on the path of holiness, we pray: ◆ For civil leaders, that they may responsibly seek the common good of all peoples, we pray: ◆ For all those who are ill, that the word of God may be a source of comfort for all who suffer in any way, we pray: ◆ For all religious, married couples, and single peoples, that all may live the virtue of chastity according to their state of life, we pray: ◆ For our faith community, that through prayer and the sacraments, Jesus Christ may quiet our hearts to give us lasting peace, we pray: ◆ For the grace this week to be free of anxiety and to seek the things of the Lord without distraction, we pray: ◆

Our Father . . .

Good and loving Father,
open our hearts to hear your voice
and to fulfill your holy will,
as we strive to remain always
united in communion with you.
Grant us the daily grace, Lord,
to live in your Triune life
in the glory of the Resurrection.
We ask this through Christ our Lord.
Amen.

✞ Praise the Lord, who heals the brokenhearted.

✝ Those who sow in tears shall reap rejoicing.

Psalm 34 *page 406*

Reading *Mark 6:53–56*

After making the crossing to the other side of the sea, Jesus and his disciples came to land at Gennesaret and tied up there. As they were leaving the boat, people immediately recognized him. They scurried about the surrounding country and began to bring in the sick on mats to wherever they heard he was. Whatever villages or towns or country-side he entered, they laid the sick in the marketplaces and begged him that they might touch only the tassel on his cloak; and as many as touched it were healed.

Reflection *Jill Maria Murdy*

One might scoff at being healed by touching a tassel, but if you have ever been with someone struggling with a life-threatening illness, grasping at straws or trying new medical proce-dures is common. Here the people are making a spiritual pilgrimage, hoping to be healed by Jesus, just as the sick go to Lourdes or another shrine seeking a miracle.

Prayers *others may be added*

God our Father, through your Son, Jesus Christ, you invite us to share in the mission of the Trinity. Hear our prayers, as we pray:

◆ Lord, send out your Spirit, and renew the face of the earth.

That the Church may continue to fulfill the mission of Jesus Christ, we pray: ◆ That all cultures may be open to the work of the Holy Spirit who breathes new life upon his people, we pray: ◆ For all who suffer despair and loneliness, that the Lord may rise up and save them from their pain, we pray: ◆ For all who are persecuted for the faith, that they may be strengthened in faith, and that their witness may bring others to the truth of the Gospel, we pray: ◆ For our local community, that each and every one of us may not be afraid to speak of the good things God has done in our lives, we pray: ◆

Our Father . . .

Good and loving Father,
by the witness of your saints
you give us an example of how to live
in holiness and fulfill your will.
Through the prayers of the Martyrs
Saint Paul Miki and his companions,
may we be strengthened to give testimony
to your Son, Jesus Christ, the word
of truth.
May our lives give all glory to you.
We ask this through Christ our Lord.
Amen.

✝ Those who sow in tears shall reap rejoicing.

✟ How lovely is your dwelling place, Lord, mighty God!

Psalm 63   *page 410*

Reading   *Mark 7:5–13*

The Pharisees and the scribes questioned [Jesus], "Why do your disciples not follow the tradition of the elders but instead eat a meal with unclean hands?" He responded, "Well did Isaiah prophesy about you hypocrites, as it is written: / *This people honors me with their lips,* / *but their hearts are far from me;* / *In vain do they worship me,* / *teaching as doctrines human precepts.* / You disregard God's commandment but cling to human tradition." He went on to say, "How well you have set aside the commandment of God in order to uphold your tradition! For Moses said, / *Honor your father and your mother,* / and *Whoever curses father or mother shall die.* / Yet you say, 'If a person says to father or mother, "Any support you might have had from me is *qorban*"' [meaning, dedicated to God], you allow him to do nothing more for his father or mother. You nullify the word of God in favor of your tradition that you have handed on. And you do many such things."

Reflection

Jesus admonishes the Pharisees for their hypocrisy. He criticizes their hardness of heart in the way that they are only concerned with fulfilling the external rituals without a genuine interior disposition. Sometimes we, too, can be tempted toward legalism and toward living our lives in hypocrisy. However, Jesus reminds us today to be Christians of integrity, whose hearts are united to the Lord in both worship and in action.

Prayers   *others may be added*

God our Father, you touch us and heal us through your Son, Jesus Christ. Let us pray:

◆ Lord, hear our prayer.

For the Church, that, united to the Holy Spirit, she may remain ever fruitful in the life of Christ Jesus, we pray: ◆ For all political leaders, that they may not seek their own desires, but rather the good of the individuals of society, we pray: ◆ For those who suffer from physical disabilities, that they may recognize the great gifts they have to offer to the Church and to the world, we pray: ◆ That our local community may grow in deeper respect of the blessings and gift of children, we pray: ◆

Our Father . . .

Good and loving God,
through your Son, Jesus Christ,
you heal us and set us free.
By the working of the Holy Spirit,
you reveal your power and majesty.
We beg you to pour out your
mercy upon us, your children.
Open our ears to hear your word,
as you call our name to rise up
to the light of your everlasting life.
We ask this through Christ our Lord.
Amen.

✟ How lovely is your dwelling place, Lord, mighty God!

Wednesday, February 8, 2012
Weekday

✟ The mouth of the just murmurs wisdom.

Psalm 95   *page 413*

Reading   *Mark 7:14–15, 21–23*

Jesus summoned the crowd again and said to them, "Hear me, all of you, and understand. Nothing that enters one from outside can defile that person; but the things that come out from within are what defile. . . .

"From within the man, from his heart, come evil thoughts, unchastity, theft, murder, adultery, greed, malice, deceit, licentiousness, envy, blasphemy, arrogance, folly. All these evils come from within and they defile."

Reflection

Sometimes it is easy to appear to be a good and holy Christian on the outside, when on the inside our hearts and thoughts are filled with sinfulness and negativity. By his grace, Jesus invites us to allow him to free us from our sin and sadness—all that keeps us from experiencing the freedom of true life. Let us rise up from the darkness of our selfishness, vanity, egos, and anxiety, for God calls us to purity of life.

Prayers   *others may be added*

Every day is an opportunity to encounter the Lord more profoundly. With open hearts, we pray:

◆ Renew our faith in you, O Lord.

For the Church, especially in times of persecution, may she remain faithful to the service of the truth, we pray: ◆ For all who work for the good of their country, we pray: ◆ For all families, that their homes may be places of mutual love and sacrifice and gift of self, we pray: ◆ For those who suffer from illness or disease, that they may be renewed in faith as they await healing and consolation of Jesus Christ, we pray: ◆ For our local community, that we may receive the grace to live a virtuous life despite what others may think of us, we pray: ◆

Our Father . . .

Father in heaven,
you send us Jesus Christ
to heal our physical infirmities
and to free us from our sins.
Open our hearts to receive your grace.
Increase in us the gift of faith
through the power of the Holy Spirit,
sent forth for the forgiveness of sins.
We ask this through our Lord Jesus
    Christ, your Son,
who lives and reigns with you in the unity
    of the Holy Spirit,
one God, forever and ever.
Amen.

✟ The mouth of the just murmurs wisdom.

✝ Remember us, O Lord, as you favor your people.

Psalm 95 page 413

Reading Mark 7:24–30

Jesus went to the district of Tyre. He entered a house and wanted no one to know about it, but he could not escape notice. Soon a woman whose daughter had an unclean spirit heard about him. She came and fell at his feet. The woman was a Greek, a Syrophoenician by birth, and she begged him to drive the demon out of her daughter. He said to her, "Let the children be fed first. For it is not right to take the food of the children and throw it to the dogs." She replied and said to him, "Lord, even the dogs under the table eat the children's scraps." Then he said to her, "For saying this, you may go. The demon has gone out of your daughter." When the woman went home, she found the child lying in bed and the demon gone.

Reflection

Jesus cannot escape notice. This is what we hear in today's Gospel. Even when Jesus tries not to be noticed, the people recognize his presence and they come to him, bringing him their sick and asking for help and healing. Do we recognize Jesus' presence among us today? Do we go to him and beg for his healing power for ourselves and for our loved ones?

Prayers *others may be added*

Father, you send out your Spirit to affect the mission of Jesus Christ throughout all the world. Hear the prayers we offer today:

◆ Heal us, O Lord; grant us peace.

For the Church, that she may tirelessly continue Christ's apostolic work to preach the Good News, we pray: ◆ For the nations of the world, that all cultures may be open to hearing the word of God, we pray: ◆ For those who suffer the loss of abandonment, estrangement, or loneliness, that the true and real friendship of Christ may fill their emptiness, we pray: ◆ That we may not forget that our personal apostolic endeavors must include our families, friends, and coworkers, we pray: ◆ For the grace to remain always faithful to God with our whole heart and soul, we pray: ◆

Our Father . . .

God our Father,
you are the vine dresser
who calls each of us to work in
    your vineyard.
To each you give a unique task to fulfill.
Keep us faithful to your call,
and may we always persevere
to love you with our whole
heart and with our whole soul.
We ask this through Christ our Lord.
Amen.

✝ Remember us, O Lord, as you favor your people.

✟ Deep waters cannot quench love, nor floods sweep it away. (*Song of Songs 8:7*)

Psalm 100   *page 414*

Reading   *Luke 10:38–42*

Jesus entered a village where a woman whose name was Martha welcomed him. She had a sister named Mary who sat beside the Lord at his feet listening to him speak. Martha, burdened with much serving, came to him and said, "Lord, do you not care that my sister has left me by myself to do the serving? Tell her to help me." The Lord said to her in reply, "Martha, Martha, you are anxious and worried about many things. There is need of only one thing. Mary has chosen the better part and it will not be taken from her."

Reflection

Today the Gospel teaches us how we grow in life with Christ through a balance of both contemplation and service. Jesus does not rebuke Martha for her service, but rather, for her anxiousness, because she is "worried about many things." This passage does not intend to present a dichotomy between these two necessary forms of prayer; however, through a united balance of both active service and quiet meditation, we grow ever deeper in union with the life of God.

Prayers   *others may be added*

God our Father, you speak your word to us through your Son, Jesus Christ. In faith, we pray to you:

◆ Open our hearts, to hear your voice.

That the Church, guided by the Holy Father, may grow in unity through increased prayer and service of all her members, we pray: ◆ For nations that suffer devastation from storms, earthquakes, hurricanes, and natural disasters, we pray: ◆ For those who suffer from anxiety and depression, that the peace of Christ may fill them with new freedom, we pray: ◆ That siblings may enjoy a holy and genuine fraternal love for one another, we pray: ◆ For the grace this week to take time out from the cares and responsibilities of daily life to sit at the Lord's feet and listen to him speak, we pray: ◆

Our Father . . .

Good and loving God,
You give us the gift of prayer,
so that we may draw ever closer
into union with you, our Triune God.
Through the intercession
    of Saint Scholastica,
teach us how to pray,
and how to serve you
with all of our hearts in every moment
and every circumstance of our lives.
We ask this through Christ our Lord.
Amen.

✟ Deep waters cannot quench love, nor floods sweep it away.

✝ As a mother comforts her [child], so will I comfort you. (*Isaiah 66:13*)

Psalm 103 *page 415*

Reading *John 2:1–8, 10*

There was a wedding in Cana in Galilee, and the mother of Jesus was there. Jesus and his disciples were also invited to the wedding. When the wine ran short, the mother of Jesus said to him, "They have no wine." And Jesus said to her, "Woman, how does your concern affect me? My hour has not yet come." His mother said to the servers, "Do whatever he tells you." Now there were six stone water jars there for Jewish ceremonial washings, each holding twenty to thirty gallons. Jesus told them, "Fill the jars with water." So they filled them to the brim. Then he told them, "Draw some out now and take it to the headwaiter." So they took it. . . . The headwaiter called the bridegroom and said to him, "Everyone serves good wine first, and then when people have drunk freely, an inferior one; but you have kept the good wine until now."

Reflection

Jesus has given us his own mother, whose maternal presence is always available to us through her prayers and intercession. She leads us to her Son and teaches us how we ought to live and fulfill the will of God. "Do whatever he tells you," she says. May we come ever closer to Mary who always guides us to deeper unity with the sacred heart of her Son.

Prayers *others may be added*

In confidence that there is nothing that is impossible for God, we present our prayers and petitions, as we pray:

◆ Heal us, O Lord, and set us free.

For the Church, that she may continue to be a source of peace and healing for all the faithful, we pray: ◆ For nations torn apart by war, terrorism, poverty, and disease, we pray: ◆ For all those who suffer, especially for all the sick throughout the world, that, through the intercession of Our Lady of Lourdes, they may receive comfort, healing, and fortitude through the healing power of Jesus Christ, we pray: ◆ That our local parish may dedicate itself more fully to service to one another, especially to the poor and sick of the community, we pray: ◆

Our Father . . .

Father of mercy,
in your great wisdom you give us
the sacrament of the Holy Eucharist,
as the source of healing and peace.
Through the prayers of Mary,
Our Lady of Lourdes,
may we come to him,
your Son, present in the Eucharist,
to receive the healing waters
    of forgiveness
and peace that flow from his most
    sacred heart.
We ask this through Christ our Lord.
Amen.

✝ As a mother comforts her [child], so will I comfort you.

✝ I turn to you, Lord, in time of trouble.

Psalm 145   *page 422*

Reading   *Mark 1:40–45*

A leper came to Jesus and kneeling down begged him and said, "If you wish, you can make me clean." Moved with pity, he stretched out his hand, touched him, and said to him, "I do will it. Be made clean." The leprosy left him immediately, and he was made clean. Then, warning him sternly, he dismissed him at once. Then he said to him, "See that you tell no one anything, but go, show yourself to the priest and offer for your cleansing what Moses prescribed; that will be proof for them." The man went away and began to publicize the whole matter. He spread the report abroad so that it was impossible for Jesus to enter a town openly. He remained outside in deserted places, and people kept coming to him from everywhere.

Reflection

God desires us to be made clean. He desires that we be whole, that we enjoy freedom and a full life rich in joy and fulfillment. God sees our weaknesses and infirmities, but he also wants us to come to him in humility to request what we need. In gratitude for all his blessings, we likewise should be driven by the desire to share what great gifts and healing we have received.

Prayers   *others may be added*

Father in heaven, you know our needs even before we speak them. In humble faith we come before you, as we pray:

◆ Make us clean, O Lord.

For the Holy Father, all bishops, priests, and deacons, that they may remain pure in body, mind, and spirit, we pray: ◆ That government officials may work with responsibility and charity as they seek means to foster peace among nations, we pray: ◆ For the sick and all those who care for them, that God may give them healing and patient fortitude to bear their suffering, we pray: ◆ For our church community, that together rejoicing in the gifts the Lord has given us, we may be united together in praise of God, we pray: ◆

Our Father . . .

God, our Father,
in your Son, Jesus Christ,
you bring us healing and love.
Pour your Holy Spirit upon us,
that we may be strengthened in faith and
    solid in hope,
as we await the day when you will be all
    in all.
We ask this through our Lord Jesus
    Christ, your Son,
who lives and reigns with you in the unity
    of the Holy Spirit,
one God, forever and ever.
Amen.

✝ I turn to you, Lord, in time of trouble.

Monday, February 13, 2012
Weekday

✝ Be kind to me, Lord, and I shall live.

Psalm 19   *page 403*

Reading   *Mark 8:11 – 13*

The Pharisees came forward and began to argue with Jesus, seeking from him a sign from heaven to test him. He sighed from the depth of his spirit and said, "Why does this generation seek a sign? Amen, I say to you, no sign will be given to this generation." Then he left them, got into the boat again, and went off to the other shore.

Reflection

We need to read this scripture many times until we can hear that deep, deep sigh of Jesus as the profound expression of frustration that it was. We've created a false, sugar-coated Jesus who is covered with so many layers of sweetness that contemplating him is bound to give us cavities. But the real Jesus is a man of strength who expects of us what we are able to give. The Pharisees were smart enough to know better and so he had to walk away from their tricks and the malice in their hearts. Make no mistake about it; Jesus also knows what we can give. And he won't settle for any less.

Prayers   *others may be added*

God has a human heart. In confidence in his mercy and love, we offer our prayers and petitions, as we pray:

◆ Lord, we believe; help our unbelief.

For the Church, that she may be a guiding light for all sinners and seekers of forgiveness, we pray: ◆ For the leaders of nations, that they may be inspired with creativity to seek new means of dialogue, as together they work for peace and justice, we pray: ◆ For those who suffer from mental illness and for all who care for them, we pray: ◆ For all parents, that they may have love and patience and forgiveness toward their children, we pray: ◆ For our local community, that, by the power of the Spirit, we may grow together in virtue, we pray: ◆ For the grace to be rededicated in our work and duties this week, as we seek to serve the Lord with renewed love and cheerfulness, we pray: ◆

Our Father . . .

Most loving God,
you speak the word of your incarnate Son
by the power of the most Holy Spirit.
Breathe this same Spirit upon us,
that we may be open to hear and receive
    your word.
Forgive us our sins and keep us from
    all evil,
that we may never wound the most sacred
    heart of your Son, Jesus Christ,
who lives and reigns with you in the unity
    of the Holy Spirit,
one God, forever and ever.
Amen.

✝ Be kind to me, Lord, and I shall live.

✝ Go out to all the world and tell the Good News.

Psalm 27 *page 405*

Reading *Mark 8:14–21*

The disciples had forgotten to bring bread, and they had only one loaf with them in the boat. Jesus enjoined them, "Watch out, guard against the leaven of the Pharisees and the leaven of Herod." They concluded among themselves that it was because they had no bread. When he became aware of this he said to them, "Why do you conclude that it is because you have no bread? Do you not yet understand or comprehend? Are your hearts hardened? Do you have eyes and not see, ears and not hear? And do you not remember, when I broke the five loaves for the five thousand, how many wicker baskets full of fragments you picked up?" They answered him, "Twelve." "When I broke the seven loaves for the four thousand, how many full baskets of fragments did you pick up?" They answered him, "Seven." He said to them, "Do you still not understand?"

Reflection

Today the Church celebrates the memorial of two brothers who worked as missionaries in the Slavic countries. But today is also Saint Valentine's Day, a feast from the Roman martyrology. As Jesus says, let us not allow our hearts to be hardened. Rather, may we be open to see and understand God's love for us through others.

Prayers *others may be added*

Father, you are the only true source of our happiness and joy. Hear our prayers, as we pray:

◆ Fill us with your love, O Lord.

For the Church, that she may be a light to bring understanding and truth where there is darkness and doubt, we pray: ◆ For all the Slavic nations, that the Lord will raise up more people to be bearers and teachers of faith as witnesses and bearers of peace, we pray: ◆ For all nations torn apart by violence, that all evils may be conquered by love, we pray: ◆ For those who are sick and for all who care for them, that they may be strengthened by God's love for each and every person, we pray: ◆ For the poor and the lonely, that they may experience God's love through the charity of others, we pray: ◆ For all young people in relationships, and for all engaged and married couples, that they may love one another with pure and holy hearts, we pray: ◆

Our Father . . .

Most good and loving Father,
in the person of Jesus Christ,
you reveal to us love Incarnate.
By listening to your most holy word
in openness of heart,
you teach us how to love.
Through the prayers of Saints Cyril
    and Methodius,
may we be bearers of your love to all
    the nations.
We ask this through Christ our Lord.
Amen.

✝ Go out to all the world and tell the Good News.

✞ They who do justice shall walk in the presence of God.

Psalm 27 — page 405

Reading — Mark 8:22–26

When Jesus and his disciples arrived at Bethsaida, people brought to him a blind man and begged him to touch him. He took the blind man by the hand and led him outside the village. Putting spittle on his eyes he laid his hands on him and asked, "Do you see anything?" Looking up he replied, "I see people looking like trees and walking." Then he laid hands on his eyes a second time and he saw clearly; his sight was restored and he could see everything distinctly. Then he sent him home and said, "Do not even go into the village."

Reflection

It is important for us to pray for others and for ourselves, to pray that God may heal our blindness and make us see. In today's Gospel the people bring Jesus a blind man and beg him to touch him and heal him. In fervent prayer, let us likewise bring him our needs and beg him to heal us and our families and friends. It is he who has the power to restore peace and order to all things.

Prayers — *others may be added*

O God, you know our needs even before we ask them. Coming before you in faith, we beg you to hear the petitions we offer, as we pray:

◆ Heal us, O Lord, that we may see.

For the Holy Father, that he may be strengthened in his ministry to offer insight and clarity to the word of God in this world of blindness, we pray: ◆ For all world leaders, that they may discover new solutions to bring about peace and justice in areas of conflict and discord, we pray: ◆ For the sick and the suffering, that Jesus may come and touch them in their illness, bringing them healing and new life, we pray: ◆ For all those who are spiritually blind, that with the eyes of faith they may see the truth of Jesus Christ, we pray: ◆ For our local community, that all may be renewed in dedication to daily prayer of intercession for our community of family and friends, we pray: ◆

Our Father . . .

Lord Jesus Christ,
you teach us to pray.
Bless all those who suffer in your name
and give sight to all those who seek
　　your face.
We ask this in your holy name,
you who live and reign with the Father in
　　the unity of the Holy Spirit,
one God, forever and ever.
Amen.

✞ They who do justice shall walk in the presence of God.

Thursday, February 16, 2012
Weekday

✝ The Lord hears the cry of the poor.

Psalm 34
page 406

Reading
Mark 8:27–33

Jesus and his disciples set out for the villages of Caesarea Philippi. Along the way he asked his disciples, "Who do people say that I am?" They said in reply, "John the Baptist, others Elijah, still others one of the prophets." And he asked them, "But who do you say that I am?" Peter said to him in reply, "You are the Christ." Then he warned them not to tell anyone about him.

He began to teach them that the Son of Man must suffer greatly and be rejected by the elders, the chief priests, and the scribes, and be killed, and rise after three days. He spoke this openly. Then Peter took him aside and began to rebuke him. At this he turned around and, looking at his disciples, rebuked Peter and said, "Get behind me, Satan. You are thinking not as God does, but as human beings do."

Reflection

Too frequently, we want to avoid the reality that, as Christians, suffering will and must come. In today's Gospel, after Peter identifies Jesus as the Messiah, Jesus speaks openly of the fact that he will have to suffer and die. Jesus does not avoid the reality of the cross, but instead prepares and teaches us so that we may learn to think as God does, who always brings resurrection and new life, redeeming us from suffering.

Prayers
others may be added

Father, you prepared the ages for the coming of your Son, the Messiah. Let us pray:

◆ You are the Christ, O Lord.

For the Church, that, strengthened by the cross of Christ, she may endure the persecutions and difficulties from those who do not understand, we pray: ◆ For all nations, that, through the work of the Holy Spirit, they may peacefully dialogue in order to serve all individuals, we pray: ◆ For all who suffer under the weight of heavy crosses, that they may receive comfort and solace through union with Christ's work of redemption, we pray: ◆ For the grace to use our tongues to speak with kindness and charity in order to build up our family and friends, we pray: ◆ For those who will die today, and all the faithful departed, that, by Christ's cross, their sufferings will merit true and everlasting life, we pray: ◆

Our Father . . .

God our Father,
your redemption is the greatest mystery.
Through your Holy Spirit,
grant us supernatural faith and
    understanding.
Help us not to fear the cross,
but to take on our burdens in faith,
knowing you will redeem us by your
    ever-flowing and loving grace.
We ask this through Christ our Lord.
Amen.

✝ The Lord hears the cry of the poor.

✝ Faith without works is dead.
(*James 2:26*)

Psalm 63   page 410

Reading   Mark 8:34–9:1

Jesus summoned the crowd with his disciples and said to them, "Whoever wishes to come after me must deny himself, take up his cross, and follow me. For whoever wishes to save his life will lose it, but whoever loses his life for my sake and that of the Gospel will save it. What profit is there for one to gain the whole world and forfeit his life? What could one give in exchange for his life? Whoever is ashamed of me and of my words in this faithless and sinful generation, the Son of Man will be ashamed of when he comes in his Father's glory with the holy angels." He also said to them, "Amen, I say to you, there are some standing here who will not taste death until they see that the Kingdom of God has come in power."

Reflection

Again, Jesus speaks clearly and openly to his disciples about the necessity of suffering. It is a great mystery that in order to attain true freedom and true life, we must deny ourselves and take up our cross daily. However, in this mystery, the cross of Jesus Christ gives meaning to the otherwise absurdity of suffering: from death God brings life.

Prayers   *others may be added*

Jesus invites us to joyfully follow after him. Let us pray:

◆ Strengthen us in faith, O Lord.

For the Holy Father, that he may lead the Church through his word and example to pick up one's cross and follow in the footsteps of the Lord, we pray: ◆ For all civic leaders who work to bring hope and resolution to nations suffering from violence, war, and unrest, we pray: ◆ For the sick, that they may receive patience as they await healing, and that their sufferings may bear much fruit as they offer it to the Lord in union with Christ's cross, we pray: ◆ For unbelievers, that they may come to an understanding of the truth of Jesus Incarnate who brings meaning and purpose to every aspect of humanity, we pray: ◆ For all Christians, that they may not fear to follow Christ, we pray: ◆

Our Father . . .

Loving God,
purify our hearts and empty us
of all that keeps us from you.
Give us the grace to rid ourselves
of all that is an obstacle of your grace.
Send us your Spirit
and grant us deeper faith in you.
We ask this through our Lord Jesus
    Christ, your Son,
who lives and reigns with you in the unity
    of the Holy Spirit,
one God, forever and ever.
Amen.

✝ Faith without works is dead.

Saturday, February 18, 2012
Weekday

✝ You will protect us, Lord.

Psalm 95
page 413

Reading
Mark 9:2–8

Jesus took Peter, James, and John and led them up a high mountain apart by themselves. And he was transfigured before them, and his clothes became dazzling white, such as no fuller on earth could bleach them. Then Elijah appeared to them along with Moses, and they were conversing with Jesus. Then Peter said to Jesus in reply, "Rabbi, it is good that we are here! Let us make three tents: one for you, one for Moses, and one for Elijah." He hardly knew what to say, they were so terrified. Then a cloud came, casting a shadow over them; then from the cloud came a voice, "This is my beloved Son. Listen to him." Suddenly, looking around, they no longer saw anyone but Jesus alone with them.

Reflection

Drawing close to God can be terrifying. We may not like to hear it, but it's true. God is pure love and pure anything is quite foreign to our human nature that's so adulterated and compromised by sin. So, in the face of Love itself, we *will* tremble. Peter does. When Jesus is revealed in all his glory standing beside the icons of the Prophets (Elijah) and the Law (Moses), Peter is reduced to babbling. And the voice from heaven hasn't even spoken. When it does, it says two important things: Jesus is "Beloved," for he is part of the eternal dance of love we call the Trinity. The second point is just as clear: Love must be heeded. If we would live, we have to "listen to him!"

Prayers
others may be added

Heavenly Father, in our daily lives you reveal to us the your glory through your Son. Send your Spirit as we pray:

◆ Lord, it is good that we are here.

For the Church, that she may stand solid and strong, we pray: ◆ For civic leaders, that they may work together to discover new methods that will construct societies of justice and stability, we pray: ◆ For the sick and for those who are unable to receive proper medical care, that the Lord Jesus Christ may give them strength in their suffering, we pray: ◆ For all children and youth, that they will not fear to stand up in the name of the Lord, we pray: ◆ For our parish community, that we may have the grace to place the interests of others above ours, we pray: ◆

Our Father . . .

God our Father,
you reveal to us your Triune glory
by your Incarnate Son and the
    Holy Spirit.
Give us a true gratitude for all of
    your gifts.
Open our eyes to see your glory and
    goodness.
Open our ears to listen to your voice,
that we may be transformed into union
with you.
We ask this through Christ our Lord.
Amen.

✝ You will protect us, Lord.

✝ Lord, heal my soul, for I have sinned against you.

Psalm 100 *page 414*

Reading *Mark 2:1–12*

When Jesus returned to Capernaum after some days, it became known that he was at home. Many gathered together so that there was no longer room for them, not even around the door, and he preached the word to them. They came bringing to him a paralytic carried by four men. Unable to get near Jesus because of the crowd, they opened up the roof above him. After they had broken through, they let down the mat on which the paralytic was lying. When Jesus saw their faith, he said to the paralytic, "Child, your sins are forgiven." Now some of the scribes were sitting there asking themselves, "Why does this man speak that way? He is blaspheming. Who but God alone can forgive sins?" Jesus immediately knew in his mind what they were thinking to themselves, so he said, "Why are you thinking such things in your hearts? Which is easier, to say to the paralytic, 'Your sins are forgiven,' or to say, 'Rise, pick up your mat and walk'? But that you may know that the Son of Man has authority to forgive sins on earth"—he said to the paralytic, "I say to you, rise, pick up your mat, and go home." He rose, picked up his mat at once, and went away in the sight of everyone. They were all astounded and glorified God, saying, "We have never seen anything like this."

Reflection

Who else is there like God? It is only he who comes to us out of love and in his power frees us both spiritually and physically. Today's Gospel recounts the healing of the paralytic. First, Jesus heals him of the spiritual affliction of his sins, and then Jesus heals him of his physical infirmity. In obedience to the Lord's call, let us also rise up and walk with him.

Prayers *others may be added*

With confidence, we pray:

◆ Heal us, O Lord, and have mercy.

For the Church and her people, that they may continue to follow Christ's mission of the healing and forgiveness of sins, we pray: ◆ That all nations may give glory to God for the great works he has done among all peoples, we pray: ◆ For those who await mental, physical, emotional, and spiritual healing, that God's grace may touch them to bring them freedom from their suffering, we pray: ◆ For those who are estranged from the home of the Church, that they may return with forgiveness and healing in the sacrament of Confession, we pray: ◆

Our Father . . .

God, our Father,
without your grace we are nothing.
Continue to heal us and give us your life.
We ask this through Christ our Lord.
Amen.

✝ Lord, heal my soul, for I have sinned against you.

✝ The precepts of the Lord give joy to the heart.

Psalm 103   *page 415*

Reading   *Mark 9:19–29*

[Jesus] said to [the crowd and the scribes] in reply, "O faithless generation, how long will I be with you? How long will I endure you? Bring him to me." They brought the boy to him. And when he saw him, the spirit immediately threw the boy into convulsions. As he fell to the ground, he began to roll around and foam at the mouth. Then he questioned his father, "How long has this been happening to him?" He replied, "Since childhood. It has often thrown him into fire and into water to kill him. But if you can do anything, have compassion on us and help us." Jesus said to him, " 'If you can!' Everything is possible to one who has faith." Then the boy's father cried out, "I do believe, help my unbelief!" Jesus, on seeing a crowd rapidly gathering, rebuked the unclean spirit and said to it, "Mute and deaf spirit, I command you: come out of him and never enter him again!" Shouting and throwing the boy into convulsions, it came out. He became like a corpse, which caused many to say, "He is dead!" But Jesus took him by the hand, raised him, and he stood up. When he entered the house, his disciples asked him in private, "Why could we not drive it out?" He said to them, "This kind can only come out through prayer."

Reflection

In our weaknesses, we take part in this faithless generation that doubts God's power and his work among us. However, through fervent prayer and perseverance we can beg the Lord like the man in the Gospel to give us faith and to help our unbelief.

Prayers   *others may be added*

We cry out to God:

◆ Lord, I believe; help my unbelief.

That the Church will fulfill her mission for the needs of all peoples, we pray: ◆ That civic leaders may be aware of their responsibility to seek the common good of all peoples, we pray: ◆ That the sick may receive the medical care they need, we pray: ◆ That prisoners and those who serve them may receive spiritual liberation in Christ Jesus, we pray: ◆ That those without faith will soften their hearts to receive this gift, we pray: ◆

Our Father . . .

Heavenly Father,
anything is possible to the one who
    has faith.
Heal our sins and free us from all
    physical infirmity,
that we may enjoy the freedom of
    serving you.
We ask this through Christ our Lord.
Amen.

✝ The precepts of the Lord give joy to the heart.

✝ Throw your cares on the Lord, and he will support you.

Psalm 19   *page 403*

Reading   *Mark 9:31–37*

[Jesus] was teaching his disciples and telling them, "The Son of Man is to be handed over to men and they will kill him, and three days after his death he will rise." But they did not understand the saying, and they were afraid to question him.

They came to Capernaum and, once inside the house, he began to ask them, "What were you arguing about on the way?" But they remained silent. They had been discussing among themselves on the way who was the greatest. Then he sat down, called the Twelve, and said to them, "If anyone wishes to be first, he shall be the last of all and the servant of all." Taking a child he placed it in their midst, and putting his arms around it he said to them, "Whoever receives one child such as this in my name, receives me; and whoever receives me, receives not me but the One who sent me."

Reflection

Tomorrow is the first day of Lent. Jesus told his apostles that soon he would have to suffer, die, and rise. Not understanding what Jesus said, they argued about who was the greatest. Jesus also teaches us of his deep love and humble self-sacrificial service for us through his Passion, death, and Resurrection, which we begin to contemplate anew during this holy time.

Prayers   *others may be added*

Lord, you teach us that the first shall be last and the last shall be first. Let us pray:

◆ Give us a servant's heart, O Lord.

For the Church, that through the work of all the bishops, priests, deacons, and lay ministers, she may imitate the self-giving service of her Bridegroom, Jesus Christ, we pray: ◆ For government officials and leaders of all nations, that they may constantly renew their efforts to serve the poor and the weakest of society, we pray: ◆ For the poor, the sick, the lonely, and all who suffer, that they may know that to them belongs the kingdom of God, we pray: ◆ That the lives of all children may be received by all people in joy and love, we pray: ◆ For the grace of safety, sobriety, and temperance for all peoples, we pray: ◆

Our Father . . .

Merciful God,
as we prepare to meditate more deeply
on the mystery of your Son's Passion,
    death, and Resurrection,
teach us the true meaning of service
    and love.
Pour out the wisdom of your Spirit
    upon us,
that we may seek you through a life
    of virtue.
We ask this through Christ our Lord.
Amen.

✝ Throw your cares on the Lord, and he will support you.

✝ A clean heart create for me, God.
(*Psalm 51:12*)

Psalm 51   page 409

Reading   *Matthew 6:2, 5a–5b, 6, 16*

"When you give alms, do not blow a trumpet before you, as the hypocrites do in the synagogues and in the streets to win the praise of others. . . .

"When you pray, do not be like the hypocrites, who love to stand and pray in the synagogues and on street corners so that others may see them . . . But when you pray, go to your inner room, close the door, and pray to your Father in secret. And your Father who sees in secret will repay you.

"When you fast, do not look gloomy like the hypocrites."

Reflection   *Graziano Marcheschi*

Each year as we begin a season when many make (often public) resolutions to deny themselves of favorite foods or TV programs, or to adopt some practice of prayer, we hear this gospel that warns of the dangers of hypocrisy and of public shows of piety. Don't bother, says Jesus, if you're doing it for the admiration of the crowd. If that's your motive, you've already got your reward, so don't expect a thing from God. Such dangers are real, and so is the damage they do. But if your motives are pure, keep your goodness to yourself. God will know. And that will be enough.

Prayers   *others may be added*

Acknowledging our sins, we turn to you, O God, to heal us. Let us pray:

◆ Be merciful, O God, for we have sinned.

For the Holy Father, that he may be strengthened in his mission to continue to lead the Church to follow in the footsteps of Christ, we pray: ◆ That the graces of this holy time may bring conversion to all leaders of nations, that they may truly seek the common good for all peoples, we pray: ◆ For all the poor, the sick, and the suffering; for those who are weighed down by the burden of illness and pain, that they may find comfort in the compassion of our Great High Priest who suffers in and with us, we pray: ◆ For our local community, that we may be intent on performing works of charity, we pray: ◆ That each day this Lent may be an opportunity us to turn more deeply to the Lord and to respond in love to his gifts of freedom and life for us, we pray: ◆

Our Father . . .

God our Father,
you send us your Son, Jesus Christ,
to free us from our sins and
to give us everlasting life.
As we begin this holy time of Lent,
may the Holy Spirit convert our hearts
as we enter into the mystery of
the Passion, death, and Resurrection
of your Son, Jesus Christ,
through whom we ask this prayer.
Amen.

✝ A clean heart create for me, God.

✝ Blessed are they who hope in the Lord.

Psalm 51 *page 409*

Reading *Luke 9:22–25*

Jesus said to his disciples, "The Son of man must suffer greatly and be rejected by the elders, the chief priests, and the scribes, and be killed and on the third day be raised."

Then he said to all, "If anyone wishes to come after me, he must deny himself and take up his cross daily and follow me. For whoever wishes to save his life will lose it, but whoever loses his life for my sake will save it. What profit is there for one to gain the whole world yet lose or forfeit himself?"

Reflection

All the riches of the world are nothing in comparison to the glory of communion and life with God. Today in the liturgy, Jesus teaches that, in order to attain this union with him, we must be willing to deny ourselves and follow in his footsteps. By dying to our selfish desires and to our own will, the life of Christ can dwell within us.

Prayers *others may be added*

Father, in your Son you show us true self denial. Let us pray:

◆ Help us to follow after you, O Lord.

For the Holy Father, that each day he may persevere in carrying his cross as he fulfills his role as the Vicar of Christ, we pray: ◆ For civil leaders, that they may not seek their own interests and desires, but instead may they may serve the good of all peoples, especially those most in need, we pray: ◆ For all those who suffer under the weight of heavy crosses that they may persevere in offering their sufferings to the Lord who accompanies them and gives strength and healing, we pray: ◆ For all those that work, that the challenges of each day may be little opportunities of self-denial following in the footsteps of Christ, we pray: ◆ For those who have died, that they may enjoy the glory given to all who persevere to the end, we pray: ◆

Our Father . . .

God our Father, in your great mercy
you have sent your Son among us
to teach us the path of love and joy.
By following in his footsteps
in our little sufferings and trials,
may we come to enjoy forever
the glory of communion with you,
where you live and reign with your Son,
    our Lord Jesus Christ,
in the unity of the Holy Spirit,
one God, forever and ever.
Amen.

✝ Blessed are they who hope in the Lord.

✝ A heart contrite and humbled,
   O God, you will not spurn.

Psalm 51   *page 409*

Reading   *Matthew 9:14–15*

The disciples of John approached Jesus and said, "Why do we and the Pharisees fast much, but your disciples do not fast?" Jesus answered them, "Can the guests mourn as long as the bridegroom is with them? The days will come when the bridegroom is taken away from them, and then they will fast."

Reflection

Fasting is one of the primary Lenten disciplines. By fasting, which should always be united to prayer, we become less attached to the things of the world, and we become freer to serve God and others. Jesus himself fasted for 40 days when in the desert, and during this season of Lent we accompany Christ in this journey of preparation.

Prayers   *others may be added*

In preparation for the Passion, death, and Resurrection, we present our petitions to the Father as we pray:

◆ Purify our hearts, O Lord.

For the Holy Father, that, in imitation of Christ, he may offer prayer and sacrifice for the conversion of all peoples, we pray: ◆ For governors, rulers, and leaders of all nations, that they may work for justice in order to create a civilization of love, we pray: ◆ For those who suffer in body, mind, and spirit, that their sufferings may be offered in union with the offering of the Sacrificial Lamb, we pray: ◆ For the needs of the families and friends of our community, especially for those who suffer loss, we pray: ◆ For the grace to dedicate ourselves to moments of silent prayer in order to hear the voice of the Lord, we pray: ◆

Our Father . . .

Lord,
we are a sinful people.
Without your grace we are nothing
and we are capable of nothing.
Through our Lenten sacrifice,
come more deeply into our hearts,
that your life may dwell within us.
We ask this through your Son Jesus
    Christ, our Lord,
who lives and reigns with you in the unity
    of the Holy Spirit,
one God, forever and ever.
Amen.

✝ A heart contrite and humbled,
   O God, you will not spurn.

☩ The LORD will guide you always and give you plenty even on the parched land. (*Isaiah 58:11*)

Psalm 51   *page 409*

Reading   *Luke 5:27–32*

Jesus saw a tax collector named Levi sitting at the customs post. He said to him, "Follow me." And leaving everything behind, he got up and followed him. Then Levi gave a great banquet for him in his house, and a large crowd of tax collectors and others were at table with them. The Pharisees and their scribes complained to his disciples, saying, "Why do you eat and drink with tax collectors and sinners?" Jesus said to them in reply, "Those who are healthy do not need a physician, but the sick do. I have not come to call the righteous but sinners."

Reflection

Lent invites us once again to return to the Lord with all our hearts. As sinners, we are all in need of God's mercy and grace, and so during this penitential season we turn again to the Lord in repentance to ask him to heal and free our souls from sin. In these grace-filled days, may we have the courage to follow the Lord like Matthew, also called Levi, leaving behind all our attachments to sin.

Prayers   *others may be added*

Father, you sent your Son Jesus as healer of our bodies and souls. We pray:

◆ Free us from our sins, O God.

For the Church throughout the world, that she may continue to be dedicated to works of charity for those in need, we pray: ◆ For civil leaders, that they may guide their citizens in justice and truth, we pray: ◆ For all those who suffer mentally, emotionally, physically, or spiritually, that the Divine Physician may bring them peace and freedom, we pray: ◆ That our local community may become more united in prayer and good works this Lent, we pray: ◆ For the perseverance to remain faithful to our Lenten observances, we pray: ◆

Our Father . . .

God our Father,
we turn back to you with joyful hearts,
confident that you forgive us our sins
and renew us in your fatherly love.
Teach us your ways, O Lord,
so that we may walk in your truth.
May we always radiate your joy
   and peace.
We ask this through Christ our Lord.
Amen.

☩ The LORD will guide you always and give you plenty even on the parched land.

Sunday, February 26, 2012
First Sunday of Lent

✝ Your ways, O Lord, are love and truth to those who keep your covenant.

Psalm 91 page 412

Reading Mark 1:12–15

The Spirit drove Jesus out into the desert, and he remained in the desert for forty days, tempted by Satan. He was among wild beasts, and the angels ministered to him.

After John had been arrested, Jesus came to Galilee proclaiming the gospel of God: "This is the time of fulfillment. The kingdom of God is at hand. Repent, and believe in the gospel."

Reflection

We have begun our Lenten journey. We spiritually enter into the desert to accompany Jesus in prayer and fasting. Now is the time of repentance; now is the time to turn away from our sins and to turn to the Lord. Assisted by the angels and united to the whole Church, with Christ, we make our way toward Calvary and toward the glorious Resurrection.

Prayers others may be added

Father, you sent us your Son to free us from our sins. Let us pray:

◆ Heal us, O Lord, and save us.

For the Church, that, as we begin our Lenten journey, we may remain faithful in prayer throughout our earthly pilgrimage, we pray: ◆ For all governmental officials and social workers, that they may be renewed in a spirit of service in promoting justice and human dignity for all peoples, we pray: ◆ For all who suffer in mind, body, and spirit, that they may not become hard-hearted, but rather offer their sacrifices to the Lord, who brings life out of all suffering and death, we pray: ◆ For our local community, that this Lent may be a fruitful time of repentance and fellowship, we pray: ◆ For the grace this week to serve God and others through the little suffering of each day, we pray: ◆

Our Father . . .

God our Father,
you know our weakness and sinfulness.
Stay close to us through the
difficulties and trials of life.
Keep us faithful during our
    Lenten practice,
and give us the grace to pick up our
daily crosses and follow after your Son,
    our Lord Jesus Christ,
who lives and reigns with you in the unity
    of the Holy Spirit,
one God, forever and ever.
Amen.

✝ Your ways, O Lord, are love and truth to those who keep your covenant.

✝ Your words, O Lord, are Spirit and Life.

Psalm 130 page 420

Reading Matthew 25:31–34

Jesus said to his disciples: "When the Son of Man comes in his glory, and all the angels with him, he will sit upon his glorious throne, and all the nations will be assembled before him. And he will separate them one from another, as a shepherd separates the sheep from the goats. He will place the sheep on his right and the goats on his left. Then the king will say to those on his right, 'Come, you who are blessed by my Father. Inherit the kingdom prepared for you from the foundation of the world.'"

Reflection Graziano Marcheschi

In the end, there are only two categories for us all: sheep and goats. Perhaps today Jesus would use different imagery, but the point would be the same: love puts us on God's "right" side; selfishness puts us on the wrong side. We're given a lifetime to make the choices that will put us on one side or the other. But each lifetime is different and the years that will comprise it are unknown to anyone but God. The words of the King in the gospel are reassuring: "Inherit the kingdom." But what if we're not on that side? What if we end up on the wrong side? Here's the good news: it's not the end, and we still have today to make the *right* choice.

Prayers *others may be added*

Jesus Christ will come again in glory to judge the sheep from the goats. Let us pray:

◆ **Good Shepherd, hear our cry for mercy.**

For the Church, that she may continue to work in service for the littlest and the poorest, we pray: ◆ For leaders of all nations, that they may seek means of feeding the hungry and clothing the naked, we pray: ◆ For all doctors, nurses, and caregivers who provide help and healing for the sick, we pray: ◆ For an ever deeper spirit of generosity and charity, we pray: ◆

Our Father . . .

Loving and merciful God,
may our hearts not remain hardened
at the sight of our brothers and sisters
    in need.
Open our eyes to see, and may our wills
be moved to love as you love.
Teach us to be holy, Lord,
that we may enjoy the happiness of life
you give to all who hope in you.
We ask this through Christ our Lord.
Amen.

✝ Your words, O Lord, are Spirit and Life.

Tuesday, February 28, 2012
Lenten Weekday

✝ From all their distress, God rescues the just.

Psalm 51
page 409

Reading
Matthew 6:7–15

Jesus said to his disciples: "In praying, do not babble like the pagans, who think that they will be heard / because of their many words. Do not be like them. Your Father knows what you need before you ask him.

"This is how you are to pray: / Our Father who art in heaven, / hallowed be thy name, / thy Kingdom come, / thy will be done, / on earth as it is in heaven. / Give us this day our daily bread; / and forgive us our trespasses, / as we forgive those who trespass against us; / and lead us not into temptation, but deliver us from evil. /

"If you forgive men their transgressions, your heavenly Father will forgive you. But if you do not forgive men, neither will your Father forgive your transgressions."

Reflection

Today in the Gospel, Jesus teaches us how to pray. When we pray we are to say, "Our Father." God the Father has become our Father through Jesus Christ. Together with Jesus we can call God our Father. Likewise, all people can call upon the Father, and so together with all believers throughout the world and throughout all time we pray to God in Jesus Christ.

Prayers
others may be added

God, our Father, you know all our needs before we ask them. Hear us as we pray:

◆ Thy will be done, O God.

For the Church, that during these days of Lent, all her members may be more strongly united in prayer, we pray: ◆ For the Holy Father, that, as the Vicar of Christ on earth, he may lead us to God the Father through Christ Jesus, we pray: ◆ For people of all nations, that they may be drawn into unity as children of a single universal family, we pray: ◆ For all who grieve or suffer the loss or absence of their fathers, that the love and power of God the Father may heal all wounds, we pray: ◆ For our families, that they may be renewed in forgiveness and peace, we pray: ◆ For the humility and boldness to ask for what we need in prayer, confident in the goodness of God's providence, we pray: ◆

Our Father . . .

Loving God,
in your Son, Jesus Christ,
you have become our Father.
Banish our mistaken ideas of fatherhood
    and teach us who you are.
Instruct us how to live as your children
    and to be united to one another and to
    your Son,
who lives and reigns with you in the unity
    of the Holy Spirit,
one God, forever and ever.
Amen.

✝ From all their distress, God rescues the just.

✝ A heart contrite and humbled,
O God, you will not spurn.

Psalm 91 *page 412*

Reading *Luke 11:29–31*

While still more people gathered in the crowd, Jesus said to them, "This generation is an evil generation; it seeks a sign, but no sign will be given it, except the sign of Jonah. Just as Jonah became a sign to the Ninevites, so will the Son of Man be to this generation. At the judgment the queen of the south will rise with the men of this generation and she will condemn them, because she came from the ends of the earth to hear the wisdom of Solomon, and there is something greater than Solomon here."

Reflection

Today in the Gospel, Jesus refuses to give the people a sign other than the sign of the prophet Jonah. Jonah was sent by God to proclaim repentance throughout the corrupt city of Nineveh. He repented when they heard Jonah's words. Jesus says that today's evil generation will be condemned even more severely than the city of Nineveh, because the Ninevites repented of their sins.

Prayers *others may be added*

God our Father, you sent us your Son, the great Prophet and King as messenger of your word. Let us pray:

◆ Convert our hearts, O Lord.

That the Church, together with the Pope, bishops, and priests, may tirelessly proclaim Christ's mission as priest, prophet, and king, we pray: ◆ For all countries, nations, and cities, that they may hear the word of God and be drawn to repentance, we pray: ◆ For all those who suffer from violence, poverty, or abuse, we pray: ◆ For the grace to humbly turn to the Lord, rather than refusing to acknowledge our sins through excuses, we pray: ◆

Our Father . . .

Heavenly Father,
the people of Niveveh heard the words
of the prophet Jonah and they converted.
Send your Holy Spirit upon us today,
that we may not remain deaf to your word
that you speak through your Son,
the great priest, prophet, and king,
who lives and reigns with you in the unity
of the Holy Spirit,
one God, forever and ever.
Amen.

✝ A heart contrite and humbled,
O God, you will not spurn.

Thursday, March 1, 2012
Lenten Weekday

✝ Lord, on the day I called for help, you answered me.

Psalm 130 page 420

Reading Matthew 7:7–12

Jesus said to his disciples: "Ask and it will be given to you; seek and you will find; knock and the door will be opened to you. For everyone who asks, receives; and the one who seeks, finds; and to the one who knocks, the door will be opened. Which one of you would hand his son a stone when he asked for a loaf of bread, or a snake when he asked for a fish? If you then, who are wicked, know how to give good gifts to your children, how much more will your heavenly Father give good things to those who ask him?

"Do to others whatever you would have them do to you. This is the law and the prophets."

Reflection

Through these Lenten Gospel readings, Jesus continues to teach us how to pray to his Father, who, through Christ, has become our Father as well. Jesus tells us that we need only to ask and it will be given to us, provided that it be for our good and according to God's most perfect will. As little children, let us come before our Father to beg him for all of our needs and desires.

Prayers *others may be added*

Good and loving Father, you promise that we need only to ask. With child-like confidence, hear our prayer.

◆ Remember you promise, O Lord.

For the Church throughout the world and her people, that they may serve God faithfully and be kept safe from harm, we pray: ◆ For all nations, especially those torn by war and violence, that governments work unselfishly for peace and justice, we pray: ◆ For all who are alone, especially all of the sick, and for those who have no one to help them, we pray: ◆ For our local community, that its people may become ever more united to one another through personal prayer and the celebration of the liturgy, we pray: ◆ For the humility and courage to come before our Father to request what we need, we pray: ◆

Our Father . . .

God our Father,
we cry out to you in faith,
"Save us from the hand of our enemies,
turn our mourning into gladness
and our sorrows into wholeness"
    (Esther 12:24–25).
Help, us Lord; you are our only hope.
We ask this through Christ our Lord.
Amen.

✝ Lord, on the day I called for help, you answered me.

Friday, March 2, 2012
Lenten Weekday

✝ Out of the depths I call to you, LORD.
(*Psalm 130:1*)

Psalm 51 page 409

Reading *Matthew 5:20, 23–24*

Jesus said to his disciples: "I tell you, unless your righteousness surpasses that of the scribes and Pharisees, you will not enter into the Kingdom of heaven.

"Therefore, if you bring your gift to the altar, and there recall that your brother has anything against you, leave your gift there at the altar, go first and be reconciled with your brother, and then come and offer your gift."

Reflection *Graziano Marcheschi*

Jesus said his "yoke" was sweet and his "burden" light. But are they? Don't we often labor mightily under the weight of our burdens? Yes. But are they burdens Jesus asks us to carry or ones we place upon ourselves? Anger and resentment become a heavy weight upon us. The "yoke" of love and the "burden" of forgiveness Jesus places on us are infinitely sweeter and lighter than the yokes of resentment we place on ourselves and the burdens of anger we carry when we reject his invitation to repent and forgive. Every time we receive the Eucharist, let us first examine our hearts and lay down whatever anger toward our neighbor still resides there.

Prayers *others may be added*

You send us Jesus Christ to teach us love and forgiveness. Let us pray:

◆ Heal us, O Lord.

For the Church, that she may be a source of forgiveness and healing for all through the holy sacrament of Reconciliation, we pray: ◆ For all leaders of nations, that they may work to restore all discord and division, we pray: ◆ For all the sick, that God may alleviate their pain, we pray: ◆ For all who suffer anger, that God may bring them healing and peace, we pray: ◆ For all who give their lives in service to the poor and lowly, we pray: ◆ For families everywhere to become schools of love and forgiveness, through the power of the Holy Spirit, we pray: ◆

Our Father . . .

Forgiving Father,
you establish your kingdom here on earth through your Son, Jesus Christ.
Pour out the fire of your Holy Spirit to send workers into your vineyard to work in generous service for
    your kingdom.
We ask this through Christ our Lord.
Amen.

✝ Out of the depths I call to you, LORD.

Saturday, March 3, 2012
Lenten Weekday
Optional memorial of Saint Katherine Drexel, Virgin

✝ Blessed are they who follow the law of the Lord!

Psalm 91   *page 412*

Reading   *Matthew 5:43–48*

Jesus said to his disciples: "You have heard that it was said, *You shall love your neighbor and hate your enemy.* But I say to you, love your enemies, and pray for those who persecute you, that you may be children of your heavenly Father, for he makes his sun rise on the bad and the good, and causes rain to fall on the just and the unjust. For if you love those who love you, what recompense will you have? Do not the tax collectors do the same? And if you greet your brothers and sisters only, what is unusual about that? Do not the pagans do the same? So be perfect, just as your heavenly Father is perfect."

Reflection

Today Jesus gives us a tall order: to love our enemies and to pray for those who persecute us. He calls us to perfection, so that we may share in his life with the Father, which is true happiness and true fulfillment. In imitation of the saints, may our lives also be examples of holiness and Christian love and joy.

Prayers   *others may be added*

Lord, you have called us to remain in your love. Let us pray:

◆ Holy Spirit, bear fruit in our lives.

For the Church, that she may be a beacon of light and love to the nations, we pray: ◆ For all people to choose to lay down their lives in love and service to God and others, we pray: ◆ For government officials, that they may work to build up civilizations of love, we pray: ◆ For those who suffer in mind and body, that God may render their sufferings fruitful for the salvation of many souls, we pray: ◆ For our local community to be a place of apostolic joy and genuine love and friendship, we pray: ◆ For the courage to truly love with all our hearts, we pray: ◆

Our Father . . .

Loving God,
we see the definition of true love in
     your Son,
who lays down his life for his friends.
In our sinfulness, we have not merited
     your friendship,
yet we beg you for the grace to remain
     always in your love.
Pour your Holy Spirit upon us,
that we may live a life of joy and peace
     beyond all understanding.
We give our lives to you.
May we bear fruit in holiness.
We ask this through Christ our Lord.
Amen.

✝ Blessed are they who follow the law of the Lord!

✝ I will walk before the Lord, in the land of the living.

Psalm 130   *page 420*

Reading   *Mark 9:2–10*

Jesus took Peter, James, and John and led them up a high mountain apart by themselves. And he was transfigured before them, and his clothes became dazzling white, such as no fuller on earth could bleach them. Then Elijah appeared to them along with Moses, and they were conversing with Jesus. Then Peter said to Jesus in reply, "Rabbi, it is good that we are here! Let us make three tents: one for you, one for Moses, and one for Elijah." He hardly knew what to say, they were so terrified. Then a cloud came, casting a shadow over them; from the cloud came a voice, "This is my beloved Son. Listen to him." Suddenly, looking around, they no longer saw anyone but Jesus alone with them.

As they were coming down from the mountain, he charged them not to relate what they had seen to anyone, except when the Son of Man had risen from the dead So they kept the matter to themselves, questioning what rising from the dead meant.

Reflection

Today on this Second Sunday of Lent, we hear the Gospel of the Transfiguration, which prefigures the glory of Christ's Resurrection. The Father speaks from the cloud, "Listen to him." Yes, "it is good that we are here" during this time of Lent to listen and follow Christ as we accompany him in preparation for his Passion, death, and Resurrection.

Prayers   *others may be added*

Father, you who did not spare to give us your own Son will not spare to give us everything else along with him. In faith, we pray:

◆ **Hear the cry of the faithful who long to see your face.**

For the Church, that, guided by the pastoral work of the Pope, all of her suffering may be transformed into glory, we pray: ◆ For all nations, especially those who suffer violence, terrorism, and war, that the merits of Christ's sufferings may bear fruit in peace and justice, we pray: ◆ For all the sick and the lonely, that they may hear the Father's voice, we pray: ◆ For our faith community gathered in prayer, that God may answer each of our needs, we pray: ◆ For all who have died, that they may forever enjoy Christ's divine glory with the company of all the angels and saints, we pray: ◆

Our Father . . .

Heavenly Father,
keep us faithful to prayer and penance
as we continue our Lenten journey.
We ask this through our Lord Jesus
    Christ, your Son,
who lives and reigns with you in the unity
    of the Holy Spirit,
one God, forever and ever.
Amen.

✝ I will walk before the Lord, in the land of the living.

✝ Your words, Lord, are spirit and life;
you have the words of everlasting life.

Psalm 130   *page 420*

Reading   *Luke 6:36–38*

Jesus said to his disciples: "Be merciful, just as your Father is merciful.

"Stop judging and you will not be condemned. Forgive and you will be forgiven. Give and gifts will be given to you; a good measure, packed together, shaken down, and overflowing, will be poured into your lap. For the measure with which you measure will in return be measured out to you."

Reflection   *Graziano Marcheschi*

One of scripture's most misunderstood passages is in this Gospel. It's often thrown like a dart at anyone who is perceived to be narrow and judgmental, using Jesus' words to tell others not to judge. But Jesus is advocating *right* judgment, not telling us to abdicate common sense. Being human requires exercising judgment, and in many places scripture admonishes us to judge . . . but to judge right and prudently. Judgmentalism, i.e., judging from a presumed place of superiority; judging out of anger and resentment; judging that is not motivated by love of the other, these are what Jesus eschews. Jesus himself was always judging behavior . . . but he did it out of love. And love makes the difference between judging and being judgmental.

Prayers   *others may be added*

Father, you sent us your Son to free us from our sins. Let us pray:

◆ Heal us, O Lord, and save us.

For the Church and all her members as we begin our Lenten journey, that we may remain faithful in prayer throughout our earthly pilgrimage, we pray: ◆ For all governmental officials and social workers, that they may be renewed in a spirit of service in promoting justice and human dignity for all peoples, we pray: ◆ For all who suffer in mind, body, and spirit, that they may not become hard-hearted, we pray: ◆ For our local community, that this Lent may be a fruitful time of repentance and fellowship, we pray: ◆ For the grace this week to serve God and others through the little suffering of each day, we pray: ◆

Our Father . . .

God our Father,
you know our weaknesses and sinfulness.
Stay close to us through the difficulties
    and trials of life.
Keep us faithful during our
    Lenten practice,
and give us the grace
to pick up our daily crosses and follow
    after our Lord, Jesus Christ, your Son,
who lives and reigns with you in the unity
    of the Holy Spirit,
one God, forever and ever.
Amen.

✝ Your words, Lord, are spirit and life;
you have the words of everlasting life.

✝ To the upright I will show the saving power of God.

Psalm 51   *page 409*

Reading   *Matthew 23:1–3, 8b–12*

Jesus spoke to the crowds and to his disciples, saying, "The scribes and the Pharisees have taken their seat on the chair of Moses. Therefore, do and observe all things whatsoever they tell you, but do not follow their example. For they preach but they do not practice. . . . You have but one teacher, and you are all brothers. Call no one on earth your father; you have but one Father in heaven. Do not be called 'Master'; you have but one master, the Christ. The greatest among you must be your servant. Whoever exalts himself will be humbled; but whoever humbles himself will be exalted."

Reflection

Unfortunately, sometimes those who appear to be holy can be hypocritical, like the scribes and Pharisees in today's Gospel. However, Jesus tells us to do what they say to do, but not to follow their example. Jesus Christ is our true Teacher. The test of the one who is truly the greatest is the one who is willing to be the servant of the others.

Prayers   *others may be added*

Father, come to the aid of your children amid the various teachings of the world. Let us pray:

◆ Lord, hear our prayer.

For the Church and all her members, that they may be freed from the temptation to seek power and authority rather than the true authority that comes from humble service, we pray: ◆ For the Holy Father and all the bishops, priests, and deacons, that they may firmly fight in defense of truth, and that at all times and in all places they may give good example by practicing what they preach, we pray: ◆ For governments run by false ideologies such as relativism, materialism, and the degradation of the human person, we pray: ◆ For children who suffer because of the scandal caused by teachers or other adults, we pray: ◆ For the grace to fight against the temptation of laziness, so as to live Christian lives of integrity, we pray: ◆

Our Father . . .

Jesus, our Master and Teacher,
by your word you set us free along the
    way of life.
Convert our hearts to turn back to you.
Wash us clean of our sins as you
    have said:
"Though your sins be like scarlet,
they may become white as snow"
    (Isaiah 1:18).
You live and reign forever and ever.
Amen.

✝ To the upright I will show the saving power of God.

Wednesday, March 7, 2012
Lenten Weekday

✝ Save me, O Lord, in your kindness.

Psalm 91 *page 412*

Reading *Matthew 20:20–23*

The mother of the sons of Zebedee approached Jesus with her sons and did him homage, wishing to ask him for something. He said to her, "What do you wish?" She answered him, "Command that these two sons of mine sit, one at your right and the other at your left, in your kingdom." Jesus said in reply, "You do not know what you are asking. Can you drink the chalice that I am going to drink?" They said to him, "We can." He replied, "My chalice you will indeed drink, but to sit at my right and at my left, this is not mine to give but is for those for whom it has been prepared by my Father."

Reflection *Graziano Marcheschi*

Even a mother's politicking can't win her boys the special place she seeks for them. Jesus seems to open the door a crack: "Can you drink the chalice?" he asks. But their overeager "yes" still doesn't suffice. Work for the kingdom must be its own reward. Even if you give your life, there won't be guarantees of special honors and distinctions. The greatest honor is belonging to Christ. The greatest distinction is spilling our blood—whether literally or figuratively—for him. To desire any more is futile. If there are places of honor in the kingdom, it will be the Father who assigns them. Jesus' task, and ours, is to make sure we get there.

Prayers *others may be added*

Holy God, in the Paschal Mystery of your Son we see true greatness. Let us pray:

◆ You will redeem me, O Lord, O faithful God.

For the Church throughout the world, that, as the Mystical Body of Christ, she may be a faithful witness to Christ's outpouring and total gift of self, we pray: ◆ For civic leaders, that they may achieve true greatness by serving the weakest and poorest of their countries, we pray: ◆ For all who suffer physically, spiritually, materially, or emotionally, and for those who care for them, we pray: ◆ For all of us during this season of Lent, that we may spiritually accompany Christ through prayer and service, as he nears closer to Calvary, we pray: ◆

Our Father . . .

O God, our Father,
we wish to sit beside you in the kingdom
 of heaven.
Enliven us with your Holy Spirit,
that we may not fear to pick up our cross
every day through humble service
as we follow the Master, your Son.
We ask this through Christ our Lord.
Amen.

✝ Save me, O Lord, in your kindness.

✝ Blessed are they who hope in the Lord.

Psalm 130 page 420

Reading Luke 16:19–24

"There was a rich man who dressed in purple garments and fine linen and dined sumptuously each day. And lying at his door was a poor man named Lazarus, covered with sores, who would gladly have eaten his fill of the scraps that fell from the rich man's table. Dogs even used to come and lick his sores. When the poor man died, he was carried away by angels to the bosom of Abraham. The rich man also died and was buried, and from the netherworld, where he was in torment, he raised his eyes and saw Abraham far off and Lazarus at his side. And he cried out, 'Father Abraham, have pity on me. Send Lazarus to dip the tip of his finger in water and cool my tongue, for I am suffering torment in these flames.'"

Reflection *Graziano Marcheschi*

This story won't end well: the rich man remains in torment while Lazarus is couched in the bosom of Abraham. The rich man humbles himself to ask Lazarus for help, he'll even ask Abraham to send messengers to his brothers so they won't make the same mistakes. But the sobering message is that the brothers have enough warning—as did the rich man himself. Truth is all around us; we have only to open our eyes. Jesus warns that there can be a time when it's too late to see. And for the rich man, it was.

Prayers *others may be added*

God our Father, all the prophets of old have spoken your word. Let us pray:

◆ Here we are, Lord, we come to do your will.

For the Mystical Body of Christ, that all those in heaven, on earth, and in purgatory may be united with Christ present in the Holy Eucharist, we pray: ◆ For all nations, that they may heed God's word and further his kingdom throughout all the earth, we pray: ◆ For all those who suffer physical or mental agony, that God may send his angels to alleviate their pain, we pray: ◆ For all who have died, that they may enjoy the eternal rest in the union of the Trinity, we pray: ◆

Our Father . . .

God of all people,
it is you who probes the mind and tests the heart.
It is you who rewards everyone according to his or her deeds.
You understand the complexity of humans,
and it is you who have the power to heal us.
Come and save your people, Lord.
We ask this through Christ our Lord. Amen.

✝ Blessed are they who hope in the Lord.

Friday, March 9, 2012
Lenten Weekday

✝ Remember the marvels the Lord has done.

Psalm 51   *page 409*

Reading   *Matthew 21:33–40*

Jesus said to the chief priests and the elders of the people: "Hear another parable. There was a landowner who planted a vineyard, put a hedge around it, dug a wine press in it, and built a tower. Then he leased it to tenants and went on a journey. When vintage time drew near, he sent his servants to the tenants to obtain his produce. But the tenants seized the servants and one they beat, another they killed, and a third they stoned. Again he sent other servants, more numerous than the first ones, but they treated them in the same way. Finally, he sent his son to them, thinking, 'They will respect my son.' But when the tenants saw the son, they said to one another, 'This is the heir. Come, let us kill him and acquire his inheritance.' They seized him, threw him out of the vineyard, and killed him. What will the owner of the vineyard do to those tenants when he comes?"

Reflection

Today in the Gospel, Jesus angers the Pharisees by his parable of the vineyard. But, Jesus does not fear to speak out with boldness about the truth of his kingdom. Some regarded him as a prophet; however, the scribes and Pharisees were angered by him and wanted to arrest him. Likewise, we too can be angered by Jesus, when we become content in our own ways and do not want to convert from a way of life that may be more comfortable than what Jesus is asking of us.

Prayers   *others may be added*

Through our Lenten practice, we strive to turn away from sin and to turn to the loving unity of the Trinity.

◆ Have mercy on us, Lord.

For the Pope, that he may remain a faithful witness of holiness, and that he may have the physical strength to persevere in leading the Church, we pray: ◆ For all countries that are stricken by poverty and violence, that the Lord will send laborers into the vineyard to serve their needs and bring them aid, we pray: ◆ For all the poor and suffering, for those whose human dignity is unacknowledged by others, we pray: ◆ For all prisoners, we pray: ◆ For all those who are doing good work to serve humanity, we pray: ◆

Our Father . . .

Good and gracious God,
give us grateful hearts and cheerful faces
as we strive to serve you
through the sacrifices and trials of
    this day.
May everything be an opportunity
    for love.
We ask this through Christ our Lord.
Amen.

✝ Remember the marvels the Lord has done.

Saturday, March 10, 2012
Lenten Weekday

✟ The Lord is kind and merciful.

Psalm 91 page 412

Reading Luke 15:31–32

[The father said to the oldest son,] " 'My son, you are here with me always; everything I have is yours. But now we must celebrate and rejoice, because your brother was dead and has come to life again; he was lost and has been found.' "

Reflection

Today Jesus teaches us that his Father will meet us even in the midst of our sinfulness, our foolishness, and our weakness. He is a Father who welcomes sinners back into unity with him and desires to give us life even more and more abundantly.

Prayers *others may be added*

May we come to understand the mercy of the Father. Let us pray:

◆ Turn our hearts back to you, O Lord.

That the Church may be supported in grace to continue to welcome all peoples into her motherly embrace, we pray: ◆ That all peoples may be holy instruments of God's grace and forgiveness, we pray: ◆ That civil leaders may use their God-given authority to foster unity, peace, and justice, we pray: ◆ That those who suffer from illness and disease may not grow hardened, and that they may receive full and complete healing from the Lord, we pray: ◆ That all fallen-away Catholics may return home to the Father's embrace through the sacrament of Reconciliation, we pray: ◆

Our Father . . .

Loving Father,
you are a God who welcomes and feasts
    with sinners.
Help us to have the courage to forgive as
    you forgive
and to love as you love until we attain the
    glorious unity
of life everlasting with you.
We ask this through Christ our Lord.

✟ The Lord is kind and merciful.

✝ Lord, you have the words of everlasting life.

Psalm 130
page 420

Reading
John 2:13–17

Since the Passover of the Jews was near, Jesus went up to Jerusalem. He found in the temple area those who sold oxen, sheep, and doves, as well as the moneychangers seated there. He made a whip out of cords and drove them all out of the temple area, with the sheep and oxen, and spilled the coins of the moneychangers and overturned their tables, and to those who sold doves he said, "Take these out of here, and stop making my Father's house a marketplace." His disciples recalled the words of Scripture, "Zeal for your house will consume me."

Reflection

In today's Gospel, we see the just anger of Jesus as he drives the money changers from the temple. This season of Lent is likewise a time for Jesus to drive out our sins, which contaminate the temple of our bodies and souls. Through our practice of prayer and mortification, God purifies us so that we can be holy dwellings of the Holy Spirit.

Prayers
others may be added

God the Father sent the Son to save us from our sins. In faith and penitence, we pray:

◆ Purify us, O Lord, and make us clean.

For Christ's Bride, our Holy Mother Church, that she may remain pure and holy, we pray: ◆ For all nations, that they may cease attempts of violence, war, terrorism, and disrespect of human rights, we pray: ◆ For peoples throughout the world, that they may respond with generosity to help the poor and those who lack necessary resources, we pray: ◆ For all those who suffer physical, emotional, or spiritual illnesses, that they may be quickly healed, we pray: ◆ For the grace this week to persevere in charity among one's family and coworkers, we pray: ◆

Our Father . . .

O God,
sometimes we fear the pain involved
in allowing you to purify our hearts.
Help us to cease to makes excuses
and free us from our laziness
    and complacency.
Give us a great hatred for sin,
that we may avoid evil at all costs,
so as to live in joyful unity with you.
We ask this through Christ our Lord.
Amen.

✝ Lord, you have the words of everlasting life.

✝ Athirst is my soul for the living God.

Psalm 51   *page 409*

Reading   *Luke 4:24–30*

Jesus said to the people in the synagogue at Nazareth: "Amen, I say to you, no prophet is accepted in his own native place. Indeed, I tell you, there were many widows in Israel in the days of Elijah when the sky was closed for three and a half years and a severe famine spread over the entire land. It was to none of these that Elijah was sent, but only to a widow in Zarephath in the land of Sidon. Again, there were many lepers in Israel during the time of Elisha the prophet; yet not one of them was cleansed, but only Naaman the Syrian." When the people in the synagogue heard this, they were filled with fury. They rose up, drove him out of the town, and led him to the brow of the hill on which their town had been built, to hurl him down headlong. But he passed through the midst of them and went away.

Reflection   *Graziano Marcheschi*

It's a truism of the spiritual life that those who bring the truth go unrecognized. Perhaps it's for the sake of the "prophet" that this occurs; rejection may foster greater reliance on God. Being "chosen" brings temptations as well as responsibilities and perhaps rejection helps us steer clear of temptations. Jesus' experience offers comfort and courage to anyone who bears the prophetic burden of speaking the truth.

Prayers   *others may be added*

O God, you send your Son as Prophet to announce the glory of your kingdom. Let us pray:

◆ **Heal us, O Lord.**

That all who serve the Church may be faithful witnesses in Christ's prophetic ministry, we pray: ◆ That government officials may work to serve the poor, weak, and marginalized of their countries, we pray: ◆ That all who suffer from illness and disease may be restored to health of mind, body, and spirit, we pray: ◆ That our local community may draw from the healing living waters of the sacraments during this time of Lent, we pray: ◆

Our Father . . .

God our Father,
our souls are longing for your healing and
    life-giving waters.
Give us patience as we await your coming
    in glory
and help us to accept your will in
    moments of suffering
through faith and the love of our Lord
    Jesus Christ, your Son,
who lives and reigns with you in the unity
    of the Holy Spirit
one God, forever, and ever.
Amen.

✝ Athirst is my soul for the living God.

Tuesday, March 13, 2012
Lenten Weekday

✝ Remember your mercies, O Lord.

Psalm 91
page 412

Reading
Matthew 18:21–22

Peter approached Jesus and said to him, "Lord, if my brother sins against me, how often must I forgive him? As many as seven times?" Jesus answered, "I say to you, not seven times but seventy-seven times."

Reflection
Graziano Marcheschi

People walked away from Jesus when he spoke the "hard saying" about eating his body and blood. But his teaching on forgiveness may be an even "harder" saying for many of us. We may not walk away because of these words, but do we close our ears and harden our hearts to them? It's not a reasonable request to forgive so often. It seems to violate our dignity to let someone hurt and hurt again. "Seventy-seven times" means a limitless number. Is that possible? Is it even right? Jesus thinks so. Of course, he's not talking about becoming a floor-mat and taking the abuse of others. But true repentance must be met with true forgiveness. When we start to think, "Okay, this is one too many times!" perhaps we should remember how many times God has forgiven us.

Prayers
others may be added

O God, you are just and merciful.
Let us pray:

◆ Remember your mercies, O Lord.

That the Church may be blessed through this time of preparation for the Lord's Resurrection, we pray: ◆ That warring nations can come to resolutions of peace and justice through forgiveness and dialogue, we pray: ◆ That those who suffer alone may receive the help they need through the presence of family and friends, we pray: ◆ That all young people and children who have suffered mistreatment may be granted healing, we pray: ◆ That we may be given the grace to love and forgive as God has loved and forgiven us, we pray: ◆

Our Father . . .

God our Master,
deal with us with patience and mercy
despite our constant failings
    and sinfulness.
Give us generous hearts to offer
the mercy we have received from you
as mercy and forgiveness to others.
Free us from all bitterness
    and resentment,
through the gift of your Holy Spirit, and
give us the peace and joy of
    forgiving love.
We ask this through Christ our Lord.
Amen.

✝ Remember your mercies, O Lord.

✝ Praise the Lord, Jerusalem.

Psalm 130   *page 420*

Reading   *Matthew 5:17–19*

Jesus said to his disciples: "Do not think that I have come to abolish the law or the prophets. I have come not to abolish but to fulfill. Amen, I say to you, until heaven and earth pass away, not the smallest letter or the smallest part of a letter will pass from the law, until all things have taken place. Therefore, whoever breaks one of the least of these commandments and teaches others to do so will be called least in the Kingdom of heaven. But whoever obeys and teaches these commandments will be called greatest in the Kingdom of heaven."

Reflection

In Jesus Christ, the entire Law comes to fulfillment. Since the beginning of creation, God has been guiding and forming his people. By the covenants made with his people throughout all of salvation history, the Father has prepared his people for the greatest covenant, the death and Resurrection of his Son Jesus, who fulfills all the promises and prophecies made throughout the ages.

Prayers   *others may be added*

The season of Lent recalls the ages of preparation before the culmination of God's promise fulfilled in Christ Jesus. Let us pray:

◆ Remember your promise, O Lord.

That the Church, guided by the leadership and prayer of the Holy Father, may not be seen as a legalistic institution, but rather as the humble servant to the truth of Jesus Christ, we pray: ◆ That all national leaders and politicians may use their authority to establish and preserve laws that serve the common good of each person, we pray: ◆ That the sick in nursing homes, hospitals, or at home may have the patience to await the promise of new life, we pray: ◆ That all teachers may live lives of integrity worthy of imitation, we pray: ◆ That all who have died may swiftly attain glorious union with God, we pray: ◆

Our Father . . .

Good and loving Father,
throughout all time and all ages,
you father your people by revealing
your love to us through your covenant.
In these last days you have sent us
    your Son
to free us from our sins and bring us to
    new and everlasting life.
Continue to fulfill your will in us
through the work of our Lord Jesus
    Christ, your Son,
who lives and reigns with you in the unity
    of the Holy Spirit,
one God, forever and ever.

✝ Praise the Lord, Jerusalem.

Thursday, March 15, 2012
Lenten Weekday

✝ If today you hear his voice, harden not your hearts.

Psalm 91
page 412

Reading
Luke 11:14–20

Jesus was driving out a demon that was mute, and when the demon had gone out, the mute man spoke and the crowds were amazed. Some of them said, "By the power of Beelzebul, the prince of demons, he drives out demons." Others, to test him, asked him for a sign from heaven. But he knew their thoughts and said to them, "Every kingdom divided against itself will be laid waste and house will fall against house. And if Satan is divided against himself, how will his kingdom stand? For you say that it is by Beelzebul that I drive out demons. If I, then, drive out demons by Beelzebul, by whom do your own people drive them out? Therefore they will be your judges. But if it is by the finger of God that I drive out demons, then the Kingdom of God has come upon you."

Reflection

Jesus tell us, a "kingdom divided against itself will be laid waste and house will fall against house." Therefore, our whole being and our whole life must be for the Lord. Lent is the opportune time to turn back to the Lord, because if we are not for him we are against him.

Prayers
others may be added

The kingdom of God is at hand. Let us repent and turn back to the Lord as we pray:

◆ Redeem us, O Lord.

For the Holy Father, that he may be strengthened by the love and prayers of his flock throughout the world, we pray: ◆ For civic leaders, that they may continually grow in natural virtues as they serve humanity in the midst of economic, social, and environmental challenges, we pray: ◆ For the poor, the sick, the lonely, the marginalized, and the oppressed, that God may rescue them and give them his peace, we pray: ◆ For all those in special need, for travelers, the imprisoned, and for those struggling with family difficulties, we pray: ◆ For all those who will die today, we pray: ◆

Our Father . . .

Loving God,
we praise you for the gift of your Son,
by whose love and unity with you
is the source of all goodness and wisdom.
Send down your Holy Spirit upon us to
draw us into the beauty of your
Trinitarian life.
We ask this through Christ our Lord.
Amen.

✝ If today you hear his voice, harden not your hearts.

✞ I am the Lord your God: hear
my voice.

Psalm 91
page 412

Reading
Mark 12:28–33

One of the scribes came to Jesus and asked him, "Which is the first of all the commandments?" Jesus replied, "The first is this: / *Hear, O Israel! / The Lord our God is Lord alone! / You shall love the Lord your God with all your heart, / with all your soul, / with all your mind, / and with all your strength.* The second is this: *You shall love your neighbor as yourself. /* There is no other commandment greater than these." The scribe said to him, "Well said, teacher. You are right in saying, / *He is One and there is no other than he. / And to love him with all your heart, / with all your understanding, / with all your strength, / and to love your neighbor as yourself / is worth more than all burnt offerings and sacrifices.*"

Reflection

Again, in this Gospel we see how Jesus does not come to abolish the law, but rather to fulfill it. When asked what is the greatest commandment, Jesus responds with the "Shema" ("Hear, O Israel"), the summary of the Jewish Law. In Jesus, we see the greatest example of this love of God and love of neighbor in his total obedience to the Father through his outpouring of self for us on the cross.

Prayers
others may be added

The greatest commandment is to love: first God, then our neighbor. Let us pray:

◆ Lord God, teach us how to love.

For the Church, that she may be a witness to the love of Christ to every sector of the world, we pray: ◆ For leaders of all nations, that they may serve the common good and dignity of each human person, we pray: ◆ For all who seek work, and those who struggle economically, we pray: ◆ For all doctors, nurses, and caretakers, that they may do the work of the Lord with patience and love, we pray: ◆ For all catechumens as they prepare for the reception of the sacraments, we pray: ◆ For all Christians, that they may bring others to the joy of Jesus Christ through their love and charity and cheerfulness, we pray: ◆

Our Father . . .

Merciful Father,
we are nothing without your grace.
Open our hearts to hear your word.
Bring us into deeper union with you
    through prayer,
and teach us how to love as you have
    loved us in our Lord Jesus Christ,
    your Son,
who lives and reigns with you in the unity
    of the Holy Spirit,
one God, forever and ever.
Amen.

✞ I am the Lord your God: hear
my voice.

✝ It is mercy I desire, and not sacrifice.

Psalm 130   *page 420*

Reading   *Luke 5:4–10*

After [Jesus] had finished speaking, he said to Simon, "Put out into deep water and lower your nets for a catch." Simon said in reply, "Master, we have worked hard all night and have caught nothing, but at your command I will lower the nets." When they had done this, they caught a great number of fish and their nets were tearing. They signaled to their partners in the other boat to come to help them. They came and filled both boats so that the boats were in danger of sinking. When Simon Peter saw this, he fell at the knees of Jesus and said, "Depart from me, Lord, for I am a sinful man." For astonishment at the catch of fish they had made seized him and all those with him, and likewise James and John, the sons of Zebedee, who were partners of Simon. Jesus said to Simon, "Do not be afraid; from now on you will be catching men."

Reflection

Today we celebrate the memorial of Saint Patrick, the great Bishop and missionary of Ireland. Through his work and teaching, he converted the country of Ireland and rid it of pagan worship and practices. During our Lenten practice, may we turn away from the idols of sin and return to God, who is Father, Son, and Holy Spirit.

Prayers   *others may be added*

With faithful confidence that God always hears our prayers, we pray:

◆ O God, be merciful to me, a sinner.

For the missionary Church throughout the world, that she may bring the light of Christ to all peoples, we pray: ◆ For all nations, that they may practice natural human virtues and Gospel values, we pray: ◆ For all the sick and suffering, that they may be comforted, we pray: ◆ For all the Irish, that they may be renewed in the truth brought to them by their Catholic traditions, we pray: ◆ For all of our deceased relatives and friends, we pray: ◆

Our Father . . .

Lord our God,
by your saints, you inspire us to holiness.
Through the prayers of Saint Patrick,
may we work in service of your name
and come into deeper union in the Trinity.
We ask this through our Lord Jesus
    Christ, your Son,
who lives and reigns with you in the unity
    of the Holy Spirit,
one God, forever and ever.
Amen.

✝ It is mercy I desire, and not sacrifice.

✝ Let my tongue be silenced, if I ever forget you!

Psalm 51   *page 409*

Reading   *John 3:14–21*

Jesus said to Nicodemus: "Just as Moses lifted up the serpent in the desert, so must the Son of Man be lifted up, so that everyone who believes in him may have eternal life."

For God so loved the world that he gave his only Son, so that everyone who believes in him might not perish but might have eternal life. For God did not send his Son into the world to condemn the world, but that the world might be saved through him. Whoever believes in him will not be condemned, but whoever does not believe has already been condemned, because he has not believed in the name of the only Son of God. And this is the verdict, that the light came into the world, but people preferred darkness to light, because their works were evil. For everyone who does wicked things hates the light and does not come toward the light, so that his works might not be exposed. But whoever lives the truth comes to the light, so that his works may be clearly seen as done in God.

Reflection

During this season of Lent, we have been preparing and contemplating the mystery of Jesus' Passion, death, and Resurrection. Today's Gospel teaches us what the heart of Lent is about: "For God so loved the world. . . ." In his love, God has sent us his Son Jesus so that we can be freed from our sins; that we may live and share his eternal life and union with him.

Prayers   *others may be added*

Father you have sent your Son to give us eternal life. Let us pray:

◆ **Save us, O Lord, and grant us your salvation.**

For the Church, that she may overflow in joyful evangelization, proclaiming God's love to all the nations, we pray: ◆ For ecumenical consciousness and unity throughout the world, we pray: ◆ For those who suffer illness and pain, that they may look upon the cross and be healed by Christ's Blood, we pray: ◆ For our parish community, that it may become a source of joy and support through friendship with one another, we pray: ◆ For the grace this week to be a wellspring of love and encouragement, we pray: ◆

Our Father . . .

Heavenly Father,
we thank you and praise you for the gift of your Son,
whom you send us by your love to free us and bring us salvation.
Increase our faith and lead us to the joy of eternal union with you.
We ask this through Christ our Lord.
Amen.

✝ Let my tongue be silenced, if I ever forget you!

✝ Blessed are those who dwell in your house, O Lord; they never cease to praise you.

Psalm 91 *page 412*

Reading *Matthew 1:16, 18–21, 24a*

Now this is how the birth of Jesus Christ came about. When his mother Mary was betrothed to Joseph, but before they lived together, she was found with child through the Holy Spirit. Joseph her husband, since he was a righteous man, yet unwilling to expose her to shame, decided to divorce her quietly. Such was his intention when, behold, the angel of the Lord appeared to him in a dream and said, "Joseph, son of David, do not be afraid to take Mary your wife into your home. For it is through the Holy Spirit that this child has been conceived in her. She will bear a son and you are to name him Jesus, because he will save his people from their sins." When Joseph awoke, he did as the angel of the Lord had commanded him and took his wife into his home.

Reflection *Graziano Marcheschi*

The woman you love is found to be pregnant and you know you're not the father. Running into a brick wall couldn't be more painful. The "righteous" Joseph knows what he must do, but he loves Mary enough to want to spare her pain. It's only a dream that sets him straight. Imagine the faith it took to believe an angelic messenger encountered in a dream! Now Joseph's faith stands as a model for us.

Prayers *others may be added*

God our Father, you sent your Son into the world to be born into an earthly family. Let us pray:

◆ Help us to be saints, O Lord.

That the Church, through the intercession of Saint Joseph, the patron of the universal Church, may be strengthened in grace and protected from all evil, we pray: ◆

For all civic leaders, that they may use wisdom and care to serve their people with concern for each human person, we pray: ◆

For the poor, the sick, the lonely, the homeless, and those in difficulty, that through the prayers of Saint Joseph, God may provide for all their needs, we pray: ◆

For all fathers, priests, seminarians, and young boys, that, through the example of Saint Joseph, they may have the courage to be true and holy men of God, we pray: ◆

For all families, and all dating and engaged couples, that Saint Joseph may protect and care for them as he cared for the Holy Family, we pray: ◆

Our Father . . .

Heavenly Father,
through the intercession of Saint Joseph,
give us the grace to live holy lives of
    justice, purity, and love,
that we too may be numbered among
    your saints in union with you.
We ask this through Christ our Lord.
Amen.

✝ Blessed are those who dwell in your house, O Lord; they never cease to praise you.

Tuesday, March 20, 2012
Lenten Weekday

✟ A clean heart create for me, O God; give me back the joy of your salvation.

Psalm 130   *page 420*

Reading   *John 5:2–9*

Now there is in Jerusalem at the Sheep Gate a pool called in Hebrew Bethesda, with five porticoes. In these lay a large number of ill, blind, lame, and crippled. One man was there who had been ill for thirty-eight years. When Jesus saw him lying there and knew that he had been ill for a long time, he said to him, "Do you want to be well?" The sick man answered him, "Sir, I have no one to put me into the pool when the water is stirred up; while I am on my way, someone else gets down there before me." Jesus said to him, "Rise, take up your mat, and walk." Immediately the man became well, took up his mat, and walked.

Reflection

Sometimes it seems as if God makes us wait a long time before he answers our prayers. The man in today's Gospel had been sick for 38 years, before Jesus healed him by telling him to rise, pick up his mat, and walk. Jesus teaches the man that sin is a far greater evil than any sickness.

Prayers   *others may be added*

Lord and Master, you heal the sick man by the power of your word. Let us pray:

◆ Heal us from all our sins, O Lord.

For the Holy Mother Church, that all her members may honor her with obedience to Christ present in his Church, we pray: ◆ That all civic leaders may serve the impoverished, the ill, and the marginalized of their nations, we pray: ◆ For all those who suffer sickness in body, mind, or spirit, that they may be quickly healed, and that they may be given the patience to suffer in reparation for sinners, we pray: ◆ That this time of Lent may be a time of deep interior conversion, we pray: ◆

Our Father . . .

God our Father,
all healing and forgiveness
comes from you through your Son.
Heal us and help us rise from our sins,
so as to walk in the new life of your
   Holy Spirit
and to follow you in the way of truth.
We ask through Jesus Christ our Lord.
Amen.

✟ A clean heart create for me, O God; give me back the joy of your salvation.

✝ The Lord is gracious and merciful.

Psalm 51 *page 409*

Reading *John 5:25–30*

[Jesus said to the Jews:] "Amen, amen, I say to you, the hour is coming and is now here when the dead will hear the voice of the Son of God, and those who hear will live. For just as the Father has life in himself, so also he gave to the Son the possession of life in himself. And he gave him power to exercise judgment, because he is the Son of Man. Do not be amazed at this, because the hour is coming in which all who are in the tombs will hear his voice and will come out, those who have done good deeds to the resurrection of life, but those who have done wicked deeds to the resurrection of condemnation.

"I cannot do anything on my own; I judge as I hear, and my judgment is just, because I do not seek my own will but the will of the one who sent me."

Reflection

Jesus is at work among us even now fulfilling the will and work of the Father. Jesus teaches in today's Gospel about his life in union with God the Father. He teaches that he likewise gives life as the Father raises the dead and gives life. Through these words, Jesus prepares the people for his Resurrection, through which we too receive everlasting life through faith in his mystery.

Prayers *others may be added*

Jesus, you teach us that whoever believes in your word shall pass from death to new life. In faith we pray:

◆ Give us new life, O Lord.

For the Church, the Holy Father, all priests and bishops, that they may live the calling of their priestly ministry as "other Christs," leading all peoples to the love of Father, we pray: ◆ For all nations that are persecuted for the faith, that the witness and sufferings of believers may bring about the kingdom of God, we pray: ◆ For all the homeless, the poor, the hungry, and the lonely, that they may know the Father's care and love for them, we pray: ◆ For all judges and lawyers, that they may practice the law with the same justice and mercy as Jesus Christ, we pray: ◆

Our Father . . .

God, our Father,
you raise the dead and give new life.
By the power of your Holy Spirit,
may each one of us come to share
in the unity you share with your Son,
Jesus Christ, in whose name we pray.
Amen.

✝ The Lord is gracious and merciful.

✝ Remember us, O Lord, as you favor your people.

Psalm 91 *page 412*

Reading *John 5:39–47*

[Jesus said:] "You search the Scriptures, because you think you have eternal life through them; even they testify on my behalf. But you do not want to come to me to have life.

"I do not accept human praise; moreover, I know that you do not have the love of God in you. I came in the name of my Father, but you do not accept me; yet if another comes in his own name, you will accept him. How can you believe, when you accept praise from one another and do not seek the praise that comes from the only God? Do not think that I will accuse you before the Father: the one who will accuse you is Moses, in whom you have placed your hope. For if you had believed Moses, you would have believed me, because he wrote about me. But if you do not believe his writings, how will you believe my words?"

Reflection

Why is it that we do not want to come to Christ to have life? What is it that prevents us from drawing joy from his wellspring of love? God the Father testifies to the truth of Jesus Christ through his signs and works. Why is it that we remain hardhearted like the Israelites in the Old Testament who constructed idols and were reluctant to believe in the God who saves?

Prayers *others may be added*

God, our Father, you testify to your Son, Jesus Christ, whom we know is truth. With contrite hearts, we pray:

◆ Illuminate our minds and hearts to your truth.

For the Church, that she may always render faithful witness to the truth of Jesus Christ, we pray: ◆ For people of every nation, that they may render God glory and praise, we pray: ◆ For all those who are in pain, that they may be given the grace to be joyful as they seek the face of Christ in their suffering, we pray: ◆ For all the elderly and those facing old age, that they may be sources of wisdom for their friends and families, we pray: ◆ For all who will die today, that they may be brought to new life, we pray: ◆

Our Father . . .

Heavenly Father,
we thank you for the truth you give us,
   revealed in your Son, Jesus Christ.
Accompany us on our Lenten journey
as we strive to grow in the Spirit
through prayer, fasting, and almsgiving.
We ask this through Christ our Lord.
Amen.

✝ Remember us, O Lord, as you favor your people.

✝ The Lord is close to the brokenhearted.

Psalm 130
page 420

Reading
John 7:25–30

Some of the inhabitants of Jerusalem said, "Is [Jesus] not the one they are trying to kill? And look, he is speaking openly and they say nothing to him. Could the authorities have realized that he is the Christ? But we know where he is from. When the Christ comes, no one will know where he is from." So Jesus cried out in the temple area as he was teaching and said, "You know me and also know where I am from. Yet I did not come on my own, but the one who sent me, whom you do not know, is true. I know him, because I am from him, and he sent me." So they tried to arrest him, but no one laid a hand upon him, because his hour had not yet come.

Reflection

In today's Gospel, we hear that the Jews were planning to kill Jesus, making it dangerous for Jesus to go into Jerusalem. However, Jesus continues to go and to speak among the people. It is Jesus' identity with the Father and his knowledge of his mission that drives him to continue to fulfill his Father's will.

Prayers
others may be added

Lord Jesus, we know you are sent from the Father. Hear our prayers we offer you today as we pray:

◆ Deliver us, O Lord, from all evil.

That the Church led by the Holy Father may continue to proclaim the truth of Jesus Christ even in moments of difficulty, we pray: ◆ That all nations, especially those countries in which the Church is persecuted, may have the courage to remain steadfast in faith, we pray: ◆ That those who suffer persecution, abuse, mistreatment, or discrimination may forgive all who fail to respect their dignity, we pray: ◆

Our Father . . .

God our Father,
you sent your Son into the world
to fulfill your plan of salvation.
Strengthen us in faith as you send us
to participate in the work of your Son,
who lives and reigns with you in the unity
   of the Holy Spirit,
one God, forever and ever.
Amen.

✝ The Lord is close to the brokenhearted.

✝ O Lord, my God, in you I take refuge.

Psalm 51 *page 409*

Reading *John 7:44–52*

Some of [the crowd] even wanted to arrest [Jesus], but no one laid hands on him.

So the guards went to the chief priests and Pharisees, who asked them, "Why did you not bring him?" The guards answered, "Never before has anyone spoken like this man." So the Pharisees answered them, "Have you also been deceived? Have any of the authorities or the Pharisees believed in him? But this crowd, which does not know the law, is accursed." Nicodemus, one of their members who had come to him earlier, said to them, "Does our law condemn a man before it first hears him and finds out what he is doing?" They answered and said to him, "You are not from Galilee also, are you? Look and see that no prophet arises from Galilee."

Reflection

As Jesus reveals that he is a great prophet by his words and deeds, the people begin to argue whether he is truly the Messiah. This same dispute happens even today. Some people think Jesus is only a good philanthropist, some are faithful followers, others want to put him to death. However, despite disagreements, Jesus continues to reveal himself as the Anointed One sent from the Father.

Prayers *others may be added*

Father of all wisdom, in times of confusion and doubt, we place our petitions before you, as we pray:

◆ Reveal yourself to us, O God.

For the Church, that she may instruct and teach with all wisdom and clarity, we pray: ◆ For all public leaders, that they may be inspired by the Holy Spirit to make good and just decisions for the common good of all society, we pray: ◆ For those who suffer persecution, hunger, and poverty, that the kingdom of God may be established among them, God's chosen ones, we pray: ◆ For all families, that anger, criticism, and resentfulness may be replaced by love, encouragement, and forgiveness, we pray: ◆

Our Father . . .

O just God,
searcher of heart and soul,
bring us to deeper conversion,
that we may truly believe that your Son,
Jesus Christ, is our Messiah and Lord,
who lives and reigns with you in the unity
   of the Holy Spirit,
one God, forever and ever.
Amen.

✝ O Lord, my God, in you I take refuge.

Sunday, March 25, 2012
Fifth Sunday of Lent

✝ Create a clean heart in me, O God.

Psalm 91 *page 412*

Reading *John 12:23–24*

Jesus [said], "The hour has come for the Son of Man to be glorified. Amen, amen, I say to you, unless a grain of wheat falls to the ground and dies, it remains just a grain of wheat; but if it dies, it produces much fruit."

Reflection

In today's Gospel, Jesus prepares for his death. In order that his disciples understand, he teaches them that first a seed must die before it can bear fruit. The seed is the Word of God, Jesus Incarnate. Through his death and Resurrection the Father is glorified and we are given the grace to follow after Christ and share in his eternal life.

Prayers *others may be added*

God of love, you sent your Son to bring new life to the world. Let us pray:

◆ Father, glorify your name.

For the Church, that she may be fruitful in good works of charity and service, we pray: ◆ For all countries that suffer the evils of war, human trafficking, poverty, and hunger, that Christ will draw all peoples and nations to himself in unity and love, we pray: ◆ For those who suffer in body, mind, and spirit, that they may be like seeds that blossom in abundant fruitfulness after the trial of their suffering, we pray: ◆ For all catechumens who are preparing to enter the Church this Easter, that they may die to their old self and rise to new life through the sacraments, we pray: ◆ For the grace this week to die to our selfishness and greed for material possessions, we pray: ◆

Our Father . . .

Father of glory,
we want to see Jesus.
By your Son's death and Resurrection,
draw all people to yourself,
that we may share in your eternal life of
    glory forever.
We ask this through our Lord Jesus
    Christ, your Son,
who lives and reigns with you in the unity
    of the Holy Spirit,
one God, forever and ever.
Amen.

✝ Create a clean heart in me, O God.

✝ Here I am, Lord; I come to do your will.

Psalm 130   *page 420*

Reading   *Luke 1:26–38*

The angel Gabriel was sent from God to a town of Galilee called Nazareth, to a virgin betrothed to a man named Joseph, of the house of David, and the virgin's name was Mary. And coming to her, he said, "Hail, full of grace! The Lord is with you." But she was greatly troubled at what was said and pondered what sort of greeting this might be. Then the angel said to her, "Do not be afraid, Mary, for you have found favor with God. Behold, you will conceive in your womb and bear a son, and you shall name him Jesus. He will be great and will be called Son of the Most High, and the Lord God will give him the throne of David his father, and he will rule over the house of Jacob forever, and of his Kingdom there will be no end."

Reflection

Today we celebrate the solemnity of the Annunciation of the Lord, in which we honor the grandeur of God's plan of salvation through the humble "yes" of the young Blessed Virgin Mary. By Mary's receptive openness to God's Word, Jesus Christ, the Word Incarnate, is made flesh within her womb, and the mystery of the Incarnation takes place in the small town of Nazareth.

Prayers   *others may be added*

Father, in your majesty you choose human beings to participate in your work of salvation. With open hearts, we pray:

◆ Hear I am Lord; I come to do your will.

That through the prayers of Mary, Mother and model of the Church, the Church may be renewed in the outpouring of the Spirit in gifts of faith and fruitfulness, we pray: ◆ That all public officials may imitate Mary's obedience by following God's will to establish justice and peace for all nations, we pray: ◆ For those who suffer illness, poverty, and persecution, that the prayers of the Virgin Mary may offer them maternal comfort and consolation, we pray: ◆ For all consecrated virgins, religious sisters, mothers, young women, and girls, that by looking to the example of Mother Mary, they may learn to be receptive to God's will, we pray: ◆

Our Father . . .

Our Father,
you sent us your Son, born of a woman.
By the prayers of the Mother of God,
open our hearts to receive your Word
with obedience and generosity,
that your will may be done in our lives
through the power of the Holy Spirit.
We ask this through Christ our Lord.
Amen.

✝ Here I am, Lord; I come to do your will.

✝ O Lord, hear my prayer, and let my cry come to you.

Psalm 51 *page 409*

Reading *John 8:21–24*

Jesus said to the Pharisees: "I am going away and you will look for me, but you will die in your sin. Where I am going you cannot come." So the Jews said, "He is not going to kill himself, is he, because he said, 'Where I am going you cannot come'?" He said to them, "You belong to what is below, I belong to what is above. You belong to this world, but I do not belong to this world. That is why I told you that you will die in your sins. For if you do not believe that I AM, you will die in your sins."

Reflection

The Father and the Son are one and share the same eternal life. God's glory is manifested in Jesus Christ, true God and true man, when he is lifted upon the cross and gains us our salvation. In today's Gospel, the Pharisees cannot come to understand because of their sin and hardness of heart; however, Jesus continues to teach and many come to believe in him.

Prayers *others may be added*

Father, you lift up the Son of Man so that all may believe through him. Let us pray:

◆ O Lord, hear my prayer and let my cry come to you.

For the Holy Father, that his work may be offered in union with the work of Christ, our great High Priest, for the salvation of all souls, we pray: ◆ For all nations, that they may respect the value and dignity of human life, we pray: ◆ For those who suffer addiction, depression, or fear, that they may receive freedom and peace, we pray: ◆ For all young children, especially those who go without food or proper medical care, we pray: ◆ For all those who have died, that they may share in the eternal life of the Father, Son, and Holy Spirit, we pray: ◆

Our Father . . .

O God,
you remain always united to your Son,
and in him you perfectly fulfill your
   plan of salvation.
By the work of the Holy Spirit,
give us a share in the sonship of Christ,
that we too may become children of God.
We ask this through Christ our Lord.
Amen.

✝ O Lord, hear my prayer, and let my cry come to you.

✝ Glory and praise for ever!

Psalm 91   *page 412*

Reading   *John 8:31–33*

Jesus said to those Jews who believed in him, "If you remain in my word, you will truly be my disciples, and you will know the truth, and the truth will set you free."

Reflection

Jesus is sent to reveal the Father to us. By his Passion and Resurrection, we share in Christ's sonship and likewise become children of God. This is the truth that sets us free. With God as our Father, we are free from every anxiety and fear. Let us remain in his love.

Prayers   *others may be added*

Calling upon our Father as humble children, we confidently entrust to him our needs and concerns:

◆ Loving Father, hear our prayer.

For Holy Mother Church, that all of her children throughout the world may be gathered into the family of God, we pray: ◆ For government leaders, that they may always seek the truth, which will lead their countries to be nations of true freedom, we pray: ◆ For all those who suffer, that they may remain in Christ's love and safety through their trials, we pray: ◆ For those who are persecuted for the truth, that they may be faithful witnesses to God's constant love, we pray: ◆ For all nations, especially those countries in which the Church is persecuted, that all Christians may have the courage to remain steadfast in faith, we pray: ◆ For all those who suffer persecution, abuse, mistreatment, or discrimination, that they may have forgiveness for all who fail to respect their dignity, we pray: ◆ For the grace to see the good of each human person created in the image and likeness of God, we pray: ◆ For all peoples, that they may serve the common good and dignity of each human person, we pray: ◆ For all who seek work, and those who struggle economically, we pray: ◆ For all doctors, nurses, and caretakers, that they may do the work of the Lord with patience and love, we pray: ◆ For all catechumens, as they prepare for the reception of the sacraments, we pray: ◆ For all Christians, that they may bring others to the joy of Jesus Christ through their love and charity and cheerfulness, we pray: ◆

Our Father . . .

Father God,
you have created us in your image
    and likeness
and called us to share in your life forever,
not as slaves, but as your children.
Give us the grace to imitate Christ,
that we may live and worship you
as children of the light in spirit and
    in truth.
With joy, we abandon ourselves to your
    providential love.
We ask this through our Lord Jesus
    Christ, your Son,
who lives and reigns with you in the unity
    of the Holy Spirit,
one God, forever and ever.
Amen.

✝ Glory and praise for ever!

Thursday, March 29, 2012
Lenten Weekday

✝ The Lord remembers his covenant for ever.

Psalm 130 *page 420*

Reading *John 8:51–58*

[Jesus said:] "Amen, amen, I say to you, whoever keeps my word will never see death." So the Jews said to him, "Now we are sure that you are possessed. Abraham died, as did the prophets, yet you say, 'Whoever keeps my word will never taste death'? Are you greater than our father Abraham, who died? Or the prophets, who died? Who do you make yourself out to be?" Jesus answered, "If I glorify myself, my glory is worth nothing; but it is my Father who glorifies me, of whom you say, 'He is our God.' You do not know him, but I know him. And if I should say that I do not know him, I would be like you a liar. But I do know him and I keep his word. Abraham your father rejoiced to see my day; he saw it and was glad." So the Jews said to him, "You are not yet fifty years old and you have seen Abraham?" Jesus said to them, "Amen, amen, I say to you, before Abraham came to be, I AM."

Reflection

As Jesus continues to reveal himself as the one whom God sent to do the Father's will, the Jews persecute and criticize him. In today's Gospel, they think he is possessed because of his claims of equality with God, and they want to kill him. Despite their disbelief, Jesus does not tire in teaching and speaking the truth.

Prayers *others may be added*

Father of all history, in Jesus Christ you fulfill your covenants through the prophets. Let us pray:

◆ Save us, O Lord, and heal us from our sin.

That the Holy Father, all priests, bishops, and deacons may remain steadfast in proclaiming and clarifying the truth of the Church's treasury of faith, especially in moments of difficulty, we pray: ◆ That all national disputes may be resolved through open dialogue and mutual respect between civil leaders, we pray: ◆ That those who suffer for righteousness' sake may be rewarded with God's grace and love, we pray: ◆ That all fallen-away Catholics may receive the grace this Lenten season to return home to the welcoming embrace of Holy Mother Church, we pray: ◆

Our Father . . .

Everlasting Father,
we praise you and thank you
for your glory and majesty
in sending us your Son, the true Prophet,
to free us from our sins.
Strengthen us to keep your word
and share in your everlasting life.
We ask through Jesus Christ our Lord.
Amen.

✝ The Lord remembers his covenant for ever.

✟ In my distress I called upon the Lord, and he heard my voice.

Psalm 51 *page 409*

Reading *John 10:31–42*

The Jews picked up rocks to stone Jesus. Jesus answered them, "I have shown you many good works from the Father. For which of these are you trying to stone me?" The Jews answered him, "We are not stoning you for a good work but for blasphemy. You, a man, are making yourself God." Jesus answered them, "Is it not written in your law, 'I said, "You are gods" '? If it calls them gods to whom the word of God came, and Scripture cannot be set aside, can you say that the one whom the Father has consecrated and sent into the world blasphemes because I said, 'I am the Son of God'? If I do not perform my Father's works, do not believe me; but if I perform them, even if you do not believe me, believe the works, so that you may realize and understand that the Father is in me and I am in the Father." Then they tried again to arrest him; but he escaped their power.

He went back across the Jordan to the place where John first baptized, and there he remained. Many came to him and said, "John performed no sign, but everything John said about this man was true." And many there began to believe in him.

Reflection

In these last Gospel readings, we see the progression toward the cross as the Jews increase in anger and desire to kill Jesus. They cannot accept that Jesus is both man and God, and that he makes himself out to be one with the Father. However, Jesus' works reveal the truth of his teaching that he is God, and that through him we too are called to become sons and daughters of God.

Prayers *others may be added*

We present our prayers to God, and say:

◆ Have mercy on us.

That the Church may be fruitful in good works, we pray: ◆ That all nations may be converted to the truth of Jesus Christ, we pray: ◆ That those who suffer from persecution, hunger, human trafficking, poverty, war, and oppression may be given freedom and solace through God's grace, we pray: ◆ That evangelization initiatives in our parish, in our homes, and throughout the world may be strengthened in faith, we pray: ◆

Our Father . . .

Jesus, Son of God,
you have the words of everlasting life.
Give us the grace to be holy and upright,
that we may live in freedom as sons and
    daughters of God.
You live and reign forever.
Amen.

✟ In my distress I called upon the Lord, and he heard my voice.

Saturday, March 31, 2012
Lenten Weekday

✝ The Lord will guard us, as a shepherd guards his flock.

Psalm 91   page 412

Reading   John 11:45–53

Many of the Jews who had come to Mary and seen what Jesus had done began to believe in him. But some of them went to the Pharisees and told them what Jesus had done. So the chief priests and the Pharisees convened the Sanhedrin and said, "What are we going to do? This man is performing many signs. If we leave him alone, all will believe in him, and the Romans will come and take away both our land and our nation." But one of them, Caiaphas, who was high priest that year, said to them, "You know nothing, nor do you consider that it is better for you that one man should die instead of the people, so that the whole nation may not perish." He did not say this on his own, but since he was high priest for that year, he prophesied that Jesus was going to die for the nation, and not only for the nation, but also to gather into one the dispersed children of God. So from that day on they planned to kill him.

Reflection

The chief priests and Pharisees formally plan to kill Jesus. And so Jesus fulfills his mission to free all the nations from sin by dying on the cross so all may be one in the glory and freedom of the children of God. The high priest's words prove to be ironically and providentially prophetic.

Prayers   others may be added

With sorrow and repentance for our sins, we pray:

◆ In your mercy, blot out our offense.

For the Church, that she may be protected in faith and holiness to give life to all her children through the graces of the sacraments, we pray: ◆ For all the dispersed nations of the world, that they may be gathered into one in the unity of the children of God, we pray: ◆ For the freedom of all those who suffer from addiction, we pray: ◆ For the poor, the lonely, the sick, and the homeless, that they may receive the material and spiritual goods they need through the generosity and charity of others, we pray: ◆ For all of us, that we may not become wrapped up in the busyness and hurriedness of work and daily life, but may set aside time for rest, prayer, and contemplation as we enter into these sacred days of Holy Week, we pray: ◆

Our Father . . .

God our Father,
by your Son's Passion and death,
    you fulfill
and reveal the great mystery of your plan
    of salvation for all peoples.
By the prayers of the Virgin Mary,
help us to come closer to your Son, Jesus,
who is the Way, the Truth, and the Life.
We ask this through the same Christ
    our Lord.
Amen.

✝ The Lord will guard us, as a shepherd guards his flock.

✝ Blessed is he who comes in the name of the Lord.

Psalm 22
page 403

Reading
Mark 11:1–2, 7–10

When Jesus and his disciples drew near to Jerusalem, to Bethpage and Bethany at the Mount of Olives, he sent two of his disciples and said to them, "Go into the village opposite you, and immediately on entering it, you will find a colt tethered on which no has ever sat. Untie it and bring it here." . . . So they brought the colt to Jesus and put their cloaks over it. And he sat on it. Many of the people spread their cloaks on the road, and others spread leafy branches that they had cut from the fields. Those preceding him as well as those following kept crying out: / "Hosanna! / Blessed is he who comes in the name of the Lord! / Blessed is the kingdom of our father David that is to come! / Hosanna in the highest!"

Reflection

Today begins our solemn remembrance of Holy Week in which we accompany Jesus during his last days on earth before his death and Resurrection. Jesus makes his way into Jerusalem to fulfill his Father's will, prepared throughout the ages by the prophets. Together we cry out, "Hosanna in the highest!" to our Messiah and King. May we persevere and remain faithful to accompany him in his journey.

Prayers
others may be added

God has sent his Son to fulfill the plan of salvation prepared since the beginning of time. In jubilation, we cry out:

◆ Blessed are you, O Lord!

For the pilgrim Church on earth, that she may follow in the footsteps of Christ until at last we reach the heavenly glory, we pray: ◆ For all countries, that their leaders may serve their people with the humility and meekness of Christ, we pray: ◆ For all those who suffer illness, poverty, hunger, and financial crisis, that they may turn to Jesus the Messiah who brings hope, we pray: ◆ For our local community, that this Holy Week may be a grace-filled time of conversion for all individuals and all families, we pray: ◆

Our Father . . .

Jesus, our great King and Messiah,
Son of David and ruler of all the nations,
you reveal your humility and meekness
as you enter the city of Jerusalem riding
    on a donkey.
Grant us the grace to follow in your
    footsteps
along the humble road to Calvary in our
    daily lives.
You who live and reign with God the
    Father,
in the unity of the Holy Spirit,
one God, forever and ever.
Amen.

✝ Blessed is he who comes in the name of the Lord.

Monday, April 2, 2012
Monday of Holy Week

† The Lord is my light and my salvation.

Psalm 22 *page 403*

Reading *John 12:1–3*

Six days before Passover Jesus came to Bethany, where Lazarus was, whom Jesus had raised from the dead. They gave a dinner for him there, and Martha served, while Lazarus was one of those reclining at table with him. Mary took a liter of costly perfumed oil made from genuine aromatic nard and anointed the feet of Jesus and dried them with her hair; the house was filled with the fragrance of the oil.

Reflection *Graziano Marcheschi*

Jesus often took refuge at the home of his friends Mary, Martha, and Lazarus and it's no surprise that he would come here just prior to the unfolding of his Passion. He had no home of his own, but Mary and Martha made their home his home. Judas will criticize Mary for "wasting" the expensive oil on Jesus. But Jesus surrenders to his friends' attention and their care, just as he will soon surrender to judgment, pain, and death. The oil that Mary uses to anoint him fills the house with its rich fragrance. Perhaps we have a metaphor for the effect of Jesus on the human heart. When we surrender to his call, his grace spills over us and its sweet fragrance fills us, permeating every corner of our beings. Breathe deeply and inhale the sweet, sweet scent of that holy oil.

Prayers *others may be added*

"Jesus humbled himself becoming obedient unto death, even death on a Cross" (*Philippians 2*). Let us pray:

◆ Pour out your love upon us, O Lord.

For the Holy Father, that through our faithful prayers he may receive strength, health, and stamina throughout the liturgical celebrations of Holy Week, we pray: ◆ For civic leaders, that they may work tirelessly to discover solutions to eliminate hunger and poverty, we pray: ◆ For all those who are sick and suffering, especially for the bedridden and those who care for them, that the Holy Spirit may send his anointing to bring healing and peace, we pray: ◆ For our community, that we may be renewed in radical generosity and charity toward our neighbor, we pray: ◆ For perseverance with prayer and works of mercy, that we may faithfully seek the suffering face of Christ, we pray: ◆

Our Father . . .

God, our Father,
in your Son you reveal
your outpouring of love and life upon us.
Give us the gift of your Spirit.
We ask this through Christ our Lord.
Amen.

† The Lord is my light and my salvation.

Tuesday, April 3, 2012
Tuesday of Holy Week

✝ I will sing of your salvation.

Psalm 22 *page 403*

Reading *John 13:31–33; 36–38*

Jesus said, "Now is the Son of Man glorified, and God is glorified in him. If God is glorified in him, God will also glorify him in himself, and he will glorify him at once. My children, I will be with you only a little while longer. You will look for me, and as I told the Jews, 'Where I go you cannot come,' so now I say it to you."

Simon Peter said to him, "Master, where are you going?" Jesus answered him, "Where I am going, you cannot follow me now, although you will follow later." Peter said to him, "Master, why can I not follow you now? I will lay down my life for you." Jesus answered, "Will you lay down your life for me? Amen, amen, I say to you, the cock will not crow before you deny me three times."

Reflection

We have entered into the solemn week in which we commemorate God's most mysterious and penetrating act of love for humanity, in which the Father glorifies the Son through his death and glorious Resurrection. Let us not abandon Jesus during these final days, but rather let us accompany him through prayer as we rest upon his heart and contemplate his mystery.

Prayers *others may be added*

Jesus, you are the suffering servant through whom the Father shows his glory. Let us pray:

◆ You are our hope, O Lord.

For the Church and her members, that she may warmly welcome sinners back into full communion with the Trinity, we pray: ◆ For nations that suffer from war, dictatorship, and violence, that the dignity of each person may be respected, we pray: ◆ For those who suffer in body, mind, and spirit, that in their suffering they may accompany Jesus on his way to Calvary, we pray: ◆ For all to offer and receive forgiveness and reconciliation, we pray: ◆ For all to stop and spend extra time this week to wonder about the great mystery of Jesus' Passion and death, we pray: ◆

Our Father . . .

Heavenly Father,
your Son is glorified through his
    obedience to you in life and in death.
We thank you for the mystery of
    redemption.
Never let us reject or abandon you
    through sin,
but bring us into eternal glory and union
    with you.
We ask this through Christ our Lord.
Amen.

✝ I will sing of your salvation.

Wednesday, April 4, 2012
Wednesday of Holy Week

† Lord, in your great love, answer me.

Psalm 22 page 403

Reading Matthew 26:20–25

When it was evening, [Jesus] reclined at table with the Twelve. And while they were eating, he said, "Amen, I say to you, one of you will betray me." Deeply distressed at this, they began to say to him one after another, "Surely it is not I, Lord?" He said in reply, "He who had dipped his hand into the dish with me is the one who will betray me. The Son of Man indeed goes, as it is written of him, but woe to that man by whom the Son of Man is betrayed. It would be better for that man if he had never been born." Then Judas, his betrayer, said in reply, "Surely it is not I, Rabbi?" He answered, "You have said so."

Reflection

Today is traditionally called "Spy Wednesday," which is the day that recalls when Judas decided to betray Jesus and pay the high priests 30 pieces of silver to hand him over to be killed. With each one of our sins, we make ourselves out to be betrayers, like Judas. Let us pray for the grace to remain faithful and to persevere to the end.

Prayers others may be added

Merciful God, your Son has paid the price for our sins through his death on the cross. Hear our prayers as we pray:

◆ Preserve us in your grace, O God.

For the Church, under the guidance of the Holy Father, that she may always remain faithful, we pray: ◆ For civic leaders, that they may work with honesty and integrity in serving the common good for all peoples, we pray: ◆ For those who suffer the pain of betrayal from friends or family members, we pray: ◆ For the poor and those who suffer from hunger, that our community may reach out in generosity to help those in need, we pray: ◆

Our Father . . .

Loving God,
your Son has taken on our human
    weakness
to bring us out from our suffering
    and pain
and into the joy of new life.
Keep us faithful in times of trial,
and help us to persevere until the end,
so we may be united to you who lives and
    reigns with the Son in the unity of the
    Holy Spirit,
one God, forever and ever.
Amen.

† Lord, in your great love, answer me.

Thursday, April 5, 2012

Holy Thursday: Evening Mass of the Lord's Supper

✝ I will offer a sacrifice of thanksgiving and call on the name of the LORD. *(Psalm 116:17)*

Psalm 22 *page 403*

Reading *John 13:1–4*

Before the feast of Passover, Jesus knew that his hour had come to pass from this world to the Father. He loved his own in the world and he loved them to the end. The devil had already induced Judas, son of Simon the Iscariot, to hand him over. So, during supper, fully aware that the Father had put everything into his power and that he had come from God and was returning to God, he rose from supper and took off his outer garments. He took a towel and tied it around his waist. Then he poured water into a basin and began to wash the disciples' feet and dry them with the towel around his waist.

Reflection

On Holy Thursday, we commemorate the day when Jesus celebrated the Passover feast with his apostles and instituted the sacraments of Holy Eucharist and the priesthood. During the Last Supper before he died, Jesus offered us his Body and Blood in the sacrament of the Eucharist, which culminated in his free gift of himself upon the cross.

Prayers *others may be added*

Father, in your Son you give us your life present in the Eucharist. Hear our prayers as we pray:

◆ Master and Teacher, wash us clean.

For the Holy Father, all bishops, priests, and deacons, that they may always remain faithful to the sacred call they have received through the priesthood to be holy servants willing to wash the feet of others in charity and service, we pray: ◆ For all nations, that, through the diverse languages, cultures, and traditions, all people may be one in Jesus Christ, we pray: ◆ For all who suffer from illness and pain, that they may be comforted, we pray: ◆ For young men who are discerning a call to the priesthood, that the Holy Spirit may illuminate their path, we pray: ◆ That each and every one of us may love one another as Christ has loved us, we pray: ◆

Our Father . . .

Heavenly Father,
on this holy day we honor your Son,
who gives us his Body and Blood
in the sacrament of the Holy Eucharist.
Purify our hearts to receive you worthily
and strengthen our faith in your
    true presence.
We ask this through our Lord Jesus
    Christ, your Son,
who lives and reigns with you in the unity
    of the Holy Spirit,
one God, forever and ever.
Amen.

✝ I will offer a sacrifice of thanksgiving and call on the name of the LORD.

Friday, April 6, 2012
Good Friday of the Passion of the Lord

✝ To all my foes I am a thing of scorn,
to my neighbors, a dreaded sight,
a horror to my friends. (*Psalm 31:12*)

Psalm 22   *page 403*

Reading   *John 19:38–42*
After [the crucifixion], Joseph of Arimathea, secretly a disciple of Jesus for fear of the Jews, asked Pilate if he could remove the body of Jesus. And Pilate permitted it. So he came and took his body. Nicodemus, the one who had first come to him at night, also came bringing a mixture of myrrh and aloes weighing about one hundred pounds. They took the body of Jesus and bound it with burial clothes along with the spices, according to the Jewish burial custom. Now in the place where he had been crucified there was a garden, and in the garden a new tomb, in which no one had yet been buried. So they laid Jesus there because of the Jewish preparation day; for the tomb was close by.

Reflection
O great mystery of the Cross! Again, Jesus speaks to us of love, by his Body and Blood. What folly that God dies to free us from death! From darkness to light, we have now become children of the Light. His Father is our Father. Come, Spirit Come! The Bride says, "Come!" Not your will but thine be done!

Prayers   *others may be added*
God has loved us to the end, becoming obedient even unto death, even death on a cross. Let us pray:

◆ Father, forgive us.

For the Church, the Holy Father, all bishops, priests, and clergy, that the Lord may guide them in strength in their ministry, we pray: ◆ For all nations, for those who serve in civil office, and for all unbelievers, that all who seek truth may be one in the unity of faith, we pray: ◆ For all those in special need, especially the poor, the dying, the sick, all travelers, and those who suffer violence and injustice, we pray: ◆ For those preparing for the sacraments of initiation, that the Holy Spirit may breathe new life in them by the merits of Christ's Passion, death, and Resurrection, we pray: ◆

Our Father . . .

Father of heaven and earth,
pour down your blessing upon
     your people
who today remember the death of
     your Son.
Free us from sin and continue your work
of healing and forgiveness within us
as we await the glory of the Resurrection.
We ask this through Christ our Lord,
who lives and reigns with you in the unity
     of the Holy Spirit,
one God, forever and ever. Amen.

✝ To all my foes I am a thing of scorn;
to my neighbors, a dreaded sight,
a horror to my friends.

Saturday, April 7, 2012
Holy Saturday:
Vigil of the Solemnity of the Resurrection of the Lord

✟ Let us sing to the Lord; he has covered himself in glory.

Psalm 22 *page 403*

Reading *Mark 16:1, 5–7*

When the sabbath was over, Mary Magdalene, Mary, the mother of James, and Salome bought spices so that they might go and anoint [Jesus] . . . On entering the tomb they saw a young man sitting on the right side, clothed in a white robe, and they were utterly amazed. He said to them, "Do not be amazed! You seek Jesus of Nazareth, the crucified. He has been raised; he is not here. Behold the place where they laid him. But go and tell his disciples and Peter, 'He is going before you to Galilee; there you will see him, as he told you.'"

Reflection

Holy Saturday often becomes a busy day of final preparations, last-minute shopping, and errands before the solemnity of Easter. We can easily overanticipate Christ's Resurrection without stopping to consider the mystery of what we have just experienced on Good Friday. Today, however, is the solemn day in which the Church waits and grieves with the Blessed Mother at Jesus' tomb. Today we keep watch with Mary in hope and faith as we await the coming glory of the Resurrection.

Prayers *others may be added*

Before the mystery of Christ buried in the tomb, we wait and pray:

◆ Bring us to new life, O Lord.

That the Church dispersed throughout the world may be gathered into the unity of Christ, who has died and is risen, we pray: ◆ For all who have fallen away from the faith, that they may be received into the welcoming arms of Holy Mother Church, we pray ◆ For the sick and suffering, that they may receive patience and hope as they await healing, we pray: ◆ For those who will enter into the Mystical Body of Christ through the sacraments of Baptism, Confirmation, and first Holy Communion, we pray: ◆ For all mothers and fathers who grieve the loss of a child, that, through the intercession of Mary, they may receive peace and comfort, we pray: ◆ For all who have died, that they may receive eternal life in the heavenly banquet, we pray: ◆

Our Father . . .

Loving Father,
through your Son,
you enter into the depths
of our loneliness, weakness, and pain.
Increase our faith in you.
Raise us to new life in your Son,
who lives and reigns with you in the unity
   of the Holy Spirit,
one God, forever and ever. Amen.

✟ Let us sing to the Lord; he has covered himself in glory.

Sunday, April 8, 2012
Easter Sunday:
Solemnity of the Resurrection of the Lord

✝ Alleluia! Give thanks to the LORD!
(Psalm 118:1)

Psalm 118 *page 418*

Reading *John 20:1–9*

On the first day of the week, Mary of Magdala came to the tomb early in the morning, while it was still dark, and saw the stone removed from the tomb. So she ran and went to Simon Peter and to the other disciple whom Jesus loved, and told them, "They have taken the Lord from the tomb, and we don't know where they put him." So Peter and the other disciple went out and came to the tomb. They both ran, but the other disciple ran faster than Peter and arrived at the tomb first; he bent down and saw the burial cloths there, and the cloth that had covered his head, not with the burial cloths but rolled up in a separate place. Then the other disciple also went in, the one who had arrived at the tomb first, and he saw and believed. For they did not yet understand the Scripture that he had to rise from the dead.

Reflection *Graziano Marcheschi*

From this moment on, everything changes. Life will never be the same. That would be our conviction if we really believed in the Resurrection. God has done the impossible yet again. And what God did for Christ will also be our destiny. Death is dead. Sin is conquered. Eternal life is possible. Peter saw the cloths; John saw the empty tomb. Mary saw the stone moved aside. Two millennia later we continue to rely on their testimony. But not only that, for faith in Christ brings resurrection daily into our lives. We know that death is not the final word. And so we sing, Alleluia!

Prayers *others may be added*

God has conquered the chains of death, in joy, we cry:

◆ Alleluia! He is risen!

For the Catholic Church, that she may forever be renewed in the light of the risen Christ, we pray: ◆ That all nations may be freed from every kind of injustice, poverty, and violence, we pray: ◆ For those who share in Christ's Passion through illness or sorrow, that, by the power of the Resurrection, they may be brought healing and new life, we pray:◆ For the newly baptized, that they may be a light to all peoples, we pray: ◆ That the light of the risen Christ may illuminate our lives more profoundly so that we may be witnesses to the hope and joy that God gives us through his Resurrection, we pray: ◆

Our Father . . .

God our Father,
today you raise your Son to new life through the mystery of the Resurrection.
Increase in us the graces we received
    at our Baptism,
that we may ever more share in your life,
    light, and joy.
We ask this through Christ our Lord.
Amen. Alleluia!

✝ Alleluia! Give thanks to the LORD!

Monday, April 9, 2012
Monday within the Octave of Easter

✝ Keep me safe, O God; you are my hope. Alleluia!

Psalm 118 *page 418*

Reading *Matthew 28:8–10*

Mary Magdalene and the other Mary went away quickly from the tomb, fearful yet overjoyed, and ran to announce the news to his disciples. And behold, Jesus met them on their way and greeted them. They approached, embraced his feet, and did him homage. Then Jesus said to them, "Do not be afraid. Go tell my brothers to go to Galilee, and there they will see me."

Reflection *Graziano Marcheschi*

Fearful that the body had been stolen, they run with the news to the apostles. But Jesus intercepts them. Such a dramatic reversal must have shaken them deeply. Dead . . . stolen . . . now alive! No wonder they embrace his feet; they had to make sure he was real; they had to inhale his fragrance and touch him to make sure it wasn't their imaginations run amok. Jesus makes these caring women the first heralds of his Resurrection. But "Go tell my brothers . . . " wasn't a marching order just for these chosen few, for many brothers and sisters still await the good news of Christ's Resurrection.

Prayers *others may be added*

With confidence that Christ is truly risen, we raise our prayers to God, as we say:

◆ Praise be to the Lord; Alleluia!

For the Church, illuminated by the light of the risen Christ, that she may be renewed in the fruitfulness of the life of the Trinity, we pray: ◆ For all the nations of the world, especially those that suffer violence, persecution, poverty, and hunger, that the light of the resurrected Christ may illuminate the darkness, we pray: ◆ For all the sick who await the resurrection of new life in their bodies, we pray: ◆ For our local community and for our family and friends, that we may all be renewed in joy and charity by the power of Christ's Resurrection, we pray: ◆

Our Father . . .

Father of Light,
you raise your Son, Jesus Christ,
from death to give us new life.
Bless all those who suffer,
and keep us safe from all sin,
that we may share in your eternal joy,
with you who live and reign with our
   Lord Jesus Christ,
in the unity of the Holy Spirit,
one God, forever and ever.
Amen.

✝ Keep me safe, O God; you are my hope. Alleluia!

Tuesday, April 10, 2012
Tuesday within the Octave of Easter

✝ The earth is full of the goodness of the Lord. Alleluia.

Psalm 118 *page 418*

Reading *John 20:11–14*

Mary Magdalene stayed outside the tomb weeping. As she wept, she bent over the tomb and saw two angels in white sitting there, one at the head and one at the feet where the Body of Jesus had been. And they said to her, "Woman, why are you weeping?" She said to them, "They have taken my Lord, and I don't know where they laid him." When she had said this, she turned around and saw Jesus there, but did not know it was Jesus.

Reflection

In today's Gospel, Mary Magdalene—at first—does not know it is Jesus. Not until he calls her by name does she recognize her resurrected Teacher and Good Shepherd. From this encounter with the risen Lord, she goes to announce to the disciples what she has seen and touched and heard from Jesus Christ.

Prayers *others may be added*

God, our Father, hear our humble prayers, as we cry:

◆ Shine your light upon us.

That, through the encounter with the resurrected Lord, the Church may be renewed in the Spirit to fulfill her mission of evangelization, we pray: ◆ That, through the efforts and prayers of missionaries throughout the world, all the nations shall hear the Good News of Christ's Resurrection, we pray: ◆ That those who have no faith and suffer the emptiness and loneliness of estrangement from God may receive the light of the risen Christ, we pray: ◆ That all who suffer the loss of a loved one during this Easter season may be brought the comfort and hope of the risen Christ, we pray: ◆

Our Father . . .

Loving God,
in the quiet humility of your Son's Resurrection,
you reveal the glory and majesty of your love.
Pour into our hearts your light and your life,
that we may become faithful witnesses of your truth to all the ends of the earth.
We ask this through our Lord Jesus Christ, your Son,
who lives and reigns with you in the unity of the Holy Spirit,
one God, forever and ever.
Amen.

✝ The earth is full of the goodness of the Lord. Alleluia.

† Rejoice, O hearts that seek the Lord.
Alleluia.

Psalm 118   page 418

Reading   Luke 24:13–16

That very day, the first day of the week, two of Jesus' disciples were going to a village seven miles from Jerusalem called Emmaus, and they were conversing about all the things that had occurred. And it happened that while they were conversing and debating, Jesus himself drew near and walked with them, but their eyes were prevented from recognizing him.

Reflection   Graziano Marcheschi

It's just like us to want something so badly that when we finally see it, we fail to recognize it. That's what happened here. The disciples weren't just too absorbed in their "conversing and debating" to recognize the Lord. They were too absorbed in their loss, too stricken by the disappointment of his death, too angry, perhaps, that he's not been the messiah they wanted who would free them from the bonds of Rome. They got a messiah who didn't look like a messiah, so when, risen from the dead, he stood before them they had no clue it was he. There are many forms of blindness, and not recognizing the answer to our prayer is only one of them.

Prayers   *others may be added*

Lord Jesus, you walk with us along the ways of everyday life. Let us pray:

◆ Stay with us, Lord.

For all who serve the Church, that they may foster devotion to the Word of God present in the scriptures and love of the Word Incarnate present in the Eucharist, we pray: ◆ For all civic leaders, that they may use their authority to serve the common good of all peoples through patient and open dialogue with one another, we pray: ◆ For the sick and all who suffer, that they may be surrounded by the love of people who will not be afraid to accompany them in their illness and sorrow, we pray: ◆ For our parish, that we may grow in deeper devotion to the Most Holy Eucharist, we pray: ◆ For all our minds and hearts to be opened to knowledge and understanding of the living Word in the scriptures, we pray: ◆

Our Father . . .

Heavenly Father,
by your Son, you teach us and bring us to
    the truth of salvation.
Instruct us by your Word
and give us wisdom through
    the sacraments.
We ask this through our Lord Jesus
    Christ, your Son,
who lives and reigns with you in the unity
    of the Holy Spirit,
one God, forever and ever.
Amen.

† Rejoice, O hearts that seek the Lord.
Alleluia.

✝ O Lord, our God, how wonderful your name in all the earth! Alleluia.

Psalm 118   *page 418*

Reading   *Luke 24:35–39*

The disciples of Jesus recounted what had taken place along the way, and how they had come to recognize him in the breaking of bread.

While they were still speaking about this, he stood in their midst and said to them, "Peace be with you." But they were startled and terrified and thought that they were seeing a ghost. Then he said to them, "Why are you troubled? And why do questions arise in your hearts? Look at my hands and my feet, that it is I myself. Touch me and see, because a ghost does not have flesh and bones as you can see I have."

Reflection   *Graziano Marcheschi*

How would you write the script: a miracle happens and the martyred leader is restored to his followers? How would they react: relieved, ecstatic, or doubting? But Jesus has to work to persuade his friends that it is really he. That's how we know this is *not* a script we're dealing with. The shock of his presence overwhelms them. It must be a ghost, they think. And somehow that seems more credible than Jesus' Resurrection. So Jesus calms their fears, for fear can lead us far afield, and he presents himself to them. Jesus still presents himself; he still waits for us to overcome our fears and surrender to the possibility that he has truly risen from the dead.

Prayers   *others may be added*

The disciples touch Jesus' hands and feet and recognize that he has truly been raised from the dead. Let us pray:

◆ Increase our faith, O Lord.

For the Church, that she may be driven by the love of Christ to proclaim to the world that Jesus Christ is truly risen, we pray: ◆ For all people, that they may recognize the dignity of God's creation through proper care for the environment and respect for the dignity of life, we pray: ◆ For the poor, the sick, the homeless, the hungry, and those who suffer violence and persecution, that the power of Jesus Christ, who conquers all evil, may establish his reign of peace throughout the world, we pray: ◆ For the members of our faith community, that they may encounter the risen Lord through word and sacrament, we pray: ◆

Our Father . . .

Lord Jesus Christ,
you come to meet us in our daily lives,
and you reveal to us your presence
even in the material goods of your created
    world.
Give us your peace as we strive to continue
to proclaim your goodness and glory to
    those around us in the ordinary events
    of daily life.
You live and reign forever.
Amen.

✝ O Lord, our God, how wonderful your name in all the earth! Alleluia.

Friday, April 13, 2012
Friday within the Octave of Easter

✟ The stone rejected by the builders has become the cornerstone.
Alleluia.

Psalm 118 *page 418*

Reading *John 21:12–14*

Jesus said to [his disciples], "Come, have breakfast." And none of the disciples dared to ask him, "Who are you?" because they realized it was the Lord. Jesus came over and took the bread and gave it to them, and in like manner the fish. This was the third time Jesus was revealed to his disciples after being raised from the dead.

Reflection *Graziano Marcheschi*

The disciples are still not settled with the reality of Christ's Resurrection. When he appears to them at the end of their fruitless night of fishing and tells them where to seek a catch, they suddenly realize this stranger must be Jesus. But they don't dare ask, "Who are you?" Of course not. To ask that would betray their lack of vision and their lack of faith. They've walked besides him for three years and yet they can't recognize him now that he's risen. They've made fools of themselves before and they're loathe to do it once again. When we doubt and fail to see, there may be some small comfort in knowing we're in good company.

Prayers *others may be added*

The risen Lord reveals himself to us by meeting us in our human needs. Let us pray:

◆ Feed us with the Bread of Life, O Lord.

That the Holy Father, all bishops, and priests may feed the flock of the Catholic Church in word and sacrament, we pray: ◆ That all government leaders may work to serve the needs of all human persons, we pray: ◆ For all the poor, the sick, and especially those who go hungry today, may their cries be heard and their needs provided for, we pray: ◆ That our parish, gathered together in prayer, may become a welcoming community toward all people, we pray: ◆ That all fishermen and those who work and travel by sea may be guided and protected by the Star of the Sea, we pray: ◆

Our Father . . .

Father of mercies,
The light of your risen Son shines upon us this Easter day.
Help us confidently surrender ourselves to your providential love.
We ask through our Lord Jesus Christ, your Son,
who lives and reigns with you in the unity of the Holy Spirit,
one God, forever and ever.
Amen.

✟ The stone rejected by the builders has become the cornerstone.
Alleluia.

✝ I will give thanks to you, for you have answered me. Alleluia.

Psalm 118 *page 418*

Reading *Mark 16:9–15*

When Jesus had risen, early on the first day of the week, he appeared first to Mary Magdalene, out of whom he had driven seven demons. She went and told his companions who were mourning and weeping. When they heard that he was alive and had been seen by her, they did not believe.

After this he appeared in another form to two of them along their way to the country. They returned and told the others; but they did not believe them either.

But later, as the Eleven were at table, he appeared to them and rebuked them for their unbelief and hardness of heart because they had not believed those who saw him after he had been raised. He said to them, "Go into the whole world and proclaim the Gospel to every creature."

Reflection

The mystery of the Resurrection is so great that the disciples cannot believe it. But Jesus comes to them and encounters them at table, and he reveals that he is truly risen. This is the great message of joy that we are called to likewise share among the nations: Jesus Christ has conquered death! Alleluia! He is truly risen!

Prayers *others may be added*

By the Resurrection, Jesus turns our mourning into joy. Let us rejoice as we say:

◆ Alleluia! He is truly risen!

That the whole Church throughout the world, illuminated by the light of Christ raised from the dead, may shine radiantly to testify to the glory of our risen King, we pray: ◆ That the Holy Spirit may prepare the soil of all the nations to receive the fruitful seed of the Word of the Resurrected Christ, we pray: ◆ That all those who suffer loneliness may encounter the constant presence of the living God, we pray: ◆ That Mary, Mother of the risen Lord, may intercede for us to attain a deeper and stronger faith in the mystery of the Resurrection, we pray: ◆

Our Father . . .

Merciful Father,
we thank you for the greatness of your mercy that you pour upon your children.
Have patience with our weaknesses and teach us
to rejoice in the joy of this Easter season,
confident that you are always with us.
We ask this through our Lord Jesus Christ, your Son,
who lives and reigns with you in the unity of the Holy Spirit,
one God, forever and ever.
Amen.

✝ I will give thanks to you, for you have answered me. Alleluia.

Sunday, April 15, 2012
Second Sunday of Easter/Sunday of the Divine Mercy

✝ Give thanks to the Lord for he is good; his love is everlasting. Alleluia.

Psalm 118 *page 418*

Reading *John 20:20b–23*

The disciples rejoiced when they saw the Lord. Jesus said to them again, "Peace be with you. As the Father has sent me, so I send you." And when he had said this, he breathed on them and said to them, "Receive the Holy Spirit. Whose sins you forgive are forgiven them, and whose sins you retain are retained."

Reflection

Today we celebrate the great feast of Divine Mercy, in which Jesus offers wellsprings of mercy to those who come to him asking even for a single drop from the ocean of his love. The risen Lord reveals himself to us through his mercy in forgiving our sins and giving us his peace. He shows us his wounds as signs of his merciful love.

Prayers *others may be added*

Father, in your Son you reveal to us your love and mercy. Coming to you in faith, we pray:

◆ Jesus, we trust in you.

For the Church, that the Holy Father, all bishops, priests, deacons, religious, and laity may be sent to announce the loving mercy of the risen Christ, we pray: ◆
For all civic leaders, rulers, and government officials, that they may serve their people with mercy and justice, we pray: ◆
For the sick and suffering who await God's healing mercy, that they may receive comfort through their surrender and trust in the divine providence of God who brings good out of every evil, we pray: ◆ For those who have died, that God may bring them home into the eternal love of heaven, we pray: ◆

Our Father . . .

Jesus Christ, King of mercy,
upon the cross streams of living water
and your precious blood flowed from your
    pierced side as a sign of your mercy
    and love.
Help us to trust in you,
especially in moments of difficulty and
    despair.
You live and reign forever.
Amen.

✝ Give thanks to the Lord for he is good; his love is everlasting. Alleluia.

Monday, April 16, 2012
Easter Weekday

✝ Blessed are all who take refuge in the Lord.

Psalm 66
page 410

Reading
John 3:1–8

There was a Pharisee named Nicodemus, a ruler of the Jews. He came to Jesus at night and said to him, "Rabbi, we know that you are a teacher who has come from God, for no one can do these things that you are doing unless God is with him." Jesus answered and said to him, "Amen, amen, I say to you, unless one is born from above, he cannot see the Kingdom of God." Nicodemus said to him, "How can a man once grown old be born again? Surely he cannot reenter his mother's womb and be born again, can he?" Jesus answered, "Amen, amen, I say to you, unless one is born of water and Spirit he cannot enter the Kingdom of God. What is born of flesh is flesh and what is born of spirit is spirit. Do not be amazed that I told you, 'You must be born from above.' The wind blows where it wills, and you can hear the sound it makes, but you do not know where it comes from or where it goes; so it is with everyone who is born of the Spirit."

Reflection

By the sacrament of Baptism, the Father gives us the light of his resurrected Son by the life of the Spirit. As we celebrate this Easter season, may this light of Christ grow within us by God's work within us.

Prayers
others may be added

Asking God to renew us in the life and light of the resurrected Christ, we pray:

◆ Lord, send out your Spirit and renew the face of the earth.

For the Church, that she may ever more become the radiant and glorious Mystical Body of Christ, we pray: ◆ For all nations, that they may discover new and creative means of dialogue in order to work through difficulties in peace and justice, we pray: ◆ For all who suffer sickness and illness, that God's Spirit may breathe new life in their bodies and souls, we pray: ◆ For all those recently baptized this Easter, that the graces they received may continue to grow and blossom in charity and good works, we pray: ◆

Our Father . . .

God of mercy,
all honor and praise belong to you.
By the grace of your sacraments,
lead us from the things of this earth
to the eternal glory of your heavenly
    kingdom.
May your Spirit breathe upon us
so that we may be brought to new life
    in you.
We ask this through Christ our Lord.
Amen.

✝ Blessed are all who take refuge in the Lord.

✝ The Lord is king; he is robed in majesty.

Psalm 118 *page 418*

Reading *John 3:7b–15*

Jesus said to Nicodemus: "You must be born from above." The wind blows where it wills, and you can hear the sound it makes, but you do not know where it comes from or where it goes; so it is with everyone who is born of the Spirit." Nicodemus answered and said to him, "How can this happen?" Jesus answered and said to him, "You are the teacher of Israel and you do not understand this? Amen, amen, I say to you, we speak of what we know and we testify to what we have seen, but you people do not accept our testimony. If I tell you about earthly things and you do not believe, how will you believe if I tell you about heavenly things? No one has gone up to heaven except the one who has come down from heaven, the Son of Man. And just as Moses lifted up the serpent in the desert, so must the Son of Man be lifted up, so that everyone who believes in him may have eternal life."

Reflection *Graziano Marcheschi*

Jesus teaches Nicodemus about the necessity of his future death and Resurrection. When serpents afflicted the Israelites in the desert, God told Moses to mount a bronze serpent on a pole and all who had been bitten would be healed. In like manner, Jesus, when he is "lifted up" upon the pole of the cross, will provide healing from the venom of sin and death. Not only are we healed by his death and Resurrection, but we are born again in his Holy Spirit.

Prayers *others may be added*

O God, by your Spirit we are born to new life from above. Let us pray:

◆ Increase our faith, O Lord.

For the Church, that she may remain stalwart in faith through new life in the Spirit, we pray: ◆ For all political leaders of nations, that they may not be solely concerned with worldly affairs, but rather look toward the things of above to further establish the kingdom of God through natural and human values, we pray: ◆ For all the sick in body, mind, and spirit, that they may experience the presence of God's Spirit who dwells within them in their moments of suffering, we pray: ◆ For all scientists and mathematicians, that their work may be a means of serving and glorifying God who reveals himself through his creation, we pray: ◆

Our Father . . .

Heavenly King,
our praise adds nothing to your greatness,
yet we thank you for the life
you pour upon us through the gift of
   your Spirit,
made present to us through the sacraments.
Shine the light of your life
more deeply into our hearts until the day
we attain the glory of your kingdom.
You live and reign forever.
Amen.

✝ The Lord is king; he is robed in majesty.

✝ The Lord hears the cry of the poor.

Psalm 66 *page 410*

Reading *John 3:16–21*

God so loved the world that he gave his only-begotten Son, so that everyone who believes in him might not perish but might have eternal life. For God did not send his Son into the world to condemn the world, but that the world might be saved through him. Whoever believes in him will not be condemned, but whoever does not believe has already been condemned, because he has not believed in the name of the only-begotten Son of God. And this is the verdict, that the light came into the world, but people preferred darkness to light, because their works were evil. For everyone who does wicked things hates the light and does not come toward the light, so that his works might not be exposed. But whoever lives the truth comes to the light, so that his works may be clearly seen as done in God.

Reflection

Jesus, the Light of the World, enters the story of salvation history to bring us the freedom of truth. Jesus Christ, as truth incarnate, offers us the gift of eternal life so that we may live in the light of his truth. This great mystery must be lived each day in faith and as we encounter God who comes to meet us in our humanity.

Prayers *others may be added*

Father, you send us your Son as Light of the World. Let us pray:

◆ Save your people, O God.

For the Church, that she may remain faithful to the teachings and truth of Christ, we pray: ◆ For all nations, that they may hear the Good News of salvation that Christ is risen from death to save all peoples and bring them to everlasting life, we pray: ◆ For those who suffer hunger, poverty, and lack of material needs, especially for all the sick and for young children, we pray: ◆ For all who have died by suicide and for their loved ones who grieve their loss, we pray: ◆ For our local parish community, that we may experience the light and life of Christ through friendship and unity with one another, we pray: ◆

Our Father . . .

Risen Lord,
you reign victorious over sin and death,
and your radiant light shines upon all
    the world.
By the grace of your Spirit of truth,
teach all peoples to love,
that we may one day attain the everlasting
    joys of salvation.
You live and reign forever.
Amen.

✝ The Lord hears the cry of the poor.

✝ The Lord hears the cry of the poor.

Psalm 118　　　　　　　*page 418*

Reading　　　　　　*John 3:31–36*

The one who comes from above is above all. The one who is of the earth is earthly and speaks of earthly things. But the one who comes from heaven is above all. He testifies to what he has seen and heard, but no one accepts his testimony. Whoever does accept his testimony certifies that God is trustworthy. For the one whom God sent speaks the words of God. He does not ration his gift of the Spirit. The Father loves the Son and has given everything over to him. Whoever believes in the Son has eternal life, but whoever disobeys the Son will not see life, but the wrath of God remains upon him.

Reflection

In these days of Easter Time, the Gospel continues to speak of the life that Jesus gives to us by the merits and power of his death and Resurrection. The Father has given everything over to the Son. The more that we are united to his Son, through prayer and the sacraments, the more we also will share life with him in the Father and the Spirit.

Prayers　　　*others may be added*

United to the vine of Jesus Christ,
we share in the life of God's sonship.
Let us pray:

◆ Your words are spirit and life,
　O Lord.

For the Church throughout the world, that all churches, parishes, and dioceses may become more united through the life of the Spirit, we pray: ◆ For all nations that suffer from violence, abuse, dictatorship, hunger, and poverty, that civic leaders may work for the common good so that all peoples may experience the freedom of the children of God, we pray: ◆ For all those who suffer from mental illness, drug abuse, alcoholism, and addiction, we pray: ◆ For the needs of our community, especially for families who are experiencing difficulties, we pray: ◆ For the grace to use our tongue and our words for the glory of God and the building up of others, we pray: ◆

Our Father . . .

Father,
you call us to be your sons and daughters through our union with Jesus Christ.
Give us the gift of your Spirit,
that we may live that Easter joy
with an open heart and a
　cheerful countenance.
We ask this through our Lord Jesus
　Christ, your Son,
who lives and reigns with you in the unity
　of the Holy Spirit,
one God, forever and ever.
Amen.

✝ The Lord hears the cry of the poor.

✝ One thing I seek: to dwell in the house of the Lord.

Psalm 66
page 410

Reading
John 6:11–15

Then Jesus took the loaves, gave thanks, and distributed them to those who were reclining, and also as much of the fish as they wanted. When they had had their fill, he said to his disciples, "Gather the fragments left over, so that nothing will be wasted." So they collected them, and filled twelve wicker baskets with fragments from the five barley loaves that had been more than they could eat. When the people saw the sign he had done, they said, "This is truly the Prophet, the one who is to come into the world." Since Jesus knew that they were going to come and carry him off to make him king, he withdrew again to the mountain alone.

Reflection
Graziano Marcheschi

We see a prefiguration of the Eucharist in Jesus' multiplication of loaves and fishes. The demonstrated bounty of the kingdom is a bounty that will not only meet but exceed our needs and expectations. Jesus begins with little, feeds a multitude, and ends with more than he began. He does the same in our lives. We offer the "little" faith we have and Jesus makes it more than enough. This is not a lesson in sharing but a lesson in God's bounty that compensates for human lack. It tells us of the need to rely wholly on God who feeds us with food that leads to everlasting life.

Prayers
others may be added

Father, you give the Living Bread come down from heaven. Let us pray:

◆ **Strengthen our faith, O Lord.**

For the Church, that the Pope, all the clergy, and lay faithful may fulfill their duties and ministries with humility, united to Christ with whom all things are possible, we pray: ◆ For all military personnel, that they may work faithfully in service to their country with perseverance, we pray: ◆ For the sick, the poor, and those who go without food today, that their needs may be transformed into overflowing abundance by the help and charity of others, we pray: ◆ For all to be humble and accept the grace of God in our lives, who transforms our weakness and littleness to perform great miracles, we pray: ◆

Our Father . . .

Father,
in your Son you give us the
Living Bread come down from heaven.
In this season of Easter joy,
may your grace transform us into
the light of your heavenly glory,
you who live and reign
with your Son, Jesus Christ,
in the unity of the Holy Spirit,
one God, forever and ever.
Amen.

✝ One thing I seek: to dwell in the house of the Lord.

Saturday, April 21, 2012
Easter Weekday

✝ Lord, let your mercy be on us, as we place our trust in you.

Psalm 118 *page 418*

Reading *John 6:16–21*

When it was evening, the disciples of Jesus went down to the sea, embarked in a boat, and went across the sea to Capernaum. It had already grown dark, and Jesus had not yet come to them. The sea was stirred up because a strong wind was blowing. When they had rowed about three or four miles, they saw Jesus walking on the sea and coming near the boat, and they began to be afraid. But he said to them, "It is I. Do not be afraid."

Reflection

Today's Gospel describes an unusual event where the disciples see Jesus walking on the water during a storm at sea. This event can be applied figuratively to teach us that Jesus comes to encounter us even in the difficulties and storms within our lives. And though we may be frightened, Jesus tells us not to be afraid. Soon after, we may find that we have arrived safely back on shore.

Prayers *others may be added*

During this Easter Time, the Church is filled with new life and joy. Let us pray:

◆ Come to our aid, O God.

For the Church, that she may be a refuge for all the poor, the weak, the rich, and the powerful who seek security from the storms of sin and evil, we pray: ◆ For the leaders of all nations to discover new and creative means of aiding their citizens by bringing safety and security for the welfare of all peoples, we pray: ◆ For those who suffer sadness, loneliness, and depression, that they may be comforted and may receive abounding peace, we pray: ◆
For all Christians, that they may be urged on by the love of the resurrected Christ to rise from the tomb of selfishness, in order to serve others in openness, charity, and generosity, we pray: ◆

Our Father . . .

Lord of wind and sea,
you are our loving God
who does not abandon us
in the storms and trials of life.
By the intercession of
Our Lady, Star of the Sea,
may we safely reach our
heavenly home in union with you.
We ask this through Christ our Lord.
Amen.

✝ Lord, let your mercy be on us, as we place our trust in you.

Sunday, April 22, 2012
Third Sunday of Easter

✝ Lord, let your face shine on us.

Psalm 66 *page 410*

Reading *Luke 24:35–39*

The two disciples recounted what had taken place on the way and how he was made known to them in the breaking of bread.

While they were still speaking about this, he stood in their midst and said to them, "Peace be with you." But they were startled and terrified and thought that they were seeing a ghost. Then he said to them, "Why are you troubled? And why do questions arise in your hearts? Look at my hands and my feet, that it is I myself. Touch me and see, because a ghost does not have flesh and bones as you can see I have."

Reflection

God is not afraid of our questions and doubts. Rather, he gives us his living Son who comes to us in flesh and blood, so that we may see and touch and know and believe that he is the Christ, the fulfillment of all the Law and the Prophets. In the glory of Easter, Jesus illuminates us with the gift of peace and understanding.

Prayers *others may be added*

In the glory of Jesus Christ raised from the dead, we present our petitions as we pray:

◆ Lord, let your face shine on us.

For the Holy Catholic Church, that, filled with the light of the risen Lord, she may shine ever more brilliantly as a beacon of knowledge and truth to all peoples, we pray: ◆ For all nations that suffer war, terrorism, and dictatorship, that, guided by upright government officials, they may enjoy peace, security, and justice, we pray: ◆ For all who suffer serious illness, for those who care for them, and for their family members and friends, that their hearts may not be troubled, we pray: ◆ For all our loved ones who have died, that they may behold the light and glory of our resurrected Lord, we pray: ◆ For the grace this week to live our lives as Christians transformed by the miracle of the Resurrection, we pray: ◆

Our Father . . .

Father of Light,
the light of your resurrected Son
shines upon us and the whole Church.
May the grace of this Easter Time
stir into flame the gifts we have received
through your Son, Jesus Christ our Lord,
who lives and reigns with you in the unity
   of the Holy Spirit,
one God, forever and ever.
Amen.

✝ Lord, let your face shine on us.

Monday, April 23, 2012
Easter Weekday

✝ Blessed are they who follow the law of the Lord!

Psalm 118   *page 418*

Reading   *John 6:22–29*

[After Jesus had fed the five thousand men, his disciples saw him walking on the sea.] The next day, the crowd that remained across the sea saw that there had been only one boat there, and that Jesus had not gone along with his disciples in the boat, but only his disciples had left. Other boats came from Tiberias near the place where they had eaten the bread when the Lord gave thanks. When the crowd saw that neither Jesus nor his disciples were there, they themselves got into the boats and came to Capernaum looking for Jesus. And when they found him across the sea they said to him, "Rabbi, when did you get here?" Jesus answered them and said, "Amen, amen, I say to you, you are looking for me not because you saw signs but because you ate the loaves and were filled. Do not work for food that perishes but for the food that endures for eternal life, which the Son of Man will give you. For on him the Father, God, has set his seal." So they said to him, "What can we do to accomplish the works of God?" Jesus answered and said to them, "This is the work of God, that you believe in the one he sent."

Reflection

Our lives can easily become cluttered with insignificant and trivial concerns and activities. However, in today's Gospel, Jesus tells us that we ought to work for what will endure for eternal life. The gift of faith to believe in Jesus Christ, sent from the Father, is the beginning of the work of God within us, which allows us to accomplish his works to bear fruit that will remain.

Prayers   *others may be added*

With confidence in your majesty, we pray:

◆ Lord, hear our prayer.

For the Church, that she may be renewed in faith to serve God in charity toward one another, we pray: ◆ For all peoples who are persecuted for their faith, we pray: ◆ For all the sick, we pray: ◆ For those with no faith, we pray: ◆ For our parish community, we pray: ◆

Our Father . . .

Father God,
strengthen us in faith,
that, united to you,
our work may bear fruit to accomplish
    your will.
We ask this through your Son, Jesus
    Christ our Lord,
who lives and reigns with you in the unity
    of the Holy Spirit,
one God, forever and ever.
Amen.

✝ Blessed are they who follow the law of the Lord!

✝ Into your hands, O Lord, I commend my spirit.

Psalm 66   *page 410*

Reading   *John 6:30–35*

The crowd said to Jesus: "What sign can you do, that we may see and believe in you? What can you do? Our ancestors ate manna in the desert, as it is written: / *He gave them bread from heaven to eat.*" / So Jesus said to them, "Amen, amen, I say to you, it was not Moses who gave the bread from heaven; my Father gives you the true bread from heaven. For the bread of God is that which comes down from heaven and gives life to the world."

So they said to Jesus, "Sir, give us this bread always." Jesus said to them, "I am the bread of life; whoever comes to me will never hunger, and whoever believes in me will never thirst."

Reflection

What great mystery that God in the Eucharist becomes our food! God nourishes us with his own Body and Blood, so that physically united to him in Holy Communion we enter into the divine life of the Trinity. Present in the Eucharist, Christ remains with us always. May we have the faith to believe and to accept the true and Real Presence of the resurrected Lord in the holy sacrament of the Eucharist.

Prayers   *others may be added*

Father, you give us the true Bread come down from heaven. We, your children, humbly pray:

◆ Give us this day, our daily bread.

For the Church, that she may grow in deeper devotion to the Eucharist, we pray: ◆ For civic leaders, that they may work together to solve the problems of world hunger, we pray: ◆ For those who suffer from injuries from automobile accidents, for their healing and continued safety, we pray: ◆ For all families, that they may be united in love and gratitude for one another, we pray: ◆ For all who have died, and for those who grieve their loss, that they may receive new life and comfort from the risen Christ, we pray: ◆ For each of us to be drawn more closer in faith to Christ present in the Eucharist, the font and source of all healing and peace, we pray: ◆

Our Father . . .

Father of life,
you sent us your Son,
the true Bread come down from heaven.
Nourished by your Eucharistic life,
may we be brought into the eternal glory
of the Holy Trinity.
We ask this through Christ our Lord.
Amen.

✝ Into your hands, O Lord, I commend my spirit.

Wednesday, April 25, 2012
Feast of Saint Mark, Evangelist

✝ Let all the earth cry out to God
with joy.

Psalm 118 *page 418*

Reading *John 16:15–20*

Jesus said to his disciples: "Go into the whole world and proclaim the Gospel to every creature. Whoever believes and is baptized will be saved; whoever does not believe will be condemned."

Reflection

Today we celebrate the feast of the apostle and evangelist Saint Mark. The word *apostle* means "sent." Just like he sent the apostles out, Jesus also sends each of us out to proclaim the Gospel through our word and example as apostles in our daily lives. United to him, we will be able to accomplish great works for his glory and for the good of many people.

Prayers *others may be added*

Father, you give us the witness of your saints to encourage us in following your will. Let us pray:

◆ Sanctify us, O Lord.

That the Church throughout the world may be filled with saints of every race, culture, age, and profession, who give witness to God as they strive to live the Gospel each day, we pray: ◆ For all politicians, that they may use their authority in humble service for the poor and needy, we pray: ◆ For all writers, notaries, glass workers, basket weavers, and opticians, that, through the intercession of Saint Mark, they may do their work for the glory of God, we pray: ◆ That our local community will be transformed by the word of God through meditation on the Holy Gospels, we pray: ◆ For the leaders of all nations to discover new and creative means of aiding their citizens by bringing safety and security for the welfare of all peoples, we pray: ◆ For those who suffer sadness, loneliness, and depression, that they may be comforted and may receive abounding peace, we pray: ◆ For all Christians, that they may be urged on by the love of the resurrected Christ to rise from the tomb of selfishness, in order to serve others in openness, charity, and generosity, we pray: ◆ For all those who have died, we pray: ◆

Our Father . . .

Loving God,
the witness of your saints
strengthens our faith and
encourages us on to holiness.
Through the intercession of Saint Mark,
apostle and evangelist, may we live
the call to proclaim the Gospel
to every living creature.
We ask this through Christ our Lord,
who lives and reigns with you in the unity
of the Holy Spirit,
one God, forever and ever.
Amen.

✝ Let all the earth cry out to God
with joy.

✝ Let all the earth cry out to God
with joy.

Psalm 66 *page 410*

Reading *John 6:44–51*

Jesus said to the crowds: "No one can
come to me unless the Father who sent
me draw him, and I will raise him on the
last day. It is written in the prophets: /
They shall all be taught by God. /
Everyone who listens to my Father and
learns from him comes to me. Not that
anyone has seen the Father except the
one who is from God; he has seen the
Father. Amen, amen, I say to you, whoever believes has eternal life. I am the
bread of life. Your ancestors ate the
manna in the desert but they died; this
is the bread that comes from heaven so
that one may eat it and not die. I am the
living bread that came down from
heaven; whoever eats this bread will live
forever; and the bread that I will give is
my Flesh for the life of the world."

Reflection

The Gospel readings continue to recount
Jesus' eucharistic discourses. The
Father draws us to his Son, Jesus Christ,
whom we encounter in the eucharistic
feast. Jesus, our Living Bread, gives us
his Flesh and Blood so that we may partake in his eternal life. Jesus, our divine
teacher, teaches us by this encounter
with his person, and brings us into
union with the Father and the Spirit.

Prayers *others may be added*

Father God, draw us into your life as
we pray:

◆ Living Bread of Life, hear our prayer.

For the Church, that she may always
guard, honor, and worship the great
treasure of Jesus Christ present in the
Holy Eucharist, we pray: ◆ For all social
justice programs that work to solve the
problems of world hunger, we pray: ◆
For all priests, that they may be constantly
renewed in their ministry through love
and devotion to the Mass and Eucharist,
we pray: ◆ For all the homeless and those
who go without food, that they may
receive the material and spiritual nourishment and shelter they need, we pray: ◆
For those in our parish who bring the
Eucharist to the sick and dying, we pray:
◆ For all those who have died, that they
may be brought into the eternal life and
glory of the resurrected Lord, we pray: ◆

Our Father . . .

Draw us, O Loving Father.
Open our hearts to listen,
so that, receptive to your word,
you may instruct us in the riches,
depth, and mystery of your love.
O Triune God, draw us into your life
of union,
you who live and reign together as one,
Father, Son, and Holy Spirit.
We ask this in Jesus' name.
Amen.

✝ Let all the earth cry out to God
with joy.

Friday, April 27, 2012
Easter Weekday

✝ Go out to all the world and tell the Good News.

Psalm 118
page 418

Reading
John 6:53–59

Jesus said to [the crowds], "Amen, amen, I say to you, unless you eat the Flesh of the Son of Man and drink his Blood, you do not have life within you. Whoever eats my Flesh and drinks my Blood has eternal life, and I will raise him up on the last day."

Reflection

Jesus Christ has come to give us life—a full life, rich in blessings and fulfillment. This does not mean that a life following Jesus will be absent of pain and suffering, because we will never be without the cross. However, all the little crosses will have meaning and will be transformed by the power of Christ's Resurrection, which conquers and transforms death into life. In the Eucharist, we receive and remain in Jesus' abundant life of the Father and the Spirit.

Prayers
others may be added

Father, your abundant life remains always with us in the Real Presence of your Son in the Holy Eucharist. In adoration of your goodness, we pray:

◆ Stay with us, Lord.

For the Holy Father, that he may guide the Church to union with Jesus Christ in the Eucharist, we pray: ◆ For all political leaders, that they may respect the human person in every aspect and in each stage of life, we pray: ◆ For those who suffer illness and pain in mind and body, that their sufferings may be transformed into healing and new life, we pray: ◆ For those who hunger and thirst for meaning and answers, we pray: ◆ For our local community, that they may be renewed in devotion and love for the liturgy, we pray: ◆ For gratitude for those who worship and pray before the Blessed Sacrament for the salvation of souls, we pray: ◆

Our Father . . .

Loving Father,
you have poured your mercy into your
    Son, Jesus Christ,
whom you send to us so we may share in
    your same life.
May we always remain in you
by the love of your Holy Spirit.
We ask this through Christ our Lord.
Amen.

✝ Go out to all the world and tell the Good News.

Saturday, April 28, 2012
Easter Weekday

✝ How shall I make a return to the Lord for all the good he has done for me?

Psalm 66
page 410

Reading
John 6:60–69

Many of the disciples of Jesus who were listening said, "This saying is hard; who can accept it?" Since Jesus knew that his disciples were murmuring about this, he said to them, "Does this shock you? What if you were to see the Son of Man ascending to where he was before? It is the Spirit that gives life, while the flesh is of no avail. The words I have spoken to you are Spirit and life. But there are some of you who do not believe." Jesus knew from the beginning the ones who would not believe and the one who would betray him. And he said, "For this reason I have told you that no one can come to me unless it is granted him by my Father."

As a result of this, many of his disciples returned to their former way of life and no longer walked with him. Jesus then said to the Twelve, "Do you also want to leave?" Simon Peter answered him, "Master, to whom shall we go? You have the words of eternal life. We have come to believe and are concerned that you are the Holy One of God."

Reflection

"This saying is hard," the disciples say in response to Jesus' teaching on the Eucharist. And the disciples are right. It is difficult to accept the truth that the Eucharist is truly the Body and Blood, of Jesus Christ. However, Jesus does not force us to believe, but gives us the freedom to deny his teaching, as many of the disciples did because of this hard saying.

Prayers
others may be added

Loving God, hear our prayers and petitions as we pray:

◆ Lord, you have the words of everlasting life.

For the Church, we pray: ◆ For world leaders, we pray: ◆ For those away from the Church, we pray: ◆ For those who suffer, we pray: ◆

Our Father . . .

Good and loving Father,
increase our faith so that we may
remain faithful to always follow
your Son in the newness of life
that we receive from the Eucharist.
We ask this through your Son, Jesus
    Christ our Lord,
who lives and reigns with you in the unity
    of the Holy Spirit,
one God, forever and ever.
Amen.

✝ How shall I make a return to the Lord for all the good he has done for me?

Sunday, April 29, 2012
Fourth Sunday of Easter

✝ The stone rejected by the builders has become the cornerstone.

Psalm 118   *page 418*

Reading   *John 10:11–16*

Jesus said: "I am the good shepherd. A good shepherd lays down his life for the sheep. A hired man, who is not a shepherd and whose sheep are not his own, sees a wolf coming and leaves the sheep and runs away, and the wolf catches and scatters them. This is because he works for pay and has no concern for the sheep. I am the good shepherd, and I know mine and mine know me, just as the Father knows me and I know the Father; and I will lay down my life for the sheep. I have other sheep that do not belong to this fold. These also I must lead, and they will hear my voice, and there will be one flock, one shepherd."

Reflection

Jesus reveals the mystery of who he is through the image of a shepherd. Jesus is the Good Shepherd, who guides and protects his sheep, who calls them by name and who leads them out to green pasture. Jesus knows his sheep in the same way in which the Father knows the Son. We, too, are called into filial love with God. Jesus, the Good Shepherd, lays down his life for his sheep and calls all peoples so that they may be part of one flock, one sheepfold.

Prayers   *others may be added*

With filial love we present our petitions:

◆ Good Shepherd, hear our prayer.

For the Pope, all bishops, priests, and deacons, that they may be holy and faithful shepherds to guide and lead the sheep of the flock entrusted to them by the Good Shepherd, we pray: ◆ For vocations to the priesthood, that young men may respond with generosity to serve the flock of the Church, we pray: ◆ For those who suffer illness or the sorrows of loneliness and estrangement, that the Good Shepherd may seek out his lost and suffering sheep and bring them back upon his shoulders, we pray: ◆ For all children, that they may know the love and protection of the Good Shepherd who calls them by name, we pray: ◆ For the grace to open our hearts to hear the voice of the Shepherd who personally calls us to follow him, we pray: ◆

Our Father . . .

Lord Jesus,
you are our Good Shepherd
who cares for us and protects us.
In the eucharistic celebration,
you lay down your life for us
and give yourself to us through
the gifts of bread and wine.
Lead all peoples to come into unity
    with you.
You live and reign forever.
Amen.

✝ The stone rejected by the builders has become the cornerstone.

✝ Athirst is my soul for the living God.

Psalm 118   *page 418*

Reading   *John 10:1–10*

Jesus said: "Amen, amen, I say to you, whoever does not enter a sheepfold through the gate but climbs over elsewhere is a thief and a robber. But whoever enters through the gate is the shepherd of the sheep. The gatekeeper opens it for him, and the sheep hear his voice, as he calls his own sheep by name and leads them out. When he has driven out all his own, he walks ahead of them, and the sheep follow him, because they recognize his voice. But they will not follow a stranger; they will run away from him, because they do not recognize the voice of strangers." Although Jesus used this figure of speech, they did not realize what he was trying to tell them.

So Jesus said again, "Amen, amen, I say to you, I am the gate for the sheep. All who came before me are thieves and robbers, but the sheep did not listen to them. I am the gate. Whoever enters through me will be saved, and will come in and go out and find pasture. A thief comes only to steal and slaughter and destroy; I came so that they might have life and have it more abundantly."

Reflection

Jesus the Good Shepherd has come so that we may have life, but not a life of mediocrity. He has come so that we might have life more abundantly. Our Good Shepherd calls his sheep by name, and they recognize his voice and follow him. Jesus uses this parable to reveal himself to us. We must listen to the voice of the Shepherd, and he will lead us to peace and safety.

Prayers   *others may be added*

Jesus, you are our Good Shepherd who provides for all our needs. Let us pray:

◆ **Hear our prayer, O Good Shepherd.**

For the Church, that she may witness to the goodness and love of the Good Shepherd, we pray: ◆ For those who work for the end of violence, terrorism, and war throughout the world, we pray: ◆ For all the sick, the poor, the homeless, the lonely, and those who suffer from abuse and addiction, we pray: ◆ For the grace to listen to the voice of the Shepherd who calls us by name in our daily lives and through our work, we pray: ◆

Our Father . . .

Sweet and gentle Jesus,
you are our Good Shepherd
who cares for us and protects us
from the snares of all evil and harm.
Gather us all into one flock so that
all may be one in you.
You live and reign forever.
Amen.

✝ Athirst is my soul for the living God.

Tuesday, May 1, 2012
Easter Weekday
Optional memorial of Saint Joseph the Worker

✝ Lord, give success to the work of our hands.

Psalm 66   *page 410*

Reading   *Matthew 13:54–58*
Jesus came to his native place and taught the people in their synagogue. They were astonished and said, "Where did this man get such wisdom and mighty deeds? Is he not the carpenter's son? Is not his mother named Mary and his brothers James, Joseph, Simon, and Judas? Are not his sisters all with us? Where did this man get all this?" And they took offense at him. But Jesus said to them, "A prophet is not without honor except in his native place and in his own house." And he did not work many mighty deeds there because of their lack of faith.

Reflection
Today we celebrate the memorial of Saint Joseph the Worker. Saint Joseph is the model for all who work, because in his humble and simple work as a carpenter, he cared for the holy family and provided for the needs of Mary and Jesus. Through Saint Joseph, we can learn the importance of diligence and faithfulness in our daily life and work.

Prayers   *others may be added*
Through the intercession of the saints, we offer our petitions as we pray:

◆ Bless the work of our hands, O God.

For the Church, that she may continue to persevere in the work of God throughout the world, we pray: ◆ For civic leaders throughout the world, that they will work for the common good to protect their people against all evil and harm, we pray: ◆ For thanksgiving for all fathers who work hard to provide and care for their families, that they may be blessed through the intercession of Saint Joseph, we pray: ◆ For all the sick and suffering, that they may recognize the great and necessary work that they do in offering their sufferings and prayers for the good of others, we pray: ◆ For the unemployed, those who are looking for jobs, and for those who seek just work situations, we pray: ◆

Our Father . . .

Loving God,
the work of your creation
gives you praise and glory.
Through the intercession of Saint Joseph, the Worker,
help us to serve you faithfully
through our daily life and work.
We ask this through our Lord Jesus Christ, your Son,
who lives and reigns with you in the unity of the Holy Spirit,
one God, forever and ever.
Amen.

✝ Lord, give success to the work of our hands.

✝ O, God, let all the nations praise
you!

Psalm 118   *page 418*

Reading   *Matthew 10:22–25*

Jesus said to the Twelve: "You will be
hated by all because of my name, but
whoever endures to the end will be
saved. When they persecute you in one
town, flee to another. Amen, I say to
you, you will not finish the towns of
Israel before the Son of Man comes. No
disciple is above his teacher, no slave
above his master. It is enough for the
disciple that he become like the teacher,
and the slave that he become like the
master. If they have called the master
of the house Beelzebub, how much more
those of his household!"

Reflection

Today we celebrate the feast of Saint
Athanasius, the Bishop and Doctor of
the Church who fought tirelessly against
the Arian heresy in the period of the
early Church. Today's Gospel teaches
us that we will face contradiction and
persecution on account of Jesus' name;
however, those who persevere to the end
will be saved. Saint Athanasius is an
example of a great saint who courageously persevered to the end by fighting heresy and error and by defending
and clarifying the truth about Jesus
Christ despite many persecutions and
difficulties.

Prayers   *others may be added*

In diligence and perseverance, we
pray:

◆ Keep us faithful to you, O Lord.

For God to raise up more holy men and
courageous women throughout the world
to protect and defend the truth of the
Catholic Church with fortitude and
apostolic zeal, we pray: ◆ For all peoples
of nations who are persecuted for their
faith, that their sufferings and persevering
witness may bring conversion, we pray: ◆
For all the poor, the sick, the elderly, and
the homeless; for those who experience
the loneliness of suffering, that they may
recognize the constant presence of the
risen Lord, we pray: ◆ For our parish
community to grow in devotion to the
maternal care of the Blessed Mother
Mary during this month of May,
we pray: ◆

Our Father . . .

Lord Jesus,
you do not fail to teach us
that a life following after you
will also involve the suffering of
    the cross.
Through the prayers of Saint Athanasius,
give us strength and courage to persevere
through the trials and persecutions that
    must come,
that, by your grace, after we have been
    proved faithful,
we may enjoy the glory of your
    eternal kingdom.
You live and reign forever.
Amen.

✝ O, God, let all the nations praise
you!

† Their message goes out through all the earth.

Psalm 66 *page 410*

Reading *John 14:6–14*

Jesus said to Thomas, "I am the way and the truth and the life. No one comes to the Father except through me. If you know me, then you will also know my Father. From now on you do know him and have seen him." Philip said to him, "Master, show us the Father, and that will be enough for us." James said to him, "Have I been with you for so long a time and you still do not know me, Philip? Whoever has seen me has seen the Father. How can you say, 'Show us the Father'? Do you not believe that I am the Father and the Father is in me? The words that I speak to you I do not speak on my own. The Father who dwells in me is doing his works. Believe me that I am in the Father and the Father is in me, or else, believe because of the works themselves. Amen, amen, I say to you, whoever believes in me will do the works that I do, and will be greater ones than these, because I am going to the Father. And whatever you ask in my name, I will do, so that the Father may be glorified in the Son. If you ask anything of me in my name, I will do it."

Reflection

Jesus reveals the mystery of his filial union with the Father. Philip's desire to see the Father is not foolish, but Jesus wants to bring him into the deeper understanding that the Father and he are so united, that in seeing Jesus, he too has seen the Father. The Father fulfills his works in the Son, and likewise, the Father works through all those who are united to him in Jesus.

Prayers *others may be added*

In faith, we ask:

♦ Lord, hear our prayer.

For the Church, that she may fulfill the Father's works for the glory of his name, we pray: ♦ For civic leaders, that they may promote peace and justice, we pray: ♦ For all the sick, the suffering, the poor, and needy, that the Father may provide for all their needs, we pray: ♦ For all those who have died from our parish community, we pray: ♦

Our Father . . .

Lord Jesus,
you are the Way, the Truth, and the Life.
In you we see and encounter the Father,
because you and the Father are one.
Give us knowledge and understanding of
    your great mystery,
that we may proclaim your goodness and
    do your work.
We ask this through Christ our Lord.
Amen.

† Their message goes out through all the earth.

Friday, May 4, 2012
Easter Weekday

✝ You are my Son; this day I have begotten you.

Psalm 118   *page 418*

Reading   *John 14:1–6*

Jesus said to his disciples: "Do not let your hearts be troubled. You have faith in God; have faith also in me. In my Father's house there are many dwelling places. If there were not, would I have told you that I am going to prepare a place for you? And if I go and prepare a place for you, I will come back again and take you to myself, so that where I am you also may be. Where I am going you know the way." Thomas said to him, "Master, we do not know where you are going; how can we know the way?" Jesus said to him, "I am the way and the truth and the life. No one comes to the Father except through me."

Reflection

What words of consolation Jesus speaks to us today! "Do not let your hearts be troubled." Jesus reveals his intimate love for us that longs for us to be with him. He is the Bridegroom who goes to prepare a place for us, and returns to take us to himself so we may dwell in his Father's house. He desires that we always be with him.

Prayers   *others may be added*

Jesus, you are the Way, the Truth, and the Life. Let us pray:

◆ Show us the way to the Father.

For the Church to be a home to all non-Christians and Christians alike on this earthly pilgrimage toward the Father's house, we pray: ◆ For leaders of all nations, that they may tirelessly work to provide housing, food, and security for those in need, we pray: ◆ For all the homeless, that, united to Christ who had no place to lay his head, they may find shelter and housing, we pray: ◆ For those who suffer from anxiety, depression, and mental illnesses, that they may be brought peace through faith in God, we pray: ◆ For all children of broken homes, that they may know the security of being united to Christ, we pray: ◆ For all those who have died, that they may soon enjoy the glory of eternal life in the heavenly home of the Father, we pray: ◆

Our Father . . .

In you, O Lord, our souls find rest.
In you, O Father, we have a home.
Be with us, O God, and never leave us.
Protect us against temptations of worry,
and keep us free from all anxiety.
Make us know your intimate love for us,
that desires for us to be always with you.
May we never be separated from you.
We ask this through Christ our Lord.
Amen.

✝ You are my Son; this day I have begotten you.

Saturday, May 5, 2012
Easter Weekday

✝ All the ends of the earth have seen the saving power of God.

Psalm 66   *page 410*

Reading   *John 14:7–14*

Jesus said to his disciples: "If you know me, then you will also know my Father. From now on you do know him and have seen him." Philip said to Jesus, "Master, show us the Father, and that will be enough for us." Jesus said to him, "Have I been with you for so long a time and you still do not know me, Philip? Whoever has seen me has seen the Father. How can you say, 'Show us the Father'? Do you not believe that I am in the Father and the Father is in me? The words that I speak to you I do not speak on my own. The Father who dwells in me is doing his works. Believe me that I am in the Father and the Father is in me, or else, believe because of the works themselves. Amen, amen, I say to you, whoever believes in me will do the works that I do, and will do greater ones than these, because I am going to the Father. And whatever you ask in my name, I will do, so that the Father may be glorified in the Son. If you ask anything of me in my name, I will do it."

Reflection

The month of May is dedicated to the Blessed Virgin Mary, our Mother and Queen. As the Father willed that the power of the Holy Spirit come upon her, and that the Son of God take flesh within her womb, Mary lived in inti-mate union with the Father, the Son, and the Holy Spirit. This month of May provides us with an opportunity to honor her with increased love and devotion, so that she may teach us and lead us closer to God through her example and prayers.

Prayers   *others may be added*

Hear our prayers that we ask in your name with confidence and faith:

◆ Father, fulfill your good work in us.

For the Church, that, through the work of holy thinkers, she may discover new and creative ways to proclaim the joyous message of the Gospel, we pray: ◆ For all cultures, that they may be renewed in festive celebration of the richness of their traditions, we pray: ◆ For all those who will die today, and for all our loved ones who have died from our parish community, we pray: ◆

Our Father . . .

Loving Father,
you sent us your Son, born of a woman,
to save us and give us new life.
You teach us that anything we ask
in your name you will grant
for the glory of your name.
Through the prayers of the
    Blessed Virgin,
hear our prayer and grant us
    your salvation.
We ask this through Christ our Lord.
Amen.

✝ All the ends of the earth have seen the saving power of God.

Sunday, May 6, 2012
Fifth Sunday of Easter

✝ I will praise you, Lord, in the assembly of your people.

Psalm 118
page 418

Reading
John 15:1–5

Jesus said to his disciples: "I am the true vine, and my Father is the vine grower. He takes away every branch in me that does not bear fruit, and every one that does he prunes so that it bears more fruit. You are already pruned because of the word that I spoke to you. Remain in me, as I remain in you. Just as a branch cannot bear fruit on its own unless it remains on the vine, so neither can you unless you remain in me. I am the vine, you are the branches. Whoever remains in me and I in him will bear much fruit, because without me you can do nothing."

Reflection

This Sunday, Jesus entreats us to remain in his love. He tells us to stay united in his life in the same way in which a branch must remain united to the vine in order to grow, live, and bear fruit. By remaining united to him, the sap of his divine life runs within us so that we may flourish in good works for the glory of the Father.

Prayers
others may be added

Without you, Lord, we can do nothing. Let us pray:

◆ Keep us united in your love, O Lord.

For the Holy Father, that he may lead and guide Holy Mother Church with strength and courage against misunderstandings against the Church's wellspring of grace for all people, we pray: ◆ For government leaders, that they may work to seek the common good of all peoples, and to promote a life of security and justice for each individual, we pray: ◆ For all those who suffer illness in mind, body, or spirit, that the life of the Holy Spirit may flow within in them to bring healing by means of the life of the sacraments, we pray: ◆ For all our military personnel overseas or in harm's way, that they may be protected and brought safely home, we pray: ◆ For the grace this week to remain united to Jesus Christ through prayer and worship in the midst of our daily duties and activities, we pray: ◆

Our Father . . .

Heavenly Father,
in this Easter Time we rejoice
in the light and life of the risen Lord.
May we always remain united to
    Jesus Christ,
the True Vine, so that, united with him,
we may bear abundant fruit.
We ask this through Christ our Lord.
Amen.

✝ I will praise you, Lord, in the assembly of your people.

Monday, May 7, 2012
Easter Weekday

✝ Not to us, O Lord, but to your name give the glory.

Psalm 66   *page 410*

Reading   *John 14:21–26*

Jesus said to his disciples: "Whoever has my commandments and observes them is the one who loves me. Whoever loves me will be loved by my Father, and I will love him and reveal myself to him." Judas, not the Iscariot, said to him, "Master, then what happened that you will reveal yourself to us and not to the world?" Jesus answered and said to him, "Whoever loves me will keep my word, and my Father will love him, and we will come to him and make our dwelling with him. Whoever does not love me does not keep my words; yet the word you hear is not mine but that of the Father who sent me.

"I have told you this while I am with you. The Advocate, the Holy Spirit whom the Father will send in my name—he will teach you everything and remind you of all that I told you."

Reflection

What great promises Jesus makes today! United in love with Jesus, the Word Incarnate, we will also receive the love of the Father, and God will come to us to make his dwelling within us. Jesus, furthermore, promises the gift of the Spirit sent by the Father to teach us and intercede for us on our behalf.

Prayers   *others may be added*

Hear our prayers and grant the petitions we place before you today:

◆ Holy Spirit, teach us to keep your commands.

For the Church, that, illuminated by the light of the Spirit given to us by the risen Christ, she may continue to proclaim the truth of God's glory with bold and humble clarity, we pray: ◆ For nations and families torn apart by war, violence, and political unrest, we pray: ◆ For all doctors, nurses, and medical assistants, that they may be blessed for their good work and service, and that they may be instruments of healing for all their patients, we pray: ◆ For all the charitable and apostolic endeavors of our parish, that they may be fruitful in giving aid to many people in need, we pray: ◆ For the repose of all who have died, we pray: ◆

Our Father . . .

Lord Jesus,
you are the Way, the Truth, and the Life.
In you we see and encounter the Father,
because you and the Father are one.
Give us knowledge and understanding of
    your great mystery,
that we may proclaim your goodness and
    do your work.
We ask this through Christ our Lord.
Amen.

✝ Not to us, O Lord, but to your name give the glory.

✝ Your friends make known, O Lord, the glorious splendor of your kingdom.

Psalm 118 *page 418*

Reading *John 14:27–31a*

Jesus said to his disciples: "Peace I leave with you; my peace I give to you. Not as the world gives do I give it to you. Do not let your hearts be troubled or afraid. You heard me tell you, 'I am going away and I will come back to you.' If you loved me, you would rejoice that I am going to the Father; for the Father is greater than I. And now I have told you this before it happens, so that when it happens you may believe. I will no longer speak much with you, for the ruler of the world is coming. He has no power over me, but the world must know that I love the Father and that I do just as the Father has commanded me."

Reflection

Today Jesus commands, "Do not let your hearts be troubled or afraid." By his Resurrection, Jesus has conquered the evil of the world, and in him we have nothing to fear. Jesus gives us his peace. He leaves us his peace that is a true and lasting and fulfilling peace, unlike the peace the world may give.

Prayers *others may be added*

Calling upon our Father, we pray:

◆ Lord, hear us.

That the Holy Father may receive rest and renewal in the midst of his constant responsibilities of service for the people of his flock, the Church, we pray: ◆ That political leaders may discover new ways to achieve world peace, we pray: ◆ That those who face the anxieties and worries of surgery, medical treatment, or serious illness may encounter the peace beyond all understanding of the Divine Physician, we pray: ◆ That those who suffer from anxiety, depression, addiction, and mental illness may be given peace, we pray: ◆ That our Lady, Queen of Peace, may teach us how to live peaceful lives to foster solidarity and communion with one another, we pray: ◆

Our Father . . .

Your friends make known, O Lord, the glorious splendor of your kingdom. Lord Jesus, King of peace, you command us not to be troubled or afraid, for you are with us. You have conquered over the world, and all power and authority belong to you. Give us this peace beyond understanding until we rejoice to see you face to face in the glory of the heavenly rest with you. You live and reign forever. Amen.

✝ Your friends make known, O Lord, the glorious splendor of your kingdom.

Wednesday, May 9, 2012
Easter Weekday

✝ Let us go rejoicing to the house of the Lord.

Psalm 66
page 410

Reading
John 15:1-8

Jesus said to his disciples: "I am the true vine, and my Father is the vine grower. He takes away every branch in me that does not bear fruit, and everyone that does he prunes so that it bears more fruit. You are already pruned because of the word that I spoke to you. Remain in me, as I remain in you. Just as a branch cannot bear fruit on its own unless it remains on the vine, so neither can you unless you remain in me. I am the vine, you are the branches. Whoever remains in me and I in him will bear much fruit, because without me you can do nothing. Anyone who does not remain in me will be thrown out like a branch and wither; people will gather them and throw them into a fire and they will be burned. If you remain in me and my words remain in you, ask for whatever you want and it will be done for you. By this is my Father glorified, that you bear much fruit and become my disciples."

Reflection

The union we possess in Jesus is like that of a vine and its branches. If we remain in him and his words, we can ask for anything; it will be granted to us by the Father in accordance with his glorious will. The Father desires that we remain united in his Son so that we will bear much fruit that will remain.

Prayers
others may be added

Father, you are the vine grower who, through the power of your word, prunes your choice vine so that we may bear more fruit. Let us pray:

◆ **Remain with us, O Lord.**

For all the members of the Church, that they may remain united to Jesus Christ through his word and sacrament, we pray: ◆ For all those who work for the good of their countries, that their efforts may bear fruit in the flourishing of peace and justice, we pray: ◆ For all those who long for healing, we pray: ◆ For all children who are preparing for first Holy Communion, that they may remain united to the love of the eucharistic Lord, we pray: ◆ For the grace to surrender ourselves to the love of Our Father, we pray: ◆

Our Father . . .

Jesus, our True Vine,
without you we can do nothing.
Keep us always united in your love,
that, grafted into your Triune life,
we may bear abundant fruit for the glory
of your Father, our loving Vine Grower.
You live and reign forever.
Amen.

✝ Let us go rejoicing to the house of the Lord.

✝ Proclaim God's marvelous deeds to all the nations.

Psalm 118
page 418

Reading
John 15:9–17

Jesus said to his disciples: "As the Father loves me, so I also love you. Remain in my love. If you keep my commandments, you will remain in my love, just as I have kept my Father's commandments and remain in his love.

"I have told you this so that my joy might be in you and your joy might be complete."

Reflection
Graziano Marcheschi

Love requires relationship and relationships require obedience. Love does not mean never having to say you're sorry, nor does it give license to do whatever we will. Love places demands on us and Jesus says the first is to obey his commandments. We keep the commandments because they help us to love. They help us enter more deeply into our relationships, both with God and one another. Love frees us to be our best selves, frees us even enough that we might be willing to surrender our lives for the sake of our beloved.

Prayers
others may be added

Through the sacraments, we are grafted into the divine life of God. Let us pray to remain ever united to Christ Jesus, the source of our joy:

◆ Keep us united in you, O Lord.

For the Church, that she may proclaim the word of God with charity, audacity, and clarity, we pray: ◆ For all wealthy nations, that they may generously share their riches and resources with those who are in need, we pray: ◆ For those in the midst of marital or familial strife, that they have the grace to remain united together and work through their difficulties, we pray: ◆ For those who suffer from sadness, depression, and anxiety, that they may encounter the person of Christ Jesus who brings complete and full joy, we pray: ◆ For the members of our parish community, that they may remain united to Christ through the practice of quiet prayer and contemplation, we pray: ◆

Our Father . . .

Good Father,
you love us with the same love
with which you love your Son.
Teach us how to remain in your love.
Fill us with your joy, and make our
    joy complete,
that we may be faithful witnesses
to render testimony to your glory.
We ask this through Christ our Lord.
Amen.

✝ Proclaim God's marvelous deeds to all the nations.

Friday, May 11, 2012
Easter Weekday

✝ I will give you thanks among the peoples, O Lord.

Psalm 66 *page 410*

Reading *John 15:12–17*

Jesus said to his disciples: "This is my commandment: love one another as I love you. No one has greater love than this, to lay down one's life for one's friends. You are my friends if you do what I command you. I no longer call you slaves, because a slave does not know what his master is doing. I have called you friends, because I have told you everything I have heard from my Father. It was not you who chose me, but I who chose you and appointed you to go and bear fruit that will remain, so that whatever you ask the Father in my name he may give you. This I command you: love one another."

Reflection

Jesus commands us to love. He has commanded us to love one another as he has loved us. These are strong words, because Jesus has held nothing back in emptying out his life for us. Upon the cross, and through the sacraments, he has given us his whole self and offered us his own resurrected life. God has chosen us and appointed us to love and to bear fruit that will remain if we remain in him.

Prayers *others may be added*

Hear our prayers as we say:

◆ Keep us in your love, O Lord.

For the missionary Church, that she may be strengthened in her work as the "universal sacrament of salvation," by bringing all peoples into communion with the Holy Trinity, we pray: ◆ For all men and women, that they may generously respond to Christ's radical call to love through the holy vocations of marriage and priestly and religious life, we pray: ◆ For the United States, that its people may continue to be an example of love for one another through respect for life and service toward the poor, we pray: ◆ For those who suffer from abuse, neglect, or poverty, that they may be supported through the presence and consolation of friends, we pray: ◆ For meditation on the life of Christ, that we may learn the true meaning of friendship and have the courage to die to ourselves daily out of love for one another, we pray: ◆

Our Father . . .

Jesus, our Master and Teacher,
you call us to follow your example
and to imitate your life of love for
   all peoples.
Teach us how to love so that in you
we may bear fruit that will remain
for the glory of the Father.
You live and reign forever.
Amen.

✝ I will give you thanks among the peoples, O Lord.

Saturday, May 12, 2012
Easter Weekday

✝ Let all the earth cry out to God with joy.

Psalm 118 page 418

Reading John 15:18–21

Jesus said to his disciples: "If the world hates you, realize that it hated me first. If you belonged to the world, the world would love its own; but because you do not belong to the world, and I have chosen you out of the world, the world hates you. Remember the word I spoke to you, 'No slave is greater than his master.' If they persecuted me, they will also persecute you. If they kept my word, they will also keep yours. And they will do all these things to you on account of my name, because they do not know the one who sent me."

Reflection

We do not belong to the world; rather, Jesus has chosen us out of the world, and we belong to him. Therefore, we ought not to be surprised if we are criticized or rebuked for our faith, because our Lord and Master Jesus was likewise persecuted. Whether we are loved or hated by others for Christ's name, the truth remains the same: we belong to the Lord.

Prayers *others may be added*

Let us pray:

◆ Reveal to us your Father's love.

For the Church throughout the world, especially in areas of persecution, war, and tyranny, that Christians may remain steadfast, and that their witness and suffering may bring about the salvation of souls, we pray: ◆ For the whole world, that peoples of all nations may come to know the love of the Father, we pray: ◆ For those who suffer on account of Jesus' name, we pray: ◆ For all mothers of our community who are awaiting the birth of a child, for those with difficult pregnancies or difficulties in trying to conceive, we pray: ◆ For those who have never known the love of God, that Christians may not be afraid to speak about the joy of belonging to the Lord, we pray: ◆

Our Father . . .

Father,
we praise and worship you for your
    goodness and mercy.
Keep us safely united to you in times of
    difficulty and persecution.
May our faith never waver out of vanity
    or desire for human respect.
May all peoples come to know your
    fatherly love and care,
that you reveal in your Son, Jesus Christ,
who lives and reigns with you in the unity
    of the Holy Spirit,
one God, forever and ever.
Amen.

✝ Let all the earth cry out to God with joy.

Sunday, May 13, 2012
Sixth Sunday of Easter

☩ The Lord has revealed to the nations his saving power.

Psalm 66
page 410

Reading
John 15:9–10

Jesus said to his disciples: "As the Father loves me, so I also love you. Remain in my love. If you keep my commandments, you will remain in my love, just as I have kept my Father's commandments and remain in his love."

Reflection

Today Jesus gives us a new commandment: to love one another. The new law of Jesus is fundamentally a law of love. Jesus invites us to remain in his love. We are called to remain in the love that he has revealed to us through the outpouring of the cross and the glory of his Resurrection. Through love, we enter into complete joy and life. May the love of the Father bear fruit in our lives as we remain united in Christ and the Holy Spirit.

Prayers
others may be added

Jesus, you teach us that whatever we ask the Father in your name, you will grant us. Hear the petitions we place before you as we say:

◆ Father, send us your Spirit of love.

For the Church, that, through the work of all missionaries, priests, religious, and laity, she may be sent into the world to bring all peoples to the truth found in Jesus Christ, we pray: ◆ For all ecumenical endeavors among nations, that, through dialogue and conflict resolution, they may achieve new ways of finding peace and unity, we pray: ◆ For all the sick, that, united to Christ, they may be able to find joy in their sufferings through patience and perseverance, we pray: ◆ For all wealthy nations, that they may generously share their riches and resources with those who are in need, we pray: ◆ For those in the midst of marital or familial strife, that they have the grace to remain united together and work through their difficulties, we pray: ◆ For those who suffer from sadness, depression, and anxiety, that they may encounter the person of Christ Jesus who brings complete and full joy, we pray: ◆ For the members of our parish community, that they may remain united to Christ through the practice of quiet prayer and contemplation, we pray: ◆

Our Father . . .

Heavenly Father,
you are the source of unending love.
In your Son, you have appointed us to go
and to bear much fruit that will remain.
Send your Spirit upon us,
that we may always remain in the eternal
    love of the Trinity,
and go out to share your love with those
    around us.
We ask through our Lord Jesus Christ,
    your Son,
who lives and reigns with you in the unity
    of the Holy Spirit,
one God, forever and ever.
Amen.

☩ The Lord has revealed to the nations his saving power.

Monday, May 14, 2012
Feast of Saint Matthias, Apostle

† The Lord will give him a seat with the leaders of his people.

Psalm 118
page 418

Reading
John 15:9–17

Jesus said to his disciples: "As the Father loves me, so I also love you. Remain in my love. If you keep my commandments, you will remain in my love, just as I have kept my Father's commandments and remain in his love.

"I have told you this so that my joy might be in you and your joy might be complete. This is my commandment: love one another as I love you. No one has greater love than this, to lay down one's life for one's friends. You are my friends if you do what I command you. I no longer call you slaves, because a slave does not know what his master is doing. I have called you friends, because I have told you everything I have heard from my Father. It was not you who chose me, but I who chose you and appointed you to go and bear fruit that will remain, so that whatever you ask the Father in my name he may give you. This I command you: love one another."

Reflection

Today we hear how to be a saint: remain in Christ's love. Jesus' new commandment of love is the heart of the Gospel message. First, we must remain in his love. He tells us that there is no greater love than to give one's life for one's friends. Through his death on the cross and through his glorious Resurrection, Jesus has shown us the true meaning of friendship as he has given us his life and poured out his love for us. May we remain in his love and live in his joy to bear much fruit.

Prayers
others may be added

Father, in your Son, you sent us the Advocate, the Spirit of truth, to give testimony. Hear the prayers we present before you today:

◆ Come, Holy Spirit; renew the face of the earth.

For the Church, that she may continue to hand on the truth of Jesus to all peoples through holy and faithful testimony of its members, we pray: ◆ For all Christians persecuted for the name of Jesus, that their testimony may bring about conversion and a deeper knowledge of the Father, we pray: ◆ For all who make a living through manual labor, that, through the work of their hands, they may give glory to God, we pray: ◆ For those who suffer silently in pain and sadness, that the Holy Spirit may be their Advocate to bring them peace, freedom, and healing, we pray: ◆ For all the military who have died in active duty, we pray: ◆

Our Father . . .

Heavenly Father,
we rejoice in the life of your Son,
Jesus Christ, risen from the dead,
and we praise you with music
and song for the glory your name.
We ask this through Christ our Lord.
Amen.

† The Lord will give him a seat with the leaders of his people.

✝ Your right hand saves me, O Lord.

Psalm 66   *page 410*

Reading   *John 16:5–11*

Jesus said to his disciples: "Now I am going to the one who sent me, and not one of you asks me, 'Where are you going?' But because I told you this, grief has filled your hearts. But I tell you the truth, it is better for you that I go. For if I do not go, the Advocate will not come to you. But if I go, I will send him to you. And when he comes he will convict the world in regard to sin and righteousness and condemnation: sin, because they do not believe in me; righteousness, because I am going to the Father and you will no longer see me; condemnation, because the ruler of this world has been condemned."

Reflection

In today's Gospel, Jesus consoles his apostles who are saddened that he must return to the Father. But Jesus returns to the Father in glory to send us the gift of the Spirit. Although we do not physically see Jesus as the apostles did, Jesus remains present among us, and he sends his Spirit upon us. The Holy Spirit is the Consoler, who comforts us in our sorrow and turns our hearts to the Lord in truth and righteousness.

Prayers   *others may be added*

Father, you send us your Holy Spirit in Jesus Christ to convict the world of sin and righteousness and condemnation. Let us pray:

◆ Holy Spirit, console us in our sorrow.

For the Church, the Holy Father, all priests and deacons, that they may always offer true and holy testimony to the truth, we pray: ◆ For government officials, that they may work together in unity to bring about righteousness, justice, and peace throughout the world, we pray: ◆ For all those who are grieving, that Our Lady, Comfort of the Afflicted, will be present to them in their pain to offer consolation and relief, we pray: ◆ For all farmers, that, through the prayers of Saint Isidore, their toil of the land may render rewards in bountiful harvest in the glory of all God's creation, we pray: ◆

Our Father . . .

Good and loving Father,
you provide us with everything we need.
By your Word, you comfort your people,
and you send us the Advocate, the Spirit
to lead us to all truth.
You are our only consolation, Lord.
Strengthen us and keep us faithful to you.
We ask this through Christ our Lord.
Amen.

✝ Your right hand saves me, O Lord.

✝ Heaven and earth are full of your glory.

Psalm 118 *page 418*

Reading *John 16:12–15*

Jesus said to his disciples: "I have much more to tell you, but you cannot bear it now. But when he comes, the Spirit of truth, he will guide you to all truth. He will not speak on his own, but he will speak what he hears, and will declare to you the things that are coming. He will glorify me, because he will take from what is mine and declare it to you. Everything that the Father has is mine; for this reason I told you that he will take from what is mine and declare it to you."

Reflection

God shares his Trinitarian life with us. Everything the Father has belongs to the Son, and what belongs to the Son the Spirit gives to us. We receive this life through our participation in the liturgy. We must be disposed and prepared to receive the sacraments, so that we may be able to bear and accept the greatness of the mystery that God desires to share with us.

Prayers *others may be added*

Lord Jesus, you have many things to tell us, yet we cannot yet bear to receive it. Let us pray:

◆ Open our hearts to receive your Spirit.

That the Holy Spirit may lead and guide the Church as a beacon of light to lead all people to the truth, we pray: ◆ That civic leaders may be guided by the Holy Spirit to seek innovative ways to serve the common good of society, we pray: ◆ That Christians may be the hands and feet of the resurrected Lord toward the ill, bedridden, poor, hungry, homeless, and despairing, we pray: ◆

Our Father . . .

Father,
through the prayers of the Blessed
    Mother Mary,
open our hearts to receive
the gift of your Spirit of truth.
Convict us of the truth
and bring us to everlasting life
through your Son, Jesus Christ,
who lives and reigns with you in the unity
    of the Holy Spirit,
one God, forever and ever.
Amen.

✝ Heaven and earth are full of your glory.

✝ God mounts his throne to shouts of joy.

Psalm 66 *page 410*

Reading *Mark 16:15–16*

Jesus said to his disciples: "Go into the whole world and proclaim the gospel to every creature. Whoever believes and is baptized will be saved; whoever does not believe will be condemned."

Reflection

We hear Mark's version of the risen Christ's final commission of his apostles. In the fuller text (what you just heard was an excerpt of the larger reading) are the signs that will accompany their work: exorcism, the ability to speak new languages, preservation from dangers, and healings. The work they are to do is precisely what Jesus did. Mark also tells of Jesus' return to heaven and his enthronement at the right hand of God.

Prayers *others may be added*

Father, you do not promise us happiness in this life, but you promise us joy that the world cannot give. Let us pray:

◆ Come, Holy Spirit, come.

That the Church throughout the world may become more and more a living community that respects and accepts each of its brothers and sisters as members of the same human family, we pray: ◆ That government officials may work to alleviate the evils of world hunger, poverty, and war, we pray: ◆ For all who suffer from sickness, abandonment, abuse, and neglect, we pray: ◆ For those who suffer for righteousness' sake, that God may reward them in their faithfulness, we pray: ◆ For all the faithful departed, and for those who grieve their loss, that they may be comforted and be given new life in Christ, we pray: ◆ For our parish community as we prepare to celebrate Pentecost, we pray: ◆

Our Father . . .

Father,
by the Resurrection of your Son Jesus,
you give us hope that all things
work for good for those who love you.
By the power of your Spirit,
enflame us with solid faith
to remain steadfast in moments
    of difficulty,
confident that all our tears will be turned
into laughter and our sorrows into cries
    of joy.
We ask through Jesus Christ our Lord,
who lives and reigns with you in the unity
    of the Holy Spirit,
one God forever and ever.
Amen.

✝ God mounts his throne to shouts of joy.

Friday, May 18, 2012
Easter Weekday

✝ God is king of all the earth.

Psalm 118 *page 418*

Reading *John 16:20–23*

Jesus said to his disciples: "Amen, amen, I say to you, you will weep and mourn, while the world rejoices; you will grieve, but your grief will become joy. When a woman is in labor, she is in anguish because her hour has arrived; but when she has given birth to a child, she no longer remembers the pain because of her joy that a child has been born into the world. So you also are now in anguish. But I will see you again, and your hearts will rejoice, and no one will take your joy away from you. On that day you will not question me about anything. Amen, amen, I say to you, whatever you ask the Father in my name he will give you."

Reflection

There is nothing fun about suffering. However, in Jesus Christ all suffering has purpose and meaning. The Resurrection gives us faith that a glory better than we could ever imagine can be brought out of each and every kind of suffering. Even though, in the midst of great pain, this can be difficult to believe, we must remember in faith that our grief will be turned to joy—a joy so great we will not even remember the past pain.

Prayers *others may be added*

Father, in your Son Jesus, you turn our suffering into joy and new life, as we pray:

◆ Lord, hear our prayer.

For all who serve the Church, that they may be humble servants filled with the Spirit of God's generous service, we pray: ◆
For all peoples, that they may come to respect the presence of God in each human person and recognize the beauty of creation throughout the world, we pray: ◆
For all those who suffer great pain— mentally, physically, or emotionally— for those who mourn the loss of children, family members, or friends, that they may receive comfort and that their sorrow may be turned into joy, we pray: ◆
For those of our parish who feel the pressure and stress of economic difficulties, we pray: ◆ For all women expecting babies, for all unwed mothers, and for those in crisis pregnancies, that they may have a safe and healthy delivery, we pray: ◆

Our Father . . .

Father,
send us your Holy Spirit, the Comforter,
to transform our grief into abundant joy
as we await the glory of your heavenly
    kingdom,
where there shall be no more pain or death,
where every tear shall be wiped away, and
where every tongue proclaims the glory
    of your name.
We ask this through Christ our Lord.
Amen.

✝ God is king of all the earth.

✝ God is king of all the earth.

Psalm 66 *page 410*

Reading *John 16:23b–24*

Jesus said to his disciples: "Amen, amen, I say to you, whatever you ask the Father in my name he will give you. Until now you have not asked anything in my name; ask and you will receive, so that your joy may be complete."

Reflection

We are loved by the Father. We are children of God. This is the great mystery of love that Jesus Christ reveals to us. God the Father loves each one of us. Therefore, let us ask and receive. Our Father is pleased to bestow lavish and abundant good gifts upon us, his children.

Prayers *others may be added*

Jesus, you assure us that anything we ask the Father in your name he will grant to us. Coming before you in confidence and faith, we beg you to hear our prayers:

◆ Lord, hear our prayer.

For the Church and all her members, that they may become more and more united in love and joy, we pray: ◆ For world peace, we pray: ◆ For the complete healing of all the sick in hospitals, nursing homes, and clinics, we pray: ◆ For those who suffer the loneliness, emptiness, and dissatisfaction of a life without God, we pray: ◆ For those who are facing difficult decisions, that they may be guided by the life of Christ to see clearly the right path to choose, we pray: ◆ For all wealthy nations, that they may generously share their riches and resources with those who are in need, we pray: ◆ For those in the midst of marital or familial strife, that they may have the grace to remain united together and work through their difficulties, we pray: ◆ For those who suffer from sadness, depression, and anxiety, that they may encounter the person of Christ Jesus who brings complete and full joy, we pray: ◆ For the members of our parish community, that they may ever remain united to Christ through the practice of quiet prayer and contemplation, we pray: ◆

Our Father . . .

Holy God,
in your Son, Jesus Christ,
you reveal to us your fatherly love.
You are our Father, and we are
    your children.
By the power of your Spirit,
grant us the grace to live
in the freedom and joy
of the children of God.
We ask this through our Lord Jesus
    Christ, your Son,
who lives and reigns with you in the unity
    of the Holy Spirit,
one God, forever and ever.
Amen.

✝ God is king of all the earth.

✝ The Lord has set his throne in heaven.

Psalm 47 *page 408*

Reading *Mark 16:15–20*

Jesus said to his disciples: "Go into the whole world and proclaim the gospel to every creature. Whoever believes and is baptized will be saved; whoever does not believe will be condemned. These signs will accompany those who believe: in my name they will drive out demons, they will speak new languages. They will pick up serpents with their hands, and if they drink any deadly thing, it will not harm them. They will lay hands on the sick, and they will recover."

Then the Lord Jesus, after he spoke to them, was taken up into heaven and took his seat at the right hand of God. But they went forth and preached everywhere, while the Lord worked with them and confirmed the word through accompanying signs.

Reflection

Forty days after the Resurrection, Jesus ascended into heaven in glory and took his place at the right hand of the Father. He commissioned his apostles to go out to all the nations to proclaim the Gospel. Today, Jesus sends us out to speak his words and performs his good deeds as he accompanies us and works among us.

Prayers *others may be added*

Jesus, ascended to the Father, hear our prayers as we pray:

♦ Come, Holy Spirit, fill the hearts of your faithful.

For the Church, that through the glory of the Ascension, she may be filled with the light of Christ to proclaim the mystery of God to all peoples, we pray: ♦ For all missionaries, civic leaders, clergy, and catechists; for all who work for justice and peace, that they may announce the Gospel to all creation, we pray: ♦ For those who are ill, that, through the prayers and aid of others, they may be healed for the glory of God, we pray: ♦ For the missionary activities of our parish, that the Holy Spirit may ignite the hearts of all who serve in missions throughout the world and in our own community, we pray: ♦ As we await the solemnity of Pentecost, that we may ask and pray for the gift of the Holy Spirit to clothe us from on high with his power and love, we pray: ♦

Our Father . . .

Heavenly Father,
today your Son ascends to the throne
    of heaven
where he takes his seat with you in glory.
Send out your Spirit upon all peoples,
that we may have the boldness
    to proclaim
the Good News of the Gospel to
    all creation.
We ask this through Christ our Lord.
Amen.

✝ The Lord has set his throne in heaven.

Monday, May 21, 2012
Easter Weekday

✝ Sing to God, O kingdoms of the earth.

Psalm 47   *page 408*

Reading   *John 16:29–33*

The disciples said to Jesus, "Now you are talking plainly, and not in any figure of speech. Now we realize that you know everything and that you do not need to have anyone question you. Because of this we believe that you came from God." Jesus answered them, "Do you believe now? Behold, the hour is coming and has arrived when each of you will be scattered to his own home and you will leave me alone. But I am not alone, because the Father is with me. I have told you this so that you might have peace in me. In the world you will have trouble, but take courage, I have conquered the world."

Reflection

What words of comfort Jesus speaks to us today: "Take courage, I have conquered the world." In Jesus we receive peace, and he gives us fortitude to persevere in difficulties great and small. By the Resurrection, Jesus has conquered all evil and all death. Let us not leave Jesus alone, but rather remain united to him in whom the victory is won.

Prayers   *others may be added*

Jesus, you do not promise us peace in this world, but rather we receive peace united in you. Let us pray:

◆ Come, Spirit of piety and fortitude.

For the Church, that she may remain united in the light of the resurrected Christ who has conquered all evil and brings us his peace, we pray: ◆ For all those who suffer from mental disorders, AIDS, cancer, and terminal illnesses, that by the power of the Passion, death, Resurrection, and Ascension of Jesus they may receive full healing and peace, we pray: ◆ For those who are weighed down by the cares of the world, we pray: ◆ For the grace and strength to flee from all occasions of sin that can separate us from his love, we pray: ◆

Our Father . . .

King Jesus,
by your Paschal Mystery
we see your strength and your glory.
You are the victor over all sin and evil.
United to you, we have peace in you
who have conquered the world.
Send us your Spirit so that we may have
courage to remain always united to you,
who live and reign with the Father
in the unity of the Holy Spirit,
one God, forever and ever.
Amen.

✝ Sing to God, O kingdoms of the earth.

Tuesday, May 22, 2012
Easter Weekday

✝ Sing to God, O kingdoms of the earth.

Psalm 47
page 408

Reading
John 17:1–5

Jesus raised his eyes to heaven and said, "Father, the hour has come. Give glory to your son, so that your son may glorify you, just as you gave him authority over all people, so that your son may give eternal life to all you gave him. Now this is eternal life, that they should know you, the only true God, and the one whom you sent, Jesus Christ. I glorified you on earth by accomplishing the work that you gave me to do. Now glorify me, Father, with you, with the glory that I had with you before the world began."

Reflection

The Father has sent the Son among us to give us abundant life in him who is life itself. In today's Gospel, Jesus prays for us. He asks the Father to bless and protect us in the world so that we may have eternal life through knowledge of him and his Father. In this way, the Father is glorified in the Son, and the Son is glorified in the Father who gives life to us who belong to him.

Prayers
others may be added

Father, may you be glorified in your Son, and may your Son be glorified in you throughout all the world. Let us pray:

◆ Come, Spirit of wonder and awe.

For the Church, that she may accomplish the work and mission given to her by Jesus Christ for the glory of God, we pray: ◆ For the people of all countries, that they may see each other as fellow members of the same human family and come to the aid of those in need, we pray: ◆ For all the sick, the weak, poor, hungry, homeless, and the downtrodden, that their sufferings may be for the glory of God who transforms suffering into life, we pray: ◆ For all those who struggle with familial or marital distress, that the Lord may bring peace to all family relationships, we pray: ◆

Our Father . . .

Heavenly Father,
through the witness of your saints,
you teach us how to persevere in holiness.
May we learn patience in suffering,
peace in the midst of difficulties,
and may we have unwavering faith that
nothing is impossible with you, O God.
We ask this through Christ our Lord.
Amen.

✝ Sing to God, O kingdoms of the earth.

✝ Sing to God, O kingdoms of the earth.

Psalm 47 *page 408*

Reading *John 17:14–19*

[Jesus said] "I gave them your word, and the world hated them, because they do not belong to the world any more than I belong to the world. I do not ask that you take them out of the world but that you keep them from the Evil One. They do not belong to the world any more than I belong to the world. Consecrate them in the truth. Your word is truth. As you sent me into the world, so I sent them into the world. And I consecrate myself for them, so that they also may be consecrated in truth."

Reflection

In the Gospel, Jesus prays for us and entrusts us to the care of the Father, so that he may keep us in his name and protect and guard us from the evil one. How beautiful to hear the words of Jesus' prayer to the Father for us. With great love and fervor, Jesus consecrates us in the truth, and he sends us forth into the world under the protection of his word.

Prayers *others may be added*

Father, your word is truth. Consecrate us in the truth of your Son, Jesus Christ. Let us pray:

◆ Come, Spirit of love and joy.

For the Church, that she may provide social services to care for the good of all her members in need, we pray: ◆
For Christians, Muslims, Jews, and people of every creed and denomination everywhere, that we may be united as one as brothers and sisters of the same God, we pray: ◆ For those who work to preserve, protect, and defend the truth in all areas of human life, we pray: ◆ For all young people and university students, that, during this time of their youth, they may be protected from all evil and guided to the truth through the pursuit of knowledge, genuine friendship, and the discovery of the goodness of life, we pray: ◆

Our Father . . .

Holy Father,
your Son, Jesus Christ,
intercedes for us on our behalf,
begging you to keep us safe.
Send us your Spirit of truth,
and consecrate us in your truth
so that we may fully share in your joy.
We ask this through Christ our Lord.
Amen.

✝ Sing to God, O kingdoms of the earth.

✟ Keep me safe, O God; you are
my hope.

Psalm 47   page 408

Reading   John 17:20–26

Lifting up his eyes to heaven, Jesus prayed saying: "I pray not only for these, but also for those who will believe in me through their word, so that they may all be one, as you, Father, are in me and I in you, that they also may be in us, that the world may believe that you sent me. And I have given them the glory you gave me, so that they may be one, as we are one, I in them and you in me, that they may be brought to perfection as one, that the world may know that you sent me, and that you loved them even as you loved me. Father, they are your gift to me. I wish that where I am they also may be with me, that they may see my glory that you gave me, because you loved me before the foundation of the world. Righteous Father, the world also does not know you, but I know you, and they know that you sent me. I made known to them your name and I will make it known, that the love with which you loved me may be in them and I in them."

Reflection

The world does not know the great gift of life in God. Frequently, we too do not understand our Father's love for us in his Son. But, today we continue to listen to the words of Jesus' prayer for us. How beautiful to hear Jesus say that we are a gift to him! Jesus not only prays for us, but also for all our friends, our family, our acquaintances, and all those who will come to encounter God through us.

Prayers   others may be added

Father, may your love be in us as we pray:

◆ Come, Spirit of peace and kindness.

For the Church, we pray: ◆ For the end of violence, child abuse, war, terrorism, and anti-life regimes, we pray: ◆ For all the sick and suffering, we pray: ◆ For our family and friends, we pray: ◆

Our Father . . .

Righteous Father,
may the offering of our lives
be a gift to you, and may your goodness
be proclaimed throughout all the earth.
Make us faithful witnesses of your glory
as you send us out to testify to your love
so all peoples may believe in the truth
of your Son, Jesus Christ our Lord,
who lives and reigns with you in the unity
    of the Holy Spirit,
one God, forever and ever.
Amen.

✟ Keep me safe, O God; you are
my hope.

✝ The Lord has established his throne in heaven.

Psalm 47   *page 408*

Reading   *John 21:17b–19*

Jesus said to [Simon Peter], "Feed my sheep. Amen, amen, I say to you, when you were younger, you used to dress yourself and go where you wanted; but when you grow old, you will stretch out your hands, and someone else will dress you and lead you where you do not want to go." He said this signifying by what kind of death he would glorify God. And when he had said this, he said to him, "Follow me."

Reflection

During the Passion, Peter had denied Jesus three times, but after the Resurrection, Jesus asks for an affirmation of Peter's love for him followed by the command to feed and tend to his sheep. Likewise, Jesus asks us to follow him and feed his sheep.

Prayers   *others may be added*

Heavenly Father, your Son is the Good Shepherd who lays down his life for his sheep. Let us pray:

◆ Come, Spirit of patience and gentleness.

For the Pope, the Bishop of Rome, for all bishops and priests, that, following the example of Saint Peter, they may be faithful shepherds to feed and tend to Christ's flock of the Church, we pray: ◆ For all civic leaders, that they may seek the common good of all people by feeding the hungry, clothing the naked, serving the poor, sheltering the homeless, and comforting the afflicted, we pray: ◆ For all doctors, nurses, caregivers, and volunteers in hospitals and medical clinics, that their work may be blessed as they love and care for the sick, suffering, and dying, we pray: ◆ For all wealthy nations, that they may generously share their riches and resources with those who are in need, we pray: ◆ For those in the midst of marital or familial strife, that they have the grace to remain united together and work through their difficulties, we pray: ◆ For those who suffer from sadness, depression, and anxiety, that they may encounter the person of Christ Jesus who brings complete and full joy, we pray: ◆ For the members of our parish community, that they may ever remain united to Christ through the practice of quiet prayer and contemplation, we pray: ◆

Our Father . . .

Jesus, our Good Shepherd,
you ask us to love you above all things.
Nothing is more important than you.
Send your Spirit upon us to teach us
how to love you with all our hearts,
that, in union with you,
our love for you may overflow in love
for our fellow brothers and sisters.
You live and reign forever.
Amen.

✝ The Lord has established his throne in heaven.

✝ The just will gaze on your face,
O Lord.

Psalm 47
page 408

Reading
John 21:24–25

It is this disciple who testifies to these things and has written them, and we know that his testimony is true. There are also many other things that Jesus did, but if these were to be described individually, I do not think the whole world would contain the books that would be written.

Reflection

Today we celebrate the memorial of Saint Philip Neri, apostle of Rome, who had a great love for the youth, and was known for his cheerfulness and deep love for all people. He constantly told his friends and followers to flee from the vanity of the world and seek Christ, our only true happiness.

Prayers
others may be added

Father, in the witness of your saints, you teach us how to live the Gospel. Fill us with your Spirit as we pray:

◆ Come, Spirit of faithfulness and generosity.

For the Holy Father, all priests, religious, bishops, deacons, and laity, that they may be filled with the same love and cheerfulness of Saint Philip Neri to be faithful Christian witnesses of God's love, we pray: ◆ For all government officials, that they may be open to dialogue in order to discover solutions to current economic, social, environmental, and legislative problems, we pray: ◆ For all the sick and handicapped, that they may find joy in their suffering, we pray: ◆ For all youth, that they may not be swayed by the empty temptations of the world, but instead find the joy and true happiness that comes from a life united to Jesus Christ, we pray: ◆ For all those who are preparing to receive the gift of the Spirit through the sacrament of Confirmation, we pray: ◆ That, through the prayers of the Blessed Virgin Mary, all of us may be freed from the vanities of the world and be witnesses of cheerfulness and joy, we pray: ◆

Our Father . . .

Heavenly Father,
you inflamed the heart
of your servant, Saint Philip Neri,
with the burning love of the Spirit.
Grant that we, too, may increase
in love and joy in the Spirit
as we await his coming this Pentecost.
We ask through our Lord Jesus Christ,
your Son,
who lives and reigns with you in the unity
of the Holy Spirit,
one God, forever and ever.
Amen.

✝ The just will gaze on your face,
O Lord.

✝ Lord, send out your Spirit, and
renew the face of the earth.

Psalm 104 *page 416*

Reading *John 16:12–15*

[Jesus said to his disciples:] "I have much more to tell you, but you cannot bear it now. But when he comes, the Spirit of truth, he will guide you to all truth. He will not speak on his own, but he will speak what he hears, and will declare to you the things that are coming. He will glorify me, because he will take from it what is mine and declare it to you."

Reflection

After Jesus ascended to the Father in heaven, the apostles waited and prayed for the promised gift of the Spirit. On the great day of Pentecost, the Holy Spirit came upon the apostles, appearing as tongues of fire, and they went out proclaiming the Gospel, speaking new languages and performing mighty deeds for the glory of God.

Prayers *others may be added*

Lord, you send us your Spirit. Open our hearts to receive you as we pray:

◆ Lord, send out your Spirit and renew the face of the earth.

That, like that first day of Pentecost, the Church may be renewed with the same fervor and fire of the Holy Spirit to go out to proclaim with boldness and fearlessness the Good News of Jesus Christ, we pray: ◆ That nations of every race, creed, and tongue, may be enlivened by the Holy Spirit, who brings peace and unity, we pray: ◆ That the Spirit of life may breathe upon all those who are sick or suffering to restore them to health of mind and body, we pray: ◆ That the grace of this most holy feast may take root in our parish community through the fruits of fuller participation at Mass, frequent reading of the scriptures, apostolic works of mercy, and fraternal charity among one another, we pray: ◆ That we may be open to receive the gift of the Holy Spirit, who transforms our lives, our families, and our work in newness and genuine love, we pray: ◆

Our Father . . .

Father of life,
by the death and Resurrection of your Son,
you have poured upon us your Holy Spirit
through the sacrament of Baptism.
Stir into flame this gift that we
    have received,
that we may be transformed in the Spirit
with the same power with which
    you clothed
the apostles that first Pentecost day.
We ask this through our Lord Jesus
    Christ, your Son,
who lives and reigns with you in the unity
    of the Holy Spirit,
one God, forever and ever.
Amen.

✝ Lord, send out your Spirit, and
renew the face of the earth.

Monday, May 28, 2012
Weekday
Eighth Week in Ordinary Time

✝ The Lord will remember his covenant for ever.

Psalm 19 — page 403

Reading — Mark 10:17–21

As Jesus was setting out on a journey, a man ran up, knelt down before him, and asked him, "Good teacher, what must I do to inherit eternal life?" Jesus answered him, "Why do you call me good? No one is good but God alone. You know the commandments: / *You shall not kill; / you shall not commit adultery; you shall not steal; / you shall not bear false witness; / you shall not defraud; / honor your father and your mother.*" / He replied and said to him, "Teacher, all of these I have observed from my youth." Jesus, looking at him, loved him and said to him, "You are lacking in one thing. Go, sell what you have, and give to the poor and you will have treasure in heaven; then come, follow me."

Reflection

Yesterday we concluded the glorious Easter Time with the celebration of Pentecost, and today we re-enter Ordinary Time. In today's Gospel, we encounter the rich man who asks Jesus what he must do to enter the kingdom of God. The man goes away sad, because he has many material possessions and does not recognize the true riches that he would receive in giving up everything to follow Christ.

Prayers — *others may be added*

O God, with you, nothing is impossible. Instruct us what we must do to enter into your kingdom, as we pray:

◆ **Good Teacher, hear our prayer.**

That the Holy Father, all priests and bishops, religious, and lay faithful, and all the members of the Church may not be tempted by the lure of riches, but rather, that they may be detached from material goods in order to follow Christ, we pray: ◆ That all civic leaders may follow God's commandments as they seek to honor human life, support justice, protect the innocent, and defend the truth, we pray: ◆ That all the poor, the weak, and the sick may follow after Christ, who guides us into his kingdom, we pray: ◆ That our nation, our family, and all the world may be liberated from the chains of materialism that prevent us from true freedom and happiness, we pray: ◆

Our Father . . .

Loving Father,
through your Son, the Word Incarnate,
you teach us about your kingdom.
Through the prayers of Mary
    Immaculate,
open our hearts and give us courage
to respond to your Word
with a generous and loving "yes."
We ask through Christ our Lord.
Amen.

✝ The Lord will remember his covenant for ever.

Tuesday, May 29, 2012
Weekday

✝ The Lord has made known his salvation.

Psalm 144 *page 422*

Reading *Mark 10:28–31*

Peter began to say to Jesus, "We have given up everything and followed you." Jesus said, "Amen, I say to you, there is no one who has given up house or brothers or sisters or mother or father or children or lands for my sake and for the sake of the Gospel who will not receive a hundred times more now in this present age: houses and brothers and sisters and mothers and children and lands, with persecutions, and eternal life in the age to come. But many that are first will be last, and the last will be first."

Reflection

The apostles and the saints give us examples that it is possible to give up everything and follow Jesus for the sake of gaining a life richer in happiness than what the world can give. In today's Gospel, Jesus assures his blessing on those who give up the goods of the world in order to follow after him. He promises that whoever gives give up worldly goods for his sake will receive a hundred times more in heaven and also in this life.

Prayers *others may be added*

Jesus, you give us your promise of freedom and happiness. Let us pray:

◆ Give us courage to follow after you, Lord.

For the Holy Father, all priests, religious brothers and sisters, lay consecrated, and all the Church's faithful who have given up the riches of this world for the glory of the kingdom of God, that they may receive abundant blessings, we pray: ◆ For all those who serve their countries through military service, social work, and political activity, we pray: ◆ For the poor, the homeless, the sick, and those in difficulty, that they may receive the help and aid they need, we pray: ◆ For our local community, that, united in the faith, we may follow after the Lord as one body, we pray: ◆ For the grace each day to turn from our selfish desires in order to seek God in service to others, we pray: ◆

Our Father . . .

Loving Jesus,
you call our hearts by the gentle whisper of your Holy Spirit to follow after you along the way to the Father.
Through the intercession of Mary, Seat of Wisdom,
may we not become distracted by the worldly goods, but rather keep our eyes fixed on you.
We ask this through Christ our Lord. Amen.

✝ The Lord has made known his salvation.

✝ Praise the Lord, Jerusalem.

Psalm 34 *page 406*

Reading *Mark 10:32–37*

The disciples were on the way, going up to Jerusalem, and Jesus went ahead of them. They were amazed, and those who followed were afraid. Taking the Twelve aside again, he began to tell them what was going to happen to him. "Behold, we are going up to Jerusalem, and the Son of Man will be handed over to the chief priests and the scribes, and they will condemn him to death and hand him over to the Gentiles who will mock him, spit upon him, scourge him, and put him to death, but after three days he will rise." Then James and John, the sons of Zebedee, came to Jesus and said to him, "Teacher, we want you to do for us whatever we ask of you." He replied, "What do you wish me to do for you?" They answered him, "Grant that in your glory we may sit one at your right and the other at your left."

Reflection

When James and John ask to sit at Jesus' right hand in glory, Jesus teaches that the truly greatest is the servant of others. Jesus gives us his own example as his entire life reveals service, culminating in giving his life upon the cross as ransom to save us from our sins. Jesus, likewise, offers us to drink from the cup that he drinks with the firm hope that all suffering will be turned into ever more radiant glory.

Prayers *others may be added*

You teach us that the first shall be last and the last shall be first. Confident in your mercy for us, we pray:

◆ Give us a servant's heart, O Lord.

For the Holy Father, the Servant of the servants of God, that he may be strengthened to faithfully fulfill his earthly mission in service to Christ and his Church, we pray: ◆ For public officials and world rulers, that they may not lord over their authority, but rather perform their duties with service toward the common good of all society, we pray: ◆ That the poor, the sick, and the suffering may attain true greatness in their weakness by remaining united to Jesus, the Suffering Servant, we pray: ◆ For all of us, that we may not be preoccupied by desires for worldly honors and ranks of status, we pray: ◆

Our Father . . .

Lord Jesus,
you teach us that the first shall be last
and the last shall be first.
You instruct us that the greatest
among us will be the servant.
Give us hearts of service, Lord,
to seek the good of others before
the satisfaction of our own desires.
You live and reign forever.
Amen.

✝ Praise the Lord, Jerusalem.

Thursday, May 31, 2012
Feast of the Visitation of the Blessed Virgin Mary

✝ Blessed are you who believed.
(*Luke 1:45*)

Psalm 146 *page 423*

Reading *Luke 1:39–41a*

Mary set out and traveled to the hill country in haste to a town of Judah, where she entered the house of Zechariah and greeted Elizabeth. When Elizabeth heard Mary's greeting, the infant leaped in her womb, and Elizabeth, filled with the Holy Spirit, cried out in a loud voice and said, "Blessed are you among women, and blessed is the fruit of your womb. . . . "

Reflection

Today we conclude the month dedicated to Our Lady with the celebration of the feast of the Visitation. After receiving the announcement from the angel that she would be the Mother of God, Mary goes in haste to visit her cousin Elizabeth who is also pregnant with child. The Holy Spirit who overshadows Mary at the Annunciation urges her to serve her relative in charity. In their encounter, Mary and Elizabeth glorify God and proclaim the great things that God has done.

Prayers *others may be added*

The soul of Mary magnifies and glorifies your name, O Lord. Let us pray:

◆ Lord, you have done great things for us, and holy is your name.

For the Church, that she may constantly work to seek out the poor, lonely, weak, and the marginalized of society, through the service of charitable organizations and the good will of all Christians, we pray: ◆ For governmental officials, that they may respond to the cries of the needy through social justice and works of charity, we pray: ◆ For those who are sick and suffering, that they may be visited by the maternal love and presence of Our Lady, we pray: ◆ For the healing of all families and all familial relations, that, through the intercession of Mary and Elizabeth, families may become renewed in peace and charity, we pray: ◆

Our Father . . .

Heavenly Father,
in the Blessed Mother Mary
you give us the perfect example
of charity and generosity.
Send your Holy Spirit upon us
to enflame us in your gifts,
that we may no longer
think only of ourselves,
but be driven to serve and work
for the good of our neighbor.
We ask this through Christ our Lord.
Amen.

✝ Blessed are you who believed.

Friday, June 1, 2012
Memorial of Saint Justin, Martyr

✝ The Lord comes to judge the earth.

Psalm 95
page 413

Reading
Mark 11:15–17

[Jesus and his disciples] came to Jerusalem, and on entering the temple area he began to drive out those selling and buying there. He overturned the tables of the money changers and the seats of those who were selling doves. He did not permit anyone to carry anything through the temple area. Then he taught them saying, "Is it not written: / *My house shall be called a house of prayer for all peoples? / But you have made it a den of thieves.*" /

Reflection

Jesus arrives in Jerusalem, the goal of his journey. The story of the cleansing of the temple is framed by two rather perplexing incidents involving the fig tree. How could Jesus look for figs if it was not the time for figs—much less curse the tree for being fruitless? Perhaps the story is meant more to emphasize the power of Jesus' word, as well as possess a symbolic value in terms of Israel's fruitlessness. Note that the power of words is the subject of the last three sayings in today's Gospel.

Prayers
others may be added

Casting aside all doubt, we pray:

◆ Lord, hear our prayer.

That united to Jesus, the True Vine, the Church may remain in the love of the Trinity to bring forth good fruit of works of charity, holy vocations, and sacramental life for all peoples, we pray: ◆ That the work of civic leaders may not remain sterile and empty but may flourish in creating environments of justice, security, and peace, we pray: ◆ That those who suffer from injustice, abuse, illness, and neglect may be given healing, we pray: ◆ That all the silent and hidden needs of our parish, local community, and our families may be freed from all doubt and anxiety to have full confidence in our God who knows our needs better than we ourselves, we pray: ◆

Our Father . . .

Loving Father,
you know our needs even before we
    speak them.
Open our hearts to forgive one another
for the hurts they have caused us,
as you, Father, forgive us our sins.
Increase our faith in you, O Lord,
to make us faithful witnesses of your word.
We ask this through Christ our Lord.
Amen.

✝ The Lord comes to judge the earth.

✝ My soul is thirsting for you, O Lord my God.

Psalm 146   *page 423*

Reading   *Mark 11:27–33*

Jesus and his disciples returned once more to Jerusalem. As he was walking in the temple area, the chief priests, the scribes, and the elders approached him and said to him, "By what authority are you doing these things? Or who gave you this authority to do them?" Jesus said to them, "I shall ask you one question. Answer me, and I will tell you by what authority I do these things. Was John's baptism of heavenly or of human origin? Answer me." They discussed this among themselves and said, "If we say, 'Of heavenly origin,' he will say, 'Then why did you not believe him?' But shall we say, 'Of human origin'?"—they feared the crowd, for they all thought John really was a prophet. So they said to Jesus in reply, "We do not know." Then Jesus said to them, "Neither shall I tell you by what authority I do these things."

Reflection

Jesus is not outsmarted by the scribes, Pharisees, and the elders when they ask about the origins of his authority. These learned men do not truly seek an answer to the question they ask, but rather they are trying to entrap Jesus. However, Jesus stumps them with his own question for them, and thus silences their insincere questioning.

Prayers   *others may be added*

Hear the prayer we place before you:

◆ **Omnipotent God, hear our prayer.**

For the Church, we pray: ◆ For world leaders, we pray: ◆ For those who suffer, we pray: ◆ For all peoples, we pray: ◆

Our Father . . .

Lord Jesus,
all power and authority is given
to you by your Father in heaven.
Come in your power and glory
to renew the face of the earth
and restore all things in you.
You live and reign forever.
Amen.

✝ My soul is thirsting for you, O Lord my God.

☦ Blessed be the people the Lord has chosen to be his own.

Psalm 100 *page 414*

Reading *Matthew 28:16–20*

The eleven disciples went to Galilee, to the mountain to which Jesus had ordered them. When they saw him, they worshipped, but they doubted. Then Jesus approached and said to them, "All power in heaven and on earth has been given to me. Go, therefore, and make disciples of all nations, baptizing in the name of the Father, and of the Son, and of the Holy Spirit, teaching them to observe all that I have commanded you. And behold, I am with you always, until the end of the age."

Reflection

This Sunday we celebrate the mystery of the Trinity: one God in three divine Persons. By the grace given to us in the sacrament of Baptism, the Father, the Son, and the Holy Spirit dwell in our souls and invite us to participate in their Trinitarian life and love. Today, Jesus sends out his disciples to make disciples of all nations and promises that he will remain always with us even to the end of time.

Prayers *others may be added*

Triune God, you promise to remain with us always. Let us pray:

◆ Holy Trinity, draw us into your life and love.

For the Church, that she may continue to lead all people into the mystery of the Trinity through the Person of Jesus Christ, we pray: ◆ For all government officials, that they may work to resolve social conflicts so that all peoples may live in communion with one another in justice, charity, and peace, we pray: ◆ For all who suffer from poverty, injustice, illness, persecution, sadness, or doubt, that they may be assured of the presence of God who is always present to the weak and brokenhearted, we pray: ◆ For the newly baptized, that the light of the life of the Trinity may continue to grow and flourish within them in grace and good works, we pray: ◆

Our Father . . .

Holy Trinity,
we worship you as one God
in three divine Persons,
Father, Son, and Holy Spirit.
By the grace of the sacraments,
draw us more deeply into your
divine life of union so that
all peoples may be transformed
by your life and love.
We ask this through Christ our Lord.
Amen.

☦ Blessed be the people the Lord has chosen to be his own.

✝ In you, my God, I place my trust.

Psalm 103 page 415

Reading Mark 12:1–9

Jesus began to speak to the chief priests, the scribes, and the elders in parables. "A man planted a vineyard, put a hedge around it, dug a wine press, and built a tower. Then he leased it to the tenant farmers and left on a journey. At the proper time he sent a servant to the tenants to obtain from them some of the produce from the vineyard. But they seized him, beat him, and sent him away empty-handed. Again he sent them another servant. And that one they beat over the head and treated shamefully. He sent yet another whom they killed. So, too, many others; some they beat, others they killed. He had one other to send, a beloved son. He sent him to them last of all, thinking, 'They will respect my son.' But those tenants said to one another, 'This is the heir. Come, let us kill him, and the inheritance will be ours.' So they seized him and killed him, and threw him out of the vineyard. What then will the owner of the vineyard do? He will come, put the tenants to death, and give the vineyard to others."

Reflection

In today's Gospel, Jesus confounds the chief priests, scribes, and elders through the parable of the man and the vineyard. This parable reflects God the Father, like the vineyard owner, who sends his only Son who is killed and put to death—on the cross. However, Jesus, the stone rejected by the builders, rises again in majesty for the glory of the Father.

Prayers others may be added

Coming before God, we pray:

◆ Loving Father, hear our prayer.

For the Church, that, guided by the Holy Father, she may remain solid and steadfast upon the rock and cornerstone of Jesus Christ amid all conflicts, trials, and persecutions, we pray: ◆ For leaders of all nations, that they may be good tenants of the vineyard of their nations by upholding the dignity of the human person and common good of all society, we pray: ◆ For all who suffer persecution, abuse, sickness, poverty, and injustice, that the mercy of Christ may be upon them to transform their suffering into glory, we pray: ◆

Our Father . . .

Lord Jesus,
you are the cornerstone
rejected by the builders
in whom shines the glory.
Have mercy on our failings
and keep us faithful in service to you.
You live and reign forever.
Amen.

✝ In you, my God, I place my trust.

Tuesday, June 5, 2012
Memorial of Saint Boniface, Bishop and Martyr

✝ In every age, O Lord, you have been our refuge.

Psalm 145   *page 422*

Reading   *Mark 12:13–17*

Some Pharisees and Herodians were sent to Jesus to ensnare him in his speech. They came and said to him, "Teacher, we know that you are a truthful man and that you are not concerned with anyone's opinion. You do not regard a person's status but teach the way of God in accordance with the truth. Is it lawful to pay the census tax to Ceasar or not? Should we pay or should we not pay?" Knowing their hypocrisy he said to them, "Why are you testing me? Bring me a denarius to look at." They brought one to him and he said to them, "Whose image and inscription is this?" They replied to him, "Caesar's." So Jesus said to them, "Repay to Caesar what belongs to Caesar and to God what belongs to God." They were utterly amazed at him.

Reflection

To be a good Christian, we must also obey just civic laws and perform our everyday duties with virtue. In today's Gospel, Jesus teaches the importance of justice as he says to render to Caesar what is Caesar's, and to God what is God's. In this way, he teaches us the importance of giving what is due regarding our human and social responsibilities and giving our due to God through religion and worship.

Prayers   *others may be added*

Loving God, you teach us the way to happiness and eternal life. Let us pray:

◆ In your justice and mercy, Lord, hear our prayer.

For the members of the Church, that they may not be divided among each other, but be united in the worship of the one true God, we pray: ◆ For government officials, that they may always seek to promote just laws for the good of all peoples, we pray: ◆ For all travelers, prisoners, the sick, and those in need, that the Lord may hear their cry for help, we pray: ◆ For our local community, that they may not close their eyes, nor turn a deaf ear to the cries of the poor and suffering, but rather offer help and aid out of justice toward those in need, we pray: ◆ For the deepening of the virtue of justice to render what is due to God and our neighbor in charity and generosity, we pray: ◆

Our Father . . .

Lord Jesus Christ,
we worship you and give you thanks,
for you are our Master and Teacher.
Instruct us on the way to holiness
and teach us how to sanctify our daily lives
through the humble fulfillment of
　our duties.
You live and reign forever.
Amen.

✝ In every age, O Lord, you have been our refuge.

Wednesday, June 6, 2012
Weekday

✝ To you, O Lord, I lift up my eyes.

Psalm 19 *page 403*

Reading *Mark 12:18–27*

Some Sadducees, who say there is no resurrection, came to Jesus and put this question to him, saying, "Teacher, Moses wrote for us, 'If someone's brother dies, leaving a wife but no child, his brother must take the wife and raise up descendants for his brother.' Now there were seven brothers. The first married a woman and died, leaving no descendants. So the second brother married her and died, leaving no descendants and the third likewise. And the seven left no descendants. Last of all the woman also died. At the resurrection when they arise whose wife will she be? For all seven had been married to her." Jesus said to them, "Are you not misled because you do not know the Scriptures or the power of God? When they rise from the dead, they neither marry nor are given in marriage, but they are like the angels in heaven. As for the dead being raised, have you not read in the Book of Moses, in the passage about the bush, how God told him, *I am the God of Abraham, the God of Isaac, / and the God of Jacob?* He is not God of the dead but of the living. You are greatly misled."

Reflection

Jesus is the Resurrection and the life, the God of the living. God is greater than all suffering and death. He is above all the human complications we create regarding relationships and marriage. God has conquered death, and he brings life into all situations so that we may dwell in unity and peace with him and with one another.

Prayers *others may be added*

Turning to God for wisdom and counsel, we pray:

◆ Lord, hear our prayer.

For the Church, we pray: ◆ For world leaders, we pray: ◆ For all marriages and all relationships, we pray: ◆ For all those who grieve the loss of husbands, fiancés, friends, and loved ones, we pray: ◆ For all young people, we pray: ◆

Our Father . . .

Father of life,
we worship and praise you
as God of the all the living.
Free us from temptations of pessimism,
    cynicism, and despair
and grant us the grace to seek you,
our God of hope,
in the midst of suffering and confusion.
Heal us, Lord,
and grant us your salvation.
We ask this through Christ our Lord.
Amen.

✝ To you, O Lord, I lift up my eyes.

Thursday, June 7, 2012
Weekday

✝ Teach me your ways, O Lord.

Psalm 144 *page 422*

Reading *Mark 12:28–34*

One of the scribes came to Jesus and asked him, "Which is the first of all the commandments?" Jesus replied, "The first is this: / *Hear, O Israel! / The Lord our God is Lord alone! / You shall love the Lord your God with all your heart, / with all your soul, / with all your mind, and with all your strength.* / The second is this: *You shall love your neighbor as yourself.* There is no other commandment greater than these." The scribe said to him, "Well said, teacher. You are right in saying, / *He is One and there is no other than he. /* And *to love him with all your heart, / with all your understanding, / with all your strength, / and to love your neighbor as yourself /* is worth more than all burnt offerings and sacrifices." And when Jesus saw that he answered with understanding, he said to him, "You are not far from the Kingdom of God." And no one dared to ask him any more questions.

Reflection

Jesus orders and prioritizes our life. In today's Gospel a scribe asks him what is the greatest commandment. Jesus responds with the command of the Law: love God with your whole heart, and love your neighbor as yourself.

Prayers *others may be added*

Heavenly Father, your Son Jesus instructs us how to love. Hear our prayers as we pray:

◆ Teach us your ways, O Lord.

For the Holy Father, all priests, religious, and lay faithful of the Church, that they may be witnesses to the love of Christ through the example of their lives to lead others to the joy of union with God, we pray: ◆ For the people of all the world, that they may be freed of selfishness and egocentrism in order to love their neighbor as members of the same human family, we pray: ◆ For all those who suffer neglect, abuse, and disrespect, that they may experience God's love through the charity and friendship of faithful Christians, we pray: ◆ For all our loved ones who have died, that they may share in the eternal glory of the love of God, we pray: ◆ For the grace to love God and others with great intensity and with every ounce of our being, we pray: ◆

Our Father . . .

Heavenly Father,
in your Son, Jesus Christ,
you teach us what is most important.
Send your Spirit upon us to teach us
how to love you above all things
and to love our neighbor out of love
   for you.
We ask this through Christ our Lord.
Amen.

✝ Teach me your ways, O Lord.

✝ O Lord, great peace have they who love your law.

Psalm 34 *page 406*

Reading *Mark 12:35–37*

As Jesus was teaching in the temple area he said, "How do the scribes claim that the Christ is the son of David? David himself, inspired by the Holy Spirit, said: *The Lord said to my lord, / 'Sit at my right hand / until I place your enemies under your feet.' /* David himself calls him 'lord'; so how is he his son?" The great crowd heard this with delight.

Reflection

Sometimes we forget that before the Lord, we stand before a great mystery— a mystery of unfathomable depth, forever new, and inexhaustible in riches. Through the reading of the Sacred Scripture and the reception of the sacraments, we see, hear, touch, and enter into the mystery of the life of God. The Holy Spirit breathes within and through us to lead us in wisdom and understanding. May we become more sensitive to the movement of the Spirit who opens our hearts and minds to encounter this mystery.

Prayers *others may be added*

Father, your law is our delight.
Let us pray:

◆ Lord, open our hearts to hear your word.

For the lay faithful of the Church, that they may recognize the important service they offer by their Christian witness in the workplace, the home, and in public life, we pray: ◆ For all nations, that they may come to delight in the truth and beauty of the Good News of Jesus Christ, we pray: ◆ For all those in special need, especially the sick and dying, all travelers, prisoners, and those in crisis, we pray: ◆ For all artists, that, inspired by the goodness and beauty of creation, they may imitate and give glory to the Creator, we pray: ◆ For all who teach and proclaim the word of God, that they may remember that their teaching is not their own as they lead others to an encounter with God's mystery, we pray: ◆

Our Father . . .

O God,
you send us your Son, Jesus,
as our Messiah and Lord.
He is the fulfillment of all
the Law and all the Prophets.
Free us from sin and bring us
to everlasting life through the
gift of your salvation.
We ask this through Christ our Lord.
Amen.

✝ O Lord, great peace have they who love your law.

Saturday, June 9, 2012
Weekday

✝ I will sing of your salvation.

Psalm 63   *page 410*

Reading   *Mark 12:38–44*

In the course of his teaching Jesus said, "Beware of the scribes, who like to go around in long robes and accept greetings in the marketplaces, seats of honor in synagogues, and places of honor at banquets. They devour the houses of widows and, as a pretext, recite lengthy prayers. They will receive a very severe condemnation."

He sat down opposite the treasury and observed how the crowd put money into the treasury. Many rich people put in large sums. A poor widow also came and put in two small coins worth a few cents. Calling his disciples to himself, he said to them, "Amen, I say to you, this poor widow put in more than all the other contributors to the treasury. For they have all contributed from their surplus wealth, but she, from her poverty, has contributed all she had, her whole livelihood."

Reflection

Jesus compares the rich who offer large sums of money and perform rituals in order to be recognized by others to the poor widow who places her few cents in the temple treasury. Jesus praises the widow because, despite the seeming worthlessness of her small offering, she has given all she has to the Lord.

Prayers   *others may be added*

Father, with delight, you accept the littleness and weakness of our offerings of prayer and sacrifice. Hear our needs we place before you:

◆ Hear us, Lord, and grant us your salvation.

For the Church, that like the mustard seed, she may further the kingdom through the humble greatness and hidden work of her members, we pray: ◆ For all nations that have estranged themselves from the knowledge and love of God, that they may be sustained by the prayers and work of faithful Christians, we pray: ◆ For all who suffer from poverty, that, through the charity of others, they may receive the food, water, shelter, medical attention, and love they need, we pray: ◆ For all the rich, that they may not be enslaved by their riches, but rather seek God's glory through the detached use of their material possessions, with the awareness of their duty of justice to give charitably to those in need, we pray: ◆

Our Father . . .

Lord Jesus,
you teach us that true giving does not consist in the quantity of the amount,
but in the humble love with which it
     is given.
May the life of your Spirit bear fruit in our lives through the gift of
     true generosity.
You live and reign forever.
Amen.

✝ I will sing of your salvation.

Sunday, June 10, 2012
Solemnity of the Most Holy Body and Blood of Christ
(*Corpus Christi*)

✝ I will take the cup of salvation, and call on the name of the Lord.

Psalm 95   *page 413*

Reading   *Mark 14:22–25*

While they were eating, [Jesus] took bread, said the blessing, broke it, gave it to [the disciples], and said, "Take it; this is my body." Then he took a cup, gave thanks, and gave it to them, and they all drank from it. He said to them, "This is my blood of the covenant, which will be shed for many. Amen, I say to you, I shall not drink again the fruit of the vine until the day when I drink it new in the kingdom of God."

Reflection

Today we celebrate *Corpus Christi*, the solemnity of the Most Holy Body and Blood of Christ present in the Eucharist. In the eucharistic feast the gifts of bread and wine become the Body and Blood of Christ Jesus. Through this covenant of love, God draws us into his divine life and offers us food for our earthly pilgrimage to continue with the faith and hope, confident in God's ability to transform our weaknesses and sufferings into life and joy.

Prayers   *others may be added*

Lord Jesus, you give us the gift of your Body and Blood in the Eucharistic feast. With thanksgiving, we pray:

◆ Lord, hear our prayer.

For the Church, that her members may seek sustenance from the Eucharist, we pray: ◆ For all social and governmental initiatives to aid peoples and countries that suffer from the evils of hunger and poverty, we pray: ◆ For all the sick and dying, that the Eucharist may give them the strength they need to persevere along their journey to healing and new life, we pray: ◆ For all of us, that we may be renewed in faith in the true presence of Christ in the Eucharist, we pray: ◆

Our Father . . .

Heavenly Father,
in the gift of your Son present in the
    Eucharist,
you give us a means of giving you thanks.
Through the Eucharistic feast, we offer
thanks and praise through the
    sacred offering
of your Son, Priest and Victim,
    Jesus Christ.
By his Body and Blood, give us
    strength along
our earthly journey until we come
    to enjoy
the eucharistic wedding feast of heaven.
We ask this through Christ our Lord.
Amen.

✝ I will take the cup of salvation, and call on the name of the Lord.

Monday, June 11, 2012
Memorial of Saint Barnabas, Apostle
Tenth Week in Ordinary Time

† Our help is from the Lord, who made heaven and earth.

Psalm 100 *page 414*

Reading *Matthew 5:1–12a*

"Blessed are the poor in spirit, / for theirs is the Kingdom of heaven. / Blessed are they who mourn, / for they will be comforted. / Blessed are the meek, / for they will inherit the land. / Blessed are they who hunger and thirst for righteousness, / for they will be satisfied. / Blessed are the merciful, / for they will be shown mercy. / Blessed are the clean of heart, / for they will see God. / Blessed are the peacemakers, / for they will be called children of God. / Blessed are they who are persecuted for the sake of righteousness, / for theirs is the Kingdom of heaven. / Blessed are you when they insult you and persecute you / and utter every kind of evil against you falsely because of me. / Rejoice and be glad, / for your reward will be great in heaven."

Reflection

Through the Beatitudes, Jesus teaches that when we are persecuted for his name, we can still be happy and rejoice, because we will be truly blessed in heaven. The Beatitudes contain the heart of the Gospel message. Through these precepts, the follower of Jesus learns how to be a faithful Christian and how to achieve true happiness despite inevitable sufferings and persecutions.

Prayers *others may be added*

Loving Father, hear the prayers of your Church, as we pray:

◆ Keep us faithful, O Lord.

For the Church, even amid persecutions and trials, that she may rejoice and be glad, and that she may remain ever steadfast in furthering the kingdom of God, we pray: ◆ For all civic leaders and governmental officials, that they may work as peacemakers to bring unity among all of God's children, we pray: ◆ For all mothers, children, doctors, and families who silently suffer from effects of abortion, we pray: ◆ For the poor and suffering in mind, body, or spirit, for the hungry that go without bread today, and for those who suffer for righteousness' sake, that they may receive the material aid they need and the spiritual blessings of the kingdom of God, we pray: ◆

Our Father . . .

Heavenly Father,
blessed are those who follow
after your Son and keep his commands.
Give us the strength and perseverance
to live out the Beatitudes
despite sufferings, persecutions, conflict,
    and trials.
May we live with the faith and conviction
of the early Christians who were
    not afraid
to proclaim the Good News of
    Christ crucified,
through whom we ask this prayer.
Amen.

† Our help is from the Lord, who made heaven and earth.

Tuesday, June 12, 2012
Weekday

✝ Lord, let your face shine on us.

Psalm 103   *page 415*

Reading   *Matthew 5:13–16*
Jesus said to his disciples: "You are the salt of the earth. But if salt loses its taste, with what can it be seasoned? It is no longer good for anything but to be thrown out and trampled underfoot. You are the light of the world. A city set on a mountain cannot be hidden. Nor do they light a lamp and then put it under a bushel basket; it is set on a lampstand, where it gives light to all in the house. Just so, your light must shine before others, that they may see your good deeds, and glorify your heavenly Father."

Reflection
Jesus sends us out as salt and light for the world. He desires that the uniqueness of our Christian lives offer abundant richness and flavor to the world. United to him, our lives must shine out as radiant light, so that others may see the joy and beauty of being a Christian, and so all peoples may glorify God and share in the goodness of his life.

Prayers   *others may be added*
Father, you send us your Son as Light of the World. Let us pray:

◆ May your radiant Light shine upon us, Lord.

For the Church, that she may remain holy through the purifying radiance of the light of the risen Christ, we pray: ◆ For all Christians, that they may joyfully live in a manner worthy of the call they have received to illuminate and enrich all the nations with the Good News of salvation, we pray: ◆ For all the sick and those in special need, that their sufferings may be used for the glory of God as an invaluable treasure offered to the Lord, we pray: ◆ For all the evils of abuse, scandal, and violence to be brought to the light in order to bring about truth and healing, we pray: ◆ For all peoples to be salt and light to the world in our everyday encounters with one another at home and in the workplace, we pray: ◆

Our Father . . .

Lord Jesus,
you are the Light of the World.
By your death you conquer darkness,
and in your Resurrection
we arise with you in your radiance
    and glory.
Illuminate us with your love.
May the radiance of your Light
shine forth for the glory of your
    Heavenly Father,
who lives and reigns with you in the unity
    of the Holy Spirit,
one God, forever and ever.
Amen.

✝ Lord, let your face shine on us.

Wednesday, June 13, 2012
Memorial of Saint Anthony of Padua,
Priest and Doctor of the Church

✝ Keep me safe, O God; you are
my hope.

Psalm 145 — page 422

Reading — Matthew 5:17–19

Jesus said to his disciples, "Do not think that I have come to abolish the law or the prophets. I have come not to abolish but to fulfill. Amen, I say to you, until heaven and earth pass away, not the smallest letter or the smallest part of a letter will pass from the law, until all things have taken place. Therefore, whoever breaks one of the least of these commandments and teaches others to do so will be called least in the Kingdom of heaven. But whoever obeys and teaches these commandments will be called greatest in the Kingdom of heaven."

Reflection

In today's Gospel, Jesus teaches us the importance of integrity. Each and every sin is an offense against God; therefore, we must not make excuses for our sins, even those which are less serious. Jesus has come to bring fulfillment and new-ness in every aspect of our lives, and he requires that we remain faithful to him in things both small and great.

Prayers — *others may be added*

Father, you send your Son not to abolish but to fulfill the law. Hear the prayers of your children as we pray:

◆ Renew the face of the earth, O Lord.

For the Church, that she may instruct, guide, and clarify all doubt and error in order to lead all peoples to Jesus Christ, we pray: ◆ For the salvation of the whole world, we pray: ◆ For those who knowingly or unknowingly search for truth, that they may find what they seek in Jesus Christ, the font and source of salvation, fulfillment, and joy, we pray: ◆

Our Father . . .

Heavenly Father,
even the small and seemingly
    unimportant
can be transformed into greatness by
    your grace.
Through the prayers of Saint Anthony
    of Padua,
teach us to remain faithful to your word
in situations both small and great,
so that we may enjoy the eternal beatitude
of your kingdom in the company of
    your saints,
in union with you, who live and reign
    with your Son,
Jesus Christ, in the unity of the Holy Spirit,
one God, forever and ever.
Amen.

✝ Keep me safe, O God; you are
my hope.

✝ It is right to praise you in Zion,
O God.

Psalm 19 *page 403*

Reading *Matthew 5:21–26*

"You have heard that it was said to your ancestors, / *You shall not kill; and whoever kills will be liable to judgment.* / But I say to you, whoever is angry with his brother will be liable to judgment, and whoever says to his brother, *Raqa*, will be answerable to the Sanhedrin, and whoever says, 'You fool,' will be liable to fiery Gehenna. Therefore, if you bring your gift to the altar, and there recall that your brother has anything against you, leave your gift at the altar, go first and be reconciled with your brother, and then come and offer your gift. Settle with your opponent quickly while on the way to court with him. Otherwise your opponent will hand you over to the judge, and the judge will hand you over to the guard, and you will be thrown into prison. Amen, I say to you, you will not be released until you have paid the last penny."

Reflection

Jesus' teaching fulfills the old law and offers the new way of righteousness through his command to love. Jesus teaches the people that their love must be greater than that of the scribes and Pharisees, who were regarded as the most holy and learned. It is not enough for us to live complacent lives by only avoiding grave sins. Rather, our love must also root out all forms of judgment, criticism, anger, and cynicism toward one another, and our minor failings and weaknesses as well.

Prayers *others may be added*

Let us pray:

♦ Lord, hear our prayer.

That the diversity of the Mystical Body of Christ may be freed from all criticisms and attacks by her members, which destroy the Church's unity from within, we pray: ♦ That the leaders of all nations may bring about the kingdom of righteousness through service to the weak and poor, we pray: ♦ That the grace of forgiveness and charity may come among all families, we pray: ♦ That our nation may be freed from all complacency, mediocrity, and anti-Christian sentiment, we pray: ♦

Our Father . . .

Father God,
by your Son's word,
you command us to love
with a radical love that knows no bounds.
Look kindly on our weaknesses and
have mercy.
By the power of your grace,
instruct us how to follow your Son along
the path of righteousness
in the life of love that you share with him,
in unity with the Holy Spirit,
one God, forever and ever.
Amen.

✝ It is right to praise you in Zion,
O God.

✝ You will draw water joyfully from the springs of salvation.

Psalm 27 *page 405*

Reading *John 19:31–34*

Since it was preparation day, in order that the bodies might not remain on the cross on the sabbath, for the sabbath day of the week was a solemn one, the Jews asked that their legs be broken and they be taken down. So the soldiers came and broke the legs of the first and then of the other one who was crucified with Jesus. But when they came to Jesus and saw that he was already dead, they did not break his legs, but one soldier thrust his lance into his side, and immediately blood and water flowed out.

Reflection

God has loved us with a human heart. This is the mystery that we celebrate today. God is not a god who is unapproachable and inaccessible; but rather, God has drawn near to us through his Son, Jesus Christ. Through the love poured out through Christ's human heart, God fulfills our every need and gives us new life. Today, let us take time to be still, resting in the Sacred Heart in order to be filled in his love and life.

Prayers *others may be added*

Confident that God's love provides for our every need, we pray:

◆ Sacred Heart of Jesus, have mercy and hear our prayer.

For the Church, that she may forever remain under the torrents of Christ's sacramental grace and mercy that flow from his pierced side, we pray: ◆ For all priests, that they may be ever more conformed to the loving heart of Jesus through their priestly ministry and vocation, we pray: ◆ For public officials, that they may seek the common good of all people through their efforts in social and economic justice, we pray: ◆ For all the sick and suffering, that they may find comfort and peace in the merciful healing heart of Jesus, we pray: ◆ For all people, that they may love and serve others with the charity of Christ, we pray: ◆

Our Father . . .

Heavenly Father,
we thank you for the gift of Jesus Christ.
Help us to forever remain in the saving
    love and mercy
that flows from the Sacred Heart
of your Son, Jesus,
who lives and reigns with you in the unity
    of the Holy Spirit,
one God, forever and ever.
Amen.

✝ You will draw water joyfully from the springs of salvation.

Saturday, June 16, 2012

Memorial of the Immaculate Heart of the Blessed Virgin Mary

✝ My heart exults in the Lord,
my Savior.

Psalm 34 page 406

Reading Luke 2:46–51

After three days [Mary and Joseph] found [Jesus] in the temple, sitting in the midst of the teachers, listening to them and asking them questions, and all who heard him were astounded at his understanding and his answers. When his parents saw him, they were astonished, and his mother said to him, "Son, why have you done this to us? Your father and I have been looking for you with great anxiety." And he said to them, "Why were you looking for me? Did you not know that I must be in my Father's house?" But they did not understand what he said to them. He went down with them and came to Nazareth, and was obedient to them; and his mother kept all these things in her heart.

Reflection

The Blessed Virgin Mary is the true model for all Christians. She is the most faithful disciple of her Son, Jesus, and by her example and prayers, she teaches us how to follow after him in faithfulness and hope. Today as we celebrate the feast of the Immaculate Heart of Mary, let us draw close to her maternal heart, which comforts us in all our afflictions and guides us into union with the most Sacred Heart of her Son, Jesus.

Prayers others may be added

With gratitude, we celebrate the purity and faithfulness of our Blessed Mother. Let us pray:

◆ Lord, hear our prayer.

For the Church, that she may remain Mother and teacher to all peoples as the spotless Bride of Christ, we pray: ◆ For those who work for social justice, that they may seek the true needs of the human person, we pray: ◆ For all who suffer abuse, violence, illness, or injustice, we pray: ◆ For all of us that we may follow the model and example of the Blessed Virgin Mary and seek purity of heart, we pray: ◆ For a greater devotion to the Blessed Mother Mary who aids us by her prayers and guides us to her Son, Jesus, we pray: ◆

Our Father . . .

Loving God,
you chose your Son to be born
of a spotless and pure young virgin.
Through the prayers of our
    Blessed Mother,
may we grow in purity of heart, mind,
    and body,
through the Most Immaculate Heart
    of Mary,
and the Most Sacred Heart of Jesus,
    your Son,
who lives and reigns with you in the unity
    of the Holy Spirit,
one God, forever and ever.
Amen.

✝ My heart exults in the Lord,
my Savior.

✝ Lord, it is good to give thanks to you.

Psalm 63 *page 410*

Reading *Mark 4:26–34*

Jesus said to the crowds: "This is how it is with the kingdom of God; it is as if a man were to scatter seed on the land and would sleep and rise night and day and the seed would sprout and grow, he knows not how. Of its own accord the land yields fruit, first the blade, then the ear, then the full grain in the ear. And when the grain is ripe, he wields the sickle at once, for the harvest has come."

He said, "To what shall we compare the kingdom of God, or what parable can we use for it? It is like a mustard seed that, when it is sown in the ground, is the smallest of all the seeds on the earth. But once it is sown, it springs up and becomes the largest of plants and puts forth large branches, so that the birds of the sky can dwell in its shade." With many such parables he spoke the word to them as they were able to understand it. Without parables he did not speak to them, but to his own disciples he explained everything in private.

Reflection

Like the grain that mysteriously grows, sprouts, and yields fruit, and like the tiny mustard seed, so too does the kingdom of God mysteriously grow in magnificence and greatness. Through these images and parables, Jesus helps us understand and enter into the mystery of his kingdom.

Prayers *others may be added*

Father, your ways are above our ways, and your thoughts above our thoughts. With confidence in your providential care, we offer you our prayers:

◆ Your kingdom come, O Lord.

For the Church, the Holy Father, all priests, and laity, that they may be faithful laborers in the Father's vineyard to scatter the good seed of God's word through their prayers and work, we pray: ◆ For the work of public officials, that they may be guided by the Holy Spirit to bear fruit in peace and justice for all peoples, we pray: ◆ For all those who are sick or suffering in any way, that, in the seemingly barren mystery of suffering, they may have faith in God's work of yielding abundant fruit for the salvation of souls, we pray: ◆ That, during this time in which the lands yield their summer harvest, we may recognize the mystery of the kingdom through the beauty and fruitfulness of God's created order, we pray: ◆

Our Father . . .

Heavenly Father,
our Creator and God, we praise you
for your goodness and providential love.
Through the mystery of your creation,
draw us into the mystery of your kingdom,
where you live and reign with your Son,
   Jesus Christ,
in the unity of the Holy Spirit,
one God, forever and ever.
Amen.

✝ Lord, it is good to give thanks to you.

Monday, June 18, 2012
Weekday

✝ Lord, listen to my groaning.

Psalm 95   *page 413*

Reading   *Matthew 5:38–42*

Jesus said to his disciples: "You have heard that it was said, / *An eye for an eye and a tooth for a tooth.* / But I say to you, offer no resistance to one who is evil. When someone strikes you on your right cheek, turn the other one to him as well. If anyone wants to go to law with you over your tunic, hand him your cloak as well. Should anyone press you into service for one mile, go with him for two miles. Give to the one who asks of you, and do not turn your back on one who wants to borrow."

Reflection

To be a Christian is to truly be counter-cultural. Jesus' new law requires a great and radical love greater than our own human sense of justice. We must not be overly defensive, nor overwhelmingly offensive; rather, we ought to possess welcoming openness to invite others to experience and know the security and joy of a life in union with God.

Prayers   *others may be added*

Jesus, you call us to a radical type of love. Let us pray:

◆ May we love as you love, O Lord.

For the Church, that she may teach, instruct, and clarify through peaceful and charitable dialogue to bring all peoples to encounter the truth of Jesus Christ, we pray: ◆ For all efforts of social and economic justice, that they may be based upon God's law of mercy and love, we pray: ◆ For those who suffer persecution, estrangement, and criticism for the sake of Gospel and moral values, that they may persevere in healthy charity toward those who seek their harm, we pray: ◆ For the willingness to love as Christ loves, by going beyond the call of duty through our service, charity, patience, and generosity toward our friends and family, we pray: ◆

Our Father . . .

Merciful Father,
hear the prayers of your children
that we offer to you today.
Teach us the way of life so that
our daily lives may become witnesses
of your mercy and love that you share
with your Son, Jesus Christ,
in the unity of the Holy Spirit,
one God, forever and ever.
Amen.

✝ Lord, listen to my groaning.

✝ Be merciful, O Lord, for we have sinned.

Psalm 95   *page 413*

Reading   *Matthew 5:43–48*

Jesus said to his disciples: "You have heard that it was said, / *You shall love your neighbor and hate your enemy.* / But I say to you, love your enemies and pray for those who persecute you, that you may be children of your heavenly Father, for he makes his sun rise on the bad and the good, and causes rain to fall on the just and the unjust. For if you love those who love you, what recompense will you have? Do not the tax collectors do the same? And if you greet your brothers only, what is unusual about that? Do not the pagans do the same? So be perfect, just as your heavenly Father is perfect."

Reflection

In today's Gospel, Jesus continues his teaching on the new law of love. It is not enough just to love those who love us, but we must also love those who are difficult to love and those who may hate us or hold grudges against us. In this way we imitate God's love for us and we become children of the Father.

Prayers   *others may be added*

Jesus, you teach us to love our enemies and pray for those who persecute us. In obedience to your word, we ask:

◆ Perfect us in your love, O Lord.

For those who have been harmed or injured by the human weakness of members of the Church, that they may find forgiveness and healing, we pray: ◆ For governmental officials, that they may work to eliminate all violence, war, terrorism, and injustice among their political enemies to bring about world peace, we pray: ◆ For those who suffer persecution, hatred, and abuse, that God's grace of mercy may bring about healing and forgiveness, we pray: ◆ For the grace to see the face of Christ in each person, we pray: ◆

Our Father . . .

Heavenly Father,
in your Son Jesus, Word Incarnate,
you call us to love as you love
and to forgive as you forgive.
Without your grace we are nothing.
Teach us how to love,
and instruct us how to forgive
    our enemies,
that we may enter into the freedom of life
with you who are all holy and perfect.
We ask through Christ our Lord.
Amen.

✝ Be merciful, O Lord, for we have sinned.

Wednesday, June 20, 2012
Weekday

✝ Let your hearts take comfort, all who hope in the Lord.

Psalm 100
page 414

Reading
Matthew 6:1, 5–6

Jesus said to his disciples: "When you pray, do not be like the hypocrites, who love to stand and pray in the synagogues and on street corners so that others may see them. Amen, I say to you, they have received their reward. But when you pray, go to your inner room, close the door, and pray to your Father in secret. And your Father who sees in secret will repay you."

Reflection

We do not pray and do good only in order for other people to see us or think highly of us. Rather, we strive to do good out of love for God and for his glory. As his children, God knows our hearts and all our needs. He listens to us and hears our prayer. In today's Gospel, Jesus teaches us that it is not necessary for us to seek vain approval or recognition from others.

Prayers
others may be added

Father, accept our humble prayers as we say:

◆ Lord, hear our prayer.

For all the spiritual and material needs of the Church, we pray: ◆ For public officials, that they may not work solely for recognition and human praise, but rather seek the common good of the human person through their efforts of establishing justice and order, we pray: ◆ For all the sick and those in special need, that they may offer their sufferings as prayers to God who knows us in our inmost depths and hears the cry of the poor, we pray: ◆ For our local community, that they may be united together through a deepening of prayer and fraternal charity, we pray: ◆ For all of us, that we may be freed from the sin of vanity, so that we may enjoy the freedom of living totally and entirely for God and for the good of his people, we pray: ◆

Our Father . . .

Lord Jesus,
you teach us to be humble
in our work and prayer.
Protect us from the evil of vanity
so as to serve you in true freedom.
May all our thoughts, words, prayers,
and actions be for love of you,
who live and reign with the Father,
in the unity of the Holy Spirit,
one God, forever and ever.
Amen.

✝ Let your hearts take comfort, all who hope in the Lord.

Thursday, June 21, 2012
Memorial of Saint Aloysius Gonzaga, Religious

✝ Rejoice in the Lord, you just!

Psalm 103 *page 415*

Reading *Matthew 6:9–15*

[Jesus said to his disciples:] "This is how you are to pray: 'Our Father who art in heaven, / hallowed be thy name, / thy Kingdom come, / thy will be done, on earth as it is in heaven. / Give us this day our daily bread; / and forgive us our trespasses, / as we forgive those who trespass against us; / and lead us not into temptation, / but deliver us from evil.' /

"If you forgive others their transgressions, your heavenly Father will forgive you. But if you do not forgive others, neither will your Father forgive your transgressions."

Reflection

In today's Gospel, Jesus teaches us how to pray. Prayer is a loving dialogue of communion with the Father. In Jesus Christ and through the Holy Spirit, we cry, "Abba, Father!" Jesus warns us that our prayer must not become a babbling of many words. Rather, our prayer must become an unceasing union of our heart and will to that of God, our Father.

Prayers *others may be added*

In humility and trust, we present to God our petitions:

◆ Heavenly Father, hear our prayer.

For the Holy Father, that he may be strengthened by the love and prayers of his flock, as he offers prayers and sacrifices for the whole world, we pray: ◆ For all nations that suffer from the evils of poverty and hunger, that, through the work of generous Christians and the initiatives of civic leaders, they may serve the basic needs of our human brothers and sisters, we pray: ◆ For those who suffer illness, loss, and loneliness, that God our Father may hear their prayers, and that God's holy and loving will may be accomplished in their lives to bring about healing and peace, we pray: ◆ For all in need of mercy and forgiveness, that, as the Father has forgiven us in Christ Jesus, we may have the grace to forgive those who have hurt us, we pray: ◆

Our Father . . .

God, our Father,
united in your Son, Jesus Christ,
we are blessed to call you Father.
Forgive us our sins
and give us the grace to forgive others
so we may remain forever free
in the union of love with you
and your Son, Jesus Christ,
who lives and reigns with you in the unity
of the Holy Spirit,
one God, forever and ever.
Amen.

✝ Rejoice in the Lord, you just!

Friday, June 22, 2012
Weekday

✝ The Lord has chosen Zion for his dwelling.

Psalm 145   *page 422*

Reading   *Matthew 6:19–23*

Jesus said to his disciples: "Do not store up for yourselves treasures on earth, where moth and decay destroy, and thieves break in and steal. But store up treasures in heaven, where neither moth nor decay destroys, nor thieves break in and steal. For where your treasure is, there also will your heart be.

"The lamp of the body is the eye. If your eye is sound, your whole body will be filled with light; but if your eye is bad, your whole body will be in darkness. And if the light in you is darkness, how great will the darkness be."

Reflection

Life is short. The world is passing away, and in today's Gospel, Jesus teaches us that we must not cling too tightly to the things of this world. Jesus warns us not to store up treasures on earth, but rather to store up treasures in heaven that are more precious than that of the passing goods of this world. The glory to come far surpasses all of the beauties and goodness of this life.

Prayers   *others may be added*

Jesus, you teach us to store up spiritual treasures in heaven. Hear the prayers we offer you today:

◆ Free us from our sins, O Lord.

For the Church, that she may not be tempted by the riches of the world, but rather persevere to constantly seek first the kingdom of God, we pray: ◆ For all wealthy nations, that they may be driven by charity and generosity to share their goods and treasures with those in need, we pray: ◆ For the end of crime and for the protection of all children and families, we pray: ◆ For all peoples, that they may come to respect the dignity and treasure of human life, we pray: ◆ For the grace to always keep a spiritual outlook on life, so that we may not give in to temptations of fear and worldly anxiety, we pray: ◆

Our Father . . .

Lord Jesus,
you are our only treasure.
Free us from the worship of all false gods,
and convict us of the emptiness of
   worldly riches,
that we may enjoy the freedom that comes
from a life of total love and service to you,
who live and reign with the Father,
in the unity of the Holy Spirit,
one God, forever and ever.
Amen.

✝ The Lord has chosen Zion for his dwelling.

✝ For ever I will maintain my love for my servant.

Psalm 27 *page 405*

Reading *Matthew 6:24–27*

Jesus said to his disciples: "No one can serve two masters. He will either hate one and love the other, or be devoted to one and despise the other. You cannot serve God and mammon.

"Therefore I tell you, do not worry about your life, what you will eat or drink, or about your body, what you will wear. Is not life more than food and the body more than clothing? Look at the birds in the sky; they do not sow or reap, they gather nothing into barns, yet your heavenly Father feeds them. Are not you more important than they? Can any of you by worrying add a single moment to your life-span?"

Reflection

Do not worry! Today Jesus assures us that his loving Father will care for us and provide for everything we need. Just as God cares and provides for his creation, even more so will he provide and care for us who are worth more than all the lilies of the field and all the birds of the air. We belong to the Lord; therefore, do not worry about your life. Rather, seek God's kingdom of righteousness and peace and you will be provided with all that you need.

Prayers *others may be added*

You are our faithful, loving Father who gives us every good gift. With confidence that you hear our prayers and petitions, we pray:

◆ Keep us safe, O Lord.

That the Church, ever sustained by the grace of the Holy Spirit, may remain protected and steadfast amid the cares and trials of this earthly life, we pray: ◆ For nations that suffer poverty, hunger, and violence, that generous Christians may be the hands of Christ to offer food and aid to those in need, we pray: ◆ For those who suffer from anxiety, depression, stress, and worry, that they may receive peace from faith in our loving Father who knows our needs and provides for us with his loving gentle care, we pray: ◆ For those who suffer from distorted body image and eating disorders, we pray: ◆ For the grace to keep our eyes focused on Christ and the glory of his kingdom, we pray: ◆

Our Father . . .

Loving Father,
in your providential love for us,
you care for us and provide for our
    every need.
Give us the faith to surrender our lives
    to you,
the hope to believe in your promise,
and the charity to serve you in
    our neighbor.
We ask this through Christ our Lord.
Amen.

✝ For ever I will maintain my love for my servant.

✝ I praise you for I am wonderfully made.

Psalm 34   *page 406*

Reading   *Luke 1:57–66*

When the time arrived for Elizabeth to have her child she gave birth to a son. Her neighbors and relatives heard that the Lord had shown his great mercy toward her, and they rejoiced with her. When they came on the eighth day to circumcise the child, they were going to call him Zechariah after his father, but his mother said in reply, "No. He will be called John." But they answered her, "There is no one among your relatives who has this name." So they made signs, asking his father what he wished him to be called. He asked for a tablet and wrote, "John is his name," and all were amazed. Immediately his mouth was opened, his tongue freed, and he spoke blessing God. Then fear came upon all their neighbors, and all these matters were discussed throughout the hill country of Judea. All who heard these things took them to heart, saying, "What, then, will this child be?" For surely the hand of the Lord was with him.

Reflection

Today we celebrate the solemnity of the birth of Saint John the Baptist. He was the great prophet and herald of Jesus the Messiah who prepared the way of the Lord and revealed Jesus to others as both the Messiah and the Lamb of God. Saint John exemplifies the Christian life as one who proclaims the Gospel message of healing and repentance, while he points out Christ to others and shows them the way to become united with God.

Prayers   *others may be added*

Through the prayers of Saint John the Baptist, we pray:

◆ Lord, hear our prayer.

For the Church, that she may proclaim the presence of Jesus Christ here among us, who calls us to repentance and new life, we pray: ◆ For all nations, that they may recognize Jesus Christ, who comes to free us from our sins and lead us to salvation, we pray: ◆ For the end of abortion and all anti-life practices, that mothers, fathers, doctors, and all peoples may recognize the treasure of life of the born and unborn, we pray: ◆ For all friends or family members who have died, that they may enter into the glory of the heavenly rest, we pray: ◆

Our Father . . .

God of all ages,
through the life of Saint John the Baptist,
you prepared your people for the coming
of your Son, Jesus Christ, our Lord
    and Messiah.
Through his prayers, may we too be
    faithful messengers to prepare the way
    of the Lord.
We ask this through Christ our Lord.
Amen.

✝ I praise you for I am wonderfully
    made.

✝ Help us with your right hand,
O Lord, and answer us.

Psalm 63 *page 410*

Reading *Matthew 7:1–5*

Jesus said to his disciples: "Stop judging, that you may not be judged. For as you judge, so will you be judged, and the measure with which you measure will be measured out to you. Why do you notice the splinter in your brother's eye, but do not perceive the wooden beam in your own eye? How can you say to your brother, 'Let me remove that splinter from your eye,' while the wooden beam is in your eye? You hypocrite, remove the wooden beam from your eye first; then you will see clearly to remove the splinter from your brother's eye."

Reflection

God is our just and merciful judge; it is not our responsibility to judge. In today's Gospel, Jesus tells us to stop judging others, because we will be judged with the same measure with which we judge others. So frequently we see the faults of others precisely because we possess those same faults to a greater degree. But through the Gospel, we need to learn to be patient with the faults of others in the same way that God is patient with our faults and our sins against him.

Prayers *others may be added*

Father, you are all just and merciful. Hear our prayers and petitions we humbly present before you, as we pray:

◆ Have mercy on us, Lord.

For the Church, that she may proclaim the presence of Jesus Christ here among us, who calls us to repentance and new life, we pray: ◆ For the work of all civic leaders to flourish in promoting human values and a renewed social order, we pray: ◆ For those who suffer persecution and violence, we pray: ◆ For the protection and safety of all families and children, and for those who suffer domestic abuse, we pray: ◆ For God to pour out his mercy and love on all who have died, and for those who grieve their losses, we pray: ◆ For the grace to love as God loves, so as not to judge, but rather to have mercy and patience with the sins and weaknesses of our brothers and sisters, we pray: ◆

Our Father . . .

Loving God,
your Son Jesus is our merciful and
    just judge.
Give us the grace not to judge,
but rather to encourage
and strengthen our brothers as we all
    struggle together
in the joys and trials of life.
We ask this through Christ our Lord.
Amen.

✝ Help us with your right hand,
O Lord, and answer us.

Tuesday, June 26, 2012
Weekday

✝ God upholds his city for ever.

Psalm 85   *page 411*

Reading   *Matthew 7:6, 12–14*

Jesus said to his disciples: "Do not give what is holy to dogs, or throw your pearls before swine, lest they trample them underfoot, and turn and tear you to pieces.

"Do to others whatever you would have them do to you. This is the Law and the Prophets.

"Enter through the narrow gate; for the gate is wide and the road broad that leads to destruction, and those who enter through it are many. How narrow the gate and constricted the road that leads to life. And those who find it are few."

Reflection

Today's Gospel is a continuation of Jesus' teaching from the Sermon on the Mount. Jesus does not leave us to wander aimlessly as we go in search for truth and happiness, but rather he teaches us and gives us precepts to follow so that we can arrive at peace and fulfillment. Jesus encourages us to follow the "Golden Rule," to treasure that which is holy and to take the road less traveled in our Christian journey.

Prayers   *others may be added*

All the Law and Prophets are fulfilled in your Word, Lord Jesus. Let us pray:

◆ Lead us along the path of life, O Lord.

For the Holy Father, that he may love and teach the flock of the Church entrusted to him in the same way that Christ loves and teaches his people, we pray: ◆ That, through the witness and evangelization of Christians, all peoples of the world may discover the narrow gate of Jesus Christ that leads to eternal life and salvation, we pray: ◆ For all women in unhealthy relationships, that they may have the strength and courage to recognize their beauty and dignity given to them as a gift from God, we pray: ◆ For the grace to love others in charity and kindness as we ourselves would like to be loved, we pray: ◆

Our Father . . .

Lord Jesus,
narrow is the road that leads to
    eternal life,
but you, O Good Shepherd,
are the gate through which we enter into
    your heavenly glory.
Do not abandon us, O Lord, but walk
    with us
and teach us the way to your Father,
who lives and reigns with you in the unity
    of the Holy Spirit,
one God, forever and ever.
Amen.

✝ God upholds his city for ever.

✝ Teach me the way of your decrees, O Lord.

Psalm 100 *page 414*

Reading *Matthew 7:15–20*

Jesus said to his disciples: "Beware of false prophets, who come to you in sheep's clothing, but underneath are ravenous wolves. By their fruits you will know them. Do people pick grapes from thornbushes, or figs from thistles? Just so, every good tree bears good fruit, and a rotten tree bears bad fruit. A good tree cannot bear bad fruit, nor can a rotten tree bear good fruit. Every tree that does not bear good fruit will be cut down and thrown into the fire. So by their fruits you will know them."

Reflection

Jesus' teaching is often very practical. He warns us to beware of false prophets and those things that seem to be good and true, but in reality are far from the truth. Yet, Jesus simply states that we discern these things by their fruit. Those that bear good fruit are good, because a good tree cannot bear bad fruit and vice versa. In Jesus, we learn how to discern and judge between right and wrong, even in seemingly deceiving circumstances.

Prayers *others may be added*

Jesus, you are the vine and we are the branches. Let us pray:

◆ Consecrate us in your truth.

That the Church may grow and flourish by bearing good fruit in holy vocations to marriage, priesthood, and religious life, we pray: ◆ That our nation may not be deceived by relativism, secularism, and anti-life ideologies, but rather that we may courageously identify their falsehoods and work to promote the flourishing of truth and goodness, we pray: ◆ That the suffering of all the sick may bear fruit for the salvation of all the world, we pray: ◆ That those who are in the process of making important decisions and are experiencing new life changes may be graced with the gifts of discernment, counsel, and peace, we pray: ◆

Our Father . . .

Lord Jesus,
you are the vine and we are the branches.
Your Father, the vine grower, prunes and casts away
all that does not bear good fruit.
Send your Spirit of wisdom, counsel, and discernment
upon us, your people,
so that we may clearly distinguish
the light of truth from the darkness of sin and evil.
You live and reign forever.
Amen.

✝ Teach me the way of your decrees, O Lord.

Thursday, June 28, 2012
Memorial of Saint Irenaeus, Bishop and Martyr

✝ For the glory of your name, O Lord, deliver us.

Psalm 103   *page 415*

Reading   *Matthew 7:21, 24–27*

Jesus said to his disciples: "Not everyone who says to me, 'Lord, Lord,' will enter the Kingdom of heaven, but only the one who does the will of my Father in heaven.

"Everyone who listens to these words of mine and acts on them will be like a wise man who built his house on rock. The rain fell, the floods came, and the winds blew and buffeted the house. But it did not collapse; it had been set solidly on rock. And everyone who listens to these words of mine but does not act on them will be like a fool who built his house on sand. The rain fell, the floods came, and the winds blew and buffeted the house. And it collapsed and was completely ruined."

Reflection

The word of God is our security and foundation. Jesus teaches us in today's Gospel that to listen and act upon his word provides us with a stronghold to remain steadfast among the winds and rains and storms. However, those who choose not to listen are like the fool who builds on the unstable foundation of sand. Jesus reminds us that those who listen and fulfill his Father's will are the ones who will enter his kingdom.

Prayers   *others may be added*

Jesus, you teach and instruct us along the path of life. Hear our prayers and petitions, as we say:

◆ **Teach us to hear your word and do your will, O Lord.**

For the Church, that, built upon the rock of Jesus Christ, she may remain steadfast and secure amid the storms and persecutions from within and without, we pray: ◆ For civic leaders, that they may work to promote societies of justice and peace upon the secure foundation of human and Christian values, we pray: ◆ For those experiencing intense trials and difficulties, that the truth of Jesus Christ may remain their stronghold and security, we pray: ◆ For all construction workers, builders, contractors, and architects, we pray: ◆

Our Father . . .

Lord Jesus,
you teach us that we must not only call on
    your name,
but we must also fulfill the will of your
    heavenly Father.
Give us the wisdom to live our lives
securely founded on the truth of
    your word,
that in times of difficulty we may ever
    remain united to you,
our refuge and our strength.
You live and reign forever.
Amen.

✝ For the glory of your name, O Lord, deliver us.

✝ The angel of the Lord will rescue those who fear him.

Psalm 34   *page 406*

Reading   *Matthew 16:13–19*

When Jesus went into the region of Caesarea Philippi he asked his disciples, "Who do people say that the Son of Man is?" They replied, "Some say John the Baptist, others Elijah, still others Jeremiah or one of the prophets." He said to them, "But who do you say that I am?" Simon Peter said in reply, "You are the Christ, the Son of the living God." Jesus said to him in reply, "Blessed are you, Simon son of Jonah. For flesh and blood has not revealed this to you, but my heavenly Father. And so I say to you, you are Peter, and upon this rock I will build my Church, and the gates of the netherworld shall not prevail against it. I will give you the keys to the Kingdom of heaven. Whatever you bind on earth shall be bound in heaven; and whatever you loose on earth shall be loosed in heaven."

Reflection

Today's Gospel recounts Peter's profession of faith as he proclaims that Jesus is truly the Christ, the Son of God. After this affirmation, Jesus appoints Peter as the rock of the visible Church on earth to continue Jesus' mission to shepherd his flock. Saint Paul is known as the apostle to the Gentiles, through his great work of evangelization and conversion of many nations through spreading the Gospel of Christ Jesus.

Prayers   *others may be added*

Loving God, you promise to guide and protect your Church to the end of the age. Let us pray:

◆ **You are the Christ, the Son of the living God.**

For the Holy Father, the successor of Saint Peter, and for all the bishops as successors of the apostles, that they may be holy and steadfast to carry out Christ's mission of evangelization, we pray: ◆
For Christians of all nations, that they may rise up to go out to spread the Good News to all the world, we pray: ◆
For those in doubt and despair, those who suffer poverty, illness, and violence, we pray: ◆ For those inspired by the witness of the apostles, that they may go out to proclaim Christ's word in our homes, among our friends, in the workplace, and to all the nations, we pray: ◆

Our Father . . .

Lord Jesus,
you are the Christ, the Son of the
    Living God.
Through the witness of the apostles,
you give us example to offer our lives
in bold service to your holy name.
Through the prayers of Saints Peter
    and Paul,
may we have the courage and faith to
    proclaim to all the world
your goodness and glory.
You live and reign forever.
Amen.

✝ The angel of the Lord will rescue those who fear him.

✝ Lord, forget not the souls of your poor ones.

Psalm 145   *page 422*

Reading   *Matthew 8:5–13*

When Jesus entered Capernaum, a centurion approached him and appealed to him, saying, "Lord, my servant is lying at home paralyzed, suffering dreadfully." He said to him, "I will come and cure him." The centurion said in reply, "Lord, I am not worthy to have you enter under my roof; only say the word and my servant will be healed. For I too am a man subject to authority, with soldiers subject to me. And I say to one, 'Go,' and he goes; and to another, 'Come here,' and he comes; and to my slave, 'Do this,' and he does it." When Jesus heard this, he was amazed and said to those following him, "Amen, I say to you, in no one in Israel have I found such faith. I say to you, many will come from the east and the west, and will recline with Abraham, Isaac, and Jacob at the banquet in the Kingdom of heaven, but the children of the Kingdom will be driven out into the outer darkness, where there will be wailing and grinding of teeth." And Jesus said to the centurion, "You may go; as you have believed, let it be done for you." And at that very hour his servant was healed.

Reflection

Jesus is our divine physician who heals all our ills, both physical and spiritual. Today's Gospel reveals Jesus as our God who comes to earth as man to heal us of our infirmity. God chooses to spend his time in service to the sick, visiting them, being present to them, and healing them of their illnesses. Let us have faith in this great healer who is our loving God come to save us.

Prayers   *others may be added*

Father, you send your Son to heal us and grant us salvation. Let us pray:

◆ Strengthen our faith, O Lord.

For the Church, that she may be the source of salvation for all who seek physical and spiritual healing, we pray: ◆ For the success of social initiatives to improve health care, eliminate poverty, hunger, and war, and to create environments of true justice and peace, we pray: ◆ For our faith community to become ever more united through the word of God and Christian living, we pray: ◆ For all who are sick and in need of healing, that Christ the Divine Physician may restore them to health of mind and body and give them patience to endure their sufferings, we pray: ◆

Our Father . . .

Jesus Christ,
you choose to be among the weak, the sick, and the broken.
Grant us your salvation, and strengthen us in your word.
You live and reign forever.
Amen.

✝ Lord, forget not the souls of your poor ones.

✝ I will praise you, Lord, for you have rescued me.

Psalm 34 page 406

Reading Mark 5:25–29

There was a woman afflicted with hemorrhages for twelve years. She had suffered greatly at the hands of many doctors and had spent all that she had. Yet she was not helped but only grew worse. She had heard about Jesus and came up behind him in the crowd and touched his cloak. She said, "If I but touch his clothes, I shall be cured." Immediately her flow of blood dried up. She felt in her body that she was healed of her affliction.

Reflection

Today's Gospel passage recounts the event of the healing of the hemorrhaging woman who had found no healing from her affliction even after years and years. Upon hearing about Jesus, she comes to him in faith and in courage. She reaches out to touch him, confident that if she does so she will be healed. Jesus praises her faith, heals her, and tells her to go in peace.

Prayers *others may be added*

With faith in your healing power, O God, we come to you to receive your grace and your life. Let us pray:

◆ Heal us and save us, O Lord.

For the ministers of the Church, the Holy Father, all priests, bishops, and clergy, that they may be instruments of the Lord's healing power and grace, we pray: ◆ For all nations, that they may be touched by the power of the Lord, who restores all order and bring justice and peace, we pray: ◆ For all the sick who have suffered at the hands of many doctors, that they may not tire in their search to discover competent health care providers to help them in their need, we pray: ◆ For our parish community, that we may be ever strengthened in a living faith among one another, we pray: ◆ For the faith and courage to come to receive grace and life from Jesus' healing touch, we pray: ◆

Our Father . . .

Heavenly Father,
you sent your Son to heal us
in mind, body, and spirit.
Touch us with your grace,
that we may be renewed
in new life to live as your children.
We ask through our Lord Jesus Christ,
    your Son,
who lives and reigns with you in the unity
    of the Holy Spirit,
one God, forever and ever.
Amen.

✝ I will praise you, Lord, for you have rescued me.

✝ I will praise you Lord, for you have rescue me.

Psalm 85　　　　　　*page 411*

Reading　　　　　*Matthew 8:18–22*

When Jesus saw a crowd around him, he gave orders to cross to the other shore. A scribe approached and said to him, "Teacher, I will follow you wherever you go." Jesus answered him, "Foxes have dens and birds of the sky have nests, but the Son of Man has nowhere to rest his head." Another of his disciples said to him, "Lord, let me go first and bury my father." But Jesus answered him, "Follow me, and let the dead bury their dead."

Reflection

The true encounter with Jesus Christ requires a definitive response: we will either follow him or reject him. In today's Gospel, a scribe boldly professes that he will follow the Master wherever he goes. This definitive response to follow Jesus must take root and blossom through the constant renewal of this "yes" to follow Christ in the daily circumstances and opportunities of each day.

Prayers　　　　*others may be added*

Father, you send your Son to make his dwelling among us. Let us pray:

◆ Teacher, give us the grace to follow after you.

For the Church, that she may be the home and refuge for all who seek rest and truth, we pray: ◆ For all missionaries, that their work may bear fruit in encouraging many peoples to follow after Christ, we pray: ◆ For all the homeless, those who live on the streets, and for those who suffer from poverty, we pray: ◆ For all those who suffer illness in mind, body, or spirit, we pray: ◆ For the needs of our community, that throughout joys, sufferings, and sacrifices we may remain faithful to following after Christ, we pray: ◆ For all who earn their living through the work of their hands, we pray: ◆ For all those who have died, that they may enjoy the glory of the beatific vision and for the comfort of their families and friends, we pray: ◆

Our Father . . .

Heavenly Father,
you sent your Son among us
to teach us and reveal your fatherly love.
Pour your Spirit upon us,
that we may recognize that we are made
　　for heaven,
and that the sufferings and trials
of this life are nothing to be compared
with the joy and glory to come.
We ask this through Christ our Lord.
Amen.

✝ I will praise you Lord, for you have rescued me.

Tuesday, July 3, 2012
Feast of Saint Thomas, Apostle

✝ Go out to all the world and tell the Good News.

Psalm 146 *page 423*

Reading *John 20:24–29*

Thomas, called Didymus, one of the Twelve, was not with them when Jesus came. So the other disciples said to him, "We have seen the Lord." But Thomas said to them, "Unless I see the mark of the nails in his hands and put my finger into the nailmarks and put my hand into his side, I will not believe." Now a week later his disciples were again inside and Thomas was with them. Jesus came, although the doors were locked, and stood in their midst and said, "Peace be with you." Then he said to Thomas, "Put your finger here and see my hands, and bring your hand and put it into my side, and do not be unbelieving, but believe." Thomas answered and said to him, "My Lord and my God!" Jesus said to him, "Have you come to believe because you have seen me? Blessed are those who have not seen and have believed."

Reflection

Especially in this modern day and age, most of us want empirical evidence before we will believe or accept something as true. Likewise, Thomas could not believe that Jesus had truly risen until he had touched and seen the living Christ. Through the sacraments, we see, touch, and encounter the living Jesus, our Lord and our God. However, we must possess a firm faith to believe in

Christ Jesus until the day when we will see him face to face upon his return in glory.

Prayers *others may be added*

Lord, increase our faith as we pray:

◆ Lord, I believe; help my unbelief.

For the Church, that she may remain steadfast against the ideologies of empiricism, relativism, and modernism that threaten to diminish faith in Jesus Christ, we pray: ◆ For world leaders, that they may work to eliminate world hunger, social injustice, war, and poverty, we pray: ◆ For all who suffer sickness, that they may receive renewed health, enduring peace, and boundless hope in Jesus who brings healing and salvation to all who call upon his name, we pray: ◆ For the grace of relentless faith to believe in the truth of Jesus Christ even in moments of darkness and uncertainty, we pray: ◆

Our Father . . .

Eternal Father,
through the Incarnation of your Son,
we see, hear, and touch the Word of life.
Through the prayers of Saint Thomas,
may we boldly testify to Jesus Christ,
risen from the dead, our Lord and
   our God,
who lives and reigns with you in the unity
   of the Holy Spirit,
one God, forever and ever.
Amen.

✝ Go out to all the world and tell the Good News.

✝ To the upright I will show the saving power of God.

Psalm 150   *page 424*

Reading   *Matthew 8:32–34*

When Jesus came to the territory of the Gadarenes, two demoniacs who were coming from the tombs met him. They were so savage that no one could travel by that road. They cried out, "What have you to do with us, Son of God? Have you come here to torment us before the appointed time?" Some distance away a herd of many swine was feeding. The demons pleaded with him, "If you drive us out, send us into the herd of swine." And he said to them, "Go then!" They came out and entered the swine, and the whole herd rushed down the steep bank into the sea where they drowned.

Reflection

Similar to the words in today's Gospel, our modern world also frequently asks, "What have you to do with us, Son of God?" And it is a good question to consider. What does God have to do with us? Is God here only to torment us and make us feel guilty about ourselves, or does a life surrendered to God's sovereignty really lead to true freedom and happiness? God answers these important human questions for us when we are honest and humble enough to ask and listen.

Prayers   *others may be added*

Father, hear the prayers we offer to you:

◆ **Give us true freedom, O Lord.**

For the Church, that she may continue her good works of charity and evangelization for the building up and flourishing of our nation, we pray: ◆ For the United States of America, that she may remain one nation under God with true liberty and justice for all, we pray: ◆ For our President, that he may lead the people of this nation in service of the good and true dignity of each person, we pray: ◆ For all immigrants, that they may be aided and accepted as they seek a better life of freedom and opportunity, we pray: ◆ For U.S. citizens, that, united together as one nation, they may work together to share our gifts to build civilizations of love within our homes and throughout all the world, we pray: ◆

Our Father . . .

Christ our King,
you reign sovereign above all the nations.
Visit your people, O Lord,
and renew the United States
in the true freedom and peace and justice
     that comes
only through the encounter with your love
     and life.
You live and reign forever.
Amen.

✝ To the upright I will show the saving power of God.

✝ The judgments of the Lord are true, and all of them are just.

Psalm 100   *page 414*

Reading   *Matthew 9:1–8*

After entering a boat, Jesus made the crossing, and came into his own town. And there people brought to him a paralytic lying on a stretcher. When Jesus saw their faith, he said to the paralytic, "Courage, child, your sins are forgiven." At that, some of the scribes said to themselves, "This man is blaspheming." Jesus knew what they were thinking, and said, "Why do you harbor evil thoughts? Which is easier, to say, 'Your sins are forgiven,' or to say, 'Rise and walk'? But that you may know that the Son of Man has authority on earth to forgive sins"—he then said to the paralytic, "Rise, pick up your stretcher, and go home." He rose and went home. When the crowds saw this they were struck with awe and glorified God who had given such authority to men.

Reflection

Jesus asks us today in the Gospel, "Why do you harbor evil thoughts?" Too often we fall into skepticism and we harshly judge and criticize both God and our neighbor. Yet Jesus performs miracles of healing and forgiveness, like today's Gospel reading, so that we may know that he is truly Almighty God. Only through a humble openness to his word can we encounter his majesty and receive his gifts of newness and life.

Prayers   *others may be added*

Lord Jesus, you heal the paralytic by the authority and power given to you by the Father. Let us pray:

◆ Heal us and free us from sin, O God.

For the Holy Father and all priests and bishops, that, sustained by the prayers and support of all the laity, they may remain faithful to their mission of service to the Holy Mother Church, we pray: ◆ For the world, that all may know the saving and healing power of Jesus Christ, we pray: ◆ For all who suffer from paralysis, heart disease, and all illnesses, that they may have courage as they await the healing power of Jesus to restore them to perfect health in mind and body, we pray: ◆

Our Father . . .

Heavenly Father,
you manifest your greatness
in the authority and healing power
of your Son, Jesus Christ.
Heal us from all our sins and afflictions,
that we may be free to enjoy
the happiness of heaven in union with you
and your Son, who live and reign together
in the unity of the Holy Spirit,
one God, forever and ever.
Amen.

✝ The judgments of the Lord are true, and all of them are just.

Friday, July 6, 2012
Weekday

✝ One does not live by bread alone, but by every word that comes from the mouth of God.

Psalm 103   *page 415*

Reading   *Matthew 9:9–13*

As Jesus passed by, he saw a man named Matthew sitting at the customs post. He said to him, "Follow me." And he got up and followed him. While he was at table in his house, many tax collectors and sinners came and sat with Jesus and his disciples. The Pharisees saw this and said to his disciples, "Why does your teacher eat with tax collectors and sinners?" He heard this and said, "Those who are well do not need a physician, but the sick do. Go and learn the meaning of the words, / *I desire mercy, not sacrifice.* / I did not come to call the righteous but sinners."

Reflection

Jesus has come to call sinners. This is good news for us. Why do we insist on thinking that Jesus is only for those people to whom doing good and being holy comes easily? If we read the Gospel, we see that Jesus spent his time with the sinners, the sick, the weak, and the poor. Jesus has come for us: for those who are weak, those who makes mistakes, those who are imperfect. This gives us great reason for hope, so let us follow him along the path of freedom.

Prayers   *others may be added*

Jesus, you meet us where we are, and you invite us to follow after you. Hear our prayers and petitions as we pray:

◆ Come to our aid, O God.

For all who serve the Church, that they may faithfully follow after Christ in humble recognition of their weakness and their dependence on the grace and mercy of God to fulfill the greatness of their calling, we pray: ◆ For government officials, that they may always seek to serve the weak and vulnerable of society, we pray: ◆ For all the sick who experience hopelessness because of illness or suffering, that they may rejoice in the presence of Jesus, the Divine Physician, who comes to bring them help and healing, we pray: ◆ For all who have died, we pray: ◆ For the courage to follow after Christ and encounter him in the everyday circumstances of daily life, we pray: ◆

Our Father . . .

Heavenly Father,
through your Son, you free us from
    our sins
and restore us to health in mind and body.
May we be renewed in purity and love
to courageously follow after your
    Son, Jesus,
who lives and reigns with you in the unity
    of the Holy Spirit,
one God, forever and ever.
Amen.

✝ One does not live by bread alone, but by every word that comes from the mouth of God.

Saturday, July 7, 2012
Weekday

✝ The Lord speaks of peace to his people.

Psalm 145 *page 422*

Reading *Matthew 9:14–15*

The disciples of John approached Jesus and said, "Why do we and the Pharisees fast much, but your disciples do not fast?" Jesus answered them, "Can the guests mourn as long as the bridegroom is with them? The days will come when the bridegroom is taken away from them, and then they will fast."

Reflection

There is a time for everything just as in today's Gospel, there is a time for fasting and time for celebration. We do not have to do anything strange in order to live the Christian life, but by following Christ we learn the appropriate ways to live the ordinary and practical means of our everyday lives. In this way, Christ gives meaning and fulfillment in the joys and sorrows of each of our lives.

Prayers *others may be added*

Lord, your Incarnate Word teaches us and gives us clarity on how we ought to live. Hear our prayer as we ask:

◆ Sanctify your people, O Lord.

For the Church, that she may instruct and teach with clarity and wisdom to offer counsel to those who seek the truth, we pray: ◆ For civic leaders, that they may seek appropriate means to aid those in need by serving the common good of society, we pray: ◆ For all peoples, that they may come to know the truth of Jesus Christ, who brings fulfillment in the everyday duties and responsibilities of our lives, we pray: ◆ For the sick, the homebound, the lonely, and those who do not know the abundant love of the Father, we pray: ◆ For all travelers, that they may arrive safely at their destinations, we pray: ◆ For the grace to be all things to all people, as we rejoice with those who rejoice and mourn with those who mourn, we pray: ◆

Our Father . . .

Loving God,
you give us this summertime
of beauty, warmth, and harvest
in which to delight in the praise
    your name.
Open our hearts to receive your love
and free us to experience the joy of life,
united to you and your Son, who live and
    reign in the unity of the Holy Spirit,
one God, forever and ever.
Amen.

✝ The Lord speaks of peace to his people.

Sunday, July 8, 2012
Fourteenth Sunday in Ordinary Time

✝ Our eyes are fixed on the Lord,
pleading for his mercy.

Psalm 104 *page 416*

Reading *Mark 6:4–6*

Jesus said to [his disciples], "A prophet is not without honor except in his native place and among his own kin and in his own house." So he was not able to perform any mighty deed there, apart from curing a few sick people by laying his hands on them. He was amazed at their lack of faith.

Reflection

Sometimes it is our families that cause us the most pain and hurt. But we see in today's Gospel that even Jesus had difficulty among his family members as his kin took offense and criticized him. The Father has all of his children in his hand and will work his miracles among our loved ones as we continue to offer love and prayers for our families, friends, coworkers, and our country.

Prayers *others may be added*

Father, your Son came into the world, and the world did not receive him. Let us pray:

♦ Draw us into one family, O Lord.

For the Church, that she may be drawn together as one body in Christ, we pray: ♦ For the work of government officials, that they may help to aid poverty, hunger, and all anti-life practices for the unity, protection, and betterment of each person of our human family, we pray: ♦ For all those who suffer marital difficulties, domestic abuse, and family problems, that the Triune God may bring about peace, healing, and forgiveness in all conflicts among family members, we pray: ♦

Our Father . . .

Triune God,
you give us the gift of family
to imitate your Trinitarian love.
Heal our brokenness, and give us the grace to forgive
and to be forgiven by those closest to us.
Restore us to the joy and freedom of living
in communion with others and with you,
who live and reign together with your Son,
Jesus Christ, in the unity of the Holy Spirit,
one God, forever and ever.
Amen.

✝ Our eyes are fixed on the Lord,
pleading for his mercy.

Monday, July 9, 2012
Weekday

✝ The Lord is gracious and merciful.

Psalm 34
page 406

Reading
Matthew 9:18–22

While Jesus was speaking, an official came forward, knelt down before him, and said, "My daughter has just died. But come, lay your hand on her, and she will live." Jesus rose and followed him, and so did his disciples. A woman suffering hemorrhages for twelve years came up behind him and touched the tassel on his cloak. She said to herself, "If only I can touch his cloak, I shall be cured." Jesus turned around and saw her, and said, "Courage, daughter! Your faith has saved you." And from that hour the woman was cured.

Reflection

Jesus heals the sick and raises the dead to new life. This is the Good News of Jesus Christ that must be spread throughout the world. The news on television often highlights negative events; however, God is still at work among us bringing healing and new life. Let us open our eyes so that we may see the good work that God is doing within our lives and those of our families and friends.

Prayers
others may be added

To those who call upon your name, O Lord, you bring healing and newness. Let us pray:

◆ Restore us to life, O Lord.

That the Church may be renewed in a new springtime of grace and mercy for all her members and for the whole world, we pray: ◆ That cultures who suffer the emptiness of ignorance of God may be lifted up in faith by the work of missionaries, social workers, and by the prayers of all the faithful, we pray: ◆ That the Lord may touch all who are sick, to raise them up and restore them to health of mind and body, we pray: ◆ That in faith, we may boldly beg God for the graces and favors that we need, we pray: ◆

Our Father . . .

Gracious and merciful Father,
you sent your Son to bring us healing and
   new life.
May we always proclaim the Good News
   of the Gospel
with faith and courage for the glory
of your name and the salvation of all
   peoples.
We ask this through Christ our Lord.
Amen.

✝ The Lord is gracious and merciful.

Tuesday, July 10, 2012
Weekday

✝ The house of Israel trusts in the Lord.

Psalm 95
page 413

Reading
Matthew 9:35–38

Jesus went around to all the towns and villages, teaching in their synagogues, proclaiming the Gospel of the Kingdom, and curing every disease and illness. At the sight of the crowds, his heart was moved with pity for them because they were troubled and abandoned, like sheep without a shepherd. Then he said to his disciples, "The harvest is abundant but the laborers are few; so ask the master of the harvest to send out laborers for his harvest."

Reflection

How beautiful to see and encounter the tender heart of Jesus that is moved with pity and compassion for us. He is our Good Shepherd who loves his troubled sheep as he teaches us, proclaims to us the Father's message of love, and cures every disease and illness. He heals us from our sins by driving out all evil so that we may speak and proclaim the greatness of the Lord and all he has done for us.

Prayers
others may be added

Lord Jesus, our Good Shepherd, your heart is moved with pity for us, your people. Hear the prayers we present to you today:

◆ Guide and protect your flock, O Lord.

For all who serve the Church, that they may faithfully follow after Christ in humble recognition of their weakness and their dependency on the grace and mercy of God to fulfill the greatness of their calling, we pray: ◆ For government officials, that they may always seek to serve the weak and vulnerable of society, we pray: ◆ For all the sick who experience hopelessness because of illness or suffering, that they may rejoice in the presence of Jesus, the Divine Physician, who comes to bring them help and healing, we pray: ◆ For all who have died, we pray: ◆ For the courage to follow after Christ and encounter him in the everyday circumstances of daily life, we pray: ◆

Our Father . . .

Heavenly Father,
you sent your Son as the Good Shepherd
to the lost sheep of the house of Israel.
Teach us, Lord; heal us in mind,
    spirit, and body,
and restore us to the glory of union
    with you
in your kingdom where you live and reign
    with your Son,
in the unity of the Holy Spirit,
one God, forever and ever.
Amen.

✝ The house of Israel trusts in the Lord.

Wednesday, July 11, 2012
Memorial of Saint Benedict, Abbot

✝ Seek always the face of the Lord.

Psalm 100
page 414

Reading
Matthew 10:1, 5–7

Jesus summoned his Twelve disciples and gave them authority over unclean spirits to drive them out and to cure every disease and every illness. . . .

Jesus sent out these Twelve after instructing them thus, "Do not go into pagan territory or enter a Samaritan town. Go rather to the lost sheep of the house of Israel. As you go, make this proclamation: 'The Kingdom of heaven is at hand.'"

Reflection

Like the twelve apostles, Jesus also calls us and sends us out to be messengers of his Good News. By virtue of our Baptism, we have been set apart, called by name, and given a share in Christ's mission as priest, prophet, and king. Through the diligent fulfillment of our daily work, our example of charity, and our faithfulness to prayer, we offer an example as faithful apostles to others through our daily lives.

Prayers
others may be added

Jesus, you call your chosen people to continue your work on earth. Let us pray:

◆ Thy kingdom come, O Lord.

That the Holy Father and all the clergy may be renewed in their ministry to seek out the lost sheep of the world in faithful imitation of the holiness of Jesus Christ, we pray: ◆ That civic leaders may work to serve the common good of all peoples by discovering means to end war, violence, hunger, poverty, and injustice, we pray: ◆ That the Lord will send Christian disciples to bring aid, healing, and peace to all who suffer, we pray: ◆ That all Benedictines may further the kingdom of God, we pray: ◆

Our Father . . .

Loving God,
open our hearts to hear the voice
of the Good Shepherd who calls us
   by name
and invites us to follow him along the
   path of life.
Through the prayers of Saint Benedict,
may we faithfully follow the Lord
in prayer and work until we attain the
glory and eternal beatitude in heaven.
We ask this through Christ our Lord,
who lives and reigns with you in the unity
   of the Holy Spirit,
one God, forever and ever.
Amen.

✝ Seek always the face of the Lord.

✝ Let us see your face, Lord, and we shall be saved.

Psalm 103   *page 415*

Reading   *Matthew 10:7–14*

Jesus said to his Apostles: "As you go, make this proclamation: 'The Kingdom of heaven is at hand.' Cure the sick, raise the dead, cleanse the lepers, drive out demons. Without cost you have received; without cost you are to give. Do not take gold or silver or copper for your belts; no sack for the journey, or a second tunic, or sandals, or walking stick. The laborer deserves his keep. Whatever town or village you enter, look for a worthy person in it, and stay there until you leave. As you enter a house, wish it peace. If the house is worthy, let your peace come upon it; if not, let your peace return to you. Whoever will not receive you or listen to your words—go outside that house or town and shake the dust from your feet."

Reflection

We have been given everything freely by God. Therefore, we ought to give generously to others in the same manner in which God has given to us. Jesus tells us that the kingdom of God is at hand. There is no time to waste. Let us freely and generously give to those around us the peace and life that we have received from our encounter with Jesus Christ.

Prayers   *others may be added*

O God, you sent us into the vineyard to invite all peoples to life with you. Let us pray:

◆ Let your peace rest upon us, Lord.

That the Good News of the kingdom of God may be proclaimed to all the world through the faithful work of missionaries, the clergy, and all the lay faithful, we pray: ◆ That countries torn apart by war, violence, abuse, and unhealthy living situations may be aided by the good work and charity of government leaders and Christian organizations, we pray: ◆ That we may be freed from all selfishness so that we may share the gifts and blessings we have freely received from the Lord, we pray: ◆

Our Father . . .

Almighty Father,
through your Son, you call us as apostles
to bring the healing peace of your love
    and life.
Pour out the power of your Spirit upon us,
that we may be driven to serve your
    people in love
as we await the coming of your kingdom.
We ask this through our Lord Jesus
    Christ, your Son,
who lives and reigns with you in the unity
    of the Holy Spirit,
one God, forever and ever.
Amen.

✝ Let us see your face, Lord, and we shall be saved.

Friday, July 13, 2012
Weekday

✝ My mouth will declare your praise.

Psalm 145 *page 422*

Reading *Matthew 10:16–20*

Jesus said to his Apostles: "Behold, I am sending you like sheep in the midst of wolves; so be shrewd as serpents and simple as doves. But beware of men, for they will hand you over to courts and scourge you in their synagogues, and you will be led before governors and kings for my sake as a witness before them and the pagans. When they hand you over, do not worry about how you are to speak or what you are to say. You will be given at that moment what you are to say. For it will not be you who speak but the Spirit of your Father speaking through you."

Reflection

Jesus never says it's going to be easy. On the contrary, he warns us that we will most likely be persecuted and criticized by friends and even family members for the sake of his name. However, in this way we will witness to Christ, and the Holy Spirit will be present to guide us and give us the words to speak. Those who persevere to the end will reap the reward of life and salvation.

Prayers *others may be added*

Jesus, you send us as sheep among wolves. In faith, hear the prayers of your flock as we pray:

◆ Good Shepherd, send us your Spirit.

For the Holy Father, all bishops, and priests, that they may remain faithful and persevering amid the persecutions of the world, so as to be witnesses to the kingdom, we pray: ◆ For all judges and lawyers, that they may make wise and prudent decisions as they serve society through the pursuit of justice and truth, we pray: ◆ For all converts to the faith, that they may receive strength to patiently bear misunderstandings from their family and friends, we pray: ◆ For all who suffer persecution, that they may be freed from fear and filled with the Holy Spirit, who leads and guides all to truth, we pray: ◆ For the grace to be wise as serpents and gentle as doves while we seek to follow the path of the Lord, we pray: ◆

Our Father . . .

Loving Father,
protect your children who seek to
    serve you.
Give us courage in time of trial,
and send out your Holy Spirit upon us
so our mouths may proclaim your praise
as faithful witnesses to your glory.
We ask this through Christ our Lord.
Amen.

✝ My mouth will declare your praise.

Saturday, July 14, 2012
Memorial of Blessed Kateri Tekakwitha, Virgin

✝ The Lord is king; he is robed in majesty.

Psalm 150   *page 424*

Reading   *Matthew 10:24–33*

Jesus said to his Apostles: "No disciple is above his teacher, no slave above his master. It is enough for the disciple that he become like his teacher, for the slave that he become like his master. If they have called the master of the house Beelzebul, how much more those of his household!

"Therefore do not be afraid of them. Nothing is concealed that will not be revealed, nor secret that will not be known. What I say to you in the darkness, speak in the light; what you hear whispered, proclaim on the housetops. And do not be afraid of those who kill the body but cannot kill the soul; rather, be afraid of the one who can destroy both soul and body in Gehenna. Are not two sparrows sold for a small coin? Yet not one of them falls to the ground without your Father's knowledge. Even all the hairs of your head are counted. So do not be afraid; you are worth more than many sparrows. Everyone who acknowledges me before others I will acknowledge before my heavenly Father. But whoever denies me before others, I will deny before my heavenly Father."

Reflection

Do not be afraid. Over and over Jesus repeats the same words to us: do not be afraid. God is with us, and the Father will protect us, his children. We must remember that Jesus has conquered over the darkness of sin and death. If we are met by challenges, trials, and persecutions, we must not fear, for Jesus is present to us and will not test us beyond our strength.

Prayers   *others may be added*

Lord, hear the prayers we offer you today:

◆ **Free us from fear, O Lord.**

For the Church, that she may faithfully follow after Jesus, the Master and Teacher, we pray: ◆ For the conversion of all nations to the eternal love of the Trinity, we pray: ◆ For those who suffer from illnesses, especially diseases of the skin, that they may be restored to full health, through the prayers of Blessed Kateri, we pray: ◆ For all to confidently give witness to Christ, we pray: ◆

Our Father . . .

Loving Father,
you provide for all our needs.
Give us faith to trust in your merciful love.
We ask through Christ our Lord.
Amen.

✝ The Lord is king; he is robed in majesty.

✝ Lord, let us see your kindness, and grant us your salvation.

Psalm 34 *page 406*

Reading *Mark 6:7–13*

Jesus summoned the Twelve and began to send them out two by two and gave them authority over unclean spirits. He instructed them to take nothing for the journey but a walking stick—no food, no sack, no money in their belts. They were, however, to wear sandals but not a second tunic. He said to them, "Wherever you enter a house, stay there until you leave from there. Whatever place does not welcome you or listen to you, leave there and shake the dust off your feet in testimony against them." So they went off and preached repentance. [The Twelve] drove out many demons, and they anointed with oil many who were sick and cured them.

Reflection

In this part of Ordinary Time, the graces of God's mystery that we celebrate throughout the liturgical year grow and mature within our hearts. The graces of the birth, life, death, Resurrection, and Ascension of Jesus continue to wash over us through the outpouring of the Holy Spirit as Jesus invites us to ever more deeply follow him and as he sends us out to be his instrument for others in our daily lives.

Prayers *others may be added*

Jesus, you send us out as your apostles to continue your work among the world. Let us pray:

◆ **Lord, make us instruments of your peace.**

For the Church, that she may faithfully fulfill Christ's mission to bring the message of salvation to all peoples of the world, we pray: ◆ For all nations, that they may be receptive to welcome the Good News, salvation, and truth of Jesus Christ, we pray: ◆ For all who suffer from illness, poverty, abuse, hunger, and those in crisis situations, we pray: ◆ For our parish community, that they may be renewed in love for one another through generosity, support, and openness toward our neighbor, we pray: ◆ For all to choose to always follow Christ, even during times in which he invites us along a more difficult path, we pray: ◆

Our Father . . .

O God,
in your Son Jesus, you drive out demons, heal the sick, and bring peace to all peoples. May the graces of your miraculous power be made manifest to us today through our participation in the sacraments, so that, having shared in your gift of life in the Spirit, we may be sent out to do
   your work.
We ask this through Christ our Lord. Amen.

✝ Lord, let us see your kindness, and grant us your salvation.

Monday, July 16, 2012
Weekday

✝ To the upright I will show the saving power of God.

Psalm 104 *page 416*

Reading *Matthew 10:34–36*

Jesus said to his Apostles: "Do not think that I have come to bring peace upon the earth. I have come to bring not peace but the sword. For I have come to set a man against his father, a daughter against her mother, and a daughter-in-law against her mother-in-law; and one's enemies will be those of his household."

Reflection

We are still hearing from Matthew 10, Jesus' commission of the apostles. Today, the emphasis is first of all on the opposition Jesus' disciples will encounter, even from their own family members. Yet nothing—no relationship, even that of kinship—can have priority over one's relationship with Jesus. The second part of the text focuses on the blessings to be received by the people to whom the apostles are sent—if they are receptive to their words.

Prayers *others may be added*

Father, hear the prayers we offer to you:

◆ To you and to your most holy will, we surrender, O Lord.

For the Church, that all members of the Mystical Body of Christ may live out their baptismal call to follow the Lord and heed his word, we pray: ◆ For civic leaders, that they may work in service of the poor and weak, especially in areas in need of social development, we pray: ◆ For all who suffer the loneliness of sickness or pain, that, after the dark night of suffering, they may rejoice in the joy of Christ's healing light, we pray: ◆ For all the members of the Carmelite order, we pray: ◆ For our wills to become ever more united to God's will, we pray: ◆ For all the faithful departed, we pray: ◆

Our Father . . .

Heavenly Father,
in times of darkness and despondency,
send your Spirit upon us to give us strength
to surrender ourselves ever more fully
to your most holy will.
Through the prayers
of Our Lady of Mount Carmel, teach us
how to meditate and contemplate the glory
of your majesty, you who live and reign
with your Son, Jesus Christ, in the unity
of the Holy Spirit, one God, forever
and ever.
Amen.

✝ To the upright I will show the saving power of God.

✝ God upholds his city for ever.

Psalm 95 *page 413*

Reading *Matthew 11:20–24*

Jesus began to reproach the towns where most of his mighty deeds had been done, since they had not repented. "Woe to you, Chorazin! Woe to you, Bethsaida! For if the mighty deeds done in your midst had been done in Tyre and Sidon, they would long ago have repented in sackcloth and ashes. But I tell you, it will be more tolerable for Tyre and Sidon on the day of judgment than for you. And as for you, Capernaum:

Will you be exalted to heaven? / You will go down to the netherworld.

For if the mighty deeds done in your midst had been done in Sodom, it would have remained until this day. But I tell you, it will be more tolerable for the land of Sodom on the day of judgment than for you."

Reflection

Sometimes through our skepticism, doubt, and indifference, we remain hardhearted and closed off to God and his work within us. We don't want God to get too close, and so we choose to live in the deceptive emptiness of our own selfishness and isolated autonomy. However, in this way we prevent God from entering our hearts and transforming our lives into lives rich in meaning, fulfillment, and hope.

Prayers *others may be added*

Father, you send your Son to proclaim your message of repentance and salvation. Hear our humble prayers as we cry:

◆ Convert our hearts, O God.

For the healing and forgiveness of all the weak and sinful members of the Church, we pray: ◆ For those charged with the responsibility of authority, that they may use this gift in service for the good of all God's children, we pray: ◆ For ecumenical initiatives toward unity among all Christians, we pray: ◆ For all who suffer the emptiness of a life without the knowledge or belief in God, the giver of life and hope, we pray: ◆ For the grace of continual deeper conversion into the merciful and loving heart of Jesus, we pray: ◆

Our Father . . .

Heavenly Father,
by the power of your Spirit,
awaken our hearts from the lethargy
of indifference and skepticism.
Lead us into the light of your truth
so that we may see clearly the path
of righteousness as we wait in joyful hope
to behold the glory of your face forever.
We ask through Christ our Lord.
Amen.

✝ God upholds his city for ever.

Wednesday, July 18, 2012
Weekday

✝ The Lord will not abandon his people.

Psalm 146   *page 423*

Reading   *Matthew 11:25–27*

At that time Jesus exclaimed: "I give praise to you, Father, Lord of heaven and earth, for although you have hidden these things from the wise and the learned you have revealed them to the childlike. Yes, Father, such has been your gracious will. All things have been handed over to me by my Father. No one knows the Son except the Father, and no one knows the Father except the Son and anyone to whom the Son wishes to reveal him."

Reflection

Jesus teaches us that the humble, poor, weak, and childlike are the ones to whom the mysteries of the kingdom are revealed. Those who are wise and learned by the standards of the world do not necessarily know the secrets of God unless they themselves are humble and simple of heart. Jesus praises his Father for revealing the great and hidden richness of his mysteries to those who follow his Father as humble children.

Prayers   *others may be added*

Father, your thoughts are not our thoughts, nor are your ways our ways. Let us pray:

◆ Father, reveal to us the mystery of your greatness.

For the Church, that she may be united as one body through communion and solidarity with the poor, the suffering, and all in need, we pray: ◆ For all doctors, nurses, health care workers, and all who work and serve the sick, that they may be strengthened in their work of serving Christ present in his suffering people, we pray: ◆ For the poor, the weak, the sick, and the suffering, that through their humility and poverty they may be restored to health in mind and body, and that they may experience the riches and greatness of God's mysteries who reveals himself to his little ones, we pray: ◆

Our Father . . .

Loving Father God,
to you belongs all greatness, glory,
    and praise.
Do not abandon your weak and sinful
    children,
but lovingly teach us to follow you amid
the joys and sufferings of this present life.
Bless all the sick and suffering
and reveal to us the mysteries of
    your kingdom.
We ask this through Christ our Lord.
Amen.

✝ The Lord will not abandon his people.

Thursday, July 19, 2012
Weekday

✝ From heaven the Lord looks down on the earth.

Psalm 103 *page 415*

Reading *Matthew 11:28–30*

Jesus said: "Come to me, all you who labor and are burdened, and I will give you rest. Take my yoke upon you and learn from me, for I am meek and humble of heart; and you will find rest for yourselves. For my yoke is easy, and my burden light."

Reflection

How good our God is, that he gives rest to the weary and comforts those who are burdened by the cares and worries of life! In today's Gospel, Jesus speaks these words of comfort to us that ease the anxiety and weight of our troubles. We must have faith to believe and trust in God's promise of peace and rest. Jesus has promised us peace, yet we must actively accept his peace by taking up the yoke of his cross. In this way we will learn from him as we follow as his disciple along the path from Calvary to the empty tomb to the glory of the Father's kingdom in heaven.

Prayers *others may be added*

Jesus, you speak to us your words of peace. Hear our prayer as we ask you in confidence:

◆ Lord Jesus, free us from our burdens.

For the Holy Father, that he may be renewed in health and strength to lead his faithful flock along our earthly pilgrimage toward the glory of our heavenly home, we pray: ◆ For the end of war, political strife, world hunger, violence, and poverty, that the Lord will bring peace and justice and relieve all peoples of the burdens of sin, we pray: ◆ For all those who suffer from sickness, and for all who care and worry for their well-being, that God may give patience to those who suffer, and peace and trust to their loved ones, we pray: ◆ For the grace to give up all our worries to the Lord who cares for us, we pray: ◆

Our Father . . .

Sweet Jesus,
in your eternal love you protect us
and give us all that we need.
Teach us how to trust in you so that
    ·we may
be freed from all worry and anxiety.
Help us to receive your peace beyond all understanding,
which the world does not give,
as we strive to follow you as faithful
    disciples.
You live and reign forever.
Amen.

✝ From heaven the Lord looks down on the earth.

Friday, July 20, 2012
Weekday

✝ You saved my life, O Lord; I shall not die.

Psalm 145   *page 422*

Reading   *Matthew 12:1–8*

Jesus was going through a field of grain on the sabbath. His disciples were hungry and began to pick the heads of grain and eat them. When the Pharisees saw this, they said to him, "See, your disciples are doing what is unlawful to do on the sabbath." He said to them, "Have you not read what David did when he and his companions were hungry, how he went into the house of God and ate the bread of offering, which neither he nor his companions but only the priests could lawfully eat? Or have you not read in the law that on the sabbath the priests serving in the temple violate the sabbath and are innocent? I say to you, something greater than the temple is here. If you knew what this meant, *I desire mercy, not sacrifice*, you would not have condemned these innocent men. For the Son of Man is Lord of the sabbath."

Reflection

For the Jews, the temple was of central importance. However, in today's Gospel, Jesus says that there is something greater than the temple here. Jesus, referring to himself, is the new temple, the new center of worship and life. He is the fulfillment of the Old Law and brings a teaching of newness in his kingship and sovereignty even over the former laws of the Sabbath.

Prayers   *others may be added*

With wonder and awe, we present to you our prayers as we pray:

◆ Lord and King of all the nations, hear our prayer.

That the witness of evangelization of the Holy Father, all priests, and the lay faithful may blossom in conversions for all people young and old, we pray: ◆ That all peoples may recognize the Church as the sacrament of newness and life, rather than a legalistic institution devoid of relevance to our current times, we pray: ◆ That those who suffer physical injury from car accidents, work-related injuries, and all those undergoing physical therapy may be healed through God's grace, we pray: ◆ That the poor and the hungry, and those who go without food today, will be filled in mind, body, and spirit, we pray: ◆

Our Father . . .

Loving Father,
through the Holy Eucharist,
you have given us the perfect
gift of your Son, Jesus Christ.
Lead us into ever more deeper union
with your Trinitarian life through
our encounter with you in the sacraments.
May you always be the center of our lives.
We ask this through Christ our Lord.
Amen.

✝ You saved my life, O Lord; I shall not die.

Saturday, July 21, 2012
Weekday

✝ Do not forget the poor, O Lord!

Psalm 27   *page 405*

Reading   *Matthew 12:14–21*

The Pharisees went out and took counsel against Jesus to put him to death.

When Jesus realized this, he withdrew from that place. Many people followed him, and he cured them all, but he warned them not to make him known. This was to fulfill what had been spoken through Isaiah the prophet:

Behold, my servant whom I have chosen, / my beloved in whom I delight; / I shall place my Spirit upon him, / and he will proclaim justice to the Gentiles. / He will not contend or cry out, / nor will anyone hear his voice in the streets. / A bruised reed he will not break, / a smoldering wick he will not quench, / until he brings justice to victory. / And in his name the Gentiles will hope.

Reflection

Jesus Christ is our hope. We have hope in the name of our Lord Jesus, the Messiah who has come among us to bring us healing and new life through the gift of his Spirit. Jesus is the fulfillment of the Old Testament, and he reveals himself through the power of his miracles and his word of truth and love. Jesus also comes in gentleness through the whispering of his Spirit. May we have eyes to recognize his presence and ears to hear his word.

Prayers   *others may be added*

Father, in your beloved servant, your Son, we see the power of your glory. Let us pray:

◆ Lord Jesus Christ, we hope in your name.

For the Church, that she may loudly proclaim the truth of Jesus Christ through the example and prayers of all the faithful, we pray: ◆ For all civic leaders, that they may work to achieve justice and peace for all peoples, we pray: ◆ For the grace never to forget our duty and responsibility to aid our brothers and sisters spiritually and physically through the preferential option for the poor, especially those in our home and in the workplace, we pray: ◆ For all who seek a cure for illnesses of mind, body, or spirit, that Jesus may bring them healing through the work and service of skilled doctors, nurses, and health care workers, we pray: ◆ For the grace to imitate the gentleness and unprejudiced love of Jesus Christ toward all, we pray: ◆

Our Father . . .

Almighty Father,
you sent us your beloved Son among us
to serve the weak and the poor
and to announce your message of
    salvation and life.
Heal us of our ills
and free us from our sins.
We ask this through Christ our Lord.
Amen.

✝ Do not forget the poor, O Lord!

✝ The Lord is my shepherd; there is nothing I shall want.

Psalm 19 *page 403*

Reading *Mark 6:30–34*

The apostles gathered together with Jesus and reported all they had done and taught. He said to them, "Come away by yourselves to a deserted place and rest a while." People were coming and going in great numbers, and they had no opportunity even to eat. So they went off in the boat by themselves to a deserted place. People saw them leaving and many came to know about it. They hastened there on foot from all the towns and arrived at the place before them.

When Jesus disembarked and saw the vast crowd, his heart was moved with pity for them, for they were like sheep without a shepherd; and he began to teach them many things.

Reflection

In today's Gospel, we see the compassion and reasonableness of Jesus who cares for our human needs. After all their hard work, Jesus invites his apostles to come away to a deserted place to rest. These summer months can likewise provide opportunity for rest and vacation, in which we come away from our daily duties in order to draw closer to God through prayer and treasured time spent with our family and friends.

Prayers *others may be added*

Lord Jesus, you lead us to still waters and you restore our souls. Let us pray:

◆ Good Shepherd, hear our prayer.

For the Holy Father, that he may have strength and health in his ministry, we pray: ◆ For our nation's President and for his administration, that they may enact just laws for the good of all society, we pray: ◆ For the poor, the sick, and the suffering; for those who struggle economically, we pray: ◆ For all travelers; for their safety and that their time of rest and vacation may restore joy and a renewed health of mind and body through the contemplation of God's beauty in nature and all creation, we pray: ◆ For the grace of peacefulness and simplicity, that we may cease to rush around in constant busyness, so that we do not fail to recognize the blessed encounters with God and with one another that we are given every day, we pray: ◆

Our Father . . .

Lord Jesus,
all nature lifts its voice in praise of you.
Teach us how to contemplate you,
revealed through the marvels of
   your creation.
Draw us away and renew us in your peace
   and rest
to be free from the burdens and worries
   of each day.
We ask this through Christ our Lord.
Amen.

✝ The Lord is my shepherd; there is nothing I shall want.

Monday, July 23, 2012
Weekday

✝ To the upright I will show the saving power of God.

Psalm 34   page 406

Reading   · Matthew 12:38–42

Some of the scribes and Pharisees said to Jesus, "Teacher, we wish to see a sign from you." He said to them in reply, "An evil and unfaithful generation seeks a sign, but no sign will be given it except the sign of Jonah the prophet. Just as Jonah was in the belly of the whale three days and three nights, so will the Son of Man be in the heart of the earth three days and three nights. At the judgment, the men of Nineveh will arise with this generation and condemn it, because they repented at the preaching of Jonah; and there is something greater than Jonah here. At the judgment the queen of the south will arise with this generation and condemn it, because she came from the ends of the earth to hear the wisdom of Solomon; and there is something greater than Solomon here."

Reflection

Jesus reveals himself as the greatest Prophet. In Baptism, we are born into Jesus' prophetic ministry to be prophets in our modern day. We must first listen through the encounter with God in prayer. Then our lives must speak volumes primarily through the silent witness and example of living a virtuous life and secondly through our spoken words with our friends and to whomever God sends us.

Prayers   *others may be added*

· Lord, you send your prophets among us to proclaim the goodness of your name and convert our hearts to you. Let us pray:

◆ Hear I am, Lord; I come to do your will.

For all who serve the Church, that they may partake in Christ's prophetic ministry through the uniqueness and necessity of their diverse roles and states of life, we pray: ◆ For all nations and generations, that they may not remain hardened of heart, but may be open to the Word of truth who brings life and salvation, we pray: ◆ For those who suffer the evils of war, violence, abuse, poverty, hunger, and sickness, we pray: ◆ For all the imprisoned, that they may receive knowledge and conversion to Jesus Christ who comes to set all captives free, we pray: ◆

Our Father . . .

Great and merciful Father,
you sent us your Son as Prophet,
to announce your message of salvation to
     all peoples.
Soften our hearts by the anointing of
     your Spirit,
that we may not remain closed off
     and indifferent
to the Incarnate Word of your Son, Jesus,
through whom we pray.
Amen.

✝ To the upright I will show the saving power of God.

☦ Lord, show us your mercy and love.

Psalm 150 *page 424*

Reading *Matthew 12:46–50*

While Jesus was speaking to the crowds, his mother and his brothers appeared outside, wishing to speak with him. Someone told him, "Your mother and your brothers are standing outside, asking to speak with you." But he said in reply to the one who told him, "Who is my mother? Who are my brothers?" And stretching out his hand toward his disciples, he said, "Here are my mother and my brothers. For whoever does the will of my heavenly Father is my brother, and sister, and mother."

Reflection

Sometimes in Christian circles we hear the phrase "will of God." We despondently resign ourselves saying, "It's God's will," or we compliment ourselves by saying that all we want is "to do God's will." But what does it mean to do the will of the heavenly Father? God's will is his merciful plan of love for us and all humanity. Through prayer, the Father reveals his will of love for us, and it is then up to us to respond in generosity and trust by following his voice one step at a time in childlike faith.

Prayers *others may be added*

Heavenly Father, in your merciful will, you draw us into your Triune family. Let us pray:

◆ Reveal to us your loving plan, O Lord.

For the Church, that she may truly become a welcoming family of all believers regardless of race, nationality, wealth, or social status, we pray: ◆ For civic leaders, that they may work to accomplish unity among nations through dialogue and conflict resolution, so that all peoples may experience the dignity and peace of living as members of God's human family, we pray: ◆ For all children who suffer in hospitals and intensive care units, and for their families and those who care for them, we pray: ◆ For all our relatives and friends who have gone before us in death, that they may enjoy the eternal beatitude of the heavenly glory, we pray: ◆ For the wisdom and counsel to know God's will and the courage and boldness to carry it out, we pray: ◆

Our Father . . .

Heavenly Father,
you reveal to us your loving and
    merciful will.
Free our hearts from the desire of control,
and give us the grace to surrender
    ourselves to you.
We ask this through Christ our Lord.
Amen.

☦ Lord, show us your mercy and love.

✝ Those who sow in tears shall reap rejoicing.

Psalm 95 *page 413*

Reading *Matthew 20:25–28*

Jesus summoned [his disciples] and said, "You know that the rulers of the Gentiles lord it over them, and the great ones make their authority over them felt. But it shall not be so among you. Rather, whoever wishes to be great among you shall be your servant; whoever wishes to be first among you shall be your slave. Just so, the Son of Man did not come to be served but to serve and to give his life as a ransom for many."

Reflection

The Saint James we honor today is the brother of the apostle John, one of the "sons of thunder" (Mark 3:17) who were privileged witnesses of some of Jesus' greatest signs: the raising of the daughter of Jairus from the dead, the Transfiguration, the agony in the garden. James was the first apostle to suffer martyrdom, slain by Herod's orders as described in Acts. According to legend, his remains were carried away by his friends in a rudderless boat, which drifted to Spain. Many centuries later his remains were discovered, and a great cathedral was built over the spot where they were found (Santiago de Compostela, which became one of the most popular pilgrimage destinations of the Middle Ages). To this day, hundreds of thousands of pilgrims make their way to that remote corner of Spain to venerate the relics of Saint James.

Prayers *others may be added*

In confidence and faith, we pray:

◆ Make us faithful servants, O Lord.

For all seminarians preparing for the priestly ministry of service to the Church, that they may persevere in the virtues of faithfulness and chastity as they fall ever more deeply in love with the Church through their study, prayer, and formation, we pray: ◆ For the witness of the martyrs throughout all history, that they may become the fruitful soil for conversion and repentance for all the world, we pray: ◆ For those who drink the bitter cup of pain, suffering, illness, and loss, that the presence of Christ may bring them consolation, patience, and hope as they await the future glory that is nothing to be compared with the sufferings of this present age, we pray: ◆

Our Father . . .

Heavenly Father,
you desire us to dwell always with you
as you prepare a place for us in your
    kingdom.
By the prayers of Saint James, may we
    have the courage
to humbly drink the cup of service and
    self-donation
as we imitate your Son, Jesus Christ,
as apostles and witnesses of your
    presence among us.
We ask this through Christ our Lord.
Amen.

✝ Those who sow in tears shall reap rejoicing.

Thursday, July 26, 2012

Memorial of Saints Joachim and Anne, Parents of the Blessed Virgin Mary

✝ With you is the fountain of life,
  O Lord.

Psalm 95 *page 413*

Reading *Matthew 13:10–13*

The disciples approached Jesus and said, "Why do you speak to the crowd in parables?" He said to them in reply, "Because knowledge of the mysteries of the Kingdom of heaven has been granted to you, but to them it has not been granted. To anyone who has, more will be given and he will grow rich; from anyone who has not, even what he has will be taken away. This is why I speak to them in parables, because 'they look but do not see and hear but do not listen or understand.'"

Reflection

Today's Gospel is perplexing. Why is Jesus' teaching so enigmatic? Matthew sees the crowd's failure to understand the fulfilment of the words of the prophet Isaiah: Israel is deaf and blind in its own obstinacy. The disciples are blessed because they see and hear and believe.

Prayers *others may be added*

Jesus, you tell us to ask and we shall receive, to seek and we shall find. In confidence and faith, we pray:

◆ Make us faithful servants, O Lord.

For all seminarians preparing for the priestly ministry of service to the Church, that they may persevere in the virtues of faithfulness and chastity as they fall ever more deeply in love with the Church through their study, prayer, and formation, we pray: ◆ That the witness of the martyrs throughout all history may become the fruitful soil for conversion and repentance for all the world, we pray: ◆ For those who drink the bitter cup of pain, suffering, illness, and loss, that the presence of Christ may bring them consolation, patience, and hope as they await the future glory that is nothing to be compared with the sufferings of this present age, we pray: ◆

Our Father . . .

Heavenly Father,
you desire us to dwell always with you
as you prepare a place for us in your
  kingdom.
May we have the courage
to humbly drink the cup of service and
  self-donation
as we imitate your Son, Jesus Christ,
as apostles and witnesses of your
  presence among us.
We ask this through Christ our Lord.
Amen.

✝ With you is the fountain of life,
  O Lord.

✝ The Lord will guard us as a shepherd guards his flock.

Psalm 103 *page 415*

Reading *Matthew 13:18–23*

Jesus said to his disciples: "Hear the parable of the sower. The seed sown on the path is the one who hears the word of the Kingdom without understanding it, and the Evil One comes and steals away what was sown in his heart. The seed sown on rocky ground is the one who hears the word and receives it at once with joy. But he has no root and lasts only for a time. When some tribulation or persecution comes because of the word, he immediately falls away. The seed sown among thorns is the one who hears the word, but then worldly anxiety and the lure of riches choke the word and it bears no fruit. But the seed sown on rich soil is the one who hears the word and understands it, who indeed bears fruit and yields a hundred or sixty or thirtyfold."

Reflection

Jesus uses parables to reveal the mystery of his kingdom to his disciples. Through this method, Jesus teaches us in a profound way by using stories, images, and everyday examples. Within the parables, the kingdom of God remains a mystery beyond our full comprehension, yet always reveals something new to us. The parables put us in contact with that great mystery of God and invite us to more deeply understand and more fully share in God's life.

Prayers *others may be added*

Father, hear the prayers of your faithful children as we pray:

◆ Open our hearts to receive your Word, O God.

For the Church, that she may remain firmly rooted in the rock of Jesus Christ until the end of time even amid the persecutions and tribulations of our present day, we pray: ◆ For the work of missionaries, that they may be fruitful as they go out to sow the Word of God throughout all lands, so that all may come to knowledge and understanding of the kingdom, we pray: ◆ For those who suffer anxiety and the emptiness of the lure of riches and worldly possessions, that they may know the peace and freedom that comes from true union with Christ Jesus, we pray: ◆ For the grace to hear God's Word and respond to his voice as he speaks to us through the truth, beauty, and goodness of his creation, we pray: ◆

Our Father . . .

Almighty Father,
you sow the seed of your Word, Jesus
    Christ, in our hearts.
Protect us from sin and till the soil
of our hearts so that it may become fertile
    ground
for the life of your Spirit to yield
    abundant fruit
in good works for the glory of your name.
We ask this through Christ our Lord.
Amen.

✝ The Lord will guard us as a shepherd guards his flock.

✝ How lovely is your dwelling place,
Lord, mighty God!

Psalm 145   *page 422*

Reading   *Matthew 13:24–30*

Jesus proposed a parable to the crowds. "The Kingdom of heaven may be likened to a man who sowed good seed in his field. While everyone was asleep his enemy came and sowed weeds all through the wheat, and then went off. When the crop grew and bore fruit, the weeds appeared as well. The slaves of the householder came to him and said, 'Master, did you not sow good seed in your field? Where have the weeds come from?' He answered, 'An enemy has done this.' His slaves said to him, 'Do you want us to go and pull them up?' He replied, 'No, if you pull up the weeds you might uproot the wheat along with them. Let them grow together until harvest; then at harvest time I will say to the harvesters, "First collect the weeds and tie them in bundles for burning; but gather the wheat into my barn."'"

Reflection

Sometimes we blame God for the evil we see in the world similar to the slaves of today's Gospel. But God allows the weeds sown by the evil one to grow alongside the good crop of wheat. Only at the time of harvest will the weeds be uprooted, so as not to also uproot the wheat. At the last judgment, the weeds will be gathered to be burned, but the wheat will be safely gathered to dwell in the kingdom of God.

Prayers   *others may be added*

Jesus, you liken the kingdom of God to the parable of the weeds and the wheat. Let us pray:

◆ Keep us faithful to the end, O Lord.

For the Church, that she may remain vigilant and watchful to protect her children from the damage and harm of sin and evil, we pray: ◆ For all Christians living in areas of persecution, hatred, or anti-Christian sentiment, that they may persevere to the end as they faithfully await the coming of the kingdom, we pray: ◆ For all who suffer the evils of poverty, hunger, war, violence, and illness, we pray: ◆ That we may be apostles and missionaries to our friends, families, and coworkers through the faithful daily witness of our Christian lives in the midst of the world, we pray: ◆

Our Father . . .

Almighty Father,
the presence of both good and evil
in the world remains a mystery to us.
May the good seed of your Word
bear fruit in charity and perseverance until
the day of harvest when you will
collect the weeds for burning and when
the good wheat of the faithful children
   of God
will be gathered together in the
   righteousness
of the glory of your heavenly kingdom.
We ask through Christ our Lord.
Amen.

✝ How lovely is your dwelling place,
Lord, mighty God!

Sunday, July 29, 2012
Seventeenth Sunday in Ordinary Time

✝ The hand of the Lord feeds us; he answers all our needs.

Psalm 19 *page 403*

Reading *John 6:8–11*

One of [Jesus'] disciples, Andrew, the brother of Simon Peter, said to him, "There is a boy here who has five barley loaves and two fish; but what good are these for so many?" Jesus said, "Have the people recline." Now there was a great deal of grass in that place. So the men reclined, about five thousand in number. Then Jesus took the loaves, gave thanks, and distributed them to those who were reclining, and also as much of the fish as they wanted.

Reflection

God always provides. He always gives us what we need and brings abundance out of what seems to us not to be enough. In today's Gospel, Philip states the fact that two hundred days' wages would not be enough to feed the crowd of five thousand. However, with Jesus, our almighty God, human limitations cease to matter. God uses the little we have, and he performs miracles to feed and nourish all of us in abundance.

Prayers *others may be added*

Lord, you feed the crowd of thousands with five loaves and two fishes. Hear our prayer:

◆ We trust in your mercy, O Lord.

For the Church, that she may remain vigilant and watchful to protect her children from the damage and harm of sin and evil, we pray: ◆ For all Christians living in areas of persecution, hatred, or anti-Christian sentiment, that they may persevere to the end as they faithfully await the coming of the kingdom, we pray: ◆ For all who suffer the evils of poverty, hunger, war, violence, and illness, we pray: ◆ For all of us to be apostles and missionaries to our friends, families, and coworkers through the faithful daily witness of our Christian lives in the midst of the world, we pray: ◆

Our Father . . .

Loving Father,
every good and precious gift comes
    from you.
In your providential care and
    fatherly love,
you provide for our every want and need.
Give us our daily bread and protect us
from all evil as we await the glorious
coming of your Son, Jesus Christ,
who lives and reigns with you in the unity
    of the Holy Spirit,
one God, forever and ever.
Amen.

✝ The hand of the Lord feeds us; he answers all our needs.

✝ You have forgotten God who gave you birth.

Psalm 27 *page 405*

Reading *Matthew 13:31–35*

Jesus proposed a parable to the crowds. "The Kingdom of heaven is like a mustard seed that a person took and sowed in a field. It is the smallest of all the seeds, yet when full-grown it is the largest of plants. It becomes a large bush, and the 'birds of the sky come and dwell in its branches.'"

He spoke to them another parable. "The Kingdom of heaven is like yeast that a woman took and mixed with three measures of wheat flour until the whole batch was leavened."

All these things Jesus spoke to the crowds in parables. He spoke to them only in parables, to fulfill what had been said through the prophet: / *I will open my mouth in parables, / I will announce what has lain hidden from the foundation of the world.*

Reflection

How could it be possible that a tiny mustard seed, the smallest of all seeds, could grow into a bush so large that birds could dwell in its branches? This is a great mystery of creation. God our Creator likens this mystery to the mystery of the kingdom of God, which may start small and tiny, but then grows and grows into something greater than could have been ever imagined from the beginning.

Prayers *others may be added*

Lord Jesus, you give us the parables to reveal to us the mysteries of your kingdom. Full of wonder and awe, we pray:

◆ Thy kingdom come, O Lord.

For the Church throughout the world, that she may be leaven to the nations in order to raise all people's minds to the truth and goodness of the salvation given to us in Jesus Christ, we pray: ◆ For all who suffer the evils of poverty, hunger, war, violence, and injustice, that civic leaders and all Christians may work together to alleviate the sufferings of our human family in need, we pray: ◆ For all ministries, charities, educational institutes, and all people who work through these means of service, that through their small beginnings they may bear great and abundant fruit, we pray: ◆

Our Father . . .

Jesus Christ,
our Master and Lord,
you teach us the way to your Father's
    kingdom
through the means of your Gospel parables.
Open our hearts and minds to understand
the great mystery of your love as we
seek your face in wonder and
    contemplation.
You live and reign forever.
Amen.

✝ You have forgotten God who gave you birth.

Tuesday, July 31, 2012
Memorial of Saint Ignatius of Loyola, Priest

✝ For the glory of your name, O Lord, deliver us.

Psalm 34 *page 406*

Reading *Luke 14:25–26*

Great crowds were traveling with Jesus, and he turned and addressed them, "If anyone comes to me without hating his father and mother, wife and children, brothers and sisters, and even his own life, he cannot be my disciple. Whoever does not carry his own cross and come after me cannot be my disciple."

Reflection

Today we celebrate the memorial of Saint Ignatius, who taught his followers to solely seek to honor, praise, and glorify Jesus Christ. Union with Jesus Christ should be our ultimate goal, and thus we should remain indifferent to all other created things. We should strive only to have concern for them insomuch as they aid us to attain union with Jesus.

Prayers *others may be added*

Lord, by your saints, you teach us how to pick up our cross daily. Let us pray:

◆ Teach us to follow after you, O God.

For the Church and all her members, led by the Holy Father, that she may do all things for the honor and glory of God, we pray: ◆ For all military personnel, that they may be virtuous in their work of fighting in defense of security and the good of their country, we pray: ◆ For all who are sick and homebound, that these difficult times of suffering for them may become moments of conversion in which to draw closer to the presence of the Lord, we pray: ◆ For all the Jesuits, that through the prayers of their founder, the Society of Jesus may be renewed and strengthened in holiness and faithfulness to its charism, we pray: ◆

Our Father . . .

Lord Jesus,
through the witness of your saints,
teach us how to live out the Gospel.
By the prayers of Saint Ignatius
    of Loyola,
help us to detach ourselves
from all materials things,
that we may only seek to praise,
    reverence, and serve you.
You live and reign forever.
Amen.

✝ For the glory of your name, O Lord, deliver us.

Wednesday, August 1, 2012
Memorial of Saint Alphonsus Liguori, Bishop and Doctor of the Church

✝ God is my refuge on the day of distress.

Psalm 103
page 415

Reading
Matthew 13:44–46

Jesus said to his disciples: "The Kingdom of heaven is like a treasure buried in a field, which a person finds and hides again, and out of joy goes and sells all that he has and buys that field. Again, the Kingdom of heaven is like a merchant searching for fine pearls. When he finds a pearl of great price, he goes and sells all that he has and buys it."

Reflection

How might the merchant feel after having found the pearl of great price after all his searching? What is this special pearl that compels him to sell all he has in order to buy it? In today's Gospel, Jesus teaches that the kingdom of heaven is like a merchant searching for fine pearls. And in the parable prior, he compares the kingdom to a treasure buried in a field. What happiness he must experience to find this hidden treasure, and to sell everything in order to buy it! Has our search for the kingdom led us to this same joyful discovery?

Prayers
others may be added

Father, in your Son you invite us to share in the mystery of your kingdom. Hear our prayers we offer you today:

◆ Sanctify your people, O Lord.

For the Holy Father, that he may have health and strength to continue to lead and guide his flock as we await the coming of the kingdom, we pray: ◆ For all those who seek purpose and meaning in life, that they may discover the rich treasure of God's kingdom, we pray: ◆ For the message of Jesus Christ in the Gospel to reach all the ends of the earth through the faithful work of missionaries, teachers, and families, we pray: ◆ For all the Redemptorists of the Congregation of the Most Holy Redeemer, that, through the prayers of their founder Saint Alphonsus Liguori, they may be renewed in dedicating their life solely to God and faithfully living out their rule of life, we pray: ◆ For all scientists and theologians, that they may be filled with greater wonder and awe in the faith and truth of God's kingdom as they contemplate the mystery of creation and life, we pray: ◆ For all the sick, the dying, and those who care for them, we pray: ◆

Our Father . . .

Loving Father,
by the example of your saints you teach us
how to give up everything in the joy
of possessing the preciousness of your
   kingdom.
Through the prayers of Saint
   Alphonsus Liguori,
increase our devotion to the Blessed
   Mother Mary,
that she may guide us to union with
   your Son,
who lives and reigns with you in the unity
   of the Holy Spirit,
in the glory of your kingdom,
one God, forever and ever.
Amen.

✝ God is my refuge on the day of distress.

✝ Blessed is he whose help is the God of Jacob.

Psalm 141   *page 421*

Reading   *Matthew 13:47–50*

Jesus said to the disciples: "The Kingdom of heaven is like a net thrown into the sea, which collects fish of every kind. When it is full they haul it ashore and sit down to put what is good into buckets. What is bad they throw away. Thus it will be at the end of the age. The angels will go out and separate the wicked from the righteous and throw them into the fiery furnace, where there will be wailing and grinding of teeth."

Reflection

In the parables, Jesus uses human examples to explain to us the spiritual truths of the kingdom of heaven. Today he describes the kingdom as a net that collects every kind of fish. Similar to the parable of the weeds and the wheat, at the proper time at the end of the age, the angels will divide the good from the bad. These parables invite us to meditate on their meaning for our lives as we revisit them again and again to draw deeper into the mystery of the kingdom of God.

Prayers   *others may be added*

In faith and confidence that you always hear our prayer, we offer our petitions to you today as we pray:

◆ Draw us into the love of your kingdom.

For the Church, that she may remain open to welcome all peoples into the joy of the faith, we pray: ◆ For all bishops, that they may stand firm and faithful in the defense of the truths of the Catholic Church, we pray: ◆ For all fishermen, farmers, construction workers, mechanics, and for all who earn a living by the work of their hands, we pray: ◆ For all who have died, that they may enjoy the glory of the eternal heavenly kingdom, we pray: ◆

Our Father . . .

Heavenly God,
the mystery of your kingdom
comes and touches us in the practical
and material activities of every day.
Open our eyes so that we may not remain
    blind to your presence in our life,
but rather encounter you in our work,
our prayer, and our conversations with
    one another.
We ask this through Christ our Lord.
Amen.

✝ Blessed is he whose help is the God of Jacob.

Friday, August 3, 2012
Weekday

✝ Lord, in your great love, answer me.

Psalm 100 *page 414*

Reading *Matthew 13:54–58*

Jesus came to his native place and taught the people in their synagogue. They were astonished and said, "Where did this man get such wisdom and mighty deeds? Is he not the carpenter's son? Is not his mother named Mary and his brothers James, Joseph, Simon, and Judas? Are not his sisters all with us? Where did this man get all this?" And they took offense at him. But Jesus said to them, "A prophet is not without honor except in his native place and in his own house." And he did not work many mighty deeds there because of their lack of faith.

Reflection

Jesus came unto his own, but his own did not receive him. Today's Gospel describes the truth of this passage as Jesus comes among his relatives in his native place, and his own people take offense at him and do not believe his word. If Jesus is treated this way, we should not feel discouraged if our own family or friends treat us similarly, criticizing us for our faith. Rather, we ought to persevere in our work through prayer and affection for our loved ones.

Prayers *others may be added*

We, your lowly children, come before you in need of your mercy and grace. Hear our prayers, as we say:

◆ Come Lord, hear our prayer.

For the Church, that she may be drawn into one family in unity and fraternal love for one another, we pray: ◆ For civic leaders and governmental officials, that they may work for the good of all society, especially the poor, the needy, and those in crisis situations, we pray: ◆ For all the sick, the poor, all prisoners, travelers, and those in special need, we pray: ◆ For holy and faithful vocations to priesthood, religious life, and the sacrament of Matrimony, we pray: ◆ For healing and reconciliation amid all families, we pray: ◆ For the grace to persevere in finishing well the little and seemingly insignificant duties and responsibilities of each day, we pray: ◆

Our Father . . .

Lord Jesus,
you yourself were not accepted among
    your own.
Have mercy on our sins and send
    your Spirit
to open and heal our hearts so that we
    may receive
you with ever deeper love and devotion.
You live and reign forever.
Amen.

✝ Lord, in your great love, answer me.

Saturday, August 4, 2012
Memorial of Saint John Vianney, Priest

✝ Lord, in your great love, answer me.

Psalm 103 page 415

Reading Matthew 14:6–12

But at a birthday celebration for Herod, the daughter of Herodias performed a dance before the guests and delighted Herod so much that he swore to give her whatever she might ask for. Prompted by her mother, she said, "Give me here on a platter the head of John the Baptist." The king was distressed, but because of his oaths and the guests who were present, he ordered that it be given, and he had John beheaded in the prison. His head was brought in on a platter and given to the girl, who took it to her mother. His disciples came and took away the corpse and buried him; and they went and told Jesus.

Reflection

Today's Gospel recounts the beheading of Saint John the Baptist, the prophet and precursor of Jesus. Because of John the Baptist's faithfulness to preaching the truth, he was disliked by the Emperor Herod and was later beheaded because of the evil schemes against him. Today we also celebrate the memorial of Saint John Vianney, the French parish priest known for his holiness and devotion to serving hundreds of people daily in the sacrament of Reconciliation. May these saints inspire us to lives of holiness and faithfulness to God.

Prayers others may be added

You are Father of all the nations, O God. Hear our humble prayers, as we pray:

◆ Lord, in your great love, answer me.

For the Holy Father, all bishops, priests, and seminarians, that they may be holy and faithful to the holy ministry of the priesthood, we pray: ◆ For all who serve the poor, the sick, and the weak of the world, we pray: ◆ For those who suffer physical, mental, or spiritual illness, that they may quickly be restored to full health of mind and body, we pray: ◆ For all parish priests, that, through the intercession of Saint John Vianney, they may be renewed in love for their spiritual children, persevering in hope and fervent in faith, we pray: ◆ For the grace of purity and chastity for all people in every walk of life, we pray: ◆

Our Father . . .

Lord Jesus, our High Priest,
you give us the gift of the priesthood
as witness of your goodness and love.
Through the intercession of
    Saint John Vianney,
bless all priests and seminarians
to love as you love, and to serve as
    you serve.
We ask this through Christ our Lord.
Amen.

✝ Lord, in your great love, answer me.

Sunday, August 5, 2012
Eighteenth Sunday in Ordinary Time

✝ The Lord gave them bread from heaven.

Psalm 25   *page 405*

Reading   *John 6:22–35*

Jesus said to [his disciples], "Amen, amen, I say to you, it was not Moses who gave the bread from heaven; my Father gives you the true bread from heaven. For the bread of God is that which comes down from heaven and gives life to the world." . . . Jesus said to them, "I am the bread of life; whoever comes to me will never hunger, and whoever believes in me will never thirst."

Reflection

In today's Gospel, Jesus entreats us not to work for bread that perishes, but rather to work for the bread that endures for eternal life. Of course, it is necessary and important for us to work well here on earth for our human needs; however, all our material goods are means to serve the higher good of our union with God. Today, Jesus teaches us that he is the Bread of Life truly present in the Eucharist, whom we encounter at every Mass.

Prayers   *others may be added*

Father, you give us your Son, the Bread of Life, sent down from heaven. Let us pray:

◆ Give us this Bread of Life always, Lord.

For the Holy Father, all bishops and priests, and all the lay faithful, that they may be renewed in love and devotion to the Eucharist, we pray: ◆ For those who suffer from poverty and hunger, that peoples and nations may recognize their duty of justice to give and support those in need, we pray: ◆ For all who hunger and thirst for meaning, peace, and fulfillment in their lives, that they may draw from the fountain of salvation of Jesus Christ, the true source of fulfillment and life, we pray: ◆ For reparation from all the outrages and abuses made against the Eucharist, we pray: ◆

Our Father . . .

Jesus, our Bread of Life,
you give us your Body and Blood
as true food and true drink.
Increase our faith in you
in this present life until the day
when you will draw us into the
eternal banquet of heaven.
You live and reign forever.
Amen.

✝ The Lord gave them bread from heaven.

Monday, August 6, 2012
Feast of the Transfiguration of the Lord

✝ The Lord is king, the Most High over all the earth.

Psalm 19
page 403

Reading
Mark 9:2–7

Jesus took Peter, James, and his brother John, and led them up a high mountain apart by themselves. And he was transfigured before them, and his clothes became dazzling white, such as no fuller on earth could bleach them. Then Elijah appeared to them along with Moses, and they were conversing with Jesus. Then Peter said to Jesus in reply, "Rabbi, it is good that we are here! Let us make three tents: one for you, one for Moses, and one for Elijah." He hardly knew what to say, they were so terrified. Then a cloud came, casting a shadow over them; from the cloud came a voice, "This is my beloved Son. Listen to him."

Reflection
Graziano Marcheschi

He might be babbling, but Peter gets it right: It *is* good to be atop the mountain. Of course he doesn't want to leave. The glory they may have sensed in Jesus is now fully revealed. And he's in good company: Moses and Elijah, the embodiments of the Law and the Prophets, that are now fulfilled in Jesus. Such an experience is worth extending; it should be fully reveled in and absorbed. Storm clouds are gathering over Jesus as his passion approaches. But here, the cloud that hovers thunders his praise and demands we listen to him. It is good for us to be here.

Prayers
others may be added

Father, you reveal your Son's glory on the mountain of the Transfiguration. Let us pray:

◆ Transfigure us into your love, O Lord.

For the Church, that her teaching ministry may continue to instruct and guide the faithful to encounter the mystery of Jesus Christ, the fulfillment of all the Law and the Prophets, we pray: ◆ For civic leaders, that they may work to resolve issues of war, violence, and injustice to construct societies of peace, we pray: ◆ For all the sick and suffering, that, through the prayers of the Blessed Mother, they may hear the soft voice of the Lord who brings healing and remains present to them even in moments of difficulty, we pray: ◆ For all to have eyes to see and ears to hear the richness and glory of Jesus Christ, we pray: ◆

Our Father . . .

Heavenly Father,
on this holy feast of the Transfiguration,
you reveal to us the glory of your Trinity
made manifest in the Person of your Son,
    Jesus.
Draw us into your mystery so we
    may listen
to the voice of your Son, who leads us
    to union
with you, who live and reign together
in the unity of the Holy Spirit,
one God, forever and ever.
Amen.

✝ The Lord is king, the Most High over all the earth.

Tuesday, August 7, 2012
Weekday

✝ The Lord will build up Zion again, and appear in all his glory.

Psalm 150   page 424

Reading   *Matthew 14:26–33*

When the disciples saw [Jesus] walking on the sea they were terrified. "It is a ghost," they said, and they cried out in fear. At once Jesus spoke to them, "Take courage, it is I; do not be afraid." Peter said to him in reply, "Lord, if it is you, command me to come to you on the water." He said, "Come." Peter got out of the boat and began to walk on the water toward Jesus. But when he saw how strong the wind was he became frightened; and, beginning to sink, he cried out, "Lord, save me!" Immediately Jesus stretched out his hand and caught him, and said to him, "O you of little faith, why did you doubt?" After they got into the boat, the wind died down. Those who were in the boat did him homage, saying, "Truly, you are the Son of God."

Reflection

What would we do if we had no fear? Today, Jesus commands us to take courage. The Lord is with us; there is nothing to fear. With a holy fearlessness, we must follow the Lord with our eyes fixed firmly on him so that we may not sink into the temptations of discouragement, vanity, disbelief, and indifference.

Prayers   *others may be added*

Confident in your almighty power, we pray:

◆ Lord, save us!

For the Holy Father, the successor of Saint Peter, that he may have the same courage and boldness to follow after Christ by keeping his eyes fixed firmly on Jesus, even amid storms and persecutions, we pray: ◆ For government leaders, that they may look toward the weak, suffering, and needy of their countries to enact laws to promote the dignity and well-being of all peoples, we pray: ◆ For all who suffer illness, that they may receive restoration to health and healing from their sins, we pray: ◆ For all those who lack faith, that they may encounter the Lord to know him and share in his Trinitarian life, we pray: ◆ For all who are persecuted for the faith, that they may be fervent and persevering, we pray: ◆ For all who have died, we pray: ◆

Our Father . . .

Lord Jesus,
you command us not to fear.
By the power of your word,
cast out all worries and concerns
from our minds and hearts so that
we may seek to love and serve only you,
who live and reign with the Father
in the unity of the Holy Spirit,
one God, forever and ever.
Amen.

✝ The Lord will build up Zion again, and appear in all his glory.

Wednesday, August 8, 2012
Memorial of Saint Dominic, Priest

† The Lord will guard us as a shepherd guards his flock.

Psalm 141
page 421

Reading
Luke 9:57–62

As Jesus and his disciples were proceeding on their journey, someone said to him, "I will follow you wherever you go." Jesus answered him, "Foxes have dens and birds of the sky have nests, but the Son of Man has nowhere to rest his head." And to another he said, "Follow me." But he replied, "Lord, let me go first and bury my father." But he answered him, "Let the dead bury their dead. But you, go and proclaim the Kingdom of God." And another said, "I will follow you, Lord, but first let me say farewell to my family at home." Jesus answered him, "No one who sets a hand to the plow and looks to what was left behind is fit for the Kingdom of God."

Reflection

Jesus invites us, "Follow me," and yet again, "You, go and proclaim the Kingdom of God." He desires us to follow him without doubts and hesitations and without looking back. Today we honor Saint Dominic, the great founder of the Dominicans, the Order of Preachers. May Saint Dominic aid us to follow after Christ through fervent and faithful prayer and study.

Prayers
others may be added

Lord Jesus, you invite us to follow after you. Hear our prayers we offer you today:

◆ Lord, hear our prayer.

For the preaching and ministry of the Holy Father, priests, and bishops, that they may overflow from their humble study and contemplation of the word of God, we pray: ◆ For the nations of the world, that they may receive the light of truth through the instruction of holy teachers, evangelists, missionaries, and preachers, we pray: ◆ For all who suffer sickness, that they may offer their sufferings as powerful prayers for the salvation of all the world, we pray: ◆ For all Dominicans, that, through the prayers of their founder, holy Saint Dominic, they may be blessed with diligence and holiness in their study, work, and preaching, we pray: ◆ For a greater devotion to our Mother Mary and the Rosary, we pray: ◆

Our Father . . .

Lord Jesus,
you invite us to follow you along the path of life.
Through the prayers of Saint Dominic, may we have the grace to leave everything
and proclaim God's marvelous deeds to all the nations in service to you,
who live and reign with the Father
in the unity of the Holy Spirit,
one God, forever and ever.
Amen.

† The Lord will guard us as a shepherd guards his flock.

Thursday, August 9, 2012

Optional memorial of Saint Teresa Benedicta of the Cross, Virgin and Martyr

† Create a clean heart in me, O God.

Psalm 63   *page 410*

Reading   *Matthew 16:13–19*

When Jesus went into the region of Caesarea Philippi he asked his disciples, "Who do people say that the Son of Man is?" They replied, "Some say John the Baptist, others Elijah, still others Jeremiah or one of the prophets." He said to them, "But who do you say that I am?" Simon Peter said in reply, "You are the Christ, the Son of the living God." Jesus said to him in reply, "Blessed are you, Simon son of Jonah. For flesh and blood has not revealed this to you, but my heavenly Father. And so I say to you, you are Peter, and upon this rock I will build my Church, and the gates of the netherworld shall not prevail against it. I will give you the keys to the Kingdom of heaven. Whatever you bind on earth shall be bound in heaven; and whatever you loose on earth shall be loosed in heaven."

Reflection

Today we honor Edith Stein, a great philosopher who became a convert to the Catholic faith from Judaism. She entered the religious life as a Carmelite nun, taking the name Sister Teresa Benedicta of the Cross. She was later arrested with other Catholics of Jewish ancestry and was taken to the German concentration camp in Auschwitz where she was killed, giving her life for her nation and her people.

Prayers   *others may be added*

Jesus, you are the Christ, the Son of the Living God. Hear our prayers we offer, as we pray:

♦ Lord, teach me your statutes.

For the Church, that she may be a beacon of the light and truth of Christ Jesus, we pray: ♦ For all people, that they may seek truth and be converted to Jesus Christ, the Truth Incarnate, we pray: ♦ For all women, that they may be renewed in the dignity that they possess and glorify God, we pray: ♦ For all philosophers, writers, and great thinkers, that they may grow in wisdom through the use of their reason and intelligence, we pray: ♦ For those who suffer from the darkness of mental or physical illness, that they may feel the presence of Jesus, the Divine Physician, we pray: ♦ For those who are innocent victims of violence, abuse, war, or injustice, we pray: ♦ For all who have died, we pray: ♦

Our Father . . .

Lord Jesus,
through the intercession of Saint Teresa
    Benedicta of the Cross,
you give us the model of a holy woman
who used her intelligence and gifts at
    the service
of you and her people.
May our lives be evermore united to
    your cross.
You live and reign forever.
Amen.

† Create a clean heart in me, O God.

Friday, August 10, 2012
Feast of Saint Lawrence, Deacon and Martyr

✝ Blessed the man who is gracious and lends to those in need.

Psalm 95
page 413

Reading
John 12:24–26

Jesus said to his disciples: "Amen, amen, I say to you, unless a grain of wheat falls to the ground and dies, it remains just a grain of wheat; but if it dies, it produces much fruit. Whoever loves his life loses it, and whoever hates his life in this world will preserve it for eternal life. Whoever serves me must follow me, and where I am, there also will my servant be. The Father will honor whoever serves me."

Reflection

Today's Gospel sheds light upon the great mystery of God who transforms death into new life. The witness of the martyrs gives testimony to this Christian truth—that only once the grain of wheat falls to the earth and dies can it then grow and bear abundant fruit.

Prayers
others may be added

Jesus, we believe that you are the Way, the Truth, and the Life. Hear the prayers we offer you today.

◆ Bring us to new life, O Lord.

For the Church, the Holy Father, all priests, and lay faithful, that they may be bound together ever more profoundly in unity, we pray: ◆ For all social workers and those who provide services of food, shelter, education, and medical care, we pray: ◆ For those who carry heavy crosses, whether physical, mental, or spiritual, we pray: ◆ For ourselves and all peoples, that we may have the strength to deny ourselves for the good of others, we pray: ◆ For the grace to always keep a spiritual outlook with our eyes fixed firmly on the goal of heaven, we pray: ◆

Our Father . . .

Lord Jesus,
as Christians, you invite us to follow after you along the road to Calvary.
Through the prayers of the martyr Saint Lawrence, free us from all fear and convict us in faith in the joy of your Resurrection.
You live and reign forever.
Amen.

✝ Blessed the man who is gracious and lends to those in need.

Saturday, August 11, 2012
Memorial of Saint Clare, Virgin

✝ You forsake not those who seek you, O Lord.

Psalm 100 *page 414*

Reading *Matthew 19:27–30*

[Peter said to Jesus,] "We have given up everything and followed you. What will there be for us?" Jesus said to them, "Amen, I say to you that you who have followed me, in the new age, when the Son of Man is seated on his throne of glory, will yourselves sit on twelve thrones, judging the twelve tribes of Israel. And everyone who has given up houses or brothers or sisters or father or mother or children or lands for the sake of my name will receive a hundred times more, and will inherit eternal life. But many who are first will be last, and the last will be first."

Reflection

The saints and apostles give us an example of how to live the Gospel. In today's reading, Peter tells Jesus that he and the apostles have given up everything to follow Christ. Today we also celebrate the feast of Saint Clare, the companion of Saint Francis, who founded the order of Poor Clares and who lived in great poverty for the glory of the kingdom. In the Gospel, Jesus responds by saying that those who have given up the world for his sake will receive a hundred times as much in this life and in the eternal life to come.

Prayers *others may be added*

Jesus, you invite us to live solely for you. Let us pray:

◆ Come, Lord Jesus, come.

That the Church may remain the faithful spouse of Jesus Christ through the holiness and faithfulness of her members, we pray: ◆ For the work of civic leaders who provide services for the necessary needs of human life for the poor and hungry, we pray: ◆ For those who suffer physical injury and terminal or incurable illnesses, we pray: ◆ For all the Poor Clares, that with great joy they may live the evangelical counsels of poverty, chastity, and obedience through the unique calling of their vocation, we pray: ◆ For a deeper love and devotion to the most Holy Eucharist, we pray: ◆

Our Father . . .

Loving God,
you called Saint Clare to renounce
    the world
and all possessions to follow after
    your Son.
Grant that, through her intercession,
    we may
be filled with your light and love, and that
we may hear your voice and to follow
    after
you through our personal vocations.
We ask through Christ our Lord.
Amen.

✝ You forsake not those who seek you, O Lord.

Sunday, August 12, 2012
Nineteenth Sunday in Ordinary Time

✝ Taste and see the goodness of the Lord.

Psalm 103 *page 415*

Reading *John 6:41–51*

[Jesus said to the crowds:] "No one can come to me unless the Father who sent me draw him, and I will raise him on the last day. It is written in the prophets: / *They shall all be taught by God.* / Everyone who listens to my Father and learns from him comes to me. Not that anyone has seen the Father except the one who is from God; he has seen the Father. Amen, amen, I say to you, whoever believes has eternal life. I am the bread of life. Your ancestors ate the manna in the desert but they died; this is the bread that comes from heaven so that one may eat it and not die. I am the living bread that came down from heaven; whoever eats this bread will live forever; and the bread that I will give is my flesh for the life of the world."

Reflection

In today's Gospel, Jesus gives us the secret of union with God. He teaches that everyone who listens to the Father and learns from him will come to him. By listening to the Father through prayerful stillness and the experiences of his goodness within our lives, we shall all be taught by God. Furthermore, through the gift of the Eucharist, Jesus teaches us and brings us into physical and sacramental union with the Father and the Spirit.

Prayers *others may be added*

Through the eucharistic feast, we enter into union with the Trinity. Let us pray:

◆ Teach us, O Lord, and hear our prayer.

For the needs of the Church, that all her leaders and members may be drawn by the Father into deeper love and devotion of the Holy Eucharist, we pray: ◆ For all legislators and all who work in public life, that they may be successful in bringing about peace throughout the world, especially in places torn apart by war, violence, and disrespect for life, we pray: ◆ For all those who serve our country in the military; for their families and their health, safety, and protection, we pray: ◆ For all those who suffer illness and pain, that they may be taught by God how to offer their sufferings in joy to the Father for the expiation of sins and salvation of all souls, we pray: ◆ For all who have died, that they may enter into eternal life, and for the consolation of their loved ones, we pray: ◆

Our Father . . .

Teach us your ways, O Lord,
and grant us strength
to trust in you in moments of difficulty
 and despair.
Grant us your salvation and bring us into
 eternal union with you.
We ask this through Christ our Lord.
Amen.

✝ Taste and see the goodness of the Lord.

✝ Heaven and earth are filled with your glory.

Psalm 145 *page 422*

Reading *Matthew 17:22–27*

As Jesus and his disciples were gathering in Galilee, Jesus said to them, "The Son of Man is to be handed over to men, and they will kill him, and he will be raised on the third day." And they were overwhelmed with grief.

When they came to Capernaum, the collectors of the temple tax approached Peter and said, "Does not your teacher pay the temple tax?" "Yes," he said. When he came into the house, before he had time to speak, Jesus asked him, "What is your opinion, Simon? From whom do the kings of the earth take tolls or census tax? From their subjects or from foreigners?" When he said, "From foreigners," Jesus said to him, "Then the subjects are exempt. But that we may not offend them, go to the sea, drop in a hook, and take the first fish that comes up. Open its mouth and you will find a coin worth twice the temple tax. Give that to them for me and for you."

Reflection

By the Incarnation, Jesus, the Son of God, has become like us in all ways but sin. In today's Gospel, we see that even he offers the temple tax, though it was not required of him. He teaches us to be responsible and generous citizens in obedience to the just laws of the state and the Church, and by giving our due to those in need.

Prayers *others may be added*

Calling up our Father, we offer our prayers and petitions as we say:

◆ Lord, hear our prayer.

For the Church, and for the success of all charitable organizations, we pray: ◆ For our President, his administration, and for the aid of those in social crisis and economic need, we pray: ◆ For those who serve in the military, we pray: ◆ For all who suffer from poverty; for the sick, the homeless, the unemployed, and all who face financial struggles, we pray: ◆ For the members of our community, that they may learn to accept and welcome Christ through charity and service in accepting all of God's family around us, we pray: ◆ For all the dying and for those who grieve the losses of their loved ones, we pray: ◆

Our Father . . .

Providential God,
give us the grace to trust in you with
    confidence
that you will provide for our spiritual,
    material, and financial needs.
Keep us faithful as we follow the
    teachings of the Gospel.
We ask through Christ our Lord.
Amen.

✝ Heaven and earth are filled with your glory.

✝ How sweet to my taste is your promise!

Psalm 19 — page 403

Reading — *Matthew 18:1–4*

The disciples approached Jesus and said, "Who is the greatest in the Kingdom of heaven?" He called a child over, placed it in their midst, and said, "Amen, I say to you, unless you turn and become like children, you will not enter the Kingdom of heaven. Whoever humbles himself like this child is the greatest in the Kingdom of heaven."

Reflection

It is not the proud who enter the kingdom of God, but rather the humble and the childlike. In today's Gospel, we see Jesus' special love for children. He presents the child as the model for sanctity, telling us that the greatest in the kingdom of heaven are the little ones and the childlike. Furthermore, by receiving and welcoming God's children, we receive God himself, and we further the Father's will that not one of his little ones be lost.

Prayers — *others may be added*

The guardian angels of God's children constantly look upon the face of the Father. Through their intercession, we pray:

◆ Lord, hear the prayers of your children.

For the Church, that she may lay down her life for God's children with the same pure love and devotion as Jesus Christ, we pray: ◆ For all families and persons who suffer from addiction, we pray: ◆ For all journalists, media workers, and all involved in communication, through the intercession of Saint Maximilian Mary Kolbe, we pray: ◆ For the grace to generously lay down our lives in service to God and others in the daily opportunities of work and family life, we pray: ◆

Our Father . . .

Loving Father,
you teach us that the greatest
in the kingdom of heaven is the one
who humbles himself like a little child.
Through the intercession of Saint
    Maximilian Mary Kolbe, priest
    and martyr,
free us from our selfishness and pride
and open our hearts to accept you
who are present in our brothers and sisters.
We ask this through Christ our Lord.
Amen.

✝ How sweet to my taste is your promise!

Wednesday, August 15, 2012
Solemnity of the Assumption of the Blessed Virgin Mary

✝ The queen stands at your right
hand, arrayed in gold.

Psalm 27   *page 405*

Reading   *Luke 1:39–45*
Mary set out in those days and traveled to the hill country in haste to a town of Judah, where she entered the house of Zechariah and greeted Elizabeth. When Elizabeth heard Mary's greeting, the infant leaped in her womb, and Elizabeth, filled with the Holy Spirit, cried out in a loud voice and said, "Most blessed are you among women, and blessed is the fruit of your womb. And how does this happen to me, that the mother of my Lord should come to me? For at the moment the sound of your greeting reached my ears, the infant in my womb leaped for joy. Blessed are you who believed that what was spoken to you by the Lord would be fulfilled."

Reflection
Today we celebrate the great solemnity of the Assumption of the Blessed Virgin Mary. This solemnity celebrates the event when Mary was assumed, body and soul, into heaven. Her assumption is a unique participation in the glory of her Son's Resurrection, and it anticipates our own resurrection of the body.

Prayers   *others may be added*
Through the prayers of Blessed Mother Mary, Queen of heaven and earth, we pray:

◆ King of glory, hear our prayer.

For the Church, that Mary, the icon of the Church, may continue to guard and protect her members, we pray: ◆ For the world, that they may be freed from attachment to sin and evil in order to work for the coming of the kingdom of salvation, we pray: ◆ For all who suffer loneliness, addiction, illness, poverty, and special needs, that the prayers of Mary may aid all the afflicted, we pray: ◆ For a deeper devotion to our Blessed Mother Mary, who aids and leads us into union with her Son Jesus, we pray: ◆

Our Father . . .

Father of glory,
today we honor your majesty
    bestowed upon your chosen child,
    Mary, the Mother of God.
Through her intercession,
grant that we may remain free from sin
and be radiant in your grace
as we await the coming of your Son,
who lives and reigns with you in the unity
    of the Holy Spirit
one God, forever and ever.
Amen.

✝ The queen stands at your right
hand, arrayed in gold.

Thursday, August 16, 2012
Weekday

✝ Do not forget the works of the Lord!
(*Ps. 45:10*)

Psalm 34
page 406

Reading
Matthew 18:21–22

Peter approached Jesus and said to him, "Lord, if my brother sins against me, how often must I forgive him? As many as seven times?" Jesus answered, "I say to you, not seven times but seventy-seven times."

Reflection

Forgiveness is one of the deepest manifestations of true love. If we truly love, we will be willing to forgive those who have hurt us. Jesus shows us how to forgive as he hangs upon the cross, paying the debt for our sins. Because of our humanity, we may not always feel forgiveness for others; however, we can make an act of the will to forgive those who have wronged us and to ask the Lord to bless them.

Prayers
others may be added

With confidence in our Father's compassion and mercy for us, we offer our prayers as we say:

◆ God of mercy, hear our prayer.

For all those who have been wounded by members of the Church, that they may receive healing and forgiveness, we pray: ◆
For the end of war, violence, crime, and abuse throughout the world, we pray: ◆
For all who suffer sickness, poverty, marital strife, economic difficulties, or loss due to natural disasters, we pray: ◆
For the joy of Christ's presence to inspire us to treat one another with charity and kindness, we pray: ◆

Our Father . . .

Be patient with us, O God,
and show us your compassion.
Grant us your forgiveness,
for we know not what we do.
Teach us how to love one another
and grant us your lasting peace.
We ask this through our Lord Jesus
    Christ, your Son,
who lives and reigns with you in the unity
    of the Holy Spirit,
one God, forever and ever.
Amen.

✝ Do not forget the works of the Lord!

Friday, August 17, 2012
Weekday

✝ You have turned from your anger.

Psalm 63 *page 410*

Reading *Matthew 19:3–6*

Some Pharisees approached Jesus, and tested him, saying, "Is it lawful for a man to divorce his wife for any cause whatever?" He said in reply, "Have you not read that from the beginning the Creator / *made them male and female* / and said, / *For this reason a man shall leave his father and mother* / *and be joined to his wife, and the two shall become one flesh?* / So they are no longer two, but one flesh. Therefore, what God has joined together, man must not separate."

Reflection

Divorce has become so prevalent in our culture that it seems almost normal to get a divorce if one's marriage is not working out. However, in today's Gospel, we learn that God created the bond of marriage between a man and a woman to last even through all the difficulties of life. The dignity and gift of the sacrament of Marriage must be protected and understood so that men and women can live out this vocation in the fullness of its beauty as God created it to be from the beginning.

Prayers *others may be added*

Turning to our Father who always hears our prayers, we pray:

◆ Heal us of all sin and division.

For the Church, that she may tirelessly defend and protect the dignity of Marriage and of the human person, even in the face of persecution, misunderstanding, and indifference, we pray: ◆ For all nations, that they may rediscover the beauty of the family and work in service of all life, we pray: ◆ For all who suffer the pain of divorce or separation, we pray: ◆ For all religious and lay consecrated who live celibate lives for the sake of the kingdom, we pray: ◆ For young people, that they may have the courage and hope to discover that true love is possible within their families and in their relationships, we pray: ◆

Our Father . . .

Loving Father,
you create us to love one another
and to delight in your creation here
    on earth.
Free us from our selfishness and our sins,
which keep us from you and destroy our
unity with you and with one another.
We ask this through our Lord Jesus
    Christ, your Son,
who lives and reigns with you in the unity
    of the Holy Spirit,
one God, forever and ever.
Amen.

✝ You have turned from your anger.

Saturday, August 18, 2012
Weekday

✝ Create a clean heart in me, O God.

Psalm 141   *page 421*

Reading   *Matthew 19:13–15*
Children were brought to Jesus that he might lay his hands on them and pray. The disciples rebuked them, but Jesus said, "Let the children come to me, and do not prevent them; for the Kingdom of heaven belongs to such as these." After he placed his hands on them, he went away.

Reflection   *Graziano Marcheschi*
Were they afraid to waste his time; that he had more important things to do? They would have thought nothing to take his time with requests like, "Put us at your left and right in the coming kingdom." But playing with children seemed somehow wrong to them. Jesus uses the children and this moment to teach about the kingdom: it "belongs to such as these." What makes children and the childlike owners of the kingdom? Children can be brutal, especially to each other; Jesus must have known that. What else he knew of children was that they know they're needy and when their needs arise, they know where to go to get them met. A child of the kingdom has to know that, too. We need God. But some of us forget that we can only be whole within God's bosom. The joy and peace we seek is not minted in this world, but only in the kingdom of love.

Prayers   *others may be added*
With humble confidence in our Father's love and mercy, we pray:

◆ Father, hear the prayers of your children.

For the Holy Father, that he may be strengthened in his ministry to welcome and serve all the children of his flock throughout the world, we pray: ◆ For government leaders, that they may work for the protection of the dignity of all human life, especially the most vulnerable of society, we pray: ◆ For all teachers, youth ministers, social workers, nurses, doctors, and volunteers who work and serve the poor, the sick, and all of God's little ones, we pray: ◆ For all victims of child abuse, for their healing and for the conversion of their perpetrators, we pray: ◆ For all children, especially those who suffer sickness and poverty, we pray: ◆ For all teachers, nurses, day care workers, and mothers and fathers who serve Christ present in their children, we pray: ◆ For all who have died and for mothers or fathers who grieve the loss of a child, we pray: ◆

Our Father . . .

Heavenly Father,
give us the purity of heart
and the trustful abandonment of a
    little child.
Draw all of your children into
the love of your Trinitarian family.
We ask this through Christ our Lord.
Amen.

✝ Create a clean heart in me, O God.

✝ Taste and see the goodness of the Lord.

Psalm 100   *page 414*

Reading   *John 6:52–58*

The Jews quarreled among themselves, saying, "How can this man give us his flesh to eat?" Jesus said to them, "Amen, amen, I say to you, unless you eat the flesh of the Son of Man and drink his blood, you do not have life within you. Whoever eats my flesh and drinks my blood has eternal life, and I will raise him on the last day. For my flesh is true food, and my blood is true drink. Whoever eats my flesh and drinks my blood remains in me and I in him. Just as the living Father sent me and I have life because of the Father, so also the one who feeds on me will have life because of me. This is the bread that came down from heaven. Unlike your ancestors who ate and still died, whoever eats this bread will live forever."

Reflection

At Mass, we receive eternal life as we eat the living bread of Christ's Body and Blood in the Eucharist. This is the purpose of coming to Mass every Sunday: to gather together as God's people, to remember and ratify God's covenant of love and life for us, and to receive his life within us as we are nourished by the gift of his Body and Blood. Today and each Sunday we celebrate this mystery, which has been handed down from Christ through the ages until today. Within the Mass and the life of the Church, our Catholic faith celebrates and lives Christ yesterday, today, and always.

Prayers   *others may be added*

Gathering together as God's family, we ask our Father as we pray:

◆ **Lord, hear the prayers of your children.**

For the Church, guided by the wisdom of the Holy Father, that she may remain united to the Eucharistic heart of Jesus Christ, we pray: ◆ For all nations throughout the world, that they may encounter the Lord's salvation through the witness and example of holy and faithful Christians, we pray: ◆ For all military families and for those who suffer separation from their loved ones, we pray: ◆ For all the poor, hungry, and those who have no shelter, that those with more may help to relieve their need, we pray: ◆ For all who have died, that they may receive everlasting life in the Trinity, we pray: ◆

Our Father . . .

Heavenly Father,
you sent us your Son
as the Living Bread come down
    from heaven.
Increase our faith and open our hearts
to welcome the gift of your life within us.
We ask this through Christ our Lord.
Amen.

✝ Taste and see the goodness of the Lord.

Monday, August 20, 2012
Memorial of Saint Bernard, Abbot and Doctor of the Church

✝ You have forgotten God who gave you birth.

Psalm 139 page 421

Reading *Matthew 19:16, 21–22*

A young man approached Jesus and said, "Teacher, what good must I do to gain eternal life?" . . . Jesus said to him, "If you wish to be perfect, go, sell what you have and give to the poor, and you will have treasure in heaven. Then come, follow me." When the young man heard this statement, he went away sad, for he had many possessions.

Reflection

Our modern world has removed itself from the concerns of God. The questions of our modern life often ask, What must I do make more money? To be more successful? What must I do to be better looking? To lose more weight? To have more successful relationships? However, the wise man in today's Gospel is not concerned with these worldly questions that do not bring lasting peace. Instead, he asks Jesus, "What good must I do to gain eternal life?" Jesus provides him with the answer: Keep the commandments; give what you have to the poor and follow Jesus. This is the way to attain true and lasting perfect life.

Prayers *others may be added*

Calling upon God, the source of eternal life, let us pray:

◆ Hear us, O Lord.

For the Church, the Holy Father, all priests, bishops, religious, and lay faithful, that they may always seek the things of above that bring lasting life, we pray: ◆ For all civic leaders, that they may work to preserve the dignity of life through the aid and service of the common good, we pray: ◆ For all families, that they may be courageous and generous in their openness to the gift and joy of children, we pray: ◆ For the poor, the weak, and the suffering, that their poverty may not be a source of resentment, but rather a means of attaining the kingdom of God, we pray: ◆ For all who have given up the riches of the world for the treasures of heaven, we pray: ◆ For the grace to seek first the kingdom of heaven rather than material goods, we pray: ◆

Our Father . . .

Lord Jesus,
you teach us that true perfection
consists in keeping your commandments
and following after you.
Give us the grace to detach ourselves
from worldly possessions in order
to attain the treasure of everlasting life.
You live and reign forever.
Amen.

✝ You have forgotten God who gave you birth.

Tuesday, August 21, 2012
Memorial of Saint Pius X, Pope

✟ It is I who deal death and give life.

Psalm 150
page 424

Reading
Matthew 19:23–24

Jesus said to his disciples: "Amen, I say to you, it will be hard for one who is rich to enter the Kingdom of heaven. Again I say to you, it is easier for a camel to pass through the eye of a needle than for one who is rich to enter the Kingdom of God."

Reflection

"Who can be saved?" the disciples cry out to Jesus (prior to what is noted above), and likewise, we too can say these same words to Jesus today. We have been blessed with so many riches in this day and age, especially in all the current advances in technology, medicine, and science. Jesus warns us that it will be hard for those who are rich to enter into the kingdom of heaven. For this reason it seems as if salvation is impossible. But Jesus reminds us that on our own we can do nothing, yet with God all things are possible.

Prayers
others may be added

Father, look kindly on the prayers of your poor and lowly children as we pray:

✟ Fill us with the richness of your grace, O Lord.

For the Holy Father, that he may remain faithful and strong in his work to bring unity among all peoples and to lead all souls to God, we pray: ◆ For all bishops, that together they may strengthen one another in the fraternal love of their episcopal ministry, we pray: ◆ For all who strive for world peace through the work of dialogue, unity, and ecumenism, we pray: ◆ For all young children, especially those who will be receiving their first Holy Communion this year, we pray: ◆ For our parish, that it may be renewed in a deeper love and devotion to the liturgy and all the sacraments, we pray: ◆ For all those who have died, that they may be numbered among the saints for all eternity, we pray: ◆

Our Father . . .

Heavenly Father,
help us to detach ourselves from
    worldly riches
and seek the face of your Son.
May we courageously work
to renew all things in Christ,
through the help and prayers of the
    Blessed Virgin.
We ask this through Christ our Lord.
Amen.

✟ It is I who deal death and give life.

✝ The Lord is my shepherd; there is nothing I shall want.

Psalm 141
page 421

Reading
Matthew 20:1–4, 5b–6a, 7b–8, 10–13a, 15–16

Jesus told his disciples this parable: "The Kingdom of heaven is like a landowner who went out at dawn to hire laborers for his vineyard. After agreeing with them for the usual daily wage, he sent them into his vineyard. Going out about nine o'clock, he saw others standing idle in the marketplace, and he said to them, 'You too go into my vineyard, and I will give you what is just.' . . . . And he went out again around noon, and around three o'clock, and did likewise. Going out about five o'clock, he found others standing around, and said to them, 'You too go into my vineyard.' When it was evening the owner of the vineyard said to his foreman, 'Summon the laborers and give them their pay, beginning with the last and ending with the first.' When the first came, they thought that they would receive more, but each of them also got the usual wage. . . . They grumbled against the landowner, saying, 'These last ones worked only one hour, and you have made them equal to us, who bore the day's burden and the heat.' He said to one of them in reply, 'Am I not free to do as I wish with my own money? Are you envious because I am generous?' Thus, the last will be first, and the first will be last."

Reflection

Today on the memorial of the Queenship of Mary, we celebrate Mary crowned Queen of heaven and earth. Jesus is King, and Mary is the Queen who intercedes for us and pleads for us on our behalf to her obedient Son. Mary is blessed among women, because she was chosen by God to be the pure and stainless tabernacle of God Incarnate. Today we honor her as our Mother and Queen as she received the Word made Flesh and persevered to the end in faithfulness to God's unique calling.

Prayers
others may be added

We present our prayers to the Father:

◆ Lord, hear our prayer.

For the Church, we pray: ◆ For world leaders, we pray: ◆ For those who suffer, we pray: ◆ For those who have died, we pray: ◆

Our Father . . .

Almighty Father,
today we honor your daughter, the
    Immaculate Virgin Mary,
whom you crown as Queen of heaven
    and earth.
Through her prayers, may we be led
    ever closer
to Jesus Christ until we are drawn into
    his kingship.
We ask this through the same Christ
    our Lord.
Amen.

✝ The Lord is my shepherd; there is nothing I shall want.

✝ I will pour clean water on you and wash away all your sins.

Psalm 146   *page 423*

Reading   *Matthew 22:1b–9*

[Jesus said:] "The Kingdom of heaven may be likened to a king who gave a wedding feast for his son. He dispatched his servants to summon the invited guests to the feast, but they refused to come. A second time he sent other servants, saying, 'Tell those invited: "Behold, I have prepared my banquet, my calves and fattened cattle are killed, and everything is ready; come to the feast."' Some ignored the invitation and went away, one to his farm, another to his business. The rest laid hold of his servants, mistreated them, and killed them. The king was enraged and sent his troops, destroyed those murderers, and burned their city. Then the king said to his servants, 'The feast is ready, but those who were invited were not worthy to come. Go out, therefore, into the main roads and invite to the feast whomever you find.'"

Reflection

Today Jesus teaches us that heaven is like a wedding banquet. The Father extends the invitation to the good, bad, rich, and poor alike to participate in the marriage feast of his Son. However, it is necessary that the guests be prepared to partake in the celebration. Through the sacrament of Reconciliation, by keeping the commandments, and by practicing works of charity, we prepare ourselves and clothe our souls in the appropriate wedding garment of grace. Thus, we can partake of the wedding feast here on earth at the eucharistic table at every Mass, as we await the full participation in the marriage feast of the kingdom of heaven.

Prayers   *others may be added*

Awaiting the eternal feast of faith in heaven, we beg the Father:

◆ **Make us worthy of your kingdom, Lord.**

For the Church, we pray: ◆ For local, national, and world leaders, we pray: ◆ For those who suffer persecution, we pray: ◆ For all the poor, the hungry, the homeless, the abandoned, and the abused, we pray: ◆ For the protection of all travelers and for a safe return of all traveling to or from vacation, we pray: ◆ For the grace to avoid all sin, we pray: ◆

Our Father . . .

Heavenly Father,
you invite all your children
to share in the celebration
of your Son's wedding feast.
Purify us and keep us holy
until the day when we will
feast of the eternal kingdom of heaven.
We ask this through Christ our Lord.
Amen.

✝ I will pour clean water on you and wash away all your sins.

✝ Your friends made known, O Lord, the glorious splendor of your kingdom.

Psalm 146   *page 423*

Reading   *John 1:45–49*

Philip found Nathanael and told him, "We have found the one about whom Moses wrote in the law, and also the prophets, Jesus son of Joseph, from Nazareth." But Nathanael said to him, "Can anything good come from Nazareth?" Philip said to him, "Come and see." Jesus saw Nathanael coming toward him and said of him, "Here is a true child of Israel. There is no duplicity in him." Nathanael said to him, "How do you know me?" Jesus answered and said to him, "Before Philip called you, I saw you under the fig tree." Nathanael answered him, "Rabbi, you are the Son of God; you are the King of Israel."

Reflection

Today we celebrate the feast of the apostle and martyr Saint Bartholomew. In the scriptures, Bartholomew was known as Nathanael. Jesus honored his uprightness and moral character. He said, "There is no duplicity in him." Saint Bartholomew gave his life as a witness and testimony to Christ and was eventually martyred by being flayed alive. His life's witness and his martyrdom encourages us not to fear to give testimony to Christ.

Prayers   *others may be added*

Through the prayers of all the saints and martyrs, we pray:

◆ Strengthen our faith, O Lord.

For the Church, that she may send out many new apostles to continue to spread the Gospel and give witness to the truth of Jesus Christ, we pray: ◆ For civic leaders, that they will enact laws that protect and uphold the common good of all peoples, we pray: ◆ For the poor, the sick, and for those who suffer from skin diseases, we pray: ◆ For each of us in our faith community, that we may be shaken from laziness and indifference in order to boldly follow the path the Lord has chosen for us, we pray: ◆ For all who have died, especially those who have died giving witness to their faith, we pray: ◆

Our Father . . .

Loving God,
through the witness of your saints
    and martyrs,
you call us to a deeper level of holiness.
Forgive us our sins and strengthen our
    weary hearts,
so we may return to follow you in love
    and service.
We ask this through Christ our Lord.
Amen.

✝ Your friends made known, O Lord, the glorious splendor of your kingdom.

✝ The glory of the Lord will dwell in our land.

Psalm 63 *page 410*

Reading *Matthew 23:1–12*

Jesus spoke to the crowds and to his disciples, saying, "The scribes and the Pharisees have taken their seat on the chair of Moses. Therefore, do and observe all things whatsoever they tell you, but do not follow their example. For they preach but they do not practice. They tie up heavy burdens hard to carry and lay them on people's shoulders, but they will not lift a finger to move them. All their works are performed to be seen. They widen their phylacteries and lengthen their tassels. They love places of honor at banquets, seats of honor in synagogues, greetings in marketplaces, and the salutation 'Rabbi.' As for you, do not be called 'Rabbi.' You have but one teacher, and you are all brothers. Call no one on earth your father; you have but one Father in heaven. Do not be called 'Master'; you have but one master, the Christ. The greatest among you must be your servant. Whoever exalts himself will be humbled; but whoever humbles himself will be exalted."

Reflection

As the saying goes, it is easier to talk the talk than to walk the walk. This is also with the spiritual life. Many times we can be scandalized by those who seem to be good and holy Christians, yet fail to practice what they preach.

However, the Lord teaches us to forgive as we have been forgiven in Christ Jesus and for us to do and live as the "Pharisees" say, but not to follow their example.

Prayers *others may be added*

Full of hope in your promise, we present to you our needs as we pray:

◆ **Hear our prayer, O loving Father.**

For the leaders of the Church, that they may remain faithful and holy as they carry out the mission of Jesus Christ, we pray: ◆ For all civic leaders, that they may live out an example of saintly holiness in their work among the world, we pray: ◆ For those who suffer illness, depression, addiction, poverty, and unemployment, that Christ may swiftly fulfill their needs through the aid of generous Christians, we pray: ◆ For all our loved ones who have passed away, that they may soon enjoy the beatitude of eternal life, we pray: ◆

Our Father . . .

Jesus, our Master and Teacher,
you teach us that the greatest will be
the servant.
Give us the grace to humble ourselves
out of love for you and our fellow brethren.
You live and reign forever.
Amen.

✝ The glory of the Lord will dwell in our land.

✝ Taste and see the goodness of the Lord.

Psalm 150   *page 424*

Reading   *John 6:60–64a, 66–69*

Many of the disciples of Jesus who were listening said, "This saying is hard; who can accept it?" Since Jesus knew that his disciples were murmuring about this, he said to them, "Does this shock you? What if you were to see the Son of Man ascending to where he was before? It is the spirit that gives life, while the flesh is of no avail. The words I have spoken to you are Spirit and life. But there are some of you who do not believe." . . .

As a result of this, many of his disciples returned to their former way of life and no longer accompanied him. Jesus then said to the Twelve, "Do you also want to leave?" Simon Peter answered him, "Master, to whom shall we go? You have the words of eternal life. We have come to believe and are convinced that you are the Holy One of God."

Reflection   *S. Anne Elizabeth Sweet, CSO*

Today's Gospel is the conclusion of the Bread of Life discourse found in John 6. The "saying" referred to in the first line is found in the concluding verses of last Sunday's Gospel: Jesus is living bread come down from heaven; on him, believers must feed; in doing so, they live forever. Some, not understanding, find it too hard to believe. They depart from Jesus and return to their former way of life. They have made their choice. Peter too has made a choice. He has come to believe and remains with Jesus.

Prayers   *others may be added*

You, O God, have the words of everlasting life. Let us pray:

◆ Lord, we believe; help our unbelief.

For the Church, that she may stand steadfast and firm by instructing and clarifying in charity without diminishing the truths and teachings of Jesus Christ, we pray: ◆ For all nations and people who reject the teachings of the Church out of misunderstandings, selfishness, or pride, that all may be brought into unity and truth, we pray: ◆ For the sick and suffering, that they may be restored to new life through the reception of the healing sacrament of the Eucharist, we pray: ◆ For all Catholics, that they may become more deeply rooted in faith and charity, we pray: ◆

Our Father . . .

Heavenly Father,
draw us into union with you
through your Son.
Pour your Spirit and life upon us
and increase our faith so that we
may be convinced and come to believe
in your Son, Jesus, our Eucharistic Lord,
who lives and reigns with you in the unity
    of the Holy Spirit,
one God, forever and ever.
Amen.

✝ Taste and see the goodness of the Lord.

☩ Proclaim God's marvelous deeds to all the nations.

Psalm 146
page 423

Reading
Luke 7:11–17

Jesus journeyed to a city called Nain, and his disciples and a large crowd accompanied him. As he drew near to the gate of the city, a man who had died was being carried out, the only son of his mother, and she was a widow. A large crowd from the city was with her. When the Lord saw her, he was moved with pity for her and said to her, "Do not weep." He stepped forward and touched the coffin; at this the bearers halted, and he said, "Young man, I tell you, arise!" The dead man sat up and began to speak, and Jesus gave him to his mother. Fear seized them all, and they glorified God, exclaiming, "A great prophet has arisen in our midst," and "God has visited his people." This report about him spread through the whole of Judea and in all the surrounding region.

Reflection

Today we celebrate Saint Monica, the mother of Saint Augustine. Her example teaches us to be faithful in prayer. God will always hear our prayer; however, sometimes he asks us to be persevering in hope as we await his answer.

Prayers
others may be added

Filled with hope that you always hear the prayers of your faithful, let us pray:

◆ Hear our prayer and come to our aid, O God.

For the needs of the Church, that, through the patient prayer and work of all her members, all peoples may come to drink from the fountain of life, we pray: ◆ For the conversion of all nations and for all governmental officials who help to bring about peace, justice, and order, we pray: ◆ For all those who suffer anxiety, fear, depression, loss, and sickness, that they may persevere in hope as the Lord answers their needs, we pray: ◆ For all mothers, and for the safety and protection of their children, that they may be freed from all worry, confident in the Lord's care, we pray: ◆ For all who have died, that they may be numbered among the saints, we pray: ◆

Our Father . . .

Father,
your thoughts are not our thoughts,
nor are your ways our ways.
Through the intercession of
    Saint Monica,
give us the grace to persevere
in prayer and good works until the
    coming of your Son Jesus Christ,
who lives with you in the unity of the
    Holy Spirit,
one God, forever and ever.
Amen.

☩ Proclaim God's marvelous deeds to all the nations.

Tuesday, August 28, 2012
Memorial of Saint Augustine,
Bishop and Doctor of the Church

✝ The Lord comes to judge the earth.

Psalm 103
page 415

Reading
Matthew 23:23–26

Jesus said: "Woe to you, scribes and Pharisees, you hypocrites. You pay tithes of mint and dill and cummin, and have neglected the weightier things of the law: judgment and mercy and fidelity. But these you should have done, without neglecting the others. Blind guides, who strain out the gnat and swallow the camel!

"Woe to you, scribes and Pharisees, you hypocrites. You cleanse the outside of cup and dish, but inside they are full of plunder and self-indulgence. Blind Pharisee, cleanse first the inside of the cup, so that the outside also may be clean."

Reflection

Today we celebrate the great Saint Augustine who, through the prayers of his mother, Monica, converted to Christianity after a sinful life. In today's Gospel, Jesus warns us to cleanse hearts from sin and hypocrisy so that our hearts may be concerned with what is most important: the kingdom of God. The life of Saint Augustine gives us hope that, with God's grace, salvation and sanctity are possible for each and every one of us.

Prayers
others may be added

Through your grace, O God, all things are possible. Let us pray:

◆ Lord, show us your mercy and grant us your salvation.

For the Holy Father, the Bishop of Rome, that he may be strengthened in health and fortitude to fulfill his responsibility to lead all peoples to God, we pray: ◆ For our nation, that it may be converted to recognize the dignity of each human person from conception to natural death, we pray: ◆ For those who are restlessly searching for truth, that their hearts may rest in the discovery of Jesus Christ, Truth Incarnate, we pray: ◆ For the sick, the suffering, the dying, and all in special need, especially those in our local community, we pray: ◆

Our Father . . .

Merciful God,
you bring sinners back to life
through the grace of your Son Jesus.
By the prayers of Saint Augustine,
bring us deeper conversion
so we may be able to love you
with pure and faithful hearts.
We ask this through Christ our Lord.
Amen.

✝ The Lord comes to judge the earth.

✝ I will sing of your salvation.

Psalm 145 *page 422*

Reading *Mark 6:22–25*

Herodias' own daughter came in and performed a dance that delighted Herod and his guests. The king said to the girl, "Ask of me whatever you wish and I will grant it to you." He even swore many things to her, "I will grant you whatever you ask of me even to half of my kingdom." She went out and said to her mother, "What shall I ask for?" She replied, "The head of John the Baptist."

Reflection

Today we celebrate the martyrdom of Saint John the Baptist. His whole life gave witness to Jesus the Messiah by proclaiming and identifying the Lamb of God who came to free us from our sins. His life culminated in the witness of his death, in which he gave himself up for the sake of the truth in testimony to Jesus Christ. By his example, we learn how to witness to Christ faithfully even until the end.

Prayers *others may be added*

Jesus Christ, you show us the way to the Father. Let us pray:

◆ Hear us, O Lord.

For the Church in times of persecution and trial, that she may remain a faithful witness to the truth and life of Jesus Christ, we pray: ◆ For all social workers, counselors, and all involved in the work of service for the good of society, we pray: ◆ For all who suffer persecution, abuse, illness, poverty, and strife, we pray: ◆ For those who have died, that they may be brought into the eternal rest of heaven with all the angels and saints, we pray: ◆ For all to live as witnesses to the Gospel amid the little martyrdoms of each day, we pray: ◆

Our Father . . .

Lord Jesus,
through the life and work of your herald,
    John the Baptist,
you reveal to us that you
are the Messiah and Savior of the World.
By the prayers of your saints and martyrs,
help us to witness to your glory and love.
We ask this through Christ our Lord.
Amen.

✝ I will sing of your salvation.

✝ I will praise your name for ever, Lord.

Psalm 19 *page 403*

Reading *Matthew 24:42–44*

Jesus said to his disciples: "Stay awake! For you do not know on which day your Lord will come. Be sure of this: if the master of the house had known the hour of night when the thief was coming, he would have stayed awake and not let his house be broken into. So too, you also must be prepared, for at an hour you do not expect, the Son of Man will come."

Reflection

It is easy to be caught up in the monotonous routine of everyday life. However, today in the Gospel, Jesus rouses us by saying that we must stay awake! The spiritual life is one of ever increasing richness and depth, and we must not give into temptations of sadness or discouragement. We do not know the day or the hour, so let us not be found sleeping when the Bridegroom arrives!

Prayers *others may be added*

Father, we know not the day nor the hour when your Son will come again. Let us pray:

◆ Come, Lord Jesus, set us free.

For the Church, that the Pope, and all the bishops, priests, and clergy may be prudent and faithful servants as they care for all the souls entrusted to them until the Master's return, we pray: ◆ For all nations that have turned away from the Master's call, that they may return to the Lord with ready hearts, we pray: ◆ For the swift recovery of all the sick, those facing surgery and medical procedures, and all accident victims, we pray: ◆ For those who have fallen asleep in Christ, and for all who will die today, that the Lord will find them ready to come dwell with him in his eternal kingdom, we pray: ◆

Our Father . . .

Father God,
send your Spirit upon us
to rouse us from our sinfulness.
Refresh us with your living grace,
that we may enjoy the richness
of life with you in the company of
the angels.
We ask through Christ our Lord.
Amen.

✝ I will praise your name for ever, Lord.

Friday, August 31, 2012
Weekday

✝ The earth is full of the goodness of the Lord.

Psalm 25 — page 405

Reading — *Matthew 25:1–13*

Jesus told his disciples this parable: "The Kingdom of heaven will be like ten virgins who took their lamps and went out to meet the bridegroom. Five of them were foolish and five were wise. The foolish ones, when taking their lamps, brought no oil with them, but the wise brought flasks of oil with their lamps. Since the bridegroom was long delayed, they all became drowsy and fell asleep. At midnight, there was a cry, 'Behold, the bridegroom! Come out to meet him!' Then all those virgins got up and trimmed their lamps. The foolish ones said to the wise, 'Give us some of your oil, for our lamps are going out.' But the wise ones replied, 'No, for there may not be enough for us and you. Go instead to the merchants and buy some for yourselves.' While they went off to buy it, the bridegroom came and those who were ready went into the wedding feast with him. Then the door was locked. Afterwards the other virgins came and said, 'Lord, Lord, open the door for us!' But he said in reply, 'Amen, I say to you, I do not know you.' Therefore, stay awake, for you know neither the day nor the hour."

Reflection

Today in the Gospel, Jesus likens the kingdom of God to ten virgins, five who are wise and five who are foolish. By this parable, Jesus encourages us to remain watchful and prepared like the wise virgins. Let us not be like the foolish virgins who miss the Bridegroom because they were unprepared and had fallen asleep, and let us not miss Christ in the little encounters of each day where he unexpectedly comes to meet us.

Prayers — *others may be added*

Presenting our petitions, we pray:

◆ Renew us with your life, O Lord.

That the Holy Father may be crowned with wisdom we pray: ◆ That all peoples of the world may ready themselves to welcome Christ's coming, we pray: ◆ That Christ may come to heal and relieve the sufferings of all who are sick, we pray: ◆ That we may possess true wisdom through union with God, we pray: ◆

Our Father . . .

Come, Lord Jesus,
Bridegroom of our souls.
Do not delay. Ready our hearts
to receive the outpouring
of your Spirit, who lives and reigns with
　　you and the Father,
one God, forever and ever.
Amen.

✝ The earth is full of the goodness of the Lord.

✝ Blessed be the people the Lord has chosen to be his own.

Psalm 34 *page 406*

Reading *Matthew 25:14–15, 19–21*

Jesus told his disciples this parable: "A man going on a journey called in his servants and entrusted his possessions to them. To one he gave five talents; to another, two; to a third, one—to each according to his ability. Then he went away. . . . After a long time the master of those servants came back and settled accounts with them. The one who had received five talents came forward bringing the additional five. He said, 'Master, you gave me five talents. See, I have made five more.' His master said to him, 'Well done, my good and faithful servant. Since you were faithful in small matters, I will give you great responsibilities. Come, share your master's joy.'"

Reflection

In today's Gospel we learn that even the little things have significant importance. In the parable, Jesus teaches that those who are faithful in small matters will be capable to receive great responsibilities. It is through our faithfulness in the humble fulfillment of our duties that we will come to share the Master's joy.

Prayers *others may be added*

United together as God's family, we pray:

◆ Merciful Father, hear our prayer.

For the pilgrim Church, that she may be protected from all evil through the journey toward the kingdom of heaven, we pray: ◆ For all civic leaders, that they may reap abundant harvest by sowing good works of justice, reconciliation, and peace, we pray: ◆ For all who suffer difficulty because of natural disasters, financial crisis, or familial strife, we pray: ◆ For all people to use their gifts and talents for the good of family, friends, local community, and those in need, we pray: ◆

Our Father . . .

Loving God,
we praise and glorify you
for having entrusted us with the most
    precious gift
of your Son, Jesus Christ.
Open our hearts to be faithful to the voice
    of the Holy Spirit.
We ask this through Christ our Lord.
Amen.

✝ Blessed be the people the Lord has chosen to be his own.

Sunday, September 2, 2012
Twenty-second Sunday in Ordinary Time

✝ The Lord comes to rule the earth with justice.

Psalm 51   *page 409*

Reading   *Mark 7:14–15, 21–23*

Jesus summoned the crowd again and said to them, "Hear me, all of you, and understand. Nothing that enters one from outside can defile that person; but the things that come out from within are what defile.

"From within the man, from his heart, come evil thoughts, unchastity, theft, murder, adultery, greed, malice, deceit, licentiousness, envy, blasphemy, arrogance, folly. All these evils come from within and they defile."

Reflection

In our Christian witness it is important to exemplify integrity of life. Thus, our external practice is an expression of our interior disposition. In today's Gospel, Jesus criticizes religious practice that merely honors God with the lips while the heart is far from the Lord. Our beliefs must overflow in good word and deed, rather than the hypocrisy the Lord warns us to avoid.

Prayers   *others may be added*

As we celebrate together the glory of Christ's Resurrection, let us pray:

◆ Purify our hearts, O Lord.

For the Church, that she may ever remain pure and holy as the spotless Bride of Christ, we pray: ◆ For the Holy Father, all bishops, priests, religious, and lay faithful, that they may always offer holy and faithful witness to the Christian life, we pray: ◆ For government officials, that they may serve the good of all peoples by means of dialogue, charity, and service, we pray: ◆ For the poor, the homeless, the lonely, and all the sick and suffering, that they may find healing and comfort in the grace given by Jesus Christ, we pray: ◆ For all to encounter Christ in the Eucharistic celebration, that they may deeply enter the hearts of all the members of our parish community, we pray: ◆ For all the faithful departed, we pray: ◆

Our Father . . .

Heavenly Father,
may the grace of the remembrance
of the Resurrection take root in our lives
and overflow in good works of charity
    and service.
We ask through our Lord Jesus Christ,
    your Son,
who lives and reigns with you in the unity
    of the Holy Spirit,
one God, forever and ever.
Amen.

✝ The Lord comes to rule the earth with justice.

✝ Lord, I love your commands.

Psalm 95
page 413

Reading
Luke 4:17b–19

[Jesus] unrolled the scroll and found the passage where it was written: / *The Spirit of the Lord is upon me, / because he has anointed me / to bring glad tidings to the poor. / He has sent me to proclaim liberty to captives / and recovery of sight to the blind, / to let the oppressed go free, / and to proclaim a year acceptable to the Lord.*

Reflection

After reading the prophecy of Isaiah, Jesus proclaims that the reading has been fulfilled among the people that day. He reveals himself as the long-awaited Messiah, the one anointed by the Spirit of God. He was sent to bring peace, to heal the sick and broken-hearted, to free all captives, and to proclaim a message of joy. At every Mass and in our encounters with one another, Jesus Christ reveals himself in our midst, and he continues his good work among us.

Prayers
others may be added

Lord of majesty and might, hear our prayers that we entrust to you today:

◆ **Come to the aid of your people, O Lord.**

For the Holy Father, that he may govern the Church with wisdom and insight as he guides Christ's flock along the path to heaven, we pray: ◆ For government officials, that they may work together to eliminate war, violence, poverty, and abuse, we pray: ◆ For all who labor and for those who seek employment, we pray: ◆ For all the sick and dying, that they may be anointed with the healing power of the Holy Spirit, we pray: ◆ For an increase in the love and devotion given to scripture and the Mass; that all may grow in the love of God among our friends, family, and parish community, we pray: ◆

Our Father . . .

Loving God,
you blessed Pope Saint Gregory the Great
with charity and wisdom in his
    pastoral work.
By his prayers,
may we learn to follow you in courage
    and gentleness.
we ask through Christ our Lord.
Amen.

✝ Lord, I love your commands.

Tuesday, September 4, 2012
Weekday

✝ The Lord is just in all his ways.

Psalm 100 — page 414

Reading — Luke 4:31–37

Jesus went down to Capernaum, a town of Galilee. He taught them on the sabbath, and they were astonished at his teaching because he spoke with authority. In the synagogue there was a man with the spirit of an unclean demon, and he cried out in a loud voice, "What have you to do with us, Jesus of Nazareth? Have you come to destroy us? I know who you are—the Holy One of God!" Jesus rebuked him and said, "Be quiet! Come out of him!" Then the demon threw the man down in front of them and came out of him without doing him any harm. They were all amazed and said to one another, "What is there about his word? For with authority and power he commands the unclean spirits, and they come out." And news of him spread everywhere in the surrounding region.

Reflection

In today's Gospel, we hear how Jesus' word drives out demons and frees those who are oppressed. Even today we encounter this same power and authority at the Mass where we hear the word of God in the scriptures and receive Christ in the Eucharist. From the sacraments, we receive God's same healing, freedom, and new life for us today, and we can marvel at his power and authority like the disciples do in the Gospel.

Prayers — others may be added

Placing ourselves in God's presence, we present our prayers and petitions as we say:

◆ Open our hearts to hear your word, Lord.

For the Holy Father, the Bishop of Rome, and all the clergy, that they may proclaim God's word as faithful prophets to Christ Jesus, we pray: ◆ For all who serve in public office, that they may work in uprightness of character as they strive to establish social order and justice, we pray: ◆ For all those oppressed by illness, pain, loneliness, addiction, depression, and the emptiness of a life estranged from God, for their healing, we pray: ◆ For all to use their words for the benefit and building up of those around us, rather than in criticism, idle speech, or frivolity, we pray: ◆ For all the faithful departed, we pray: ◆

Our Father . . .

Lord Jesus,
your words are spirit and life.
Teach us and set us free
as you drive out all sin and evil
from our hearts and souls.
Give us the grace to love
one another in service and joy.
You live and reign forever.
Amen.

✝ The Lord is just in all his ways.

✝ Blessed the people the Lord has chosen to be his own.

Psalm 145 *page 422*

Reading *Luke 4:38–39*

After Jesus left the synagogue, he entered the house of Simon. Simon's mother-in-law was afflicted with a severe fever, and they interceded with him about her. He stood over her, rebuked the fever, and it left her. She got up immediately and waited on them.

Reflection

In today's Gospel, Jesus cures Peter's mother-in-law from a fever, and the apostles intercede with him for her healing. Jesus' fame spreads, and the people bring the sick to him to lay his hands upon them. Are we doing the same today? Do we bring others in need to Christ so that he may heal them? Do we intercede with Christ for the healing of our family and friends? Let us be modern apostles living our lives with the same closeness and faith in Jesus as the disciples in the Gospel.

Prayers *others may be added*

You lay your hands upon the sick and cure them of all their ills. Let us pray:

◆ Heal us, O Lord, and set us free.

For all the ministers of the Church, that their hands may bring about the healing of Christ, their mouths proclaim his word, and their lives witness to his Gospel, we pray: ◆ For all nations to work together to bring about justice, peace, and social order in all lands, we pray: ◆ For all who suffer illness, sorrow, and pain, that Christ may lay his healing hands upon them to bring them freedom and new life, we pray: ◆ For the gift of intercessory prayer, that the Holy Spirit may teach us how to pray and intercede for one another, we pray: ◆

Our Father . . .

God our Father,
we come before you in need of your
    healing touch.
Hear our prayers and grant our petitions,
that we ask in the name of your Son Jesus
    Christ, our Lord,
who lives and reigns with you in the unity
    of the Holy Spirit,
one God, forever and ever.
Amen.

✝ Blessed the people the Lord has chosen to be his own.

Thursday, September 6, 2012
Weekday

✟ To the Lord belongs the earth and all that fills it.

Psalm 19   *page 403*

Reading   *Luke 5:4–10*

After [Jesus] had finished speaking, he said to Simon, "Put out into deep water and lower your nets for a catch." Simon said in reply, "Master, we have worked hard all night and have caught nothing, but at your command I will lower the nets." When they had done this, they caught a great number of fish and their nets were tearing. They signaled to their partners in the other boat to come to help them. They came and filled both boats so that the boats were in danger of sinking. When Simon Peter saw this, he fell at the knees of Jesus and said, "Depart from me, Lord, for I am a sinful man." For astonishment at the catch of fish they had made seized him and all those with him, and likewise James and John, the sons of Zebedee, who were partners of Simon. Jesus said to Simon, "Do not be afraid; from now on you will be catching men."

Reflection

It is easy to fall into the complacency of routine and merely do what is necessary to get by. Jesus exhorts us to "put out into deep waters." Jesus is not satisfied with superficiality, but he desires that we draw life from the depths and richness of his love. In obedience to the Lord, the apostles do as he commands and they pull out an abundant catch.

Prayers   *others may be added*

With faith in our God of miracles, let us pray:

◆ Hear our prayer and grant our petitions.

For the Holy Father and all the clergy, that they may be faithful fishers of men as they serve God's children in the ministry of the Church, we pray: ◆ For those in governmental office, that they may boldly put out into deep waters as they work to resolve conflict and bring about peace among nations, we pray: ◆ For all who suffer illness, depression, loss, or anxiety, that God may free them from the depths of their sufferings, we pray: ◆ For our local community, that they may not remain indifferent to the needs and presence of our neighbors, we pray: ◆

Our Father . . .

Lord Jesus,
at your word, the apostles put out into
    the deep
and reap an abundant catch.
Through the events of our everyday lives,
may we also encounter your
    miraculous love
and leave everything to follow after you.
You live and reign forever.
Amen.

✟ To the Lord belongs the earth and all that fills it.

✝ The salvation of the just comes from the Lord.

Psalm 27   *page 405*

Reading   *Luke 5:33–39*

The scribes and Pharisees said to Jesus, "The disciples of John the Baptist fast often and offer prayers, and the disciples of the Pharisees do the same; but yours eat and drink." Jesus answered them, "Can you make the wedding guests fast while the bridegroom is with them? But the days will come, and when the bridegroom is taken away from them, then they will fast in those days." And he also told them a parable. "No one tears a piece from a new cloak to patch an old one. Otherwise, he will tear the new and the piece from it will not match the old cloak. Likewise, no one pours new wine into old wineskins. Otherwise, the new wine will burst the skins, and it will be spilled, and the skins will be ruined. Rather, new wine must be poured into fresh wineskins. And no one who has been drinking old wine desires new, for he says, 'The old is good.'"

Reflection

People are often critical. Even in the time of Jesus, his disciples were criticized for their way of life. However, this does not mean that we should not live out our faith in its fullness, nor does it mean that we have to do anything strange in our Christian life. What matters is how God sees us, not the opinions or judgments of others.

Prayers   *others may be added*

Father of mercy, all creation gives praise to your name. Let us pray:

◆ Hear the prayers of your children, Lord.

For the Holy Father, that he may be given health and strength to stand firm amid worldly persecutions that assail the Church, we pray: ◆ For civic leaders, that they may enact laws that protect and uphold the rights and dignity of each person, we pray: ◆ For those who suffer estrangement from family and friends, that, through forgiveness and reconciliation, all may be brought into unity, we pray: ◆ For the poor, the sick, the lonely, the homebound, all travelers, and prisoners, we pray: ◆ For all musicians, singers, and songwriters, that their music may be a means of praise and glory to God and his goodness, we pray: ◆ For the grace to remember God's presence in every moment of our lives, we pray: ◆

Our Father . . .

God our Creator,
you give us life and call us into being.
May each breath give praise to you
for the gift of salvation and life.
We ask this through our Lord Jesus
    Christ, your Son,
who lives and reigns with you in the unity
    of the Holy Spirit,
one God, forever and ever.
Amen.

✝ The salvation of the just comes from the Lord.

✝ The Lord is near to all who call upon him.

Psalm 34 *page 406*

Reading *Matthew 1:18–21*

Now this is how the birth of Jesus Christ came about. When his mother Mary was betrothed to Joseph, but before they lived together, she was found with child through the Holy Spirit. Joseph her husband, since he was a righteous man, yet unwilling to expose her to shame, decided to divorce her quietly. Such was his intention when, behold, the angel of the Lord appeared to him in a dream and said, "Joseph, son of David, do not be afraid to take Mary your wife into your home. For it is through the Holy Spirit that this child has been conceived in her. She will bear a son and you are to name him Jesus, because he will save his people from their sins."

Reflection

Today we celebrate the feast of the Nativity of the Blessed Virgin Mary. We recall the greatness of the Blessed Virgin and her importance in all of salvation history, as we remember her humble and obedient "yes" to give birth to Jesus Christ, the Savior of the world. And so on this day, we honor the life of this young woman, Mary Immaculate, called to be the Mother of God and our Mother, Queen of heaven and earth.

Prayers *others may be added*

By the witness of Mother Mary, may we learn how to live upright and holy lives. Let us pray:

◆ Lord, hear our prayer.

For the Holy Father, all priests, bishops, and clergy, that they may seek to model their lives after the purity and holiness of Mary, help of all Christians, we pray: ◆ For all the nations, especially those torn by war and violence, that they may seek resolution and justice by the prayers of Our Lady, Queen of Peace, we pray: ◆ For all military families, for those who grieve the absence of family and friends, for their safety and speedy return, we pray: ◆ For all the sick, that they may unite their sufferings to Christ through the help and prayers of Our Lady, Queen of Sorrows, we pray: ◆ For the respect and sanctity of human life in all its forms, we pray: ◆ For a deeper devotion and love of the Blessed Virgin Mary, we pray: ◆

Our Father . . .

Heavenly Father,
you chose the young Virgin Mary
to become the Mother of God.
By the grace of the Holy Spirit,
grant us the grace to accept and fulfill
our vocations of each day.
We ask this through our Lord Jesus
    Christ, your Son,
who lives and reigns with you in the unity
    of the Holy Spirit,
one God, forever and ever.
Amen.

✝ The Lord is near to all who call upon him.

Sunday, September 9, 2012
Twenty-third Sunday in Ordinary Time

✝ In God is my safety and my glory.

Psalm 22 *page 403*

Reading *Mark 7:31–37*

Jesus left the district of Tyre and went by way of Sidon to the Sea of Galilee, into the district of the Decapolis. And people brought to him a deaf man who had a speech impediment and begged him to lay his hand on him. He took him off by himself away from the crowd. He put his finger into the man's ears and, spitting, touched his tongue; then he looked up to heaven and groaned, and said to him, "*Ephphatha!*"—that is, "Be opened!"—And immediately the man's ears were opened, his speech impediment was removed, and he spoke plainly. He ordered them not to tell anyone. But the more he ordered them not to, the more they proclaimed it. They were exceedingly astonished and they said, "He has done all things well. He makes the deaf hear and the mute speak."

Reflection

Today, Jesus heals the deaf and mute man by saying, "Be opened!" It is interesting how Christ opens the man's ears in order to heal his speech impediment. This teaches us that before we are able to speak rightly, we must first listen. Prayer is essentially an act of listening to God and his word. After having listened, we are better equipped to go out and speak the word that we have heard.

Prayers *others may be added*

Jesus heals the deaf and opens their ears and mouth to proclaim God's goodness. Let us pray:

◆ Open our hearts to hear your word, O God.

For the Holy Father and all the Church, that they may draw their strength and life from quiet prayer in which God reveals his secrets to his beloved children, we pray: ◆ For all conflicts among countries to be resolved in peace through the work of just and upright national leaders, we pray: ◆ For all who suffer from physical infirmity, that God may heal them and give them the interior strength of patient endurance in their trials, we pray: ◆ For the graces of diligence and order this week as we imitate Christ, we pray: ◆

Our Father . . .

Loving Father,
you sent us your Son, Jesus Christ,
to heal us and restore us to new life.
By the power of the Holy Spirit,
open our ears to hear your word,
our eyes to see, our hearts to receive,
and our wills to respond in generous love.
We ask this through our Lord Jesus
   Christ, your Son,
who lives and reigns with you in the unity of the Holy Spirit,
one God, forever and ever.
Amen.

✝ In God is my safety and my glory.

Monday, September 10, 2012
Weekday

✝ Lead me in your justice, Lord.

Psalm 95   *page 413*

Reading   *Luke 6:6–11*

On a certain sabbath Jesus went into the synagogue and taught, and there was a man there whose right hand was withered. The scribes and the Pharisees watched him closely to see if he would cure on the sabbath so that they might discover a reason to accuse him. But he realized their intentions and said to the man with the withered hand, "Come up and stand before us." Then Jesus said to them, "I ask you, is it lawful to do good on the sabbath rather than to do evil, to save life rather than to destroy it?" Looking around at them all, he then said to him, "Stretch out your hand." He did so and his hand was restored. But they became enraged and discussed what they might do to Jesus.

Reflection

Our God is a god of life. In today's Gospel, the scribes and Pharisees are angered because Jesus heals the man with the withered hand. However, through his healings, Jesus teaches that the Sabbath is a day of renewal and a day for the restoration of life. God desires our happiness and our goodness, and he wills that we live our human lives to the fullest, which is made possible through union with him.

Prayers   *others may be added*

Through the sacraments, Christ's healing powers are made manifest here and now. Let us pray to the Lord:

◆ Restore us to new life, O God.

For the Church, that she may be the living sacrament of salvation for all peoples to come and drink from the fountain of life, we pray: ◆ For those in governmental office, that they may boldly put out into deep waters as they work to resolve conflict and bring about peace among nations, we pray: ◆ For all who suffer illness, depression, loss, or anxiety, that God may free them from the depths of their sufferings, we pray: ◆ For our local community, that they may not remain indifferent to the needs and presence of our neighbors, we pray: ◆

Our Father . . .

Lord Jesus,
in the Gospel, you heal the man with the
    withered hand.
Heal us of all our sins that have withered
    and distorted our souls.
May your Spirit bring us to new life.
You live and reign forever.
Amen.

✝ Lead me in your justice, Lord.

✝ The Lord takes delight in his people.

Psalm 100   *page 414*

Reading   *Luke 6:12–19*

Jesus departed to the mountain to pray, and he spent the night in prayer to God. When day came, he called his disciples to himself, and from them he chose Twelve, whom he also named Apostles: Simon, whom he named Peter, and his brother Andrew, James, John, Philip, Bartholomew, Matthew, Thomas, James the son of Alphaeus, Simon who was called a Zealot, and Judas the son of James, and Judas Iscariot, who became a traitor.

And he came down with them and stood on a stretch of level ground. A great crowd of his disciples and a large number of the people from all Judea and Jerusalem and the coastal region of Tyre and Sidon came to hear him and to be healed of their diseases; and even those who were tormented by unclean spirits were cured. Everyone in the crowd sought to touch him because power came forth from him and healed them all.

Reflection

In today's Gospel, we hear that after a full night in prayer, Jesus calls by name his twelve disciples. He even calls Judas Iscariot as one of his own, even though he later betrays Jesus. We also see Jesus' mercy as he heals and cures numerous people from the surrounding lands who come to him because of his great power.

Prayers   *others may be added*

God's surpassing plan of love for his people has the power to transform evil into greater good. In faith and hope, let us pray:

◆ **Great is your mercy, O Lord.**

For the members of the Church, that they may work together with the Holy Father and all bishops to bring about a culture of life and love, we pray: ◆ For the end of all violence and terrorism, for the protection of our nation and all countries, for all the military in active duty, and for all who grieve the loss of family members or friends, we pray: ◆ For all those who are victims of abuse, violence, terrorism, or tragedy, we pray: ◆ For our church community, that it may be ever more united together as members individually called into service by the Lord, we pray: ◆ For the grace to hope, trust, and accept God's plan of love and justice, we pray: ◆

Our Father . . .

Lord Jesus,
all power on heaven and earth
has been given to you by your
    heavenly Father.
Hear our prayers we offer you today.
Heal our wounds, wipe away our tears,
and bring us to the joy of new life
    with you,
where you live and reign with the Father,
in the unity of the Holy Spirit,
one God, forever and ever.
Amen.

✝ The Lord takes delight in his people.

Wednesday, September 12, 2012
Weekday

✝ Listen to me, daughter; see and bend your ear. (*Psalm 45*)

Psalm 100 *page 414*

Reading *Luke 6:20–23*

Raising his eyes toward his disciples Jesus said: / "Blessed are you who are poor, / for the Kingdom of God is yours. / Blessed are you who are now hungry, / for you will be satisfied. / Blessed are you who are now weeping, / for you will laugh. / Blessed are you when people hate you, / and when they exclude and insult you, / and denounce your name as evil / on account of the Son of Man.

"Rejoice and leap for joy on that day! Behold, your reward will be great in heaven."

Reflection

In today's Gospel, we hear the beginning of the Sermon on the Mount, where Jesus teaches us the heart of the Christian message. Through the Beatitudes, we learn how to be true and faithful Christians. Though they may seem contradictory to what the world tells us, these precepts teach us how we can attain true happiness and blessedness.

Prayers *others may be added*

Through the prayers of the Holy and Blessed Virgin Mary, the model of all Christians, we pray:

◆ Instruct us on the path of life, O God.

For all members of the Church, that they may follow the word of God as together we journey toward our heavenly home of the kingdom of heaven, we pray: ◆ For the salvation of the world, that all peoples may be brought about through the simple witness and example of holy and faithful Christians, we pray: ◆ For all the sick and suffering, that they may realize that the kingdom of heaven belongs to them, as they work in God's vineyard as his chosen little ones through the faithful and patient offering of their sufferings and prayers, we pray: ◆ For each one of us, that we may not fear to live our Christian faith in its fullness and beauty in the ordinary activities of our lives, we pray: ◆

Our Father . . .

Jesus Christ, our teacher and Lord,
you give us the means to be happy in this life
here on earth, as we journey to attain the perfect happiness of eternal life
in your kingdom where you live and reign with the Father in the unity of the Holy Spirit,
one God, forever and ever.
Amen.

✝ Listen to me, daughter; see and bend your ear.

✝ Guide me, Lord, along the everlasting way.

Psalm 42   *page 407*

Reading   *Luke 6:27–31, 35*

Jesus said to his disciples: "To you who hear I say, love your enemies, do good to those who hate you, bless those who curse you, pray for those who mistreat you. To the person who strikes you on one cheek, offer the other one as well, and from the person who takes your cloak, do not withhold even your tunic. Give to everyone who asks of you, and from the one who takes what is yours do not demand it back. Do to others as you would have them do to you . . . love your enemies and do good to them, and lend expecting nothing back; then your reward will be great and you will be children of the Most High, for he himself is kind to the ungrateful and the wicked."

Reflection

In today's Gospel, Jesus teaches us how to live as radical and true Christians. He asks us what credit it is to us if we love only those who love us, because even sinners do as much. Christ challenges us to holiness by calling us to love and to forgive when it is easy and also when it is difficult.

Prayers   *others may be added*

Lord, without your grace we can do nothing. Hear our prayers and petitions as we pray:

◆ Lord, teach us your ways of mercy and love.

For the Church, that she may be renewed with the spirit of ardent charity to reach out in service and generosity to all in need, we pray: ◆ For all those living in areas of violence, war, or political unrest, that world leaders may work to bring about resolution and peace, we pray: ◆ For all who live in poverty, that Christians everywhere may generously give to those in need, we pray: ◆ For all preachers, that, through the intercession of Saint John Chrysostum, their words may turn many hearts to the true life that comes from a relationship with God, we pray: ◆ For all of our special intentions; for blessings on our families and friends, we pray: ◆

Our Father . . .

Lord God,
you sent your Son among us to teach us
     how to be merciful and generous.
Through the prayers of Saint John
     Chrysostum,
may we proclaim your word of love
through our actions and our speech.
We ask this through our Lord Jesus
     Christ, your Son,
who lives and reigns with you in the unity
     of the Holy Spirit,
one God, forever and ever.
Amen.

✝ Guide me, Lord, along the everlasting way.

Friday, September 14, 2012

Feast of the Exaltation of the Holy Cross

✝ How lovely is your dwelling place, Lord, mighty God!

Psalm 145   *page 422*

Reading   *John 3:13–17*

Jesus said to Nicodemus: "No one has gone up to heaven except the one who has come down from heaven, the Son of Man. And just as Moses lifted up the serpent in the desert, so must the Son of Man be lifted up, so that everyone who believes in him may have eternal life."

For God so loved the world that he gave his only Son, so that everyone who believes in him might not perish but might have eternal life. For God did not send his Son into the world to condemn the world, but that the world might be saved through him.

Reflection

God sent his Son into the world so that we might receive life and salvation. Today on the feast of the Exaltation of the Holy Cross, we proclaim the Good News that God transforms suffering and death into new life. Our God is a god of victory who reigns victorious even over the evil of death. As Christians, today we rejoice in the mystery of the cross, which brings about our freedom, salvation, and life.

Prayers   *others may be added*

Because of your holy cross, you have redeemed the world. Let us pray:

◆ Lord, free us from sin, and grant us your salvation.

For the Church, the Holy Father, all priests, religious, and lay ministers, that they may keep their eyes ever fixed on the cross, our source of grace and salvation, we pray: ◆ For all to be drawn more deeply into the mystery of Christ's Passion, death, and Resurrection so that all may be one, we pray: ◆ For all who bear a part of Christ's cross in their bodies, minds, or spirits, that, through sickness or suffering, they may likewise share in the glory of his Resurrection, we pray: ◆ For all who suffer the effects of divorce, abortion, addiction, or abuse, that Christ's mercy and love may reign victorious to bring new life and freedom, we pray: ◆ For all who have died, and for the families and friends who grieve their loss, that their souls may be brought into the eternal glory of heaven, we pray: ◆

Our Father . . .

Good and merciful Father,
you sent your Son to save us from our sins
and bring us new life and salvation.
By the victory of the cross,
may we be rooted in faith to firmly believe
in your Son Jesus Christ,
who lives and reigns with you in the unity
    of the Holy Spirit,
one God, forever and ever.
Amen.

✝ How lovely is your dwelling place, Lord, mighty God!

✝ To you, Lord, I will offer a sacrifice of praise.

Psalm 19 page 403

Reading Luke 2:34–35

Simeon blessed [the Holy Family] and said to Mary his mother, "Behold, this child is destined for the fall and rise of many in Israel, and to be a sign that will be contradicted and you yourself a sword will pierce so that the thoughts of many hearts may be revealed."

Reflection

After the feast of the Exaltation of the Holy Cross, today with the Church we honor Mary, Our Lady of Sorrows. Mary, the *Stabat Mater*, standing at the foot of the cross, participated in her Son's work of redemption by uniting her pain and sorrows to those of Jesus, thus offering her life as a spiritual sacrifice to the Lord. Today we look to her as an example of how to suffer well, and we ask her to pray for us and offer us her motherly comfort and support.

Prayers *others may be added*

Placing all of our anxieties and cares before our heavenly Father, we pray:

◆ Be near to us, O Lord.

For the Church, that she may be a comforting mother and a home to all who seek solace and search for truth, we pray: ◆ For the end of war, violence, terrorism, and abuse; for the healing of all families and the protection of all children, we pray: ◆ For all the sick, the suffering, and the lonely, that the Lord would be close to the brokenhearted, we pray: ◆ For those who grieve the death of loved ones, and for all mothers who suffer the pain of miscarriage, infertility, abortion, and loss, that Our Lady of Sorrows may comfort them and bring them her Son's healing touch, we pray: ◆ For those in our parish community, that we may become more aware of the ways to help those around us who are in need of our prayers, support, and friendship, we pray: ◆

Our Father . . .

Heavenly Father,
you chose your daughter, the Blessed
    Virgin Mary,
to become the mother of your Son, Jesus.
Through the prayers of Our Lady
    of Sorrows,
may we learn how to joyfully offer all of
    our trials and difficulties to the Lord
in union with the merits of the Passion of
    Christ,
through whom we ask this prayer.
Amen.

✝ To you, Lord, I will offer a sacrifice of praise.

Sunday, September 16, 2012
Twenty-fourth Sunday in Ordinary Time

✝ Blessed be the Lord, for he has heard my prayer.

Psalm 117 *page 418*

Reading *Mark 8:27–33*

Jesus and his disciples set out for the villages of Caesarea Philippi. Along the way he asked his disciples, "Who do people say that I am?" They said in reply, "John the Baptist, others Elijah, still others one of the prophets." And he asked them, "But who do you say that I am?" Peter said to him in reply, "You are the Messiah." Then he warned them not to tell anyone about him.

He began to teach them that the Son of Man must suffer greatly and be rejected by the elders, the chief priests, and the scribes, and be killed, and rise after three days. He spoke this openly. Then Peter took him aside and began to rebuke him. At this he turned around and, looking at his disciples, rebuked Peter and said, "Get behind me, Satan. You are thinking not as God does, but as human beings do."

Reflection

People have many different ideas of the identity of Jesus. In today's Gospel, Peter responds correctly as he identifies Jesus as the Messiah, the one anointed by God and prepared for throughout all the ages. However, Jesus then teaches that in order to bring about salvation and freedom, the Messiah must suffer, die, and rise again. Jesus illuminates and deepens our understanding of the mystery of who God is.

Prayers *others may be added*

Raising our eyes to the face of God, we present our prayers and petitions as we pray:

◆ O Lord, save my life!

For the Holy Father and all the clergy, that they may be renewed in strength, diligence, and faithfulness to serve the family of God present in the Church, we pray: ◆ For all peoples, that they may be brought together in union with one another through the knowledge of the Person of Jesus Christ, we pray: ◆ For all those who share in Christ's Passion, that their suffering may be a means of sanctification and new life for themselves and for all souls, we pray: ◆ For the members of our faith community, that they may be united as they serve the needs of the parish, we pray: ◆ For all who have died, we pray: ◆

Our Father . . .

Lord God,
your ways are not our ways,
nor are your thoughts our thoughts.
Pour out your spirit of wisdom
and knowledge upon us,
that we may more deeply know who
   you are.
We ask this through our Lord Jesus
   Christ, your Son,
who lives and reigns with you in the unity
   of the Holy Spirit,
one God, forever and ever.
Amen.

✝ Blessed be the Lord, for he has heard my prayer.

Monday, September 17, 2012
Weekday

✝ Proclaim the death of the Lord until he comes again.

Psalm 34 — page 406

Reading — Luke 7:1–7

When Jesus had finished all his words to the people, he entered Capernaum. A centurion there had a slave who was ill and about to die, and he was valuable to him. When he heard about Jesus, he sent elders of the Jews to him, asking him to come and save the life of his slave. They approached Jesus and strongly urged him to come, saying, "He deserves to have you do this for him, for he loves our nation and he built the synagogue for us." And Jesus went with them, but when he was only a short distance from the house, the centurion sent friends to tell him, "Lord, do not trouble yourself, for I am not worthy to have you enter under my roof. Therefore, I did not consider myself worthy to come to you; but say the word and let my servant be healed."

Reflection

We have much to learn from the centurion in today's Gospel. First, he recognizes the goodness and value of the life of his servant. Second, not considering himself worthy to approach Jesus out of humility and respect for him, he sends his friends to ask Jesus to the heal his slave. Then, Jesus praises the centurion for his faith and his understanding of blind obedience. In return, Jesus heals the slave.

Prayers — *others may be added*

Coming to you in faith, we present our urgent needs to you today as we pray:

◆ Only say the word, Lord, and we shall be healed.

For the Holy Father and all bishops, priests, and deacons, that they may work tirelessly to perform Christ's healing ministry to all who suffer in mind, body, or spirit, we pray: ◆ For all governmental leaders, for the military, and for those in active service, that their work may bring about safe and secure societies of peace and justice, we pray: ◆ For all the sick, that those who await the healing touch of God may be sustained by the prayers and presence of family and friends, we pray: ◆ For newly ordained priests and deacons, that they may remain faithful to the call they have received and be surrounded by the love and support of friends and family, we pray: ◆ For all prisoners, the lonely, all travelers; for the unemployed and those undergoing financial or family difficulties, we pray: ◆ For all the dying, that their last days may be a time of conversion, love, and peacefulness, we pray: ◆

Our Father . . .

Lord God,
you speak and the world is made,
and all creation proclaims your glory.
Proclaim your word in our hearts today
and re-create us in the newness of
    your life.
We ask this through Christ our Lord.
Amen.

✝ Proclaim the death of the Lord until he comes again.

Tuesday, September 18, 2012
Weekday

✝ We are his people: the sheep of his flock.

Psalm 63 *page 410*

Reading *Luke 7:11–17*

Jesus journeyed to a city called Nain, and his disciples and a large crowd accompanied him. As he drew near to the gate of the city, a man who had died was being carried out, the only son of his mother, and she was a widow. A large crowd from the city was with her. When the Lord saw her, he was moved with pity for her and said to her, "Do not weep." He stepped forward and touched the coffin; at this the bearers halted, and he said, "Young man, I tell you, arise!" The dead man sat up and began to speak, and Jesus gave him to his mother. Fear seized them all, and they glorified God, exclaiming, "A great prophet has arisen in our midst," and "God has visited his people." This report about him spread through the whole of Judea and in all the surrounding region.

Reflection

What an amazing story we hear in today's Gospel. Jesus touches the coffin of a dead man and commands him to arise. Immediately, the man gets up and begins to speak, and Jesus gives the man back to the widowed mother. Jesus' words apply to us today as well. He calls us to arise from the deadness of our sins before we become buried in the evil of our complacency and indifference. What marvelous miracles God has for

us if we listen to his word and allow him to come near us.

Prayers *others may be added*

In wonder and awe at the miraculous power and majesty of God, we pray:

◆ Bring us back to life, O Lord.

For the Church, as the universal sacrament of salvation, that she may open wide her arms to all who seek healing and new life, we pray: ◆ For nations that are torn apart by violence, war, terrorism, and political unrest, that the powerful hand of God may bring justice and mercy, we pray: ◆ For all the sick, for those who await miraculous healing, and for all doctors, nurses, caregivers, friends, and family of those who are ill, that they may be strengthened and comforted in faith and prayer, we pray: ◆ For all widows, for mothers who grieve the death of a child; for those who have suffered abortion, miscarriage, or infertility, that they may be comforted in their sorrow and grief, we pray: ◆

Our Father . . .

Lord Jesus Christ,
through your miracles we see your power
and your loving concern for your people.
Continue to work powerfully
in the small details and events of
  our lives,
that we may know you more deeply,
you who live and reign with the Father,
in the unity of the Holy Spirit,
one God, forever and ever.
Amen.

✝ We are his people: the sheep of his flock.

✝ Blessed the people the Lord has chosen to be his own.

Psalm 42 *page 407*

Reading *Luke 7:31–35*

Jesus said to the crowds: "To what shall I compare the people of this generation? What are they like? They are like children who sit in the marketplace and call to one another, / 'We played the flute for you, but you did not dance. / We sang a dirge, but you did not weep.' / For John the Baptist came neither eating food nor drinking wine, and you said, 'He is possessed by a demon.' The Son of Man came eating and drinking and you said, 'Look, he is a glutton and a drunkard, a friend of tax collectors and sinners.' But wisdom is vindicated by all her children."

Reflection

It is time to shake ourselves from the spiritual lethargy and religious indifference that so easily clings to us. The everyday routine of our lives cannot be an excuse for not encountering God's presence around us. Rather, we must be renewed in faith and convinced of the truth that our God is present and near us now, today, and in this and every moment.

Prayers *others may be added*

Heavenly Father, hear the prayers of your children as we pray:

◆ Lord we believe; help our unbelief.

For the Church, that, through her people, she may be an illuminating witness to the joy that comes from a life united to God, we pray: ◆ For all world leaders, politicians, and civic rulers, that they may work to enact just laws for the common good of all peoples, we pray: ◆ For all the sick in hospitals and nursing homes, that they may quickly return to health, we pray: ◆ For those who suffer domestic abuse, that they may find safety, freedom, and peace, we pray: ◆ For our families and friends, and for all who have entrusted themselves to our prayers, we pray: ◆ For all of our loved ones who have passed away, that we may soon again be reunited to them in the eternal happiness of heaven, we pray: ◆

Our Father . . .

Loving Father,
we know that you are always near to us
and will never abandon your children.
Give us the grace never to doubt your
    presence.
May we be strengthened by this knowledge
to do your work and sing your praise ever
    more faithfully.
We ask through our Lord Jesus Christ,
    your Son,
who lives and reigns with you in the unity
    of the Holy Spirit,
one God, forever and ever.
Amen.

✝ Blessed the people the Lord has chosen to be his own.

Thursday, September 20, 2012
Memorial of the Martyrs of Korea

✝ Give thanks to the Lord, for he is good.

Psalm 116 *page 418*

Reading *Luke 7:36–47*

A certain Pharisee invited Jesus to dine with him, and he entered the Pharisee's house and reclined at table. Now there was a sinful woman in the city who learned that he was at table in the house of the Pharisee. Bringing an alabaster flask of ointment, she stood behind him at his feet weeping and began to bathe his feet with her tears. Then she wiped them with her hair, kissed them, and anointed them with the ointment. When the Pharisee who had invited him saw this he said to himself, "If this man were a prophet, he would know who and what sort of woman this is who is touching him, that she is a sinner . . . " Then he turned to the woman and said to Simon, "Do you see this woman? When I entered your house you did not give me water for my feet, but she has bathed them with her tears and wiped them with her hair. You did not give me a kiss, but she has not ceased kissing my feet since the time I entered. You did not anoint my head with oil, but she anointed my feet with ointment. So I tell you, her many sins have been forgiven; hence, she has shown great love. But the one to whom little is forgiven, loves little."

Reflection

The woman of today's Gospel models how we ought to love God. Our love for God should be like the outpouring of precious perfumed oil that the sinful woman pours over the feet of her beloved Jesus. Upon the cross, Jesus himself reveals the *kenosis* of his love as a total gift of self for us. We too are called to participate in this kind of love that generously gives all it has without holding back.

Prayers *others may be added*

Confident in your mercy and love, let us pray:

◆ **Pour out your love upon us, O Lord.**

For the Holy Father, we pray: ◆ For those who are sick and suffering, we pray: ◆ For all sinners, that they may return to the freedom of God's most abundant love and mercy, we pray: ◆ For all those in the military, we pray: ◆ For all married couples, we pray: ◆ For the life of our parish, we pray: ◆

Our Father . . .

Heavenly Father,
in your Son, Jesus Christ,
you teach us how to give of ourselves.
By the power of your Holy Spirit,
free us from our selfishness and pride,
that we may be able to pour ourselves out
   in love for you and your people.
We ask this through Christ our Lord.
Amen.

✝ Give thanks to the Lord, for he is good.

Friday, September 21, 2012

Feast of Saint Matthew, Apostle and Evangelist

✝ Lord, when your glory appears, my joy will be full.

Psalm 104 *page 416*

Reading *Matthew 9:9–13*

As Jesus passed by, he saw a man named Matthew sitting at the customs post. He said to him, "Follow me." And he got up and followed him. While he was at table in his house, many tax collectors and sinners came and sat with Jesus and his disciples. The Pharisees saw this and said to his disciples, "Why does your teacher eat with tax collectors and sinners?" He heard this and said, "Those who are well do not need a physician, but the sick do. Go and learn the meaning of the words, *I desire mercy, not sacrifice.* I did not come to call the righteous but sinners."

Reflection

Today we celebrate the feast of Saint Matthew, apostle and evangelist. Matthew was a sinner and tax collector called by God to become a great saint. Jesus reveals that he is not a distant god who is concerned only with those who are already "good" or "perfect," but he is God who calls the sinner back to new life. We honor Saint Matthew today and look to him for example and prayers.

Prayers *others may be added*

Lord God, you call sinners into life with you. Hear our prayers and petitions as we pray:

◆ Lead us to holiness, O Lord.

For all members of the Church, that she may never give scandal to others, but rather witness to the mercy of God through the power of the Holy Spirit, we pray: ◆ For all the nations of the world, that they may be blessed with God's abundant favor and blessing, we pray: ◆ For the poor, the sick, and the suffering, we pray: ◆ For those who suffer criticism, rejection, or persecution, that they may be comforted by the presence of God, we pray: ◆ For all involved in missions and apostolic works, that their efforts may yield abundant fruit for the kingdom of God, we pray: ◆ For the grace to imitate Christ's love for all people, saints and sinners alike, we pray: ◆

Our Father . . .

Lord Jesus,
you are the Good Shepherd
who calls his sheep by name.
Through the intercession of
    Saint Matthew,
open our hearts to hear your voice,
that we may turn from our sins
and enter into the sheepfold of abundant
    life with you,
who live and reign with the Father in the
    unity of the Holy Spirit,
one God, forever and ever.
Amen.

✝ Lord, when your glory appears, my joy will be full.

Saturday, September 22, 2012
Weekday

✝ I will walk in the presence of God, in the land of the living.

Psalm 118   *page 418*

Reading   *Luke 8:4–8a*

When a large crowd gathered, with people from one town after another journeying to Jesus, he spoke in a parable. "A sower went out to sow his seed. And as he sowed, some seed fell on the path and was trampled, and the birds of the sky ate it up. Some seed fell on rocky ground, and when it grew, it withered for lack of moisture. Some seed fell among thorns, and the thorns grew with it and choked it. And some seed fell on good soil, and when it grew, it produced fruit a hundredfold."

Reflection

In today's Gospel, we hear the parable of the sower and the seed. Jesus teaches us that our hearts must be open to receive his word. Jesus uses these images to reveal to us that the kingdom of God is among us, and the mysteries of this kingdom are present even within the wonders of creation.

Prayers   *others may be added*

Nourished by the Spirit, the seed of the word of God grows and bears abundant fruit. Let us pray:

◆ Open our ears to hear and our hearts to receive, O Lord.

For the Church, that she may remain ever fertile ground for the growth and furthering of the kingdom of God, we pray: ◆ For all missionaries throughout the world, that they may be strengthened in their work of spreading God's word, we pray: ◆ For the people of all nations, that they may not remain cold or indifferent, but rather may come to work and live in harmony with one another through the practice of Christian values, we pray: ◆ For the sufferings of all the sick and dying, that they may bear abundant fruit today and in the new life to come, we pray: ◆

Our Father . . .

Loving God,
you desire to spread the kingdom of your
    love
in the hearts of all peoples.
Send your Holy Spirit upon us so that we
    may
be able to receive and nourish your word.
By your power, may our lives be
    witnesses of your abundant love and
    mercy.
We ask this through our Lord Jesus
    Christ, your Son,
who lives and reigns with you in the unity
    of the Holy Spirit,
one God, forever and ever.
Amen.

✝ I will walk in the presence of God, in the land of the living.

Sunday, September 23, 2012
Twenty-fifth Sunday in Ordinary Time

✝ The Lord has done marvels for us.

Psalm 145 — page 422

Reading — Mark 9:30–35

Jesus and his disciples left from there and began a journey through Galilee, but he did not wish anyone to know about it. He was teaching his disciples and telling them, "The Son of Man is to be handed over to men and they will kill him, and three days after his death he will rise." But they did not understand the saying, and they were afraid to question him.

They came to Capernaum and, once inside the house, he began to ask them, "What were you arguing about on the way?" But they remained silent. They had been discussing among themselves on the way who was the greatest. Then he sat down, called the Twelve, and said to them, "If anyone wishes to be first, he shall be the last of all and the servant of all." Taking a child he placed it in their midst, and putting his arms around it he said to them, "Whoever receives one child such as this in my name, receives me; and whoever receives me, receives not me but the One who sent me."

Reflection

Today in the Gospel, the disciples do not easily understand Jesus' teaching. After Jesus tries to explain to them that he will have to suffer and die, they cannot understand, and they begin arguing about who is the greatest. Jesus then teaches them that the last shall be first, and that those who welcome the littlest among them receive God. We see how Jesus patiently continues to instruct his disciples toward a deeper understanding of the heart of his mystery.

Prayers — *others may be added*

O Lord, hear our prayers and grant our petitions as we pray:

◆ Teach us your ways, O Lord.

For the Church, that she may grow in ever deeper understanding of the truth of the mystery of Christ and his kingdom, we pray: ◆ For our nation, that it may come to respect the littlest and weakest among society, we pray: ◆ For all families of our parish community, that they may be open to life as they lovingly receive children as a blessing from God, we pray: ◆ For all the sick, that they may be healed by Christ, we pray: ◆

Our Father . . .

Loving Father,
you sent your Son to teach us your love.
Fill us with your Holy Spirit
as we strive to submit our human
    understanding
to that of your divine wisdom.
We ask this through our Lord Jesus
    Christ, your Son,
who lives and reigns with you in the unity
    of the Holy Spirit,
one God, forever and ever.
Amen.

✝ The Lord has done marvels for us.

Monday, September 24, 2012
Weekday

✝ The just one shall live on your holy mountain, O Lord.

Psalm 117
page 418

Reading
Luke 8:16–18

Jesus said to the crowd: "No one who lights a lamp conceals it with a vessel or sets it under a bed; rather, he places it on a lampstand so that those who enter may see the light. For there is nothing hidden that will not become visible, and nothing secret that will not be known and come to light. Take care, then, how you hear. To anyone who has, more will be given, and from the one who has not, even what he seems to have will be taken away."

Reflection

Just as a lamp is lit in order to shine light, so too are we called to shine the light of our Christian faith. Jesus is the Light of the World, and in Baptism we received his light and life. However, we have not been given this gift in order to hide or conceal its brilliance. Rather, we are luminaries of Christ called to shine his light into the world for the glory of God.

Prayers
others may be added

Approaching God's throne of glory, let us pray:

◆ Hear our prayer, and grant our petition.

For the Church, that she may forever be illuminated by the radiance of Christ Jesus, we pray: ◆ For all civic leaders, that their hearts may be open to hear the word of the Lord as they work for the betterment of society, we pray: ◆ For those who suffer loneliness, addiction, alcoholism, mental illness, or abuse, we pray: ◆ For our family and friends in need of prayer this day, we pray: ◆ For all who have died, that they may soon enter the light of glory of the heavenly kingdom, we pray: ◆

Our Father . . .

Father of light,
we praise you and thank you
for every good gift that comes from you.
Shine in our hearts the light of your
    Holy Spirit,
that we may be holy witnesses of
    your glory.
We ask this through our Lord Jesus
    Christ, your Son, the Light of
    the World,
who lives and reigns with you in the unity
    of the Holy Spirit,
one God, forever and ever.
Amen.

✝ The just one shall live on your holy mountain, O Lord.

✝ Guide me, Lord, in the way of your commands.

Psalm 27 · _page 405_

Reading _Luke 8:19–21_

The mother of Jesus and his brothers came to him but were unable to join him because of the crowd. He was told, "Your mother and your brothers are standing outside and they wish to see you." He said to them in reply, "My mother and my brothers are those who hear the word of God and act on it."

Reflection

In today's Gospel, Jesus teaches us the importance of hearing God's word and acting on it. Essentially, Jesus is describing the virtue of faith and man's response to God through the obedience of faith. By hearing his word and then obeying and carrying out his word, we become members of God's family. We are bound together as family through the bond of hearing and obeying the word of God.

Prayers _others may be added_

Confident in God, we pray:

◆ Lord, hear our prayer.

That the members of the Church, the Mystical Body of Christ, may be bound more fully together through adherence to God's word in faith and works, we pray: ◆ For all governmental officials, civic leaders, and political rulers, that they may be guided by the wisdom of God in their decisions for the common good of all peoples, we pray: ◆ For all the sick and suffering, and for those who care for them, we pray: ◆ That all families may be bound together in selfless generous love for one another, we pray: ◆ That the members of our faith community may grow in a deeper and more active participation in the liturgy and devotion to reading the Holy Scriptures, we pray: ◆

Our Father . . .

Heavenly Father,
by the gift of your Son,
you call us to enter into the freedom
of the children of God.
By the power of your Holy Spirit,
may we hear your word and be given the
courage and perseverance
to live your commands and carry out
your will.
We ask this through our Lord Jesus
Christ, your Son,
who lives and reigns with you in the unity
of the Holy Spirit,
one God, forever and ever.
Amen.

✝ Guide me, Lord, in the way of your commands.

Wednesday, September 26, 2012
Weekday

✝ Your word, O Lord, is a lamp for my feet.

Psalm 116
page 418

Reading
Luke 9:1–6

Jesus summoned the Twelve and gave them power and authority over all demons and to cure diseases, and he sent them to proclaim the Kingdom of God and to heal the sick. He said to them, "Take nothing for the journey, neither walking stick, nor sack, nor food, nor money, and let no one take a second tunic. Whatever house you enter, stay there and leave from there. And as for those who do not welcome you, when you leave town, shake the dust from your feet in testimony against them." Then they set out and went from village to village proclaiming the good news and curing diseases everywhere.

Reflection

In today's Gospel, it seems as if Jesus is teaching us a healthy attitude toward our life, our work, and our apostolate as Christians. We must do God's work faithfully; however, in those situations where we face unrelenting opposition or rejection, we can simply shake the dust from our feet, move on, and continue the work of the Lord elsewhere.

Prayers
others may be added

Confident in the power of your word, we pray:

◆ Lord, hear our prayer.

For the work of the Holy Father, bishops, priests, and deacons, that the Church may continue to proclaim the Gospel, heal the sick, and build up the kingdom of God by the ministry of Christ Jesus, we pray: ◆ For all missionaries, for their protection and safety, that their testimony may bear abundant fruit in good works for the salvation of all the world, we pray: ◆ For all the sick, the dying, and those who suffer disease, that the healing hand of God may touch them to bring them restored health through the means of doctors and nurses, and by the spiritual aid of priests and the faithful community, we pray: ◆ For those who feel entrapped by difficult, unhealthy, or tragic crisis situations, that they may be freed by God who brings us freedom and peace, we pray: ◆ For all the poor who go without food today, we pray: ◆

Our Father . . .

God of mercy,
send your Holy Spirit upon us
to anoint us with your love.
Empty us of ourselves,
that we may be transparent witnesses of
   your love.
May we decrease and you increase.
Out of love for you, enflame within us an
   intense burning love for all souls.
We ask this through Christ our Lord.
Amen.

✝ Your word, O Lord, is a lamp for my feet.

Thursday, September 27, 2012
Memorial of Saint Vincent de Paul, Priest

✝ In every age, O Lord, you have been our refuge.

Psalm 47 — *page 408*

Reading — *Luke 9:7–9*

Herod the tetrarch heard about all that was happening and he was greatly perplexed because some were saying, "John has been raised from the dead"; others were saying, "Elijah has appeared"; still others, "One of the ancient prophets has arisen." But Herod said, "John I beheaded. Who then is this about whom I hear such things?" And he kept trying to see him.

Reflection

In today's Gospel, we see how the people in the time of Jesus were questioning who he was. They recognized him to be a prophet, and some even said that John had been raised from the dead or that Elijah had returned. The Gospel states that the people kept trying to see Jesus. There is something special and attractive that makes all people desire to see Jesus. He makes us want to know who he is and what he is about. We cannot remain indifferent. Once we have seen and encountered him, we will either follow after him or refuse to listen to his word.

Prayers — *others may be added*

You are the desire of all the nations, O Lord. Let us pray:

◆ **Lord, hear our prayer.**

For Holy Mother Church, that she may ever be mindful of the call to serve the poorest and neediest of society, we pray: ◆
For civic leaders, that they will work to eliminate poverty, injustice, and war; that leaders may enact just laws to provide safety and security regarding work, family, and social life, we pray: ◆ For all the poor, the needy, the sick, and those who have no one to care for them, that God may come to them through the aid and presence of Christians, we pray: ◆ For all to seek Christ and serve him within our friends and family members around us, we pray: ◆

Our Father . . .

Lord God,
you called Saint Vincent de Paul
to work with the poor and uneducated.
By the help of his prayers,
may we dedicate our lives to your service
in love and generosity for your people.
We ask through our Lord Jesus Christ,
    your Son,
who lives and reigns with you in the unity
    of the Holy Spirit,
one God, forever and ever.
Amen.

✝ In every age, O Lord, you have been our refuge.

✝ Blessed be the Lord, my Rock!

Psalm 150 *page 424*

Reading *Luke 9:18–22*

Once when Jesus was praying in solitude, and the disciples were with him, he asked them, "Who do the crowds say that I am?" They said in reply, "John the Baptist; others, Elijah; still others, 'One of the ancient prophets has arisen.'" Then he said to them, "But who do you say that I am?" Peter said in reply, "The Christ of God." He rebuked them and directed them not to tell this to anyone. He said, "The Son of Man must suffer greatly and be rejected by the elders, the chief priests, and the scribes, and be killed and on the third day be raised."

Reflection

Who is the Person of Jesus? Whom do we consider Jesus to be? This is the question posed to us in today's Gospel. Peter responds that Jesus is the Christ of God. Jesus is the Messiah sent from the Father to redeem us and bring us freedom by his great suffering, his death, and his glorious Resurrection. Let us come to him to encounter his Person and mystery.

Prayers *others may be added*

Coming before you to encounter your mystery, we present to you our prayers and petitions as we pray:

◆ Lord, draw us into your love.

That the Holy Father may be guided by the Spirit to lead the Church in holiness toward our goal of the kingdom of heaven, we pray: ◆ For all political leaders and all who work in conflict resolution, that their efforts may further societies of justice and peace, we pray: ◆ For those who suffer injury or illness, that they may speedily be returned to full health, we pray: ◆ For all teenagers and young adults, that they may grow in virtue and good works as they discover themselves and the great work they have to offer to others, we pray: ◆ For all who have died, and for those who grieve their loss, we pray: ◆ For the grace to set aside time in solitude and prayer to contemplate the Person of Jesus Christ, we pray: ◆

Our Father . . .

Lord Jesus,
you who are true God and true Man.
Come and make your dwelling among us.
Reveal your mystery to us, so that
we may more deeply know you, and
by knowing you, we may more deeply
love you, who live and reign with
the Father, in the unity of the Spirit,
one God, forever and ever.
Amen.

✝ Blessed be the Lord, my Rock!

Saturday, September 29, 2012

Feast of Saints Michael, Gabriel, and Raphael, Archangels

✝ In every age, O Lord, you have been our refuge.

Psalm 100 *page 414*

Reading *John 1:47–51*

Jesus saw Nathanael coming toward him and said of him, "Here is a true child of Israel. There is no duplicity in him." Nathanael said to him, "How do you know me?" Jesus answered and said to him, "Before Philip called you, I saw you under the fig tree." "Rabbi, you are the Son of God; you are the King of Israel." Jesus answered and said to him, "Do you believe because I told you that I saw you under the fig tree? You will see greater things than this." And he said to him, "Amen, amen, I say to you, you will see heaven opened and the angels of God ascending and descending on the Son of Man."

Reflection

Today we celebrate the feast of the archangels, three of whom we know by name from the scriptures. The word *angel* means "messenger." Angels are messengers of God who adore and serve him in heaven and on earth. In the Bible, the angel Raphael helped Tobias; Michael battled against Lucifer; and Gabriel was sent to Mary to announce the Good News of Jesus' birth. Today's feast reminds us to be conscious of the angels who are present around us, those holy messengers who help and guide us.

Prayers *others may be added*

Lord, you give us your angels to watch us in all of our ways. Let us pray:

◆ Through the ministry of your angels, Lord, hear our prayer.

For all the spiritual and material needs of the Church and all the faithful throughout the world, we pray: ◆ For the world, that all nations may be guarded and protected from all evil through the intercession of the archangel Michael, we pray: ◆ That, through the intercession of archangel Raphael, all the sick and suffering may be relieved of their pain and restored to fullness of health, we pray: ◆ That, through the aid of Archangel Gabriel, we may come to better understand the depth and grandeur of the mystery of the Incarnation, we pray: ◆ For all peoples, that we may present all our needs, worries, and concerns to the Father who cares for us, we pray: ◆

Our Father . . .

Loving God,
your holy angels never cease to worship
  and serve you around your
  glorious throne.
By their powerful intercession,
help us to worship you in spirit and in
  truth for the glory of your name.
We ask this through our Lord Jesus
  Christ, your Son,
who lives and reigns with you in the unity
  of the Holy Spirit,
one God, forever and ever.
Amen.

✝ In every age, O Lord, you have been our refuge.

✝ Hope in God.

Psalm 116   *page 418*

Reading   *Mark 9:47–48*

"If your hand causes you to sin, cut it off. It is better for you to enter into life maimed than with two hands to go into Gehenna, into the unquenchable fire. And if your foot causes you to sin, cut it off. It is better for you to enter into life crippled than with two feet to be thrown into Gehenna. And if your eye causes you to sin, pluck it out. Better for you to enter into the kingdom of God with one eye than with two eyes to be thrown into Gehenna, where 'their worm does not die, and the fire is not quenched.' "

Reflection

In today's liturgy, Jesus warns us of the great evil of sin. It is necessary that we live good and upright Christian lives, for Jesus speaks strongly against those who give scandal to others, especially the young and innocent. Jesus emphasizes the importance of how the care for our spiritual souls is of even greater importance than our physical bodies, and how little things can be of great importance. Even giving a cup of water to someone in the name of Jesus can reap great rewards.

Prayers   *others may be added*

United together in prayer, we present you our petitions as we pray:

◆ Fill us with your life, O Lord.

For the Holy Father, that he may be sustained by the power of the Spirit to continue his ministry in service to the People of God, we pray: ◆ For all priests, that the Lord may work through their priestly ministry to perform his mighty deeds among his people, we pray: ◆ For all children, that they may be protected from all scandal, abuse, and injustice, we pray: ◆ For our parish community, that we may not remain strangers to one another, but rather live together in true Christian friendship, we pray: ◆ For all to never deny the importance of doing little things with great love for the glory of God and the service of his people, we pray: ◆ For the sick and the dying, and for the repose of all the souls of all the faithful departed, we pray: ◆

Our Father . . .

Loving God,
today we celebrate the mystery of your
    Resurrection.
Pour your life upon us and bring us more
    fully into the light of your love,
that we may live lives of integrity as
    faithful witnesses to your truth.
We ask this through our Lord Jesus
    Christ, your Son,
who lives and reigns with you in the unity
    of the Holy Spirit,
one God, forever and ever.
Amen.

✝ Hope in God.

✝ Incline your ear to me and hear
my word.

Psalm 85 *page 411*

Reading *Luke 9:46–48*

An argument arose among the disciples about which of them was the greatest. Jesus realized the intention of their hearts and took a child and placed it by his side and said to them, "Whoever receives this child in my name receives me, and whoever receives me receives the one who sent me. For the one who is least among all of you is the one who is the greatest."

Reflection

Today we celebrate the memorial of Saint Thérèse of the Child Jesus, who was a young Carmelite nun who became a great saint and Doctor of the Church through the quiet and humble offering of all her sicknesses, sufferings, and joys to the Lord with great love. Through the example of her "Little Way," Saint Thérèse inspires us to attain the depths of intimacy with our Lord Jesus through the little actions of our daily life, whether we are in the convent, the home, the office, or in mission lands.

Prayers *others may be added*

With trustful abandon and childlike confidence in your holy will, we pray:

◆ Turn your eyes upon your little children, Lord.

For the Church, that she may continue to provide service to the littlest, weakest, and those most in need, we pray: ◆ For all missionaries, that their work may be enflamed by the grace and life of the Holy Spirit, we pray: ◆ For all the sick, that, through the prayers of Saint Thérèse, they may recognize their important work of prayer and sacrifice for the Church, we pray: ◆ For all missionaries and the salvation of souls, we pray: ◆ For all young children, that they may be loved, protected, and welcomed as treasures from God, we pray: ◆ For all Christians, that they may open their hearts in generosity and love to offer spiritual and material aid to the poor, we pray: ◆ For all priests and seminarians, especially those of our community, that they may remain faithful to the call and duty they have received, we pray: ◆ For all of us, that we may journey along the way of holiness through the humble offering of the little joys and sorrows of today to the Lord, we pray: ◆

Our Father . . .

Loving Father,
by the prayers of Saint Thérèse,
draw us into intimate union with you
as you teach us your humble way of love.
Shower your graces upon us as roses
    from heaven.
We ask this through our Lord Jesus,
    your Son,
who lives and reigns with you in the unity
    of the Holy Spirit,
one God, forever and ever.
Amen.

✝ Incline your ear to me and hear
my word.

Tuesday, October 2, 2012
Memorial of the Holy Guardian Angels

✝ Let my prayer come before you, Lord.

Psalm 145
page 422

Reading
Matthew 18:1–3

The disciples approached Jesus and said, "Who is the greatest in the Kingdom of heaven?" He called a child over, placed it in their midst, and said, "Amen, I say to you, unless you turn and become like children, you will not enter the Kingdom of heaven."

Reflection

Today we celebrate the memorial of the guardian angels, who help us in difficulty and temptation, aid us by their prayers and intercession, and guide us along the path of holiness. Today we can renew our devotion to our guardian angel by being aware of his presence and asking him for help and guidance as we seek to serve the Lord ever more faithfully.

Prayers
others may be added

With hearts full of prayers and petitions, we pray:

◆ Through the intercession of the guardian angels, Lord, hear our prayer.

For the Church, that, aided by all the angels, she may stand firm in fighting the spiritual battle against sin and evil, we pray: ◆ For all politicians and civic leaders, that they may be guided in wisdom and truth by helping to create societies of justice and peace, we pray: ◆ For those who suffer illness, that they may be comforted by the presence of their guardian angel, we pray: ◆ For those in special need in our parish and for those who have asked us to pray for them, we pray: ◆ For all those who have died, that the angels may lead them into paradise, we pray: ◆

Our Father . . .

Lord God,
you send your angels to watch over us
and to guide us in all of our ways.
By their prayers, may we seek to love you
with undivided hearts as we await the day
that we will worship you in your glory
with all the angels and saints.
We ask through our Lord Jesus Christ,
   your Son,
who lives and reigns with you in the unity
   of the Holy Spirit,
one God, forever and ever.
Amen.

✝ Let my prayer come before you, Lord.

✝ Let my prayer come before you, Lord.

Psalm 27 *page 405*

Reading *Luke 9:57–62*

As Jesus and his disciples were proceeding on their journey, someone said to him, "I will follow you wherever you go." Jesus answered him, "Foxes have dens and birds of the sky have nests, but the Son of Man has nowhere to rest his head." And to another he said, "Follow me." But he replied, "Lord, let me go first and bury my father." But he answered him, "Let the dead bury their dead. But you, go and proclaim the Kingdom of God." And another said, "I will follow you, Lord, but first let me say farewell to my family at home." Jesus answered him, "No one who sets a hand to the plow and looks to what was left behind is fit for the Kingdom of God."

Reflection

Jesus calls each of us to follow him, but sometimes we think we have more important things to do first. In today's Gospel, we see Jesus calling his followers, though some are not truly interested or serious about following the Lord. Let us order our priorities by first seeking God's kingdom and then—and only then—our work, family, and our personal life will likewise fall into order.

Prayers *others may be added*

Come to our aid in our weakness as we pray:

◆ Guide us along the path of life, O Lord.

For the Church, that she may welcome all Christians into full union with the truth of the Catholic Church, we pray: ◆
For all public officials, that they may give good and faithful witness as they strive to live lives of integrity, we pray: ◆
For all who suffer the pain and loneliness of illness, that they may be comforted by the presence of friends and aided by the help of skilled physicians, we pray: ◆
For all the poor and homeless, we pray: ◆
For each of us in our parish community, that we may faithfully follow the Master's call, we pray: ◆ For the grace to seek first the kingdom of God, we pray: ◆

Our Father . . .

Heavenly Father,
we see your goodness in the beauty
   of creation.
Renew us in your love and turn our hearts
to see you ever more clearly as you
   draw us
into the intimate union of the Holy Trinity,
you who live and reign with our Lord
   Jesus Christ, your Son,
who lives and reigns in the unity of the
   Holy Spirit,
one God forever and ever.
Amen.

✝ Let my prayer come before you, Lord.

Thursday, October 4, 2012
Memorial of Saint Francis of Assisi

✝ Let my prayer come before you, Lord.

Psalm 146 *page 423*

Reading *Luke 10:1–12*

Jesus appointed seventy-two other disciples whom he sent ahead of him in pairs to every town and place he intended to visit. He said to them, "The harvest is abundant but the laborers are few; so ask the master of the harvest to send out laborers for his harvest. Go on your way; behold, I am sending you like lambs among wolves. Carry no money bag, no sack, no sandals; and greet no one along the way. Into whatever house you enter, first say, 'Peace to this household.' If a peaceful person lives there, your peace will rest on him; but if not, it will return to you. Stay in the same house and eat and drink what is offered to you, for the laborer deserves payment. Do not move about from one house to another. Whatever town you enter and they welcome you, eat what is set before you, cure the sick in it and say to them, 'The Kingdom of God is at hand for you.' Whatever town you enter and they do not receive you, go out into the streets and say, 'The dust of your town that clings to our feet, even that we shake off against you.' Yet know this: the Kingdom of God is at hand. I tell you, it will be more tolerable for Sodom on that day than for that town."

Reflection

Today we celebrate the memorial of Saint Francis, the young man who had lived a life of riches but then gave everything away for the sake of God in order to embrace a life of poverty, prayer, and penance. He gained many followers and began the Franciscan order. His life was a total and complete imitation of Christ, and he even bore Christ's wounds in his body as he endured the gift of the stigmata.

Prayers *others may be added*

Lord, you give us the example of the saints to guide us along our daily journey. Let us pray:

◆ Teach us how to be saints, O Lord.

For the Church, we pray: ◆ For all who work to establish world peace, justice, and security in society, we pray: ◆ For all young people, we pray: ◆ For all who suffer, we pray: ◆ For all Franciscans, we pray: ◆ For all to grow in the spirit of poverty and detachment from worldly things, we pray: ◆

Our Father . . .

Loving Father,
through the life of Saint Francis,
you inspire us to turn away from sin
and worldly riches that keep us from you.
By his prayers, may we come to enjoy
true freedom in union with you.
We ask this through Christ our Lord.
Amen.

✝ Let my prayer come before you, Lord.

✝ Let my prayer come before you, Lord.

Psalm 34 *page 406*

Reading *Luke 10:13–16*

Jesus said to them, "Woe to you, Chorazin! Woe to you, Bethsaida! For if the mighty deeds done in your midst had been done in Tyre and Sidon, they would long ago have repented, sitting in sackcloth and ashes. But it will be more tolerable for Tyre and Sidon at the judgment than for you. And as for you, Capernaum, 'Will you be exalted to heaven? You will go down to the netherworld.' Whoever listens to you listens to me. Whoever rejects you rejects me. And whoever rejects me rejects the one who sent me."

Reflection

What will it take for us to recognize the Lord's presence among us and turn to him? Sometimes we are so similar to, if not worse than, the people in Jesus' day who refuse to recognize the Lord despite all the wonders and signs he has worked for them. Today, let us open our eyes of faith to see his work, and may we not harden our hearts to his word.

Prayers *others may be added*

Filled with cares and concerns, we place them at your heavenly throne, O Lord. Confident that you take care of our every need, we pray:

◆ Lord, send us your Spirit.

For Holy Mother Church, that she may be illumined by the grace and light of Christ Jesus to lead all peoples into the heavenly home of the kingdom of God, we pray: ◆ For missionaries throughout the world, that they may tirelessly preach the Gospel to all the nations, we pray: ◆ For all families, that parents, children, brothers, and sisters may grow in true love for one another as they learn to forgive and to celebrate the joys of life with one another, we pray: ◆ For all the sick, infirm, those in hospitals and nursing homes, and for those who care for them, that they may receive comfort and a swift restoration of health, we pray: ◆ For our parish community, that it may be bonded ever more together in God's love, we pray: ◆ For each of us, that we may be convinced of God's constant presence and his gifts of grace for us at every moment of our lives, we pray: ◆

Our Father . . .

Holy God,
We bless you and praise you for the gift
of life that you bestow upon us today.
Pour your Spirit upon us so that we
    may live
ever more fully in your love and peace.
We ask this in Jesus' name,
who lives and reigns with you in the unity
    of the Holy Spirit,
one God, forever and ever.
Amen.

✝ Let my prayer come before you, Lord.

Saturday, October 6, 2012
Weekday

✝ Let my prayer come before you, Lord.

Psalm 8
page 402

Reading
Luke 10:17–24

The seventy-two disciples returned rejoicing and said to Jesus, "Lord, even the demons are subject to us because of your name." Jesus said, "I have observed Satan fall like lightning from the sky. Behold, I have given you the power 'to tread upon serpents' and scorpions and upon the full force of the enemy and nothing will harm you. Nevertheless, do not rejoice because the spirits are subject to you, but rejoice because your names are written in heaven." At that very moment he rejoiced in the Holy Spirit and said, "I give you praise, Father, Lord of heaven and earth, for although you have hidden these things from the wise and the learned you have revealed them to the childlike. Yes, Father, such has been your gracious will. All things have been handed over to me by my Father. No one knows who the Son is except the Father, and who the Father is except the Son and anyone to whom the Son wishes to reveal him." Turning to the disciples in private he said, "Blessed are the eyes that see what you see. For I say to you, many prophets and kings desired to see what you see, but did not see it, and to hear what you hear, but did not hear it."

Reflection

In today's Gospel, we learn how the name of Jesus is all-powerful. Jesus sends us out into the world to bring peace to others and proclaim the Gospel with the power of his name. However, he reminds us that we should rejoice not because we have been given his mighty power, but rather because our names are written in heaven. We rejoice that our Good Shepherd has called us by name, and that we are destined for greatness and holiness in his kingdom of heaven.

Prayers
others may be added

With faith in your enduring promise, we lift up our hearts as we pray:

◆ Good Shepherd, lead us to everlasting life.

For the Holy Father, we pray: ◆ For all nations, we pray: ◆ For all those who suffer, we pray: ◆ For all monks, friars, and brothers, we pray: ◆ For all the ministries and outreach projects of our parish, we pray: ◆

Our Father . . .

Good Shepherd,
you call us by name and lead us
to streams of life-giving waters.
By the prayers of Saint Bruno, help us
to follow you by lives of prayer
    and penance.
You live and reign forever.
Amen.

✝ Let my prayer come before you, Lord.

✝ The Lord will remember his covenant for ever.

Psalm 86 *page 412*

Reading *Mark 10:2–16*

The Pharisees approached Jesus and asked, "Is it lawful for a husband to divorce his wife?" They were testing him. He said to them in reply, "What did Moses command you?" They replied, "Moses permitted a husband to write a bill of divorce and dismiss her." But Jesus told them, "Because of the hardness of your hearts he wrote you this commandment. But from the beginning of creation, *God made them male and female. For this reason a man shall leave his father and mother and be joined to his wife, and the two shall become one flesh.* So they are no longer two but one flesh. Therefore what God has joined together, no human being must separate."

Reflection

In today's Gospel, Jesus speaks about the indissoluble bond of man and wife in the sacrament of Marriage. For this reason, divorce is not permitted, because the union between the man and woman remains intact by virtue of their vows to one another. In this way, the Church supports and protects the dignity of the sacrament of Marriage, by continuing to teach and promote the total gift of self in love and forgiveness toward one spouse, which results in fruitfulness and holiness among families and marriages.

Prayers *others may be added*

God, with you nothing is impossible. Hear the prayers we present to you today:

◆ Bless your chosen people, O Lord.

For the Church, that she may continue to clarify, teach, and instruct without wavering from the truth regarding difficult issues concerning the dignity of the human person, we pray: ◆ For all political leaders, that they will work to protect and ensure the safety and dignity of each human person, especially the weakest and most vulnerable of society, we pray: ◆ For all who are struggling in their marriage, especially those in our own parish community, that they may receive the support they need to make right decisions in love and forgiveness for the good of their spouse and their family, we pray: ◆ For all who have died, that they may be brought into eternal life with the Holy Trinity, we pray: ◆

Our Father . . .

Merciful Father,
today as we celebrate the memorial
of the Resurrection of your Son Jesus,
shine your healing light upon us
and renew in us your steadfast love,
that we may live in freedom and joy
with one another as your humble children.
We ask this through Christ our Lord.
Amen.

✝ The Lord will remember his covenant for ever.

✠ The Lord will remember his covenant for ever.

Psalm 118   *page 418*

Reading   *Luke 10:26–37*

[Jesus said:] "A man fell victim to robbers as he went down from Jerusalem to Jericho. They stripped and beat him and went off leaving him half-dead. A priest happened to be going down that road, but when he saw him, he passed by on the opposite side. Likewise a Levite came to the place, and when he saw him, he passed by on the opposite side. But a Samaritan traveler who came upon him was moved with compassion at the sight. He approached the victim, poured oil and wine over his wounds and bandaged them. Then he lifted him up on his own animal, took him to an inn, and cared for him. The next day he took out two silver coins and gave them to the innkeeper with the instruction, 'Take care of him. If you spend more than what I have given you, I shall repay you on my way back.'"

Reflection

We often fail to help those around us who are in need. We think that it is not our responsibility, that we don't have time, or that someone else will do something about it. The Gospel reminds us of our great call as Christians to love God and to love our neighbor with every ounce of our being.

Prayers   *others may be added*

Father, you know our weakness and brokenness. Hear our prayers we present to you this day:

◆ Lord, show us your mercy as we place our trust in you.

For the Church, that she may continue her work of charity in serving and protecting the poorest and most vulnerable of the world, we pray: ◆ For our country, that it may generously share its riches and resources with poorer nations, we pray: ◆ For all those in need who suffer abandonment, betrayal, neglect, illness, and poverty, that God may ease their pain through the presence of generous Christians willing to be instruments of God's mercy, we pray: ◆ For each of us in this parish community, that we may not turn away from neighbor, but remain open to the work of the Spirit in our lives for the good of others, we pray: ◆ For all priests, that they may faithfully bind the spiritual wounds of those entrusted to them through the healing power of the sacraments and by their pastoral ministry, we pray: ◆

Our Father . . .

Merciful Father,
in the love and compassion of your Son,
you reveal to us the mystery of true love.
Pour your Spirit upon us so that we may
be enflamed with ardent charity as
      we seek
to love you with all our heart, mind, soul,
      and strength.
We ask this through Christ our Lord.
Amen.

✠ The Lord will remember his covenant for ever.

✝ The Lord will remember his covenant for ever.

Psalm 98 *page 413*

Reading *Luke 10:38–42*

Jesus entered a village where a woman whose name was Martha welcomed him. She had a sister named Mary who sat beside the Lord at his feet listening to him speak. Martha, burdened with much serving, came to him and said, "Lord, do you not care that my sister has left me by myself to do the serving? Tell her to help me." The Lord said to her in reply, "Martha, Martha, you are anxious and worried about many things. There is need of only one thing. Mary has chosen the better part and it will not be taken from her."

Reflection

How frequently we lose faith in God and become anxious and worried about so many things. Too often we become so preoccupied with our responsibilities and what we think we ought to be doing, that we fail to recognize that Jesus is present with us. Jesus Christ is the one thing necessary. In today's Gospel, Mary has found this treasure, and it will not be taken from her as she sits in adoration and quiet silence, listening to her Lord.

Prayers *others may be added*

We present our prayers and our needs as we pray:

◆ Lord, hear our prayer.

For the Holy Father, that he may be sustained in his ministry to lead and guide the Church and all her members into deeper union with Christ Jesus, we pray: ◆ For all missionaries, especially those who serve the poorest of the poor in various countries of the world, we pray: ◆ For all the sick, that they may offer their sufferings to the Lord as a fragrant offering of love for the good of all peoples and the salvation of souls, we pray: ◆ For those who have fallen asleep in Christ, that they may reach their eternal repose in heaven, we pray: ◆ For the apostolic work of all religious orders and lay communities, that love may flow from them in deep union with God, we pray: ◆ For all who suffer from anxiety, depression, and mental illness, that Jesus Christ may come with his power to bring freedom, healing, and peace, we pray: ◆

Our Father . . .

Loving God,
protect us from all worldly care
and anxiety,
that we may listen and hear your voice.
By hearing your voice may we know how
to best serve you for your honor and glory
and for the good of our neighbor.
We ask this through Christ our Lord.
Amen.

✝ The Lord will remember his covenant for ever.

✝ The Lord will remember his covenant for ever.

Psalm 145   *page 422*

Reading   *Luke 11:1–4*

Jesus was praying in a certain place, and when he had finished, one of his disciples said to him, "Lord, teach us to pray just as John taught his disciples."

He said to them, "When you pray, say:

Father, hallowed be your name, / your Kingdom come. / Give us each day our daily bread / and forgive us our sins / for we ourselves forgive everyone in debt to us, / and do not subject us to the final test."

Reflection

In today's Gospel, the disciples ask Jesus how to pray. Jesus gives us the words for prayer by instructing us to call upon God our Father. Like the disciples, we, too, should go to Jesus and ask him to teach us how to pray, because "we do not know how to pray as we ought" (Romans 8:26). In this way, we will be drawn into the mystery of union and conversation with God, who is Father, Son, and Spirit.

Prayers   *others may be added*

Jesus, you teach us how to pray to the Father in your name through the Holy Spirit. Hear our prayers and grant our petitions we present to you this day:

◆ Thy kingdom come.

For the Church, that she may remain faithful and steadfast in proclaiming the kingdom of God and awaiting its fullness in the Parousia when God will be all in all, we pray: ◆ For the conversion of all nations, that all peoples may recognize the truth of Jesus Christ and may come to know and experience the joy of belonging to the Father as his beloved children, we pray: ◆ For all who suffer from illness, poverty, addiction, violence, and economic strife, that the Father may hear their needs and prayers for deliverance and peace, we pray: ◆ For the poor and for all those who go hungry today, we pray: ◆ For our parish community to be ever more unified as Christian brothers and sisters belonging to the same family of God our Father, we pray: ◆

Our Father . . .

Heavenly Father,
all praise and glory belongs to you.
You are our loving Father who knows our every need and desire.
Hear our prayers and give us faith
to trust and hope that you will give us
everything we need for every moment of
    our lives.
We ask this through Christ our Lord.
Amen.

✝ The Lord will remember his covenant for ever.

Thursday, October 11, 2012
Weekday

✝ Blessed be the Lord, the God of Israel; he has come to his people.

Psalm 121
page 419

Reading
Luke 11:9–13

[Jesus said:] "And I tell you, ask and you will receive; seek and you will find; knock and the door will be opened to you. For everyone who asks, receives; and the one who seeks, finds; and to the one who knocks, the door will be opened. What father among you would hand his son a snake when he asks for a fish? Or hand him a scorpion when he asks for an egg? If you then, who are wicked, know how to give good gifts to your children, how much more will the Father in heaven give the Holy Spirit to those who ask him?"

Reflection

The Holy Spirit is the Father's greatest gift given to us in Christ Jesus. In today's Gospel, Jesus tells us to ask for the gift of the Holy Spirit. With persistence and diligence, we must ask for all the graces and favors we need, but, most importantly, we must ask for the greatest gift of God himself poured upon us as life in the Spirit.

Prayers
others may be added

With hearts full of faith, we pray:

◆ Hear our prayer, O Lord.

For the gift of the Holy Spirit to be poured out in ever more abundance upon the whole Church throughout the world, we pray: ◆ For civic leaders who will work with persistence in promoting justice, order, and unity among the nations despite the obstacles and difficulties they may face, we pray: ◆ For all who serve abroad in the military, and for their family members and friends who await their safe return, we pray: ◆ For the sick and suffering who await God's healing, and for their family and friends who suffer with them, that they may not lose hope, but rather have faith in God's merciful will, we pray: ◆ For the safety and protection of all travelers, that they may be welcomed with joy and peace along their journey, we pray: ◆

Our Father . . .

Good and loving Father,
send us the sublime gift of your Holy Spirit.
Enkindle our hearts with the Spirit's divine love
that, enflamed with all your spiritual gifts,
we may go out to all the world to serve others
as instruments of your own mercy and love and life.
We ask this through Christ our Lord. Amen.

✝ Blessed be the Lord, the God of Israel; he has come to his people.

Friday, October 12, 2012
Weekday

✝ The Lord will remember his
covenant for ever.

Psalm 48   *page 408*

Reading   *Luke 11:15–20*

When Jesus had driven out a demon,
some of the crowd said: "By the power
of Beelzebul, the prince of demons, he
drives out demons." Others, to test him,
asked him for a sign from heaven. But
he knew their thoughts and said to them,
"Every kingdom divided against itself
will be laid waste and house will fall
against house. And if Satan is divided
against himself, how will his kingdom
stand? For you say that it is by Beelzebul that I drive out demons. If I, then,
drive out demons by Beelzebul, by
whom do your own people drive them
out? Therefore they will be your judges.
But if it is by the finger of God that I
drive out demons, then the Kingdom of
God has come upon you."

Reflection

We must always remember to be on
guard against the temptations of the
devil. The devil subtly tempts us toward
what appears to be good, though in reality is evil. We are led to believe that sin
is not a big deal, that what we are doing
is not really a sin; or even worse still,
we are led to believe that sin does not
even exist. Yet, sin makes us slaves to
ourselves and to evil, and it keeps us
from the freedom and true happiness
that comes from a life in union with
God.

Prayers   *others may be added*

Confident in your merciful love for us
sinners, we pray:

◆ Free us and protect us from all sin
and evil, O Lord.

For the Church, that, through the work of
the Holy Father and all deacons, priests,
and bishops, she may lead sinners back
into union with God through the sacraments of the Eucharist and Reconciliation, we pray: ◆ For all nations that suffer
from political unrest, corrupt governmental systems, war, and violence, that,
through the work of just leaders, societies
may become communities of security,
peace, and justice, we pray: ◆ For all who
suffer unjustly because of the sins of
others, we pray: ◆ For the poor, the sick,
the lonely, the homeless, and the unemployed, we pray: ◆ For all who have died,
that they may be brought into new life in
heaven, we pray: ◆

Our Father . . .

Loving Father,
you sent your Son Jesus Christ
to save us from our sins
and to bring us to new life in the Trinity.
Protect us and bless us through the merits
of your Son's Passion, death, and
    Resurrection,
who lives and reigns with you in the unity
    of the Holy Spirit,
one God, forever and ever.
Amen.

✝ The Lord will remember his
covenant for ever.

Saturday, October 13, 2012
Weekday

☩ The Lord will remember his covenant for ever.

Psalm 48 *page 408*

Reading *Luke 11:27–28*

While Jesus was speaking, a woman from the crowd called out and said to him, "Blessed is the womb that carried you and the breasts at which you nursed." He replied, "Rather, blessed are those who hear the word of God and observe it."

Reflection

Every Sunday we go to Mass and hear the word of God, yet do we allow this powerful word to penetrate our hearts to change us? In today's Gospel Jesus says, "blessed are those who hear the word of God and observe it." It is not enough only to hear; we must put into practice the life of grace that we have received.

Prayers *others may be added*

God, you call us to obey your plan of love for us. Let us pray:

◆ Open our hearts to hear and observe your word, O Lord.

For the Holy Father, the clergy, and all the lay faithful, that, together through our prayers and sacrifices for one another, the Church may be built up in holiness and virtue, we pray: ◆ For all world leaders and those who serve in public office, that they may hear the word of God and give witness to Gospel values through lives of integrity and virtue, we pray: ◆ For all expectant mothers to have a safe and healthy delivery of their children, and for all mothers and families who grieve the losses of miscarriage, abortion, or infertility, we pray: ◆ For all the sick, those who suffer from allergies during the change of seasons, and for all who suffer illnesses both small and great, that they may be restored in health and renewed energy, we pray: ◆ For all to receive the grace to open their hearts to receive the courage to live our Christian faith without fear or embarrassment, we pray: ◆ For all who have died, that angels may lead them to paradise, we pray: ◆

Our Father . . .

Heavenly Father,
you speak to us through your Son, the
  Word Incarnate.
Through the intercession of Mary
  Immaculate,
give us the grace to receive the word of God
with ever greater openness and holy purity
as we observe your law of joy and love.
We ask this through Christ our Lord.
Amen.

☩ The Lord will remember his covenant for ever.

Sunday, October 14, 2012
Twenty-eighth Sunday in Ordinary Time

✝ Fill us with your love, O Lord, and
we will sing for joy!

Psalm 42
page 407

Reading
Mark 10:17–20

As Jesus was setting out on a journey,
a man ran up, knelt down before him,
and asked him, "Good teacher, what
must I do to inherit eternal life?" Jesus
answered him, "Why do you call me
good? No one is good but God alone.
You know the commandments: *You
shall not kill; you shall not commit
adultery; you shall not steal; you shall
not bear false witness; you shall not
defraud; honor your father and your
mother.*"

Reflection

Jesus invites us to give up everything
and follow him. God desires that we
love him above all things: more than all
our riches and possessions, more than
our families and loved ones. Our treasure in heaven will be great if we do
this. By giving up everything for the
love of God, he will bless us with far
greater riches both now and in eternal
life.

Prayers
others may be added

Loving God, with you, nothing is
impossible. Hear our prayers and
petitions we place before you today:

◆ Guide us to your kingdom, O Lord.

For the universal Church, that, under the
guidance of the Holy Father, she may
visibly shine as the universal sign of
salvation for all peoples, we pray: ◆
For civic leaders, that they may work to
establish societies of peace and justice
where the growth and development of the
human person can flourish in safety and
security, we pray: ◆ For all the sick,
suffering, poor, homeless, and prisoners,
that they may receive healing and new
life, we pray: ◆ For all in doubt, for those
skeptical of the truth of Christianity, and
for those who seek empirical signs, that
they receive the gift of faith to experience
the transcendent mystery of God in and
through creation, we pray: ◆

Our Father . . .

Loving Father,
you give us this Sunday to rejoice in the
memorial of Christ's Passion and
    Resurrection.
By the celebration of this sign of love
    and life,
may we be brought into ever deeper unity
with one another and with you,
who live and reign together with your
    Son, Jesus Christ,
in the unity of the Holy Spirit,
one God, forever and ever.
Amen.

✝ Fill us with your love, O Lord, and
we will sing for joy!

Monday, October 15, 2012
Memorial of Saint Teresa of the Child Jesus,
Virgin and Doctor of the Church

✝ Blessed be the name of the Lord
forever.

Psalm 150   *page 424*

Reading   *John 15:1–5*

Jesus said to his disciples: "I am the true vine, and my Father is the vine grower. He takes away every branch in me that does not bear fruit, and every one that does he prunes so that it bears more fruit. You are already pruned because of the word that I spoke to you. Remain in me, as I remain in you. Just as a branch cannot bear fruit on its own unless it remains on the vine, so neither can you unless you remain in me. I am the vine, you are the branches. Whoever remains in me and I in him will bear much fruit, because without me you can do nothing."

Reflection

Today we celebrate the memorial of Saint Teresa of Avila, the great saint who reformed the Discalced Carmelite order with Saint John of the Cross. After her conversion from worldly vanities, her life was characterized by a deep fervor and love for God through prayer, sacrifices, and sufferings. From her deep spiritual life, she founded convents and monasteries throughout Spain. She reached the heights of mystical union with God through deep prayer and contemplation.

Prayers   *others may be added*

Without you, Lord, we can do nothing. Hear our prayers we present to you today for the glory of your Father as we pray:

◆ **May we always remain in your love, O Lord.**

For the Church, that, led by the guidance of the Holy Father, she may always draw sustenance from Jesus the True Vine, our source of life, we pray: ◆ For all priests, seminarians, and those discerning their vocation, that they may clearly hear the call of the Lord for their lives and always remain faithful and steadfast in following Christ, we pray: ◆ For all the Carmelites today as they celebrate the feast of Saint Teresa, that they may be renewed in the charism of their order and be drawn more deeply into prayer and union with God, we pray: ◆ For all the sick, the suffering, the poor, and the lonely, that, inspired by the example of Saint Teresa, we pray: ◆ For the Holy Spirit to come upon each of us to instruct us and guide us to intimacy and deep spiritual union with God through the practice of contemplative prayer, we pray: ◆

Our Father . . .

Lord God,
by the example of Saint Teresa of Avila,
you reveal to us that it is possible for
each of us to attain the heights of sanctity.
By the aid of her prayers,
bring us into deeper unity with you.
We ask this through Christ our Lord.
Amen.

✝ Blessed be the name of the Lord
forever.

✝ Let your mercy come to me, O Lord.

Psalm 23
page 404

Reading
Luke 11:37–41

After Jesus had spoken, a Pharisee invited him to dine at his home. He entered and reclined at table to eat. The Pharisee was amazed to see that he did not observe the prescribed washing before the meal. The Lord said to him, "Oh you Pharisees! Although you cleanse the outside of the cup and the dish, inside you are filled with plunder and evil. You fools! Did not the maker of the outside also make the inside? But as to what is within, give alms, and behold, everything will be clean for you."

Reflection

In today's Gospel, Jesus criticizes the Pharisees' empty ritualism, a ritual that does not concern itself with the inner disposition and intention of the heart. It is important that we, too, do not become pharisaical by only "going through the motions" or by merely performing the duties of our faith as if they were a checklist to complete. Our exterior actions ought to be signs of our interior devotion.

Prayers
others may be added

Lord, hear the prayers we present to you today:

◆ Lord, draw us into the love of your Sacred Heart.

For the Church, that she may be rekindled by God's love to go out to all the nations and be living examples of charity and forgiveness and joy, we pray: ◆ For leaders of nations, that they may use their civic authority for the common good of all peoples, we pray: ◆ For all peoples, that they may behold the loving heart of God, which is so little loved in return, we pray: ◆ For all those who suffer silently and interiorly, that the healing presence of God may free them from all fear, anxiety, and pain, we pray: ◆ For all who have died, that they may be brought into the eternal joy of heaven, we pray: ◆

Our Father . . .

Heavenly Father,
through your holy saints you reveal to us
the mystery of your divine love.
By the power of the Holy Spirit,
draw us more deeply into love
    and devotion
to the Sacred Heart of your Son Jesus,
who lives and reigns with you in the unity
    of the Holy Spirit,
one God, forever and ever.
Amen.

✝ Let your mercy come to me, O Lord.

✝ Those who follow you, Lord, will have the light of life.

Psalm 62 *page 409*

Reading *John 12:24–26*

Jesus said to his disciples: "Amen, amen, I say to you, unless a grain of wheat falls to the ground and dies, it remains just a grain of wheat; but if it dies, it produces much fruit. Whoever loves his life loses it, and whoever hates his life in this world will preserve it for eternal life. Whoever serves me must follow me, and where I am, there also will my servant be. The Father will honor whoever serves me."

Reflection

Today's Gospel sheds light upon the great mystery of God who transforms death into new life. The witness of the martyrs gives testimony to this Christian truth, that only when the grain of wheat falls to the earth and dies can it then grow and bear abundant fruit. Today is the memorial of the Church Father Saint Ignatius of Antioch, whose offering of his life in martyrdom became the fertile ground for the flourishing of the early Church.

Prayers *others may be added*

In need of God's grace and mercy, we pour our hearts out to the Lord as we pray:

◆ Make us steadfast in your truth and love, O Lord.

For the Church, that she may be a beacon of the truth of Jesus Christ in the Gospel by the witness of all the martyrs, saints, and holy men and women of today and throughout all the centuries, we pray: ◆ For public officials, that they may lead the nations toward forming societies of justice and peace through true and proper human rights, health care, and governmental and economic stability, we pray: ◆ For all those who are criticized, condemned, or persecuted for their faith, that these interior martyrdoms may be lifted up as fruitful offerings for the conversion of their persecutors, we pray: ◆ For all the sick and suffering, that they may become aware of the great power they possess in their weakness as they work as instruments for the conversion and salvation of many souls by uniting their sufferings to those of Christ Jesus on the cross, we pray: ◆ For all peoples to be free from all fear to speak the truth of the joy of our Christian faith, despite indifference, disregard, or misunderstanding we may receive from others, we pray: ◆ For all of our deceased family and friends, and for those who will die today, that, by their death, they may be brought into new life in the kingdom of God, we pray: ◆

Our Father . . .

Great and merciful father, you give us the witness of the martyrs to strengthen us along the path of holiness. By the prayers of Saint Ignatius of Antioch, may we be courageous and faithful witnesses to the truth of your word. We ask this through Christ our Lord. Amen.

✝ Those who follow you, Lord, will have the light of life.

Thursday, October 18, 2012
Feast of Saint Luke, Evangelist

✝ Your friends make known, O Lord, the glorious splendor of your Kingdom.

Psalm 19   *page 403*

Reading   *Luke 10:1–3, 8–9*

The Lord Jesus appointed seventy-two disciples whom he sent ahead of him in pairs to every town and place he intended to visit. He said to them, "The harvest is abundant but the laborers are few; so ask the master of the harvest to send out laborers for his harvest. Go on your way; behold, I am sending you like lambs among wolves. Whatever town you enter and they welcome you, eat what they set before you, cure the sick in it and say to them, 'The Kingdom of God is at hand for you.'"

Reflection

Today we celebrate the feast of Saint Luke, the evangelist and disciple of the Lord. His Gospel is unique to the other synoptic Gospel accounts, because it contains the most detail of the Infancy Narratives. Luke, furthermore, wrote the Acts of the Apostles, which narrates the events of the apostles and Saint Paul during the beginning of the early Church after Jesus' Ascension.

Prayers   *others may be added*

Lord, hear our prayers and petitions we offer you this day:

◆ Make us faithful followers of you, O Lord.

For the Church, that she may be renewed with the same fervor and zeal of the early Christians who were not afraid to proclaim the Gospel and boldly live the faith in its totality, we pray: ◆ For all to preach the Gospel to all the nations, we pray: ◆ For the sick, infirm, and injured, that, through the intercession of Saint Luke, they may receive healing and restoration of health, mind, and body through the hands of skilled physicians, we pray: ◆

Our Father . . .

Heavenly Father,
through the prayers of Saint Luke,
draw us more deeply into the mystery
of salvation as we contemplate
    Jesus Christ,
born of the Blessed Virgin Mary.
Teach us how to follow you
as faithful disciples.
We ask this through our Lord Jesus
    Christ, your Son,
who lives and reigns with you in the unity
    of the Holy Spirit,
one God, forever and ever.
Amen.

✝ Your friends make known, O Lord, the glorious splendor of your Kingdom.

Friday, October 19, 2012
Memorial of the Martyrs of North America

✝ Blessed the people the Lord has chosen to be his own.

Psalm 62 *page 409*

Reading *Matthew 28:16–20*

The eleven disciples went to Galilee, to the mountain to which Jesus had ordered them. When they saw him, they worshiped, but they doubted. Then Jesus approached and said to them, "All power in heaven and on earth has been given to me. Go, therefore, and make disciples of all nations, baptizing them in the name of the Father, and of the Son, and of the Holy Spirit, teaching them to observe all that I have commanded you. And behold, I am with you always, until the end of the age."

Reflection

Today we celebrate the memorial of Saint Isaac Jaques, Saint Jean de Brebeuf, and their companions who were Jesuit priests who worked as missionaries to convert and evangelize the Indian tribes of North America. They lived among the Indians, learning their languages and customs, and they translated the Gospel into their culture. They were brutally tortured and martyred by the Indians, yet their lives are a heroic witness of truly living and proclaiming the Gospel to all peoples no matter what the cost.

Prayers *others may be added*

Lord, hear our prayer we offer you this day:

◆ Make us faithful witnesses to your word, O Lord.

For the Church, that she may raise up more and more holy men and women ready and willing to proclaim the name of Jesus throughout the world, we pray: ◆ For all missionaries and priests who proclaim the Gospel to distant lands, especially for those in environments hostile to Christianity and for those in areas of political unrest, we pray: ◆ For all who suffer sickness, injury, neglect, and abuse, that they may aid the missions through the offering of their suffering, we pray: ◆ For each of us in our church community, that we may have the fortitude to be examples and lights of the Gospel to those around us in our homes, at work, and in our families, we pray: ◆

Our Father . . .

Lord God,
by the witness of your holy saints,
you show us the path of sanctity.
Through the prayers of the North
    American Martyrs,
may we be filled with courage to boldly
proclaim the Gospel of Christ
at all times and in all situations.
We ask this through Christ our Lord.
Amen.

✝ Blessed the people the Lord has chosen to be his own.

✝ You have given your Son rule over the works of your hands.

Psalm 34 *page 406*

Reading *Luke 12:8–12*

Jesus said to his disciples: "I tell you, everyone who acknowledges me before others the Son of Man will acknowledge before the angels of God. But whoever denies me before others will be denied before the angels of God.

"Everyone who speaks a word against the Son of Man will be forgiven, but the one who blasphemes against the Holy Spirit will not be forgiven. When they take you before synagogues and before rulers and authorities, do not worry about how or what your defense will be or about what you are to say. For the Holy Spirit will teach you at that moment what you should say."

Reflection

If we truly relied on the promise and gift of the Spirit in our lives, we could live with such freedom and peace. In today's Gospel, Jesus assures us that he will give us the words we need at the necessary moment. The Holy Spirit will teach us and guide us, so there is no need for fear or worry. God is in control. He is caring for our every need and providing us with everything necessary for this very moment.

Prayers *others may be added*

Confident that you provide us with our every need, we present to you our cares and petitions as we pray:

◆ Come, Holy Spirit.

For the Holy Father, all priests, bishops, deacons, and lay members of the Church, that they may remain solid and steadfast to proclaim the truth of the Gospel in its fullness and totality, we pray: ◆ For all nations torn apart by war, terrorism, and political unrest, we pray: ◆ For all Christians who are persecuted for their faith, we pray: ◆ For all who face difficult situations, that they may be given the courage they need to boldly speak the truth with charity, we pray: ◆ For all who serve in the military and civic service, that they receive safety and protection; and for their families, we pray: ◆ For all judges, lawyers, and attorneys, that they may always use their words to speak the truth as they defend the cause for justice, we pray: ◆ For the sick and the dying; for the comfort of their loved ones, and all who care for them, we pray: ◆

Our Father . . .

Loving God,
through the prayers of Saint Paul of the Cross,
banish from our hearts all fear and doubt.
Make us secure in your love as you
send us the gift of the Holy Spirit,
who lives and reigns together with you
and your Son, Jesus Christ,
one God, forever and ever.
Amen.

✝ You have given your Son rule over the works of your hands.

✝ Lord, let your mercy be on us, as we place our trust in you.

Psalm 116 *page 418*

Reading *Mark 10:42–45*

Jesus summoned the Twelve and said to them, "You know that those who are recognized as rulers over the Gentiles lord it over them, and their great ones make their authority over them felt. But it shall not be so among you. Rather, whoever wishes to be great among you will be your servant; whoever wishes to be first among you will be the slave of all. For the Son of Man did not come to be served but to serve and to give his life as a ransom for many."

Reflection

In today's liturgy, Jesus teaches that the one who is truly great is the one who humbles himself as a slave to be the servant of others. Jesus provides the perfect example as the messianic Suffering Servant who humbles himself even unto death on the cross (see Philippians 4). Yet, for this reason, he is greatly exalted by the Father in eternal glory. Today we remind ourselves not to expect to be served, but rather to be always ready to give ourselves in service toward others.

Prayers *others may be added*

Presenting to you our prayers and petitions, we pray:

◆ May your kindness, Lord, be upon us as we place our hope in you.

That, inspired by the word of God, the Holy Father, the clergy, and lay faithful may be united in the Mystical Body of Christ to spend themselves in service toward the poor, weak, and needy, we pray: ◆ That all government officials and civic leaders may work with dedication to serve those in need, we pray: ◆ That there will be an end of human trafficking, abuse, slavery, war, and terrorism throughout the world, we pray: ◆ That all who suffer poverty, hunger, homelessness, illness, and unemployment may be healed of their suffering, we pray: ◆ That all members of our parish community may become more willing to extend themselves in service toward the poor and needy of our community, we pray: ◆

Our Father . . .

Father of glory,
you send your Son into the world as a
    slave and servant of all
to free us from our sins
and invite us to rejoice with you in heaven.
Prepare a place for us in the glory of
    your kingdom.
We ask through our Lord Jesus Christ,
    your Son,
who lives and reigns with you in the unity
    of the Holy Spirit,
one God, forever and ever.
Amen.

✝ Lord, let your mercy be on us, as we place our trust in you.

✝ The Lord made us, we belong to him.

Psalm 48 *page 408*

Reading *Luke 12:16–21*

Then [Jesus] told [the crowd] a parable. "There was a rich man whose land produced a bountiful harvest. He asked himself, 'What shall I do, for I do not have space to store my harvest?' And he said, 'This is what I shall do: I shall tear down my barns and build larger ones. There I shall store all my grain and other goods and I shall say to myself, "Now as for you, you have so many good things stored up for many years, rest, eat, drink, be merry!"' But God said to him, 'You fool, this night your life will be demanded of you; and the things you have prepared, to whom will they belong?' Thus will it be for the one who stores up treasure for himself but is not rich in what matters to God."

Reflection

Jesus speaks strong words today as he tells us that one's life does not consist of riches, and that we must beware of all forms of greed. We live in such a materialistic society where we are constantly told by the media that our personal worth is proportionate to the amount and quality of things that we own. Yet, so often a life of only material riches can be a life of emptiness and dissatisfaction. Let us rather be rich in what matters to God.

Prayers *others may be added*

Lord, with hope and patience, we offer you our prayers and petitions:

◆ Make us rich in your blessings, Lord.

That the Holy Father, all bishops, priests, clergy, and lay faithful may not seek material wealth or prestige, but rather the blessings and riches that flow from a life of true freedom and union with God, we pray: ◆ That our nation and all nations may be freed from the slavery of materialism, we pray: ◆ That all who have been blessed economically and enjoy worldly riches may be detached from the lure of many possessions and may generously share the goods they have been given with those less fortunate, we pray: ◆ That all the poor, the homeless, the sick and injured, prisoners, and those who suffer from addiction and mental illness may be transformed by God's grace, we pray: ◆

Our Father . . .

Father of all peoples,
free our hearts from the empty desire
of worldly honors and material possessions.
May we have the eyes to give thanks to you
for every good and gracious gift you give
to us through your Son Jesus Christ,
    our Lord,
who lives and reigns together with you in
    the unity of the Holy Spirit,
one God, forever and ever.
Amen.

✝ The Lord made us, we belong to him.

Tuesday, October 23, 2012
Weekday

✝ The Lord speaks of peace to his people.

Psalm 51   *page 409*

Reading   *Luke 12:35–38*

[Jesus said to his disciples:] "Gird your loins and light your lamps and be like servants who await their master's return from a wedding, ready to open immediately when he comes and knocks. Blessed are those servants whom the master finds vigilant on his arrival. Amen, I say to you, he will gird himself, have them recline at table, and proceed to wait on them. And should he come in the second or third watch and find them prepared in this way, blessed are those servants."

Reflection

If we were to die today, would we be ready and prepared for the Lord to take us to the eternal home of heaven? We know not the day nor the hour when Christ will come again. In today's Gospel Jesus exhorts us to remain vigilant for his return. Let us be his blessed servants whom he finds prepared upon his arrival.

Prayers   *others may be added*

Calling on our Father's love, we pray:

◆ Prepare our hearts, O Lord.

For the Church, that she may be enflamed with the life of the Spirit as she continues along this earthly journey toward her heavenly home, we pray: ◆ For peoples of all nations, that they may take care to use the goods of creation so as not to abuse the resources and blessings that we have received from God, we pray: ◆ For the sick, the elderly, the poor, the lonely, and those who have no one to care for them, we pray: ◆ For all young people, that they may use this time to grow and develop their gifts and talents for the glory of God and the good of others, we pray: ◆ For all who serve our country abroad and in harm's way, that they may work to protect and promote the good of society, we pray: ◆ For all the dying, that the Bridegroom may take them to the heavenly banquet of the Lamb, we pray: ◆

Our Father . . .

Eternal Bridegroom,
by the power of your Spirit,
breathe upon us the breath of new life.
Prepare our hearts with your
    purifying love
and make us ready and open to
    receive you.
We ask this through Christ our Lord.
Amen.

✝ The Lord speaks of peace to his people.

Wednesday, October 24, 2012
Weekday

✝ You will draw water joyfully from the springs of salvation.

Psalm 118
page 418

Reading
Luke 12:39–40

Jesus said to his disciples: "Be sure of this: if the master of the house had known the hour when the thief was coming, he would not have let his house be broken into. You also must be prepared, for at an hour you do not expect, the Son of Man will come."

Reflection

As Christians, we also must expect the unexpected. Jesus tells us in today's Gospel that he will return at an hour we do not expect. Therefore, we must be ready. This demands a constant vigilance against sin and evil through the frequent reception of the holy sacraments, daily prayer, and avoiding situations where we would be led to sin. In this way, we can continually prepare our hearts for the day of the Lord.

Prayers
others may be added

With hearts full of fervor and hope, we, your loving children, come to you to ask for your blessings. Let us pray:

◆ Loving Father, hear our prayer.

That God may pour out his abundant graces upon the Church, the Holy Father, and all members of the lay faithful, so that, united in faith, we may prepare for the day in which we will celebrate together in the heavenly glory, we pray: ◆ That all the nations of the world may gather together in unity with one another free from violence and war, we pray: ◆ That those who suffer injury, illness, abuse, addiction, poverty, and persecution may be released from their suffering, we pray: ◆ That all who travel by land, sea, or air this day may safely reach their destinations, and for all who have died or suffered injury because of travel accidents, we pray: ◆

Our Father . . .

Lord God,
all creation sings your praise.
We give you thanks for your glory
that you reveal to us through the beauty
of nature during the changing seasons.
We ask this through Christ our Lord.
Amen.

✝ You will draw water joyfully from the springs of salvation.

Thursday, October 25, 2012
Weekday

✝ The earth is full of the goodness of the Lord.

Psalm 42   *page 407*

Reading: *Luke 12:49–53*

Jesus said to his disciples: "I have come to set the earth on fire, and how I wish it were already blazing! There is a baptism with which I must be baptized, and how great is my anguish until it is accomplished! Do you think that I have come to establish peace on the earth? No, I tell you, but rather division. From now on a household of five will be divided, three against two and two against three; a father will be divided against his son and a son against his father, a mother against her daughter and a daughter against her mother, a mother-in-law against her daughter-in-law and a daughter-in-law against her mother-in-law."

Reflection

How ardently Jesus desires that we live and burn with the fire of his divine love! He desires to set the whole world aflame with his love and life. His love is a purifying love that divides and separates that which is not of the Lord to bring us into true union with him in the Holy Trinity. Without first being united to God, we cannot truly experience good and pure communion with one another on earth.

Prayers   *others may be added*

Lord, you desire that we be rekindled with your life. Hear our prayers as we pray:

♦ Set our hearts on fire with your love, O Lord.

That the Holy Father's work in ecumenism may bring about dialogue and deeper understanding of Christian unity for all peoples throughout the world, we pray: ♦ That civic leaders, those who work in public office, and social workers may work together to promote peace and justice, we pray: ♦ That God will grant healing to all families divided by divorce, abuse, selfishness, and infidelity, we pray: ♦ That God will come with the sword to banish all forms of sin and evil by his mighty power we pray: ♦ That all who have died will be received into God's heavenly kingdom, we pray: ♦

Our Father . . .

Eternal and Triune God,
your love for us is everlasting
and your mercy is abundant.
By your power and grace,
enflame our hearts, our minds, and
    whole beings
with your love so that we may be
    burning examples
of your eternal love throughout the world.
We ask this through Christ our Lord.
Amen.

✝ The earth is full of the goodness of the Lord.

✝ Lord, this is the people that longs to see your face.

Psalm 107   page 417

Reading   Luke 12:54–59

Jesus said to the crowds, "When you see a cloud rising in the west you say immediately that it is going to rain—and so it does; and when you notice that the wind is blowing from the south you say that it is going to be hot—and so it is. You hypocrites! You know how to interpret the appearance of the earth and the sky; why do you not know how to interpret the present time?

"Why do you not judge for yourselves what is right? If you are to go with your opponent before a magistrate, make an effort to settle the matter on the way; otherwise your opponent will turn you over to the judge, and the judge hand you over to the constable, and the constable throw you into prison. I say to you, you will not be released until you have paid the last penny."

Reflection

If only we had eyes to see the signs and miracles the Lord is working in our lives every day! Today's Gospel tells us to use the same human wisdom in order to be perceptive to the movements of grace present in the spiritual life. Let us open our hearts to the whisperings of the Holy Spirit and his quiet, yet powerful, moments of grace in our lives.

Prayers   others may be added

God, you are always present to us.
Calling upon your holy name, we pray:

◆ Lord, send out your Spirit.

That the Holy Father and the Church's magisterium may be blessed with wisdom from on high to interpret and proclaim the word of God with clarity, depth, and fervor, we pray: ◆ That the legislative office of our country will work to enact laws that protect the human person at all stages of life, especially the elderly and the unborn, we pray: ◆ That all the poor throughout the world who suffer illness, disease, and death because of lack of health care, may be given the resources they need, we pray: ◆ That we may be filled with the virtue of cheerfulness to those around us, we pray: ◆

Our Father . . .

Everlasting God,
calling to mind the mystery
of your Son's Passion, we ask
that you may pour your mercy
upon us and fill us with your love
to make us perceptive and docile
to the grace of the Holy Spirit.
Open our eyes to see your goodness and
    glory.
We ask this through Christ our Lord.
Amen.

✝ Lord, this is the people that longs to see your face.

Saturday, October 27, 2012
Weekday

✝ Let us go rejoicing to the house of the Lord.

Psalm 27 *page 405*

Reading *Luke 13:6–9*

[Jesus told them] this parable: "There once was a person who had a fig tree planted in his orchard, and when he came in search of fruit on it but found none, he said to the gardener, 'For three years now I have come in search of fruit on this fig tree but have found none. So cut it down. Why should it exhaust the soil?' He said to him in reply, 'Sir, leave it for this year also, and I shall cultivate the ground around it and fertilize it; it may bear fruit in the future. If not you can cut it down.' "

Reflection

Jesus strongly tells us to repent. We do not want to remain barren like the fig tree that is cut down, because it does not yield any fruit. Yet, in the parable the gardener begs the owner to leave the tree for one more year so that he may tend and care for the tree. In this Gospel we learn of the mercy of God, who prunes and cultivates our souls so that we, too, may bear good and abundant fruit.

Prayers *others may be added*

Through the Lord's tender care, let us return to the Lord and allow him to bring about an abundant harvest through our lives as we pray:

◆ Turn our hearts back to you, O Lord.

That the Holy Father, all priests, missionaries, religious, and lay faithful may be witnesses to the mercy of God to show compassion and understanding to all sinners and those in need, we pray: ◆ That all the nations of the world may grow in a deeper appreciation for their individual cultures to offer richness and diversity to the beauty of all peoples throughout the world, we pray: ◆ That all who suffer isolation, rejection, despair, and anxiety may be given healing, we pray: ◆ That we may not remain stubborn, indifferent, or deaf to the voice of the Lord in our lives, we pray: ◆ That all who have died may be brought to new life in God's heavenly kingdom, and for the comfort of their loved ones, we pray: ◆

Our Father . . .

Lord Jesus,
you are the word of life.
Send your Spirit upon us to
make us fruitful in good works
through our humble offerings
and prayers of each day.
May we always remain in your love.
You live and reign forever.
Amen.

✝ Let us go rejoicing to the house of the Lord.

Sunday, October 28, 2012
Thirtieth Sunday in Ordinary Time

✝ The Lord has done great things for us.

Psalm 66 page 410

Reading Mark 10:46–47, 51b–52

As Jesus was leaving Jericho with his disciples and a sizable crowd, Bartimaeus, a blind man, the son of Timaeus, sat by the roadside begging. On hearing that it was Jesus of Nazareth, he began to cry out and say, "Jesus, son of David, have pity on me. . . . Master, I want to see." Jesus told him, "Go your way; your faith has saved you." Immediately he received his sight and followed him on the way.

Reflection S. Anne Elizabeth Sweet, CSO

In calling the blind Bartimaeus to himself, Jesus manifests an even deeper fulfillment of the promises of old than the restoration after the exile. His sight restored, Bartimaeus follows Jesus along the way—an image of true discipleship.

Prayers others may be added

Lord Jesus, you heal the blind man by his faith in you. Let us pray:

◆ Son of David, have pity on us.

That the Church may be the source of new life through the liturgical celebrations of the healing power of the sacraments, we pray: ◆ That all nations suffering poverty, hunger, economic crisis, and political instability may be given the leadership of persons dedicated to social justice and peace, we pray: ◆ That all who suffer illness, injury, and disability may be freed from their pain and restored to fullness of health, we pray: ◆ That our community members may not remain strangers to one another, but rather may grow together in holy friendship and charity through our bond of faith in Christ Jesus, we pray: ◆ That we may be given the grace to boldly and courageously ask the Lord for the gifts and needs that we desire for the good of others and for our own lives, we pray: ◆ That all those who have died, and for those who will die today, may receive the gift of salvation in the heavenly glory, we pray: ◆

Our Father . . .

Loving Father,
today we celebrate and remember
the mystery of your Son's Resurrection.
Increase in us the gift of faith and
bring us to new life by your healing power.
We ask through our Lord Jesus Christ,
    your Son,
who lives and reigns with you in the unity
    of the Holy Spirit,
one God, forever and ever.
Amen.

✝ The Lord has done great things for us.

Monday, October 29, 2012
Weekday

✝ Behave like God as his very dear children.

Psalm 62   *page 409*

Reading   *Luke 13:10–13*

Jesus was teaching in a synagogue on the sabbath. And a woman was there who for eighteen years had been crippled by a spirit; she was bent over, completely incapable of standing erect. When Jesus saw her, he called to her and said, "Woman, you are set free of your infirmity." He laid his hands on her, and she at once stood up straight and glorified God.

Reflection

The Lord's ways are not always our ways. We know that he always hears and answers our prayers, yet sometimes he requires us to wait in patience for the accomplishment of his will for us. The woman in today's Gospel had been crippled by a spirit for 18 years before she was healed and set free from the Lord. Yet, God's timing is perfect, and our patience and long suffering is not in vain, but rather is used for the greater glory of God in our lives.

Prayers   *others may be added*

With persistence and faith, we continue to ask for our needs and petitions as we pray:

◆ Lord, set us free from our infirmities.

That the Holy Father may be filled with wisdom and counsel as he guides and leads Holy Mother Church along the path of faith, we pray: ◆ That nations crippled by the evils of corrupt governmental systems and false ideologies may be set free by the truth, we pray: ◆ That all who suffer constant pain, illness, and physical and mental disabilities may be given healing in their life, we pray: ◆ That our prayer community may always be open to seeking the good of others and serving the needs of our neighbors, we pray: ◆ That all who have grown weary may persevere in hope and faith for the day of the Lord, we pray: ◆

Our Father . . .

Lord Jesus,
we rejoice in the splendid deeds
you perform for us, your humble children.
Give us hope and perseverance to
    never doubt
your presence nor your healing power
as we await the glorious coming of
    your kingdom
where you live and reign with the Father
in the unity of the Holy Spirit,
one God, forever and ever.
Amen.

✝ Behave like God as his very dear children.

✝ Blessed are those who fear the Lord.

Psalm 47   *page 408*

Reading   *Luke 13:18–21*

Jesus said, "What is the Kingdom of God like? To what can I compare it? It is like a mustard seed that a man took and planted in the garden. When it was fully grown, it became a large bush and *the birds of the sky dwelt in its branches.*"

Again he said, "To what shall I compare the Kingdom of God? It is like yeast that a woman took and mixed in with three measures of wheat flour until the whole batch of dough was leavened."

Reflection

The kingdom of God is such a mystery. Jesus compares his kingdom to a tiny mustard seed that then grows into a great bush where the birds of the air find rest and shade. It is also like yeast hidden and dispersed throughout a batch of dough that mysteriously and quietly causes the whole batch to rise and grow in size. What great mysteries to ponder and contemplate as we seek deeper understanding and meaning of Jesus' word for our lives!

Prayers   *others may be added*

With hearts and minds open to your word, together we present to you our needs and petitions. Let us pray:

◆ Thy kingdom come, O Lord.

For the Holy Father, all priests, bishops, religious, and all the lay faithful, that they may never cease to wonder about the beauty and mystery of God as they work to build up the kingdom of God through prayer and good works, we pray: ◆ For all nations, that they may not misuse the goods of creation, which give glory to God and reveal to us the mystery of his kingdom, we pray: ◆ For those who suffer pain, illness, loneliness, and sorrow, that they may not lose hope as they endure the great mystery of suffering, but rather that they may turn their eyes to Christ Jesus, the source of all hope and peace, we pray: ◆ For all who labor in God's kingdom as priests, religious, married couples, and laity, that more people may respond to the call of the Lord to live holy and saintly lives through their states of life, we pray: ◆ For all children, that they may teach us how to pray and contemplate God's beauty, as we imitate their simplicity, joy, and wonderment at the good gifts of life, we pray: ◆ For all who have died, and for those who grieve their loss, that one day we may all be reunited in the joy and glory of God's kingdom forever, we pray: ◆

Our Father . . .

Loving Father,
you are the source of all goodness,
truth, and beauty.
By the power of your Holy Spirit, draw us
    more deeply
into the mystery of your Son Jesus,
through whom we ask this prayer.
Amen.

✝ Blessed are those who fear the Lord.

✝ The Lord is faithful in all his words.

Psalm 48 *page 408*

Reading *Luke 13:23–25, 29*

Someone asked [Jesus], "Lord, will only a few people be saved?" He answered them, "Strive to enter through the narrow gate, for many, I tell you, will attempt to enter but will not be strong enough. After the master of the house has arisen and locked the door, then will you stand outside knocking and saying, 'Lord, open the door for us.' He will say to you in reply, 'I do not know where you are from.' And people will come from the east and the west and from the north and the south and will recline at table in the Kingdom of God."

Reflection

Christianity is not a religion for the weak or faint of heart. Jesus says today in the Gospel that many will try to enter but will not be strong enough. We must be persevering in faith as we stand firm against temptation, and surrender ourselves totally to Christ to guide us through the narrow gate of salvation.

Prayers *others may be added*

We can do nothing without your grace, O Lord. Hear our prayers we offer you today as we pray:

◆ Aid us in our weakness, O Lord.

That the Church, led by the Holy Father, may persevere in faith to guide and lead all peoples through the narrow gate of salvation, we pray: ◆ That political and governmental leaders may promote legislation that upholds the dignity of the human person and the common good of all society, we pray: ◆ That all those who silently suffer abuse and maltreatment may have the courage to seek the help and protection they need, we pray: ◆ That there will be an end to all evil and all anti-Christian practices, we pray: ◆ That all who struggle against sin may never cease to return to the Lord through the healing and fortifying gifts of the holy sacraments of Reconciliation and Eucharist we pray: ◆ That all children will be protected, especially today on Halloween, we pray: ◆ That all those who have died may enjoy the glory of the beatific vision, we pray: ◆ That we may have the grace to keep our eyes always focused on the Lord, we pray: ◆

Our Father . . .

Loving Father,
you promise to never leave us orphans.
Do not remove your grace from us,
but carry us along in our weakness
to enter into the joy of salvation
through the narrow gate of the
　　pierced heart
of your Son, Jesus Christ,
who lives and reigns with you in the unity
　　of the Holy Spirit,
one God, forever and ever.
Amen.

✝ The Lord is faithful in all his words.

✠ Lord, this is the people that longs to see your face.

Psalm 145 *page 422*

Reading *Matthew 5:1–2a*

When Jesus saw the crowds, he went up the mountain, and after he had sat down, his disciples came to him. He began to teach them, saying: / "Blessed are the poor in spirit, / for theirs is the Kingdom of heaven. / Blessed are they who mourn, / for they will be comforted. / Blessed are the meek, / for they will inherit the land. / Blessed are they who hunger and thirst for righteousness, / for they will be satisfied. / Blessed are the merciful, / for they will be shown mercy. / Blessed are the clean of heart, / for they will see God. / Blessed are the peacemakers, / for they will be called children of God. / Blessed are they who are persecuted for the sake of righteousness, / for theirs is the Kingdom of heaven. / Blessed are you when they insult you and persecute you and utter every kind of evil against you falsely because of me. Rejoice and be glad, for your reward will be great in heaven."

Reflection

The Beatitudes are guidelines for true joy and the attainment of sanctity in our Christian lives. We hear how to live lives of holiness so that we may attain happiness in this life, but even more happiness in the next life as we strive to likewise be numbered among the saints in heaven.

Prayers *others may be added*

The example of all the holy men and women inspires us to lives of sanctity. Hear our prayers as we ask:

◆ Make us holy, O Lord.

For the Church, that she may remain the pure and holy spotless Bride of Jesus Christ, we pray: ◆ For all nations and their governmental leaders, that they may foster Gospel values to encourage virtue and right conduct among society, we pray: ◆ For all who suffer illness, pain, poverty, or grief, that they may receive comfort and healing, we pray: ◆ For all who have died, that they may be united and numbered among all the saints of heaven, we pray: ◆

Our Father . . .

Father of all holiness and compassion,
today we celebrate all the holy men
    and women
who share in your divine Trinitarian life.
Strengthen us by the prayers of all
    the saints,
to be faithful to you and so to attain
the glories of heaven where you live
    and reign
with your Son Jesus Christ,
in the unity of the Holy Spirit,
one God, forever and ever.
Amen.

✠ Lord, this is the people that longs to see your face.

Friday, November 2, 2012
The Commemoration of All the Faithful Departed
(All Souls Day)

✝ The Lord is my shepherd; there is nothing I shall want.

Psalm 107
page 417

Reading
Luke 7:11–17

Jesus journeyed to a city called Nain, and his disciples and a large crowd accompanied him. As he drew near to the gate of the city, a man who had died was being carried out, the only son of his mother, and she was a widow. A large crowd from the city was with her. When the Lord saw her, he was moved with pity for her and said to her, "Do not weep." He stepped forward and touched the coffin; at this the bearers halted, and he said, "Young man, I tell you, arise!" The dead man sat up and began to speak, and Jesus gave him to his mother. Fear seized them all, and they glorified God, exclaiming, "A great prophet has arisen in our midst," and "God has visited his people." This report about him spread through the whole of Judea and in all the surrounding region.

Reflection

Today we celebrate the Commemoration of All the Faithful Departed, where we remember all those who have died. This day we renew our hope in the Lord's mercy both for all who have gone before us in death and also for ourselves as we continue to struggle here on earth.

Prayers
others may be added

Recalling to mind God's great love and providence, with hopefulness we offer to you our prayers:

◆ Lord, have mercy and hear our prayer.

That all the members of the Church may one day be united in the splendor of the heavenly kingdom, we pray: ◆ That all countries may respect life in all its stages and all forms, we pray: ◆ For those who will die today, that they may be transformed into new life, and that they may be brought into the glory of all the holy ones in heaven, we pray: ◆ That those who deeply grieve the loss of loved ones, family, or friends may be comforted by the presence of loving friends and supported by the prayers of faithful Christians, we pray: ◆

Our Father . . .

Lord Jesus, source of mercy,
by the power of your Resurrection,
comfort our sorrowing hearts and help us
to be faithful to you here on earth,
that we will be united to you
and all our loved ones in the glory
   of heaven
where you reign eternally with the Father
in the unity of the Holy Spirit,
one God, forever and ever.
Amen.

✝ The Lord is my shepherd; there is nothing I shall want.

Saturday, November 3, 2012
Weekday

✝ My soul is thirsting for the living God.

Psalm 116   *page 418*

Reading   *Luke 14:7–11*

[Jesus] told a parable to those who had been invited [to the Sabbath], noticing how they were choosing the places of honor at the table. "When you are invited by someone to a wedding banquet, do not recline at table in the place of honor. A more distinguished guest than you may have been invited by him, and the host who invited both of you may approach you and say, 'Give your place to this man.' and then you would proceed with embarrassment to take the lowest place. Rather, when you are invited, go and take the lowest place so that when the host comes to you he may say, 'My friend, move up to a higher position.' Then you will enjoy the esteem of your companions at the table. For everyone who exalts himself will be humbled, but the one who humbles himself will be exalted."

Reflection

Why do we make so many excuses? Jesus invites us to partake of the joy and life and blessings of his banquet table. Why do we refuse him? Maybe this is why the kingdom of God belongs to the little ones and the weak and poor, because they are humble enough to receive the true goodness and life the Lord offers. They will truly be blessed in God's kingdom.

Prayers   *others may be added*

You call us to your banquet table. Let us pray:

◆ Gather around your table of love, O Lord.

That the Church, guided by the Holy Father, the clergy, and all faithful may make ready for the coming of the Lord, we pray: ◆ That all peoples may be gathered from all nations to worship the Lord and partake of the richness of his kingdom, we pray: ◆ That the poor, crippled, blind, lame, ill, and homeless may reap blessings from the Lord and share in his banquet table, we pray: ◆ That we may cease to make excuses for not living our Christian faith to its fullest, we pray: ◆ That our faith community may become aware of the needs of the poor and generously extend ourselves to offer help and aid, we pray: ◆

Our Father . . .

Heavenly Father,
give us a greater concern for the poor
    and needy
and open our hearts to respond with joy
to come and share with you in the fullness
of your heavenly banquet of the Lamb,
Jesus Christ, your Son, who lives and
    reigns with you in the unity of the
    Holy Spirit,
one God, forever and ever.
Amen.

✝ My soul is thirsting for the living God.

Sunday, November 4, 2012
Thirty-first Sunday in Ordinary Time

✝ I love you Lord, my strength.

Psalm 34 *page 406*

Reading *Mark 12:28b–33*

One of the scribes came to Jesus and asked him, "Which is the first of all the commandments?" Jesus replied, "The first is this: / *Hear, O Israel! / The Lord our God is Lord alone! / You shall love the Lord your God with all your heart, with all your soul, / with all your mind, / and with all your strength.* / The second is this: *You shall love your neighbor as yourself.* / There is no other commandment greater than these." The scribe said to him, "Well said, teacher. You are right in saying, / 'He is One and there is no other than he.' / And 'to love him with all your heart, / with all your understanding, / with all your strength, / and to love your neighbor as yourself' / is worth more than all burnt offerings and sacrifices."

Reflection

We are created to worship and love God with our whole being. The love that we ought to have for our neighbor is an outpouring of our love for God as we recognize that each person is a reflection of God's divine image and likeness. In this way, our love toward one another becomes a joy as we worship God through service toward those around us.

Prayers *others may be added*

Coming together as God's family, we present our needs and concerns to the Lord as we pray:

◆ Teacher, instruct us in your commands.

For the Holy Father, that he may be endowed with the gifts of counsel, wisdom, and fortitude to guide God's people along the right path, we pray: ◆ For the hearts and minds of civic leaders and government officials, that they may be guided by natural law and Gospel values as they serve society in justice and truth, we pray: ◆ For the sick, the suffering, the poor, the homeless, the afflicted, and the despairing, that they may have hope and faith in our Savior who comes to save them after this momentary light affliction, we pray: ◆ For all the spiritual and material needs of our parish, families, and friends, we pray: ◆ For all those who have gone before us in death, that we may be joined in love and communion as we await the day we will celebrate the joy of salvation together in the kingdom of heaven, we pray: ◆

Our Father . . .

Loving God,
your law is our delight.
Grant that we may love you
with every fiber of our being
and serve one another in the
outpouring of selfless love.
We ask this through Christ our Lord.
Amen.

✝ I love you Lord, my strength.

✝ In you, O Lord, I have found
my peace.

Psalm 107 page 417

Reading Luke 14:12–14

On a sabbath Jesus went to dine at the home of one of the leading Pharisees. He said to the host who invited him, "When you hold a lunch or dinner, do not invite your friends or your brothers or sisters or your relatives or your wealthy neighbors, in case they may invite you back and you have repayment. Rather, when you hold a banquet, invite the poor, the crippled, the lame, the blind; blessed indeed will you be because of their inability to repay you. For you will be repaid at the resurrection of the righteous."

Reflection

In today's Gospel, Jesus tells us not to do things for the purpose of being repaid in return. We must give generously without expecting or demanding anything in return. There is great value in what we do for the poor, the weak, and those who are unable to return the favor. Let us not desire to be repaid now with earthly favors, but let us give ourselves selflessly and generously as we long for the riches of heaven.

Prayers others may be added

You teach us that the last shall be first and the first shall be last. Let us pray:

◆ Purify our hearts, O Lord.

For all the members of the Church, that they may not seek their own glory, but rather the glory of Christ Jesus as they serve the poor and needy and strive to faithfully live out the duties and responsibilities of their work, we pray: ◆ For all who feel unfulfilled, saddened, restless, or dissatisfied, that God will reveal to them the joyous path in which they should walk, and that he may give them peace, we pray: ◆ For all the military and all in the armed forces who serve at home and abroad, that they may diligently perform their duties with virtue and courage, and for their families and friends, we pray: ◆ For all those married and engaged, especially those of our parish community, that they may be strengthened by the grace of the Lord to be witnesses of true love and selfless sacrifice, we pray: ◆ For all the faithful departed, we pray: ◆

Our Father . . .

Lord Jesus,
bless us as we return to another
week of work in which to serve you
and give you glory by all that we do.
You live and reign forever.
Amen.

✝ In you, O Lord, I have found
my peace.

✝ I will praise you, Lord, in the assembly of your people.

Psalm 48   *page 408*

Reading   *Luke 14:16–21*

[Jesus] replied to him, "A man gave a great dinner to which he invited many. When the time for the dinner came, he dispatched his servant to say to those invited, 'Come, everything is now ready.' But one by one, they all began to excuse themselves. The first said to him, 'I have purchased a field and must go to examine it; I ask you, consider me excused.' And another said, 'I have purchased five yoke of oxen and am on my way to evaluate them; I ask you, consider me excused.' And another said, 'I have just married a woman, and therefore I cannot come.' The servant went and reported this to his master. Then the master of the house in a rage commanded his servant, 'Go out quickly into the streets and alleys of the town and bring in here the poor and the crippled, the blind and the lame.' "

Reflection

What are we waiting for? "Come, everything is ready," Jesus says to us today in the Gospel. Why do we hesitate to return to the Lord? He has prepared everything for us. His table is set and everything is ready for the banquet feast. Why do we delay in accepting his invitation to the joy, fruitfulness, and new life he offers?

Prayers   *others may be added*

You call us to share in your life of Trinitarian love. Let us pray:

◆ Loving God, open our hearts to respond to you in love.

For the Church, that she may become ever more unified throughout all lands and nations, we pray: ◆ For all missionaries in distant lands, that they may have courage and strength to proclaim the Gospel to all peoples, and that they may be encouraged by the support of our prayers, we pray: ◆ For all who suffer deep interior sadness, physical pain, or chronic illness, that they may be relieved of their sufferings, we pray: ◆ For all who have died and for those who grieve their losses, we pray: ◆

Our Father . . .

Loving Father,
you know our needs even before we
    speak them.
Send your Holy Spirit upon us to
    intercede for us,
for we do not know how to pray as
    we ought.
By your power, draw us into the
    glorious banquet of heaven where
    you live and reign together with
    your Son Jesus, in the unity of the
    Holy Spirit,
one God, forever and ever.
Amen.

✝ I will praise you, Lord, in the assembly of your people.

✝ The Lord is my light and my salvation.

Psalm 66 — page 410

Reading — Luke 14:25–27

Great crowds were traveling with Jesus, and he turned and addressed them, "If anyone comes to me without hating his father and mother, wife and children, brothers and sisters, and even his own life, he cannot be my disciple. Whoever does not carry his own cross and come after me cannot be my disciple."

Reflection

We must love God with undivided hearts. In order to enter into the kingdom of God, we cannot be overly attached to worldly possessions, nor even to our family members and friends. Our love for God overflows in love to our family and friends; however, in our concern or care for them, we may not place them as idols above God. Only by picking up our cross and following Christ can we experience true freedom of the heavenly glory.

Prayers — *others may be added*

You are our source of life, O God.
Hear our prayers and petitions this day as we pray:

◆ Free us from all that keeps us from you, O Lord.

For the Holy Father, all bishops, and priests, that they may be strengthened in their ministry to lay down their lives for their Bride, Holy Mother Church, with selfless love and constant fidelity, we pray: ◆ For all nations that suffer political unrest, natural disasters, war, or violence, that civic leaders may work to bring them the aid they need, we pray: ◆ For all the poor who suffer from the lack of basic human needs of food, water, housing, and health care, we pray: ◆ For all those who have died, especially this past year, we pray: ◆

Our Father . . .

Merciful Jesus,
you call us to follow you as your disciples.
Give us the strength to pick up our cross daily
and serve you through our love of those around us.
Never leave us, Lord, but stay with us
as we strive to obey your commands along the journey of this earthly life
until we will see you face to face
in the glory of heaven where you live
and reign with the Father
in the unity of the Holy Spirit,
one God, forever and ever.
Amen.

✝ The Lord is my light and my salvation.

✝ Let hearts rejoice who search for the Lord.

Psalm 33 *page 406*

Reading *Luke 15:1–7*

[Jesus said:] "What man among you having a hundred sheep and losing one of them would not leave the ninety-nine in the desert and go after the lost one until he finds it? And when he does find it, he sets it on his shoulders with great joy and, upon his arrival home, he calls together his friends and neighbors and says to them, 'Rejoice with me because I have found my lost sheep.' I tell you, in just the same way there will be more joy in heaven over one sinner who repents than over ninety-nine righteous people who have no need of repentance."

Reflection

What love our God has for us! In today's Gospel, we hear that Jesus is the Good Shepherd who leaves the other ninety-nine to go out in search of the lost sheep. Once he has found the lost sheep, he places him on his shoulders and rejoices with his friends and neighbors. This parable reveals the love and joy that God has for even one lost sinner who repents and returns to the Lord.

Prayers *others may be added*

You are the Good Shepherd who call your sheep by name. Let us pray:

◆ Bring us back, O Lord.

For the Holy Father, all bishops, and priests, that they may never cease to imitate the Good Shepherd who seeks out lost sinners as they guide and care for the members of God's flock that has been entrusted to them, we pray: ◆ For all nations and societies that have wandered far from God's truth through false ideologies, anti-Christian practice, and corrupt governmental systems, that they may return to a sense of justice and Gospel values, we pray: ◆ For all the poor, the ill, and the suffering, that Jesus the Good Shepherd may meet them in their weakness and raise them up upon his shoulders to bring them to safety, security, and fullness of life, we pray: ◆ For all the homeless who suffer from the cold as the season changes to winter, we pray: ◆

Our Father . . .

Loving Shepherd,
you lead us to verdant pastures
and springs of life-giving waters.
Restore our spirits and renew us
in your grace as we seek to hear
your voice and follow after you to
the joys and fullness of life in heaven
where you live and reign forever
with the Father in the unity of the
     Holy Spirit,
one God, forever and ever.
Amen.

✝ Let hearts rejoice who search for the Lord.

✝ The waters of the river gladden the city of God, the holy dwelling of the Most High!

Psalm 62 *page 409*

Reading *John 2:13–17*

Since the Passover of the Jews was near, Jesus went up to Jerusalem. He found in the temple area those who sold oxen, sheep, and doves, as well as the money changers seated there. He made a whip out of cords and drove them all out of the temple area, with the sheep and oxen, and spilled the coins of the money changers and overturned their tables, and to those who sold doves he said, "Take these out of here, and stop making my Father's house a marketplace." His disciples recalled the words of Scripture, *Zeal for your house will consume me.*

Reflection

Today we celebrate the feast of the dedication of the Basilica of Saint John Lateran. This church is the seat of the Pope as Bishop of Rome. The Basilica was built in honor of both Saints John the Baptist and John the Evangelist. In today's Gospel, we see the great importance of respect for God's temple through the visible signs and structures of churches and basilicas.

Prayers *others may be added*

One thing we ask; we seek to dwell in the house of the Lord. Let us pray:

◆ Consume us with zeal for your holy house, O Lord.

That the Holy Father, as Bishop of Rome, may receive strength and health to persevere and lead the members of the Church to be built up into God's holy and spiritual temple, we pray: ◆ That all peoples may respect holy places of honor, and for the end of all violence and acts of desecration against what is sacred, we pray: ◆
That our church community may be built up into a holy house of God, and for all the spiritual and material needs of our parish, we pray: ◆ That all who have gone before us in death may share in the glory and joy of God's temple of heaven, we pray: ◆

Our Father . . .

Lord Jesus,
by the power of your Resurrection,
raise us to new life and gather us
together as living stones built up
into a spiritual temple for your glory.
Grant that all the days of our life
we may dwell in your holy house,
where you live and reign with the Father
in the unity of the Holy Spirit,
one God, forever and ever.
Amen.

✝ The waters of the river gladden the city of God, the holy dwelling of the Most High!

Saturday, November 10, 2012
Memorial of Saint Leo the Great,
Pope and Doctor of the Church

☦ Blessed the man who fears the Lord.

Psalm 37 *page 407*

Reading *Luke 16:9–13*

Jesus said to his disciples: "I tell you, make friends for yourselves with dishonest wealth, so that when it fails, you will be welcomed into eternal dwellings. The person who is trustworthy in very small matters is also trustworthy in great ones; and the person who is dishonest in very small matters is also dishonest in great ones. If, therefore, you are not trustworthy with dishonest wealth, who will trust you with true wealth? If you are not trustworthy with what belongs to another, who will give you what is yours? No servant can serve two masters. He will either hate one and love the other, or be devoted to one and despise the other. You cannot serve God and mammon."

Reflection

Jesus tells us that we must be faithful in both small and great matters. Our outward actions must correspond with the inner disposition of our hearts. In this way we will be Christians of integrity rather than hypocrites like the Pharisees. Today let us renew our dedication to being upright and just in the small details, and also the great matters of our lives.

Prayers ＼ *others may be added*

Lord God, you call us to a high standard of holiness. Hear our prayers as we pray:

◆ Guide us and lead us by your grace, O Lord.

For the Pope, that, through the prayers of Pope Saint Leo the Great, he may continue to guide the Church to the truth despite difficulties and challenges of the world, we pray: ◆ For all countries that suffer from war, violence, and political unrest, that, through the help of wise and holy leaders, all nations may be brought together into unity, peace, and justice, we pray: ◆ For the poor, the homeless, the ill, and those in crisis situations, that through all the small and great offerings of their sufferings, they may win for themselves and all souls an eternal crown of glory, we pray: ◆ For all who struggle within our community, that they may find help and comfort among the Christian family, we pray: ◆ For the repose of the souls of all who have died, we pray: ◆

Our Father . . .

Lord Jesus,
through the witness of your saints,
you give us an example of holiness.
By the prayers of Saint Leo the Great,
strengthen us in all difficulties
and lead us to greatness by
faithfully accomplishing your will
in the small and great events
of our daily lives.
You live and reign forever.
Amen.

☦ Blessed the man who fears the Lord.

✝ Praise the Lord, my soul!

Psalm 146   *page 423*

Reading   *Mark 12:41–44*

Jesus sat down opposite the treasury and observed how the crowd put money into the treasury. Many rich people put in large sums. A poor widow also came and put in two small coins worth a few cents. Calling his disciples to himself, he said to them, "Amen, I say to you, this poor widow put in more than all the other contributions to the treasury. For they have all contributed from their surplus wealth, but she, from her poverty, has contributed all she had, her whole livelihood."

Reflection

Sometimes we find ourselves surrounded by people who do things only that will further their success. Often times, we ourselves do things just so others will think highly of us. But in today's reading Jesus warns against vanity, and he praises the humility of the poor woman who from her poverty offers her whole livelihood to God in sincerity rather than vainglory like the scribes and Pharisees.

Prayers   *others may be added*

Gathered together as your people, we offer our prayers and petitions at the beginning of this new week, as we pray:

◆ Shine your light upon us, O Lord.

That the Holy Father may be given wisdom and counsel to make good and wise decisions for the good of all the Church throughout the world, we pray: ◆
That the leaders of nations and all political and government officials may not seek their personal advancement, but that they may seek true success through the service to the common good of all people, we pray: ◆ That each individual of our parish community may consider to offer a small or great contribution of one's time, talent, and treasures, we pray: ◆
That all who have fallen asleep in Christ may rejoice in the splendor of heaven with all the angels and saints, we pray: ◆

Our Father . . .

Heavenly Father,
free us from all vanities.
Open our hearts to seek your face
in holy worship and praise to you.
We ask this through our Lord Jesus
   Christ, your Son,
who lives and reigns with you in the unity
   of the Holy Spirit,
one God, forever and ever.
Amen.

✝ Praise the Lord, my soul!

✝ Lord, this is the people that longs to see your face.

Psalm 34　　　　　　　*page 406*

Reading　　　　　　　*Luke 17:1–6*

Jesus said to his disciples, "Things that cause sin will inevitably occur, but woe to the one through whom they occur. It would be better for him if a millstone were put around his neck and he be thrown into the sea than for him to cause one of these little ones to sin. Be on your guard! If your brother sins, rebuke him; and if he repents, forgive him. And if he wrongs you seven times in one day and returns to you seven times saying, 'I am sorry,' you should forgive him."

And the Apostles said to the Lord, "Increase our faith." The Lord replied, "If you have faith the size of a mustard seed, you would say to this mulberry tree, 'Be uprooted and planted in the sea,' and it would obey you."

Reflection

Today's reading is filled with treasures to ponder. Jesus warns us not to be a source of scandal to others, especially to the young. He then reminds us that we must constantly forgive those who have hurt us in the same way God has forgiven us of our sins. Lastly, he teaches us that if only we had a tiny amount of faith we could work miracles. Let us beg him to increase our faith.

Prayers　　　　*others may be added*

Open to receiving your word, we present to you our prayers and petitions as we pray:

◆ Lord, increase our faith.

That the Holy Father, all bishops, priests, deacons, and all lay members of the Church may always give a holy and faithful witness to the truth of their Christian faith, through good example and integrity of life, we pray: ◆ That public officials may protect and support life at all stages, from conception to natural death, we pray: ◆ That all those, especially children, who suffer because of the sins of others, may receive healing and forgiveness, we pray: ◆ That our faith community may become united in friendship and charity toward one another, we pray: ◆ That all the faithful departed may be received in God's loving glory, we pray: ◆

Our Father . . .

Great and glorious God,
all creation gives you thanks and praise.
Increase our faith in you,
that we, too, may be numbered among
the holy ones of heaven where you
live and reign with our Lord Jesus Christ,
　　your Son,
in the unity of the Holy Spirit
one God, forever and ever.
Amen.

✝ Lord, this is the people that longs to see your face.

Tuesday, November 13, 2012
Memorial of Saint Frances Xavier Cabrini, Virgin

✝ The salvation of the just comes from the Lord.

Psalm 37
page 407

Reading
Luke 17:7–10

Jesus said to the Apostles: "Who among you would say to your servant who has just come in from plowing or tending sheep in the field, 'Come here immediately and take your place at table'? Would he not rather say to him, 'Prepare something for me to eat. Put on your apron and wait on me while I eat and drink. You may eat and drink when I am finished'? Is he grateful to that servant because he did what was commanded? So should it be with you. When you have done all you have been commanded, say, 'We are unprofitable servants; we have done what we were obliged to do.'"

Reflection

We are merely God's servants. If we truly lived as humble servants of God and his people, rather than in selfishness and ingratitude, we would experience a much greater freedom in our lives. This attitude of service should permeate our lives so that at the end of the day we may humbly say that we have only done what we have been obliged to do, and in that, the Lord will be pleased with our faithfulness.

Prayers
others may be added

Coming to you as your children, Lord, we offer to your our needs and petitions in faith as we pray:

◆ Lord of mercy and compassion, hear our prayer.

For the Holy Father, as servant of the servants of God, that he may faithfully and humbly lead, guide, and serve the Church through the guidance of the Holy Spirit and the support of our prayers, we pray: ◆ For government officials and leaders of all nations, that they may humbly serve their people in justice and truth for the good of all society, we pray: ◆ For the poor, sick, suffering, homeless, marginalized, and all emigrants and prisoners, we pray: ◆ For all who have died, especially those in the military service and in war, we pray: ◆ For the grace to fulfill our daily duties and responsibilities with humility and faithfulness in service to God and others, we pray: ◆

Our Father . . .

Father Almighty,
you sent your Son as the Suffering Servant
to save the world from sin and pride.
By the prayers of Mother Cabrini,
help us to work in service to your Church
for your honor and glory.
We ask this through Christ our Lord.
Amen.

✝ The salvation of the just comes from the Lord.

✝ The Lord is my shepherd; there is nothing I shall want.

Psalm 141   *page 421*

Reading   *Luke 17:11–19*

As Jesus continued his journey to Jerusalem, he traveled through Samaria and Galilee. As he was entering a village, ten lepers met him. They stood at a distance from him and raised their voice, saying, "Jesus, Master! Have pity on us!" And when he saw them, he said, "Go show yourselves to the priests." As they were going they were cleansed. And one of them, realizing he had been healed, returned, glorifying God in a loud voice; and he fell at the feet of Jesus and thanked him. He was a Samaritan. Jesus said in reply, "Ten were cleansed, were they not? Where are the other nine? Has none but this foreigner returned to give thanks to God?" Then he said to him, "Stand up and go; your faith has saved you."

Reflection

When was the last time we thanked God for the gifts of healing that he has worked in our lives? God is constantly pouring his blessing and healing upon us through the special graces of the Holy Spirit. Do we forget that God in his providence is governing and guiding us each day? Let us not grow indifferent and ungrateful to his work, whether great or small, within our lives.

Prayers   *others may be added*

With gratitude in our hearts to God, we present to him our prayers and petitions as we pray:

◆ Open our eyes to recognize your work, O Lord.

For the Holy Father, that he may receive the strength to continue his important work of teaching, proclaiming, and leading us into closer union with the word of God, we pray: ◆ For politicians, government officials, and all world leaders, that they may do their work humbly for the service of the common good without desiring thanks, human praise, or honor, we pray: ◆ For the work of healing that God has done throughout the world this day through the hands of doctors, the use of medicine, the presence of generous Christians, and the healing power of the sacraments, we pray: ◆ For those of our community who are experiencing difficulty, may they offer to God a sacrifice of praise and thanksgiving as they await healing and resolution, we pray: ◆ For the faithful departed, for all who will die today, and for all who grieve their losses, we pray: ◆

Our Father . . .

Loving Father,
you fill our lives with blessings.
Open our eyes to see your goodness
and fill our hearts with overflowing
gratitude for your work in our lives.
We ask this through Christ our Lord.
Amen.

✝ The Lord is my shepherd; there is nothing I shall want.

Thursday, November 15, 2012
Weekday

☦ Blessed is he whose help is the God of Jacob.

Psalm 100   *page 414*

Reading   *Luke 17:20–25*

Asked by the Pharisees when the Kingdom of God would come, Jesus said in reply, "The coming of the Kingdom of God cannot be observed, and no one will announce, 'Look, here it is,' or, 'There it is.' For behold, the Kingdom of God is among you."

Then he said to his disciples, "The days will come when you will long to see one of the days of the Son of Man, but you will not see it. There will be those who will say to you, 'Look, there he is,' or 'Look, here he is.' Do not go off, do not run in pursuit. For just as lightning flashes and lights up the sky from one side to the other, so will the Son of Man be in his day. But first he must suffer greatly and be rejected by this generation."

Reflection

We can easily find ourselves falling prey to the latest fads, wanting the newest thing, or being interested in something merely because of its novelty or attractive flashy appearance. However, today Jesus tells us not to run off in pursuit of the latest trend, whether materially or spiritually related. Jesus reminds us that the coming of the kingdom of God is not something that can be seen with our eyes, but rather that the kingdom of God is already among us.

Prayers   *others may be added*

Coming together as God's family, we offer our petitions as we pray:

◆ Lord, hear the cry of the poor.

For the Pope, that he may be supported by the love and prayers of all the members of the Church, we pray: ◆ For civic and church leaders, that they may work together for the unity of all Christians and all nations, we pray: ◆ For those who are sick and suffering; for the poor, the homeless, the handicapped, and all who care for them, we pray: ◆ For our faith community, that it may be built together in love and enflamed with the gifts of the Holy Spirit to build up God's kingdom, we pray: ◆ For all the faithful departed and for the comfort of their family members and friends who mourn in sorrow, we pray: ◆

Our Father . . .

Eternal God,
in you is the source of all light,
happiness, joy, and truth.
Lead us along the path of holiness,
We ask this through our Lord Jesus
    Christ, your Son,
who lives and reigns with you in the unity
    of the Holy Spirit,
one God, forever and ever.
Amen.

☦ Blessed is he whose help is the God of Jacob.

Friday, November 16, 2012
Weekday

✝ Blessed are they who follow the law of the Lord!

Psalm 103   *page 415*

Reading   *Luke 17:26–35*

Jesus said to his disciples: "As it was in the days of Noah, so it will be in the days of the Son of Man; they were eating and drinking, marrying and giving in marriage up to the day that Noah entered the ark, and the flood came and destroyed them all. Similarly, as it was in the days of Lot: they were eating, drinking, buying, selling, planting, building; on the day when Lot left Sodom, fire and brimstone rained from the sky to destroy them all. So it will be on the day the Son of Man is revealed. On that day, someone who is on the housetop and whose belongings are in the house must not go down to get them, and likewise one in the field must not return to what was left behind. Remember the wife of Lot. Whoever seeks to preserve his life will lose it, but whoever loses it will save it. I tell you, on that night there will be two people in one bed; one will be taken, the other left. And there will be two women grinding meal together; one will be taken, the other left."

Reflection

Our Lord does not want us to be concerned with material goods that will merely perish. Nor does he want us concerned even with our worldly lives that are worth much less than the supernatural life that God has destined us to enjoy. Jesus teaches us that he who loses his life for the sake of God and others will in fact save his life, because he will find true life and salvation in what really matters.

Prayers   *others may be added*

With faith, we offer to God our prayers:

◆ Prepare our hearts for your kingdom, O God.

For the Church, we pray: ◆ For all nations, we pray: ◆ For all who suffer injury, we pray: ◆ For those who have died, we pray: ◆

Our Father . . .

Lord Jesus,
you reveal to us the greatness of your mercy by your most Sacred Heart, which burns with love for us.
Draw us ever more closely in union with your human heart so as to come ever more united
to your divine life where you dwell as one with the Father in the unity of the Holy Spirit,
one God, forever and ever.
Amen.

✝ Blessed are they who follow the law of the Lord!

✝ Blessed the man who fears the Lord.

Psalm 145   *page 422*

Reading   *Luke 18:1–8*

Jesus told his disciples a parable about the necessity for them to pray always without becoming weary. He said, "There was a judge in a certain town who neither feared God nor respected any human being. And a widow in that town used to come to him and say, 'Render a just decision for me against my adversary.' For a long time the judge was unwilling, but eventually he thought, 'While it is true that I neither fear God nor respect any human being, because this widow keeps bothering me I shall deliver a just decision for her lest she finally come and strike me.'" The Lord said, "Pay attention to what the dishonest judge says. Will not God then secure the rights of his chosen ones who call out to him day and night? Will he be slow to answer them? I tell you, he will see to it that justice is done for them speedily. But when the Son of Man comes, will he find faith on earth?"

Reflection

We know that we ought to pray, but we can easily become lazy in our commitments to God. We begin to make excuses that we are too busy, we have no time, or we tell ourselves that we will do it later. However, communion with God in prayer is the source and nourishment for our lives. Through prayer, we enter into God's own life, and we receive the strength to serve him in our daily responsibilities. Let us renew our commitment to persevere in the discipline of prayer every day.

Prayers   *others may be added*

Calling out to our Father, who always hears our prayer, we pray:

◆ **Strengthen us in faith and perseverance, O Lord.**

For the Church, filled with the breath and new life of the Holy Spirit, that she may go out to all the nations and bring the healing Good News of Christ Jesus to all peoples, we pray: ◆ For the rulers of all nations, that, through the prayers of Saint Elizabeth of Hungary, they may govern their people with justice and charity, we pray: ◆ For the healing of all the sick and suffering, the blind, deaf, handicapped, and for those who suffer spiritual blindness on account of sin, we pray: ◆ For the needs and intentions of our family and friends, and for the repose of the souls of all the faithful departed, we pray: ◆

Our Father . . .

Lord Jesus,
in your miracles we see your power
    and glory.
By the prayers of Saint Elizabeth
    of Hungary,
may we live lives of generosity, charity,
    and service
to all of those around us for the glory of
    your name.
You live and reign forever.
Amen.

✝ Blessed the man who fears the Lord.

Sunday, November 18, 2012
Thirty-third Sunday in Ordinary Time

✝ You are my inheritance, O Lord.

Psalm 139 *page 421*

Reading *Mark 13:24–32*

Jesus said to his disciples: "In those days after that tribulation the sun will be darkened, and the moon will not give its light, and the stars will be falling from the sky, and the powers in the heavens will be shaken.

"And then they will see 'the Son of Man coming in the clouds' with great power and glory, and then he will send out the angels and gather his elect from the four winds, from the end of the earth to the end of the sky."

Reflection

As we come to the end of the liturgical year, the Gospel readings reflect on the end times. Jesus warns us to be prepared and to be ready for the Second Coming, when he will come again and God will be all in all. He reminds us that all things are passing, but that his word will never pass away.

Prayers *others may be added*

With hearts and minds watchful for the day of the Lord, let us pray:

◆ Guide and preserve your people, O Lord.

For the Church, that she may be inspired by the holy lives of Saints Peter and Paul, and that they may imitate their holiness as they follow in Christ's priestly ministry, we pray: ◆ For peoples of all nations, that they may recognize the signs of the times and turn from their sins as we await the coming of the Lord, we pray: ◆ For the sick, the dying, the homeless, the handi-capped, the poor, and elderly, and all in crisis situations, that they may offer their prayers and sufferings to the Lord as they persevere in faith and hope, we pray: ◆ For our parish community, that it may not fear the day of the Lord but await the Lord's coming with joyfulness and expectation, we pray: ◆ For all who have died, especially those of our own families and friends and for all those who have no one to pray for them, we pray: ◆

Our Father . . .

Loving God,
on the last day you will send your Son among us to gather all the nations into one. Keep us faithful so that we may partake of your glory.
We ask this through Christ our Lord. Amen.

✝ You are my inheritance, O Lord.

Monday, November 19, 2012
Weekday

✝ Those who are victorious I will feed from the tree of life.

Psalm 51   *page 409*

Reading   *Luke 18:35–43*

As Jesus approached Jericho a blind man was sitting by the roadside begging, and hearing a crowd going by, he inquired what was happening. They told him, "Jesus of Nazareth is passing by." He shouted, "Jesus, Son of David, have pity on me!" The people walking in front rebuked him, telling him to be silent, but he kept calling out all the more, "Son of David, have pity on me!" Then Jesus stopped and ordered that he be brought to him; and when he came near, Jesus asked him, "What do you want me to do for you?" He replied, "Lord, please let me see." Jesus told him, "Have sight; your faith has saved you." He immediately received his sight and followed him, giving glory to God. When they saw this, all the people gave praise to God.

Reflection

If only we had eyes to see! If only we had faith to see the good and beauty that is happening as God passes among us! The man in today's Gospel asks to see. However, this man already had true sight, because he was able to truly recognize Jesus despite his physical blindness. It is ironic that we who have physical sight can often be spiritually blind to God's presence within us and in each person around us.

Prayers   *others may be added*

Calling upon God's abundant mercy and compassion, we cry out:

◆ Give us eyes to see, O Lord!

For all the members of the Church, that we may be given the gift of faith to proclaim God's word to all peoples, through the daily duties and activities of our lives, we pray: ◆ For all the citizens of our country, that we may raise our voices and cease to accept the evils of materialism, selfishness, and all anti-life practices, we pray: ◆ For those who innocently suffer abuse or hardship because of the sins of others, we pray: ◆ For all who have died, that they may be brought to the glory of the vision of God, we pray: ◆

Our Father . . .

Lord Jesus,
by your mercy and love,
free us from our sins and all that
keeps us from union with you.
Give us eyes of faith so that we may be
able to recognize your presence among us.
Do not pass us by, O Lord.
Come to heal us and save us.
You live and reign forever.
Amen.

✝ Those who are victorious I will feed from the tree of life.

Tuesday, November 20, 2012
Weekday

✝ I will seat the victor beside me on my throne.

Psalm 121   *page 419*

Reading   *Luke 19:1–10*

At that time Jesus came to Jericho and intended to pass through the town. Now a man there named Zacchaeus, who was a chief tax collector and also a wealthy man, was seeking to see who Jesus was; but he could not see him because of the crowd, for he was short in stature. So he ran ahead and climbed a sycamore tree in order to see Jesus, who was about to pass that way. When he reached the place, Jesus looked up and said, "Zacchaeus, come down quickly, for today I must stay at your house." And he came down quickly and received him with joy. When they saw this, they began to grumble, saying, "He has gone to stay at the house of a sinner." But Zacchaeus stood there and said to the Lord, "Behold, half of my possessions, Lord, I shall give to the poor, and if I have extorted anything from anyone I shall repay it four times over." And Jesus said to him, "Today salvation has come to this house because this man too is a descendant of Abraham. For the Son of Man has come to seek and to save what was lost."

Reflection

In today's Gospel, we see that Jesus comes especially for sinners. Through Zaccheus's meeting with the Lord, his heart is converted from his attachment to his riches, and he offers Jesus half of his possessions. Through this encounter with Jesus, Zaccheus receives salvation. May we, too, have the grace to continually turn to the Lord despite our sinfulness to receive his life and grace.

Prayers   *others may be added*

Lord, we present to you our prayers and petitions:

◆ O Lord, grant us your salvation.

For the Church, we pray: ◆ For government officials, we pray: ◆ For all in special need, we pray: ◆ For our families, we pray: ◆ For those who suffer, we pray: ◆ For the faithful departed, we pray: ◆

Our Father . . .

All powerful Father,
through your holy word we encounter
the mystery and power of your Son Jesus.
Convert our hearts and free us from
    our sins,
that we may rejoice in the joy of salvation.
We ask this through Christ our Lord.
Amen.

✝ I will seat the victor beside me on my throne.

✝ Holy, holy, holy Lord, mighty God!

Psalm 95 *page 413*

Reading *Luke 1:26–33*

The angel Gabriel was sent from God to a town of Galilee called Nazareth, to a virgin betrothed to a man named Joseph, of the house of David, and the virgin's name was Mary. And coming to her, he said, "Hail, full of grace! The Lord is with you." But she was greatly troubled at what was said and pondered what sort of greeting this might be. Then the angel said to her, "Do not be afraid, Mary, for you have found favor with God. Behold, you will conceive in your womb and bear a son, and you shall name him Jesus. He will be great and will be called Son of the Most High, and the Lord God will give him the throne of David his father, and he will rule over the house of Jacob forever, and of his Kingdom there will be no end."

Reflection

Today we celebrate the tradition when Mary presented herself in the temple as a young girl. We can think of the beauty of her consecration and all of the small ways in which she must have renewed this offering through the daily actions of her sinless life. Her great "yes" in accepting to be the Mother of Jesus was possible probably because of all the other small responses of "yes" she had made to God before the angel appeared to ask her to be the Mother of God.

Prayers *others may be added*

Through the hands of the Blessed Mother, we present our prayers and petitions as we pray:

◆ Hear I am Lord, I come to do your will.

For the Church, that she may remain ever sinless and holy through the intercession of Mary, the Mother of God, we pray: ◆ For the whole world to be consecrated to the Lord and protected from all evil, we pray: ◆ For all religious and all consecrated, that they may model their lives after the purity and holiness of the Blessed Virgin Mary, we pray: ◆ For the sick and suffering, that they may receive comfort and consolation from Our Lady, and that they may have the strength to hand over their pain and hardship as an offering to the Lord, we pray: ◆ For all children and all young people, that they may hear the voice of the Lord calling them to joy, generosity, and fullness of life, we pray: ◆ For the faithful departed, we pray: ◆

Our Father . . .

Heavenly Father,
you called your daughter Mary to be the Mother of God.
Through her intercession and prayers, we consecrate our lives to you and offer to you our hearts, minds, and whole beings.
Unite us to you and bring us into everlasting life.
We ask this through Christ our Lord.
Amen.

✝ Holy, holy, holy Lord, mighty God!

Thursday, November 22, 2012
Memorial of Saint Cecilia, Virgin and Martyr

✝ The Lamb has made us a kingdom of priests to serve our God.

Psalm 98   *page 413*

Reading   ·   *Luke 19:41–44*

As Jesus drew near Jerusalem, he saw the city and wept over it, saying, "If this day you only knew what makes for peace—but now it is hidden from your eyes. For the days are coming upon you when your enemies will raise a palisade against you; they will encircle you and hem you in on all sides. They will smash you to the ground and your children within you, and they will not leave one stone upon another within you because you did not recognize the time of your visitation."

Reflection

What strong words Jesus tells us today in the Gospel! We must not remain blind to the coming of Christ and his presence already among us. We see such emotion from Jesus as he weeps over the state of the city of Jerusalem. Yet, these same words are applied for us, too. We must open our eyes to see and our ears to hear, so that we may put his word into practice through the example of our lives.

Prayers   *others may be added*

Heeding the voice of the Lord, we present our prayers and petitions as we pray:

◆ We give you thanks, O Lord.

For the work and prayers of the Holy Father, that it may bear fruit in deeper wisdom, knowledge, and conversion for all the members of the Church, we pray: ◆ For all nations and cities torn apart by war, terrorism, violence, and injustice, that civic leaders and all peoples will work in service and charity to do what is necessary to make for peace, we pray: ◆ For all musicians, that their music may give glory to God and joy to others through the intercession of Saint Cecilia, we pray: ◆ For all the poor, the sick, and lonely, and for those who suffer persecution or abuse, that they may receive healing, protection, and peace, we pray: ◆ For all those who have died, and for those who grieve the emptiness and sorrow of their loss, we pray: ◆

Our Father . . .

Lord Jesus,
through the prayers of the holy virgin and martyr, Saint Cecilia, grant, we ask, that you may strengthen us in faith and give us the courage to offer all our joys and sufferings as a song of praise and thanksgiving to you. You live and reign forever. Amen.

✝ The Lamb has made us a kingdom of priests to serve our God.

Friday, November 23, 2012
Weekday

✝ How sweet to my taste is your promise!

Psalm 103 page 415

Reading Luke 19:45–48

Jesus entered the temple area and proceeded to drive out those who were selling things, saying to them, "It is written, *My house shall be a house of prayer, but you have made it a den of thieves.*" And every day he was teaching in the temple area. The chief priests, the scribes, and the leaders of the people, meanwhile, were seeking to put him to death, but they could find no way to accomplish their purpose because all the people were hanging on his words.

Reflection

How amazing it would have been to live at the same time when Jesus walked on the earth. We could see his strength and righteous anger in protecting God's holy temple as he drove out the money changers. We could hear his teaching even as the chief priests tried to find a way to kill him. Would we, too, be found in the temple, listening to him and hanging on his words? Or would we be living the same way we do now? Do we truly believe that Jesus is present to us today and continues to teach us through the Church, the scriptures, and his presence in the Eucharist?

Prayers others may be added

Loving Father, you call us deeper into a life of prayer and belief in your Son. Let us pray:

◆ Increase our faith, O Lord.

For the Church, that she may turn from all forms of sin, religious indifference, and apathy, and that she may ever strive for true holiness to build up the kingdom of God, we pray: ◆ For those who suffer sorrow or hardship, that they may be comforted by the compassion of Christ through the presence of loving friends and Christians, we pray: ◆ For all who serve in the military and active duty, we pray: ◆ For God's protection to be upon all young people and all children, we pray: ◆ For the souls of the faithful departed, especially for those who have died suddenly or by tragedy, we pray: ◆

Our Father . . .

God of justice and mercy,
you give us hope in your Son Jesus.
Through the intercession of all your saints,
free us from sin and protect us from all evil
as we seek to follow you and live out your
    commands.
We ask this through Christ our Lord.
Amen.

✝ How sweet to my taste is your promise!

Saturday, November 24, 2012
Memorial of the Martyrs of Vietnam

✝ Blessed be the Lord, my Rock!

Psalm 86
page 412

Reading
Luke 20:27–36

Some Sadducees, those who deny that there is a resurrection, came forward and put this question to Jesus, saying, "Teacher, Moses wrote for us, *If someone's brother dies leaving a wife but no child, his brother must take the wife and raise up descendants for his brother.* Now there were seven brothers; the first married a woman but died childless. Then the second and the third married her, and likewise all the seven died childless. Finally the woman also died. Now at the resurrection whose wife will that woman be? For all seven had been married to her." Jesus said to them, "The children of this age marry and remarry; but those who are deemed worthy to attain to the coming age and to the resurrection of the dead neither marry nor are given in marriage. They can no longer die, for they are like angels; and they are the children of God because they are the ones who will rise."

Reflection

The Sadducees try to find fault with Jesus regarding the teaching on the resurrection of the dead. Jesus demonstrates a sort of apologetics as he brings new understanding and light to God's mystery by referencing the Law of Moses, Abraham, and Isaac. The people are silenced at his words and his ability to teach and instruct. Let us listen to Christ the Teacher ever more attentively and follow after his example.

Prayers
others may be added

You are not a God of the dead, but of the living. Hear our prayers as we pray:

◆ Raise us to new life, O Lord.

For the Church, we pray: ◆ For peoples of all nations, we pray: ◆ For the sick and the suffering, we pray: ◆ For all who are persecuted, we pray: ◆ For all who have died, and for all who grieve, we pray: ◆

Our Father . . .

God of all the living,
by your word, you teach and instruct us
along the path of righteousness.
Give us a living faith so we may not
succumb to discouragement or despair,
but rather rise up in the life of your Son.
We ask this through Christ our Lord.
Amen.

✝ Blessed be the Lord, my Rock!

Sunday, November 25, 2012

Solemnity of Our Lord Jesus Christ, King of the Universe

Thirty-fourth or Last Sunday in Ordinary Time

✝ The Lord is king; he is robed in majesty.

Psalm 19 *page 403*

Reading *John 18:33b–37*

Pilate said to Jesus, "Are you the King of the Jews?" Jesus answered, "Do you say this on your own or have others told you about me?" Pilate answered, "I am not a Jew, am I? Your own nation and the chief priests handed you over to me. What have you done?" Jesus answered, "My kingdom does not belong to this world. If my kingdom did belong to this world, my attendants would be fighting to keep me from being handed over to the Jews. But as it is, my kingdom is not here." So Pilate said to him, "Then you are a king?" Jesus answered, "You say I am a king. For this I was born and for this I came into the world, to testify to the truth. Everyone who belongs to the truth listens to my voice."

Reflection

Today, on this Last Sunday of Ordinary Time, we celebrate the solemnity of Jesus Christ, King of the Universe. Jesus' kingship is unlike other kings and rulers, for in today's Gospel we hear Jesus tell Pilate that his kingdom is not of this world. Jesus reveals the unique mystery of his kingship most fully on the cross as he pours out of himself for the salvation of all souls whom he desires to draw into the glory, joy, and life of his kingdom.

Prayers *others may be added*

Approaching your throne in worship and adoration as your humble servants, let us pray:

◆ Christ, our King, hear our prayer.

For all who serve the Church, we pray: ◆ For the rulers of all nations, that they may rule and govern their people in justice and truth, we pray: ◆ For all who are ill, for those who endure poverty and want, despair and doubt; and all the suffering, that Christ, our compassionate and just King, may hear their prayers for mercy, we pray: ◆ For each of us to use our gifts and talents to be faithful and diligent servants to build up the Body of Christ and further God's kingdom, we pray: ◆ For all those who have died, that they may rejoice forever with the saints and angels around the heavenly throne, we pray: ◆

Our Father . . .

Lord Jesus Christ,
We bless you and honor you,
for you are the King of kings and Lord
 of lords.
May your reign extend over all earth.
Draw us into your holy kingdom,
that, with one voice, all peoples may
 praise your blessed name.
You live and reign forever.
Amen.

✝ The Lord is king; he is robed in majesty.

✝ Lord, this is the people that longs to see your face.

Psalm 141   *page 421*

Reading   *Luke 21:1–4*

When Jesus looked up he saw some wealthy people putting their offerings into the treasury and he noticed a poor widow putting in two small coins. He said, "I tell you truly, this poor widow put in more than all the rest; for those others have all made offerings from their surplus wealth, but she, from her poverty, has offered her whole livelihood."

Reflection

Sometimes we fail to give of ourselves, because we don't think that what we have is enough. However, the Gospel is full of examples in which Jesus blesses the little, the weak, and the poor for their simple and humble offerings. We need to be humble enough to offer the little of who we are and what we have in faith in Christ Jesus who transforms our weakness and littleness into greatness and power.

Prayers   *others may be added*

Looking forward to your coming, we present to you our prayers and petitions as we pray:

◆ Transform us in your love, O Lord.

For the Church, that she may grow and extend throughout all the world through the humble service of the Pope, priests, and all the lay faithful, we pray: ◆ For the end of war, violence, and all anti-life practices, that all cultures may be renewed by the power and life of the Spirit, we pray: ◆ For the poor, the suffering, the needy, the ill, the homeless, the imprisoned, and the unemployed, that their needs may be an opportunity to come to the Lord so that he may transform their poverty into blessing, we pray: ◆ For diligence and perseverance today as we return to another week of work and service to the Lord and one another, we pray: ◆

Our Father . . .

Loving Jesus,
look with kindness upon us
in our poverty and weakness.
Heal us from our sins and give us
the strength and courage to persevere
as we strive to offer ourselves to you
by the help of your grace.
You live and reign forever.
Amen.

✝ Lord, this is the people that longs to see your face.

Tuesday, November 27, 2012
Weekday

✝ The Lord comes to judge the earth.

Psalm 23   *page 404*

Reading   *Luke 21:5–9*

While some people were speaking about how the temple was adorned with costly stones and votive offerings, Jesus said, "All that you see here—the days will come when there will not be left a stone upon another stone that will not be thrown down."

Then they asked him, "Teacher, when will this happen? And what sign will there be when all these things are about to happen?" He answered, "See that you not be deceived, for many will come in my name, saying, 'I am he,' and 'The time has come.' Do not follow them! When you hear of wars and insurrections, do not be terrified; for such things must happen first, but it will not immediately be the end."

Reflection

This week is the last week of the Church's liturgical year, and so we hear Gospel passages about when Jesus will come again at the end times. Jesus teaches us that we must not fear nor be terrified, not even when wars or disasters occur. We also must not be swayed by people who will be carried away by fanciful ideas, proclaiming that the end has come. Rather, our eyes must be set on heaven and to the truth, joy, and beauty of Jesus' coming in glory.

Prayers   *others may be added*

Jesus you are teacher and king of all the nations. Let us pray:

◆ Christ the King, come in your glory!

For the Pope, all priests, deacons, and the lay faithful, that they may help one another through the support of their prayers and service as they work to spread the Good News of Jesus Christ throughout the world, we pray: ◆ For the end of all wars, violence, and terrorism, for all nations that suffer political unrest and insecurity, that civic leaders may work to bring about justice and peace through dialogue and conflict resolution, we pray: ◆ For all who suffer loss, injury, or death from natural disasters, we pray: ◆ For the light of Christ to shine upon all the sick, the lonely, and the homebound, we pray: ◆ For all the faithful departed, and for those who grieve their loss, that, at the final resurrection, we may be reunited with all our loved ones who have gone before us from death into life, we pray: ◆

Our Father . . .

Lord Jesus,
your word is delight to our souls.
Give us courage and strength to
follow after you with faith and give us
strength not to be swayed by the fleeting
goods of this world, but rather to await
your coming in hope and expectation.
You live and reign forever.
Amen.

✝ The Lord comes to judge the earth.

Wednesday, November 28, 2012
Weekday

✝ Great and wonderful are all your works, Lord, mighty God!

Psalm 86 *page 412*

Reading *Luke 21:12–19*

Jesus said to the crowd: "They will seize and persecute you, they will hand you over to the synagogues and to prisons, and they will have you led before kings and governors because of my name. It will lead to your giving testimony. Remember, you are not to prepare your defense beforehand, for I myself shall give you a wisdom in speaking that all your adversaries will be powerless to resist or refute. You will even be handed over by parents, brothers, relatives, and friends, and they will put some of you to death. You will be hated by all because of my name, but not a hair on your head will be destroyed. By your perseverance you will secure your lives."

Reflection

Jesus doesn't deny that others may hate us for living for God and adhering to our Christian faith. He even says that we will be persecuted by our family members and those closest to us. However, we should not fear these moments, because they will be opportunities for us to offer witness and testimony. God will be present and give us wisdom and the words to speak at the precise moment. Ultimately, God will keep us safe, and our perseverance will lead to our salvation as well the salvation of others.

Prayers *others may be added*

With faith and confidence in the power of your name, we pray:

◆ Lord Jesus, hear our prayer.

For the Church, that she may remain ever steadfast against the trials and persecutions of the world, and that she may always give holy and pure witness to the power of Christ's name, we pray: ◆ For all people who are persecuted for the faith, we pray: ◆ For all missionaries that work to spread the Good News of salvation throughout the world, we pray: ◆ For all teachers, youth ministers, catechists, and all who instruct others in the faith, that they may be given wisdom and fortitude, we pray: ◆ For all the poor, the sick, all prisoners, and those who suffer injustice, we pray: ◆ For all who have died, especially for those who have given their lives in witness to Christ and service to others, we pray: ◆

Our Father . . .

All powerful and ever-loving God,
fill us with the life of your Spirit,
that we may live in freedom,
free from all fear of suffering.
You are ever present to us and instruct us
how to endure all trials with
perseverance.
Keep us close to you and bless us with
your grace.
Grant this through Christ our Lord.
Amen.

✝ Great and wonderful are all your works, Lord, mighty God!

✝ Blessed are they who are called to the wedding feast of the Lamb.

Psalm 95 *page 413*

Reading *Luke 21:25–28*

[Jesus said to his disciples:] "There will be signs in the sun, the moon, and the stars, and on earth nations will be in dismay, perplexed by the roaring of the sea and the waves. People will die of fright in anticipation of what is coming upon the world, for the powers of the heavens will be shaken. And then they will see the Son of Man coming in a cloud with power and great glory. But when these signs begin to happen, stand erect and raise your heads because your redemption is at hand."

Reflection

The Gospel readings about the end times can sometimes be frightening. However, Jesus speaks to us so that we may be prepared. We must not grow indifferent and apathetic to the evils of sin. Instead of waiting in fear, we should anticipate the day of the Lord with expectation for that will be the day in which Christ returns in glory and the faithful will receive the reward of redemption.

Prayers *others may be added*

With expectant hearts, let us pray:

◆ Lord, we long to see your face.

For the Pope, that he may guide and encourage the members of the Mystical Body of Christ with perseverance until the day of the Lord, we pray: ◆ For all nations, that they may turn to God and recognize his presence and his coming, we pray: ◆ For all who suffer the evils of war, persecution, and abuse, we pray: ◆ For the conversion of all criminals and perpetrators, that all may be brought into unity and true and lasting peace, we pray: ◆ For all those who have died, that they may be brought into the eternal beatitude of union with God, we pray: ◆

Our Father . . .

Lord Jesus,
come and visit your people.
Give us strength and perseverance
to endure all the trials of this
age so that we may be found worthy
to enter into your heavenly kingdom
when you come again in your glory.
You live and reign forever.
Amen.

✝ Blessed are they who are called to the wedding feast of the Lamb.

Friday, November 30, 2012
Feast of Saint Andrew, Apostle

✝ The judgments of the Lord are true, and all of them are just.

Psalm 91 *page 412*

Reading *Matthew 4:18–22*

As Jesus was walking by the Sea of Galilee, he saw two brothers, Simon who is called Peter, and his brother Andrew, casting a net into the sea; they were fishermen. He said to them, "Come after me, and I will make you fishers of men." At once they left their nets and followed him. He walked along from there and saw two other brothers, James, the son of Zebedee, and his brother John. They were in a boat, with their father Zebedee, mending their nets. He called them, and immediately they left their boat and their father and followed him.

Reflection

Today we celebrate the feast of the apostle and martyr Saint Andrew, brother to Simon Peter. In today's reading, we hear how Jesus called Peter and Andrew to come and follow him while they were performing their trade as fishermen. May we abandon our own and give our lives to the Lord with the same immediacy and faithfulness of the apostles.

Prayers *others may be added*

Lord God, you invite us to follow after you. Let us pray:

◆ Hear I am, Lord; I come to do your will.

For the Pope, and all who serve the Church, that they may be renewed in their priestly ministry to lay down their lives in service in the Church by the prayers and example of the holy apostles, we pray: ◆ For people of all nations, that they may turn to the Lord and heed his word through the example and witness of holy men and women throughout the world, we pray: ◆ For all who suffer illness and infirmity, for those in hospitals and nursing homes and for all who care for them, and for the poor and all those who cannot afford proper medical care, we pray: ◆ For the grace to cast off all the entanglements of sin and to follow after the Master's call with abandon, we pray: ◆

Our Father . . .

Lord Jesus,
you call us to be your faithful disciples
and to faithfully follow after you.
Through the prayers and intercession
of the holy apostle Saint Andrew,
help us by your grace to hear your word
and put it into practice in our lives.
We ask this through Christ our Lord.
Amen.

✝ The judgments of the Lord are true, and all of them are just.

✝ The judgments of the Lord are true, and all of them are just.

Psalm 51 *page 409*

Reading *Luke 21:34–36*

Jesus said to his disciples: "Beware that your hearts do not become drowsy from carousing and drunkenness and the anxieties of daily life, and that day catch you by surprise like a trap. For that day will assault everyone who lives on the face of the earth. Be vigilant at all times and pray that you have the strength to escape the tribulations that are imminent and to stand before the Son of Man."

Reflection

It is so easy to become weighed down by all the anxieties of life. These anxieties can cause us to fall into discouragement and despondency, or sometimes make us want to fill our hearts with vanities and pleasures of the world. However, today Jesus tells us to remain vigilant so that the day of his coming does not come by surprise, and so we are not caught in laziness or weariness from life's cares.

Prayers *others may be added*

Lord God, we come before your throne placing all of our cares, worries, and concerns at your feet as we pray:

◆ You are God; by your power, hear our prayer.

For all the members of the Church, that they may remain steadfast and vigilant as we enter into Advent in preparation for the day of the Lord, we pray: ◆ For civic authorities to do all they can to protect their citizens and support and uphold the common good, we pray: ◆ For all those who are weighed down by worry, depression, loss, and illness, that the burdens they carry may be lifted by the healing power of Jesus through the sacraments and through the presence and care of friends and generous Christians, we pray: ◆ For all who suffer from drug addiction and alcoholism, and for their family members and friends, that they may receive healing and freedom, we pray: ◆ For the repose of the souls of all who have died, we pray: ◆

Our Father . . .

All powerful God,
give us the grace to stand firm
against all temptations to sin and evil.
Fill us with perseverance so that
by your grace we may enter
    your heavenly
kingdom when your Son comes again.
We ask this through Christ our Lord.
Amen.

✝ The judgments of the Lord are true, and all of them are just.

✝ Marana tha! Come Lord Jesus!

Psalm 33　　　　　　　　page 406

Reading　　　　　　　　Luke 21:25–28

Jesus said to his disciples: "There will be signs in the sun, the moon, and the stars, and on earth nations will be in dismay, perplexed by the roaring of the sea and the waves. People will die of fright in anticipation of what is coming upon the world, for the powers of the heavens will be shaken. And then they will see the Son of Man coming in a cloud with power and great glory. But when these signs begin to happen, stand erect and raise your heads because your redemption is at hand."

Reflection　　　　Graziano Marcheschi

The dire images the Lectionary puts before us during Advent are quite intentional. As the year winds down, we contemplate the end of all things and the awe-inspiring circumstances that will mark that time. But while fear is an element of awe, Jesus tells us not to be afraid. Indeed, the end will come, and days of sorrow will come upon the earth. And, indeed, the time of judgment will follow. When the Son of Man returns, some, no doubt, will run in terror. But those who have clung to Christ have nothing to dread. Those who belong to him will stand tall, for when they see his face, they will be looking at the one who is their Savior.

Prayers　　　　　others may be added

As we enter this holy time of prayer and preparation, we pray:

◆ Come, Lord Jesus, hear our prayer.

That the members of the whole Church may abound in grace as we recall the mystery of the Incarnation and await Christ's Second Coming in glory, we pray: ◆ That all nations may turn to recognize Christ, the Word made Flesh, who comes to make his dwelling among us, we pray: ◆ That the sick and suffering may receive the comfort and proper care they need as they persevere in patience and await healing, we pray: ◆ That our faith community may use this time of preparation to turn from our sins through more frequent reception of the sacraments, we pray: ◆ That all may be given the grace not to give in to the temptations of worry and anxiety, we pray: ◆

Our Father . . .

Heavenly Father,
with joy and expectation, we prepare
for the coming of your Son Jesus.
Give us strength and perseverance
to ward off all temptations
of fear, anxiety, and indifference
as we await the coming of your Son
　　in glory,
who lives and reigns together with you in
　　the unity of the Holy Spirit,
one God, forever and ever.
Amen.

✝ Marana tha! Come Lord Jesus!

✝ Let us go rejoicing to the house of the Lord.

Psalm 25 *page 405*

Reading *Matthew 8:5–11*

When Jesus entered Capernaum, a centurion approached him and appealed to him, saying, "Lord, my servant is lying at home paralyzed, suffering dreadfully." He said to him, "I will come and cure him." The centurion said in reply, "Lord, I am not worthy to have you enter under my roof; only say the word and my servant will be healed. For I too am a man subject to authority, with soldiers subject to me. And I say to one, 'Go,' and he goes; and to another, 'Come here,' and he comes; and to my slave, 'Do this,' and he does it." When Jesus heard this, he was amazed and said to those following him, "Amen, I say to you, in no one in Israel have I found such faith. I say to you, many will come from the east and the west, and will recline with Abraham, Isaac, and Jacob at the banquet in the Kingdom of heaven."

Reflection

Today we honor Saint Francis Xavier, the great Jesuit missionary from Spain who followed the Lord's call to go to the lands of China, Japan, and all around the Orient preaching the Good News of Christ. By his preaching, his example, and his vast missionary work, many people converted, and he baptized thousands of people into the faith. His life is an inspiration and witness to passionately live the call of the Lord with dynamic faith and zealous evangelization regardless of our state of life.

Prayers *others may be added*

Inspired by the example of the saints, we call upon God in prayer as we say:

◆ Consume our hearts with zeal for you, O Lord.

That the Church may work to evangelize all the nations to bring about faith and salvation in Jesus Christ, we pray: ◆ That all missionaries and those involved in apostolic works may faithfully be Christ's hands and feet to bring the Good News to those who yearn for his word of truth and life, we pray: ◆ For all the sick, the disabled, those who have suffered injury, and all those in need of Christ's healing touch, we pray: ◆ That the Lord will increase in us the gift of faith during this Advent season, we pray: ◆ That all who have died may be brought into eternal salvation in heaven, we pray: ◆

Our Father . . .

Lord Jesus,
Through the prayers of Saint
    Francis Xavier,
fill us with your Spirit and urge us on
by love for you to go out to preach
your word through our words and example.
We ask this through Christ our Lord.
Amen.

✝ Let us go rejoicing to the house of the Lord.

Tuesday, December 4, 2012
Advent Weekday

✝ Justice shall flourish in his time, and fullness of peace for ever.

Psalm 1
page 402

Reading
Luke 10:21–24

Jesus rejoiced in the Holy Spirit and said, "I give you praise, Father, Lord of heaven and earth, for although you have hidden these things from the wise and the learned you have revealed them to the childlike. Yes, Father, such has been your gracious will. All things have been handed over to me by my Father. No one knows who the Son is except the Father, and who the Father is except the Son and anyone to whom the Son wishes to reveal him."

Turning to the disciples in private he said, "Blessed are the eyes that see what you see. For I say to you, many prophets and kings desired to see what you see, but did not see it, and to hear what you hear, but did not hear it."

Reflection

In today's Gospel we see the union of the Trinity as Jesus rejoices in the Holy Spirit as he gives praise to the Father. Jesus blesses the Father for revealing God's greatest mysteries to the humble, simple, and childlike. During Advent, we meditate on the greatest mystery of the Incarnation that Jesus himself, Wisdom Incarnate, was born as a little child to bring us life and freedom.

Prayers
others may be added

Coming together as God's little children, we present our needs to the Father as we pray:

◆ **Reveal your mysteries to us, O God.**

That the Church may always remain humble, and that she may learn true wisdom from the mysteries of Christ's Incarnation and sacrifice on the cross, we pray: ◆ That the eyes and ears of the rulers of all nations may be opened to see and hear the revelation and joy of Christ's mystery, we pray: ◆ That the poor, homeless, abandoned, uneducated, the sick, and all who are burdened with the cares of life may receive God's infinite wisdom and love through their weakness and suffering, we pray: ◆ That we may be brought ever more deeply into union with the Father, and that we may know and obey his gracious will, we pray: ◆

Our Father . . .

Lord Jesus Christ,
reveal to us the mystery of your life.
Bring us ever more deeply
into the Trinitarian union of life and love
that you share with your Father
in the unity of the Holy Spirit,
one God, forever and ever.
Amen.

✝ Justice shall flourish in his time, and fullness of peace for ever.

✝ Behold, our Lord shall come with power: he will enlighten the eyes of his servants.

Psalm 25 *page 405*

Reading *Matthew 15:29–37*

At that time, Jesus walked by the Sea of Galilee, went up the mountain, and sat down there. Great crowds came to him, having with them the lame, the blind, the deformed, the mute, and many others. They placed them at his feet, and he cured them. The crowds were amazed when they saw the mute speaking, the deformed made whole, the lame walking, and the blind able to see, and they glorified the God of Israel.

Jesus summoned his disciples and said, "My heart is moved with pity for the crowd, for they have been with me now for three days and have nothing to eat. I do not want to send them away hungry, for fear they may collapse along the way." The disciples said to him, "Where could we ever get enough bread in this deserted place to satisfy such a crowd?" Jesus said to them, "How many loaves do you have?" "Seven," they replied, "and a few fish." He ordered the crowd to sit down on the ground. Then he took the seven loaves and the fish, gave thanks, broke the loaves, and gave them to the disciples, who in turn gave them to the crowds. They all ate and were satisfied. They picked up the fragments left over—seven baskets full.

Reflection

Jesus is in the midst of the blind, the lame, the deformed, and all forms of disability. Jesus is not afraid of our weaknesses and deformities. He has come among us to heal us from our spiritual deformities of sin but also to care for all our other physical needs. We learn this today in the Gospel as Jesus heals the sick and miraculously feeds the thousands of people gathered to hear his word.

Prayers *others may be added*

Gathered to hear your word, we pray:

♦ Heal us, Lord, and make us whole.

For the Holy Father, that he may continue to guide and instruct God's faithful Church along the path of holiness, we pray: ♦ For civic authorities to seek ways to help the most helpless and vulnerable of society, we pray: ♦ For all the sick, we pray: ♦ For all people throughout the world, that they may receive healing, we pray: ♦

Our Father . . .

Heavenly Father,
free us from our sins and
heal us from all our ills.
Send your Holy Spirit upon us to open
our hearts to receive the gift of your Son
as we wait and prepare for his coming.
We ask this through Christ our Lord.
Amen.

✝ Behold, our Lord shall come with power: he will enlighten the eyes of his servants.

✝ Blessed is he who comes in the name of the Lord.

Psalm 37 page 407

Reading Matthew 7:21, 24–27

Jesus said to his disciples: "Not everyone who says to me, 'Lord, Lord,' will enter the Kingdom of heaven, but only the one who does the will of my Father in heaven.

"Everyone who listens to these words of mine and acts on them will be like a wise man who built his house on rock. The rain fell, the floods came, and the winds blew and buffeted the house. But it did not collapse; it had been set solidly on rock. And everyone who listens to these words of mine but does not act on them will be like a fool who built his house on sand. The rains fell, the floods came, and the winds blew and buffeted the house. And it collapsed and was completely ruined."

Reflection Graziano Marcheschi

As we continue through Advent, we keep our end-times focus and consider what it takes to be ready for Christ's return. On that day, knowing the right words to say won't be enough, Jesus tells us. It will be our lives that will be judged. Our *actions* build the foundation on which stands the building of our lives. It can be made of rock or sand, and whether we heed Christ's words determines which one we build upon. Saint Nicholas was known for the kind of self-sacrificing generosity that constitutes a firm foundation.

Prayers others may be added

With joy and expectation for your coming, let us pray:

◆ Hear the prayers of your children, Lord.

For the Holy Father, the Bishop of Rome, and all bishops and priests, that they may perform their duties and responsibilities with the love of Jesus Christ in service to all of God's people, we pray: ◆ For government officials to re-establish peace and justice through all the nations, we pray: ◆ For all the poor, and those who are unable to afford the basic necessities of life, that God may care for their every need through the generosity and aid of faithful Christians, we pray: ◆ For all children, that they may be blessed by God and that they may receive the security, love, and protection they need from their parents and brothers and sisters to grow and develop in joy and holiness, we pray: ◆ For the grace to live lives of faith built on the solid foundation of the teaching of God's holy word, we pray: ◆

Our Father . . .

Lord Jesus,
we look to the day when you will
come again.
By the prayers of Saint Nicholas,
prepare our hearts and teach us how
to fulfill
your Father's will in faith and
generous love.
We ask this through Christ our Lord.
Amen.

✝ Blessed is he who comes in the name of the Lord.

✝ The Lord is my light and my salvation.

Psalm 25   *page 405*

Reading   *Matthew 9:27–31*

As Jesus passed by, two blind men followed him, crying out, "Son of David, have pity on us!" When he entered the house, the blind men approached him and Jesus said to them, "Do you believe that I can do this?" "Yes, Lord," they said to him. Then he touched their eyes and said, "Let it be done for you according to your faith." And their eyes were opened. Jesus warned them sternly, "See that no one knows about this." But they went out and spread word of him through all that land.

Reflection

During Advent, we have the opportunity to return to the Lord through prayer and penance. In this holy time, we are encouraged to prepare our hearts for the celebration of the mystery of Christ's Incarnation. We can more fully enter this holy time by meditating on Christ's word, through frequent participation at Mass and confession, apostolic works, and the offering of little sacrifices that help prepare a place in our hearts for the coming of the Christ child.

Prayers   *others may be added*

Begging the Father to send us the gift of his Son, we cry out:

◆ Son of David, have pity on us.

For the Holy Father, that he may be inspired with wisdom and counsel as he serves the people of God, and that he may be supported by the love and prayers of all the faithful of the Church, we pray: ◆ For our government officials and all who work in the legislature, that they may protect and defend life at all stages and work to establish justice, security, and peace among the nations, we pray: ◆ For all the homeless who suffer the cold of these winter months, we pray: ◆ For all the sick, that they may receive healing and comfort, and for the physicians and their loved ones who care for them, we pray: ◆ For the intentions of our family and friends, especially those undergoing hardship or loss, we pray: ◆

Our Father . . .

Son of David,
turn your face to us;
shine the light of your countenance
    upon us.
Through the prayers of Saint Ambrose,
illuminate our hearts and open our eyes
to see you in the beauty of your creation
and to serve you in the presence of
    our neighbor.
We ask this through Christ our Lord.
Amen.

✝ The Lord is my light and my salvation.

Saturday, December 8, 2012

Solemnity of the Immaculate Conception
of the Blessed Virgin Mary

✝ Sing to the Lord a new song.

Psalm 85 *page 411*

Reading *Luke 1:26–33*

The angel Gabriel was sent from God
to a town of Galilee called Nazareth, to
a virgin betrothed to a man named
Joseph, of the house of David, and the
virgin's name was Mary. And coming
to her, he said, "Hail, favored one! The
Lord is with you." But she was greatly
troubled at what was said and pondered
what sort of greeting this might be.
Then the angel said to her, "Do not be
afraid, Mary, for you have found favor
with God. Behold, you will conceive in
your womb and bear a son, and you
shall name him Jesus. He will be great
and will be called Son of the Most High,
and the Lord God will give him the
throne of David his father, and he will
rule over the house of Jacob forever, and
of his Kingdom there will be no end."

Reflection *Graziano Marcheschi*

Obviously, Mary didn't know that she
was "favored," born without the stain
of sin, and destined to be mother of
God's son. So the angel's greeting overwhelms her and fills her with confusion.
The angel has to calm and reassure her
that she is favored. Though she lacks
the clarity with which heaven observes
this event, she will embrace the angel's
message and destiny. It's quite appropriate that we celebrate Mary's feast in
Advent, the season she made possible
with her "yes."

Prayers *others may be added*

Through the intercession of Mary
Immaculate, we present our needs
and petitions as we pray:

◆ Preserve us in your grace, O Lord.

For the Church, that she may ever remain
the holy and spotless Bride of Christ,
we pray: ◆ For all nations and lands,
that they may turn away from sin and
evil and come to know the light of truth
in Christ Jesus, we pray: ◆ For all who
suffer doubt, uncertainty, worry, mental
illness, or anxiety, that they may be
freed to enjoy the peace Christ gives,
we pray: ◆ For all expectant mothers
awaiting the birth of newborn children,
and for all families, especially those who
suffer hardship, separation, or crisis at
this time, we pray: ◆ For the grace of
openness and receptivity to God's word,
and that we may respond in love like
Mary to God's perfect and holy will,
we pray: ◆

Our Father . . .

Good and gracious Father,
you preserved your daughter Mary
    from sin.
Grant, we ask, that we too may be freed
    from the stain of all sin,
and that we may live in freedom and
    purity to one day enjoy
the glories of heaven with you,
who live and reign with your Son,
    Jesus Christ,
in the unity of the Holy Spirit,
one God, forever and ever.
Amen.

✝ Sing to the Lord a new song.

✝ Those who follow you, Lord, will have the light of life.

Psalm 1 — page 402

Reading — Luke 3:3–6

John went throughout the whole region of the Jordan proclaiming a baptism of repentance for the forgiveness of sins, as it is written in the book of the words of the prophet Isaiah: / *A voice of one in the desert: / "Prepare the way of the Lord, / make straight his paths. / Every valley shall be filled / and every mountain and hill shall be made low. / The winding roads shall be made straight, / and the rough ways made smooth, / and all flesh shall see the salvation of God."*

Reflection

On this Second Sunday of Advent, we hear about John the Baptist, the forerunner and prophet who announces the coming of Jesus the Messiah. In this holy time, we are called to make a clear and straight path for the Lord to enter our hearts. Through our prayers and sacrifices, may we prepare the way of the Lord so that we may be ready for the Lord's coming this Christmas and each day in which we encounter him in the Eucharist.

Prayers — others may be added

With repentant and contrite hearts, we offer to you our prayers and petitions as we pray:

◆ Prepare our hearts, O Lord.

For the Holy Father, that he may be given light, guidance, health, and strength to lead the universal Church along the path of salvation, we pray: ◆ For the end of all war, division, and evil, that civic authorities may dialogue to discover means to end all conflict and discord, we pray: ◆ For all the sick, injured, handicapped, the elderly, and those who are suffering in a particular way this season, that the offering of their sufferings may help to prepare the way of the Lord and straighten his paths, we pray: ◆ For all those who grieve the loss of loved ones and friends, that their tears may be turned into cries of joy, we pray: ◆ For our faith community, that they may be inspired by the example of John the Baptist to proclaim the glory of the coming of Jesus Christ, we pray: ◆

Our Father . . .

Heavenly Father,
you sent your Son among us,
born of a woman, to be our Messiah.
Open our ears to hear your word
and our eyes to recognize your coming,
that all flesh may see the salvation of God.
We ask this through Christ our Lord.
Amen.

✝ Those who follow you, Lord, will have the light of life.

Monday, December 10, 2012
Advent Weekday

✝ Lord, make us turn to you.

Psalm 37
page 407

Reading
Luke 5:17–20

One day as Jesus was teaching, Pharisees and teachers of the law, who had come from every village of Galilee and Judea and Jerusalem, were sitting there, and the power of the Lord was with him for healing. And some men brought on a stretcher a man who was paralyzed; they were trying to bring him in and set him in his presence. But not finding a way to bring him in because of the crowd, they went up on the roof and lowered him on the stretcher through the tiles into the middle in front of Jesus. When Jesus saw their faith, he said, "As for you, your sins are forgiven."

Reflection

Our God has come to save us. This is the great mystery we celebrate as we wait and prepare for the celebration of the Incarnation this Christmas. God has not left us orphans. He has not abandoned us in the helplessness of our sins, but rather he has come to us as a little child to heal us from every physical and spiritual ailment. Like those in today's Gospel, let us also glorify God and proclaim the incredible things he has done for us.

Prayers
others may be added

While we were sinners, you came to save us. Let us pray:

◆ **Come and heal us, O Lord.**

For all the members of the Church, that they may recognize God's work of healing in their lives and proclaim his goodness so that all peoples may come to know the Lord and his glory, we pray: ◆ For missionaries, social workers, religious, and lay Christian men and women, that they may be called to serve the human and social needs of society, we pray: ◆ For all who await God's healing touch, that the perseverance in their sufferings may gain them an eternal crown of glory, we pray: ◆ For all those who are seeking employment, experiencing family difficulties, or undergoing transitions and changes at this time, we pray: ◆ For all who have fallen asleep in Christ, that they may rejoice forever in the eternal rest and glory of heaven, we pray: ◆

Our Father . . .

Loving God,
you sent your Son among us
to free us from our sins and heal us from
　　all our ills.
Send your Spirit upon us
to prepare our hearts to receive you.
We ask this through Jesus Christ,
our Lord, who lives and reigns with you
in the unity of the Holy Spirit,
one God, forever and ever.
Amen.

✝ Lord, make us turn to you.

✝ Come, Lord Jesus, come!

Psalm 23 *page 404*

Reading *Matthew 18:12–14*

Jesus said to his disciples: "What is your opinion? If a man has a hundred sheep and one of them goes astray, will he not leave the ninety-nine in the hills and go in search of the stray? And if he finds it, amen, I say to you, he rejoices more over it than over the ninety-nine that did not stray. In just the same way, it is not the will of your heavenly Father that one of these little ones be lost."

Reflection

Because it is not the will of the Father that any of his little ones be lost, the Father sent his only Son to be born among us as a little child. Through the Incarnation, God seeks us, his flock, so that we might return to relationship with him. All of heaven rejoices with him as the angels sing news of glad tidings and shout, "Glory to God in the highest, / and on earth peace to people of good will."

Prayers *others may be added*

Loving God, hear the prayers of us, the little lambs of your flock, as we pray:

◆ Good Shepherd, hear our prayer.

That during Advent, the Church may lovingly welcome all people and all fallen away Catholics to return to the flock of the Church around the eucharistic table of the Good Shepherd, we pray: ◆ That missionaries, priests, religious, and lay men and women may imitate the example of the Lord to seek out the lost and abandoned of society, we pray: ◆ That all who suffer abandonment, hardship, loss, sickness, and poverty be greeted by the Good Shepherd in their weakness and trials, and be given peace and healing, we pray: ◆ That our parish community may be given the strength to endure their crosses with fortitude and faith, we pray: ◆

Our Father . . .

God our Father,
by the Incarnation, you sent your Son, the
   Good Shepherd,
to seek out all who are lost.
By the power of your Spirit,
open our hearts
to receive the healing and loving touch
of the Christ child, who lives and reigns
   with you in the unity of the Holy Spirit,
one God, forever and ever.
Amen.

✝ Come, Lord Jesus, come!

✝ My soul rejoices in my God.

Psalm 85
page 411

Reading
Luke 1:39–46

Mary set out and traveled to the hill country in haste to a town of Judah, where she entered the house of Zechariah and greeted Elizabeth. When Elizabeth heard Mary's greeting, the infant leaped in her womb, and Elizabeth, filled with the Holy Spirit, cried out in a loud voice and said, "Most blessed are you among women, and blessed is the fruit of your womb. And how does this happen to me, that the mother of my Lord should come to me? For at the moment the sound of your greeting reached my ears, the infant in my womb leaped for joy. Blessed are you who believed that what was spoken to you by the Lord would be fulfilled."

Reflection

Today we celebrate the day when Our Lady appeared to Juan Diego, in Mexico. Mary asked Juan to seek out the local Bishop and request that he build a church in the place she appeared. Upon asking the Bishop, a miraculous image appeared on Juan's cloak, and the Bishop was convinced that this request was from God. Through the intercession of Our Lady of Guadalupe, thousands of people were baptized and converted to the faith throughout Latin America.

Prayers
others may be added

Through the intercession of Our Lady of Guadalupe, let us pray:

◆ Lord Jesus, hear our prayer.

That the Church throughout the world may spread the light of Christ to all peoples and free them from the darkness of sin and evil, we pray: ◆ That Our Lady of Guadalupe's patronage and prayers may extend over all the peoples and lands of the Americas to bring others closer to her Son, Jesus, we pray: ◆ That there will be an end to abortion, euthanasia, and all anti-life practices, and for the protection of all children and the elderly, we pray: ◆ That the people of Latin America may be renewed in strength and fervor through the prayers and intercession of Mary, we pray: ◆

Our Father . . .

Loving God,
you sent your Son to be born of a
    young woman.
By the prayers of Our Lady of Guadalupe,
convert our hearts from all sin and evil
and bring us into the light of your glory,
where you live and reign with your
    Son Jesus Christ in the unity of the
    Holy Spirit,
one God, forever and ever.
Amen.

✝ My soul rejoices in my God.

✝ The Lord hears the cry of the poor.

Psalm 62 page 409

Reading Matthew 11:11–15

Jesus said to the crowds: "Amen, I say to you, among those born of women there has been none greater than John the Baptist; yet the least in the Kingdom of heaven is greater than he. From the days of John the Baptist until now, the Kingdom of heaven suffers violence, and the violent are taking it by force. All the prophets and the law prophesied up to the time of John. And if you are willing to accept it, he is Elijah, the one who is to come. Whoever has ears ought to hear."

Reflection

We meditate on the great prophet John the Baptist who heralded the coming of Jesus Christ. In today's Gospel, Jesus affirms that John the Baptist fulfills the prophecy of Elijah's return. Jesus proclaims the greatness of John the Baptist, but reminds us that the littlest and weakest of the kingdom is even greater than he.

Prayers *others may be added*

You announce to us the Good News of salvation. Let us pray:

◆ Come, Lord Jesus.

For all members of the Church, that they may go out to all the nations as heralds of the Good News of God's salvation to speak words of comfort and peace, we pray: ◆ For the Holy Father, and all the bishops and priests who share in Christ's prophetic ministry, that they may preach God's word with humility and fortitude, we pray: ◆ For government officials, that they may protect and defend the human and spiritual rights of all persons, we pray: ◆ For all who suffer blindness, poor vision, cataracts, and all ailments of the eyes, that, through the intercession of Saint Lucy, they may receive healing, and that in their sufferings they may be given the gift to spiritually see more clearly through eyes of faith, we pray: ◆ For all the weak, the sick, and the suffering, that they may be encouraged that the kingdom of God belongs to them, we pray: ◆

Our Father . . .

Loving Jesus,
through the intercession of Saint Lucy,
open our eyes to recognize your coming.
Fill us with the light of your truth
as you come to make your dwelling
    among us.
We ask this through Christ our Lord.
Amen.

✝ The Lord hears the cry of the poor.

Friday, December 14, 2012

Memorial of Saint John of the Cross,
Priest and Doctor of the Church

✝ Let the clouds rain down the Just
One, and the earth bring forth a
Savior.

Psalm 25 *page 405*

Reading *Matthew 11:16–19*

Jesus said to the crowds: "To what shall I compare this generation? It is like children who sit in marketplaces and call to one another, 'We played the flute for you, but you did not dance, we sang a dirge but you did not mourn.' For John came neither eating nor drinking, and they said, 'He is possessed by a demon.' The Son of Man came eating and drinking and they said, 'Look, he is a glutton and a drunkard, a friend of tax collectors and sinners.' But wisdom is vindicated by her works."

Reflection

Today we honor Saint John of the Cross, the great Spanish saint who reformed the Carmelite order with Saint Teresa of Avila. He lived a life devoted to penance, prayer, and asceticism. He likewise wrote and taught about the importance of detachment from all things in order to obtain freedom and union with God. Saint John of the Cross is an example of one who faithfully carried his cross daily as a disciple of the Lord.

Prayers *others may be added*

Lord God, your saints witness to your greatness. Let us pray:

◆ Through your cross, bring us to new life, O Lord.

For the Holy Father, that he may be given health and strength to faithfully carry the burdens and cares of his office as he guides the Church toward closer union with God, we pray: ◆ For all nations that suffer war, terrorism, insecurity, and political unrest, we pray: ◆ For those who are weighed down by heavy crosses, worries, and sufferings, that their burdens may be lightened through God's help and by the presence and aid of generous and charitable Christians, we pray: ◆ For all the dying, that they may persevere until the end and that all who have gone before us in death may be brought into eternal union with our Triune God, we pray: ◆ For the entire Carmelite order throughout the world, that their lives and apostolic work may bear fruit through their commitment to contemplative prayer, we pray: ◆

Our Father . . .

Loving Father,
by your cross you bring us to new life.
Through the prayers of Saint John of
    the Cross,
teach us the true wisdom that only comes
from the mystery of the Cross of your
    Son, Jesus Christ,
through whom we ask this prayer.
Amen.

✝ Let the clouds rain down the Just
One, and the earth bring forth
a Savior.

✝ I will praise you, Lord, for you have rescued me.

Psalm 85 page 411

Reading Matthew 17:9a, 10–13

As they were coming down from the mountain, the disciples asked Jesus, "Why do the scribes say that Elijah must come first?" He said in reply, "Elijah will indeed come and restore all things; but I tell you that Elijah has already come, and they did not recognize him but did to him whatever they pleased. So also will the Son of Man suffer at their hands." Then the disciples understood that he was speaking to them of John the Baptist.

Reflection

In today's Gospel, Jesus explains that John the Baptist is the new Elijah who was foretold in the ancient scriptures. The prophets wrote that Elijah would return and herald the coming of the Messiah. Therefore, as John represents Elijah, Jesus reveals that he is truly the Messiah. However, this Messiah must also suffer before entering into glory.

Prayers *others may be added*

How great is the mystery of your love, O Lord. Grant our prayers and petitions as we pray:

◆ **Come, O long-awaited Messiah.**

That the whole Church may draw upon the rich graces that the Lord offers his people during this holy season of Advent, we pray: ◆ That all nations may discover the salvation found in the little Christ child born in the humble stable of Bethlehem, we pray: ◆ That all who suffer from addiction may receive freedom and healing and for their loved ones, we pray: ◆ That the grace of patience and peacefulness may be given to the faithful during these weeks of busy preparations, we pray: ◆ That all who have died may be received into the heavenly banquet, and for grace and peace to be given to those who grieve their loss, we pray: ◆

Our Father . . .

Lord God,
you sent Saint John the Baptist
as herald of your Good News.
By your grace help us
to prepare the way of the Lord
as we await the coming of your light
and peace.
We ask through Christ our Lord.
Amen.

✝ I will praise you, Lord, for you have rescued me.

✝ Rejoice in the Lord always! I shall say it again: rejoice! (*Philippians 4:4*)

Psalm 122 *page 420*

Reading *Luke 3:15–18*

Now the people were filled with expectation, and all were asking in their hearts whether John might be the Christ. John answered them all, saying, "I am baptizing you with water, but one mightier than I is coming. I am not worthy to loosen the thongs of his sandals. He will baptize you with the Holy Spirit and fire. His winnowing fan is in his hand to clear his threshing floor and to gather the wheat into his barn, but the chaff he will burn with unquenchable fire." Exhorting them in many other ways, he preached good news to the people.

Reflection

Today we celebrate Gaudete Sunday. This Sunday is named from the first words of the Latin Entrance Antiphon to the Mass. With the whole Church, we wait and prepare with joy for Christ. In today's Gospel, the people ask Jesus, "What shall we do?" Jesus gives simple answers by saying that those who have more should share with others, and one ought to do one's duties with integrity and honesty. In preparation for Christ's coming, let us do our work well with joy and expectation of Christ's coming.

Prayers *others may be added*

Confident that you, O God, are near, we make our requests known to you with thanksgiving, as we present to you our prayers and petitions:

◆ Come Lord Jesus, fill us with your joy!

For the light of Christ to illuminate the whole Church throughout the world, we pray: ◆ For all civic authorities and government officials, that they may work to provide societies of justice and stability so that all people may enjoy security and peace, we pray: ◆ For all those who suffer sadness, depression, and anxiety, for those who are burdened by the stress of the holiday season, that the light of Christ may shine upon them to bring joy and peace, we pray: ◆

Our Father . . .

Heavenly Father,
in this Third Sunday of Advent,
we rejoice in the coming of your Son.
Grant we ask that the knowledge of
    your presence
may fill us with joy and hope in
    your promise.
We ask this through Christ our Lord.
Amen.

✝ Rejoice in the Lord always! I shall say it again: rejoice!

Monday, December 17, 2012

Advent Weekday

✟ Justice shall flourish in his time, and fullness of peace for ever.

Psalm 146 *page 423*

Reading *Matthew 1:17*

Thus the total number of generations from Abraham to David is fourteen generations; from David to the Babylonian exile, fourteen generations; from the Babylonian exile to the Christ, fourteen generations.

Reflection

God has become man, and he has come to dwell among us. This is the great mystery that we contemplate as we prepare for the solemnity of Christmas. In today's Gospel, an excerpt of the genealogy of Jesus Christ has been provided. We wonder at God's grandeur, that in order to save us from our sins, he sent his Son among us coming from the lineage of David and born of a young virgin girl. Reflecting on this mystery we are filled with joy and hope.

Prayers *others may be added*

In waiting and expectation, we pour out our hearts before you, Lord, as we pray:

◆ Come, O Wisdom, hear our prayer.

That the whole Church may be renewed in the true meaning of life as we contemplate the great mystery of the Incarnation, we pray: ◆ That there will be an end to all world hunger, poverty, war, and violence, we pray: ◆ That the poor, the homeless, and all who suffer sickness and cold in these winter months may be given strength and healing, we pray: ◆ That all men and women may experience the quiet and stillness of this holy time through dedicated prayer, despite the demands and stresses of the holiday season, we pray: ◆

Our Father . . .

O Wisdom Incarnate,
with thankful hearts we give you praise
for the love and hope that you reveal to us
through the mystery of your Incarnation.
Grant us your peace and joy.
You live and reign forever.
Amen.

✟ Justice shall flourish in his time, and fullness of peace for ever.

✝ The Lord hears the cry of the poor.

Psalm 25   *page 405*

Reading   *Matthew 1:18–21*

This is how the birth of Jesus Christ came about. When his mother Mary was betrothed to Joseph, but before they lived together, she was found with child through the Holy Spirit. Joseph her husband, since he was a righteous man, yet unwilling to expose her to shame, decided to divorce her quietly. Such was his intention when, behold, the angel of the Lord appeared to him in a dream and said, "Joseph, son of David, do not be afraid to take Mary your wife into your home. For it is through the Holy Spirit that this child has been conceived in her. She will bear a son and you are to name him Jesus, because he will save his people from their sins."

Reflection

Sometimes it can be a great challenge to be joyful. There are so many worries and concerns that burden the human heart. The knowledge of evil, war, and death can greatly discourage us and cause us to doubt God's promise of hope—even to doubt his existence. However, our joy is found in the truth that God is with us. By the Incarnation, God has entered the world. He has met us in the midst of our weakness and sinfulness and illuminates the darkness of sin and evil. The Lord is near. This truth fills us with true Christian joy.

Prayers   *others may be added*

With faith in the Word Incarnate, we lift up our prayers and petitions as we pray:

◆ Come, O Lord and Ruler, hear our prayer.

For the Pope, and all bishops and priests, that they may be renewed in their vocation to proclaim the joy of Christ who dwells among us, we pray: ◆ For all countries divided by war, violence, terrorism, and all forms of conflict, that civic leaders may dialogue with one another to bring about resolution and peace, we pray: ◆ For those who suffer sadness, illness, poverty, injury, and disability, that they may be given healing and strength as they await the day of the Lord's visitation, we pray: ◆ For each of us to receive the virtues of cheerfulness and gratitude, we pray: ◆

Our Father . . .

O Lord and Ruler,
you are the desire of all nations.
All the ages have awaited your coming.
Come and shine your light upon us.
You live and reign forever.
Amen.

✝ The Lord hears the cry of the poor.

✟ Let the Lord enter; he is the king of glory.

Psalm 85 *page 411*

Reading *Luke 1:13–17*

But the angel said to him, "Do not be afraid, Zechariah, because your prayer has been heard. Your wife Elizabeth will bear you a son, and you shall name him John. And you will have joy and gladness, and many will rejoice at his birth, for he will be great in the sight of the Lord. He will drink neither wine nor strong drink. He will be filled with the Holy Spirit even from his mother's womb, and he will turn many of the children of Israel to the Lord their God. He will go before him in the spirit and power of Elijah to turn the hearts of fathers toward children and the disobedient to the understanding of the righteous, to prepare a people fit for the Lord."

Reflection *Graziano Marcheschi*

God promised a messiah and the messiah came, but the reason so few recognized him is he didn't fit expectations. It was also prophesied that Elijah would return before the messiah's advent (see Malachi 4:5–6). Some who wondered if Jesus was the one might have been thrown by the fact that Elijah hadn't come. But Luke suggests he did. Some failed to recognize him because it was not Elijah in the flesh but the "spirit and the power of Elijah" that came in the person of John, the child of Elizabeth and Zechariah. In his life and ministry the Church believes Malachi's prophecy was fulfilled.

Prayers *others may be added*

With hopeful waiting hearts, we place our petitions and prayers at your feet, Lord, as we pray:

◆ Come, O Root of Jesse, and set us free.

For the whole Church, that in this time of quiet waiting, we may turn ever more closely to the Lord in repentance and heartfelt contrition through the holy sacraments, we pray: ◆ For all who work to increase the standard of living for all peoples, we pray: ◆ For all who suffer the hidden pain of infertility, that their patience may be rewarded with the fruitfulness of life, and that all women and families may be open to the gift of children, we pray: ◆ For the grace to have eyes of faith to perceive God's presence in our daily life, so that we may be filled with true and lasting joy, we pray: ◆ For the grace to persevere in prayer and hope in God's mysterious will, with confidence in God's perfect timing, we pray: ◆

Our Father . . .

O Flower of Jesse's Stem,
strengthen us with the light of your love.
May all our trials and sufferings bear fruit
in everlasting life where you live and reign
forever with the Father in the unity of the
   Holy Spirit,
one God, forever and ever.
Amen.

✟ Let the Lord enter; he is the king of glory.

✝ Let the Lord enter; he is the king of glory.

Psalm 25 *page 405*

Reading *Luke 1:26–33*

The angel Gabriel was sent from God to a town of Galilee called Nazareth, to a virgin betrothed to a man named Joseph, of the house of David, and the virgin's name was Mary. And coming to her, he said, "Hail, favored one! The Lord is with you." But she was greatly troubled at what was said and pondered what sort of greeting this might be. Then the angel said to her, "Do not be afraid, Mary, for you have found favor with God. Behold, you will conceive in your womb and bear a son, and you shall name him Jesus. He will be great and will be called Son of the Most High, and the Lord God will give him the throne of David his father, and he will rule over the house of Jacob forever, and of his Kingdom there will be no end."

Reflection

Sometimes God does not meet our expectations. We are left disappointed, thinking that he has failed us and has not fulfilled his word. However, is God supposed to fit our own human desires and expectations, or are we supposed to conform ourselves to the greatness and majesty of his divine and cosmic plan? With openness to God's mystery, let us more fully enter into this prayerful time of Advent.

Prayers *others may be added*

Surrendering ourselves to your holy will, we continue to place our petitions in faith and hope before you, Lord, as we pray:

◆ O Key of David, come and hear our prayer.

That the Pope, bearing the keys of Peter, may faithfully teach and instruct all the members of the pilgrim Church with courage as we joyfully journey to our heavenly home, we pray: ◆ That there will be an end to all violence, terrorism, war, and destruction, and that peace will spread throughout the world, we pray: ◆ For those who suffer sadness and anxiety, we pray: ◆ That the mentally ill, all who care for them, and the sick members of our faith community may be given healing, solace, and strength, we pray: ◆ That all who suffer from the loss of loved ones may be comforted, we pray: ◆

Our Father . . .

O Key of David,
come and shine your light upon us
in the darkness of our trials and sufferings
as we await the joy of your kingdom,
where you reign together with the Father
in the unity of the Holy Spirit,
one God, forever and ever.
Amen.

✝ Let the Lord enter; he is the king of glory.

Friday, December 21, 2012
Advent Weekday

✝ Arise, my beloved, my beautiful one, and come! (*Song of Songs 2:10*)

Psalm 85   *page 411*

Reading   *Luke 1:39–45*

Mary set out in those days and traveled to the hill country in haste to a town of Judah, where she entered the house of Zechariah and greeted Elizabeth. When Elizabeth heard Mary's greeting, the infant leaped in her womb, and Elizabeth, filled with the Holy Spirit, cried out in a loud voice and said, "Most blessed are you among women, and blessed is the fruit of your womb. And how does this happen to me, that the mother of my Lord should come to me? For at the moment the sound of your greeting reached my ears, the infant in my womb leaped for joy. Blessed are you who believed that what was spoken to you by the Lord would be fulfilled."

Reflection

Jesus, the Light of the World, is the source of all light. At his birth, this light enters into the darkness and fills the earth with its radiance. At the Crucifixion, darkness seemed to have conquered light; however, in the glory of the Resurrection, the light of Christ is more brilliant than before. Let us be imitators of God, so that we may be shining lamps of Christ's light.

Prayers   *others may be added*

Turning our eyes with hope and joy to the coming light of our Savior, we pray:

◆ Come, O Radiant Dawn.

That all the members of the Church may thrust aside the darkness of sin and evil and put on the armor and radiance of God's piercing light and truth, we pray: ◆ That all nations founded on false ideologies may be illuminated by the light of Jesus Christ, the source of truth, peace, and life, we pray: ◆ That all the sick who suffer in pain and loneliness may not fall into discouragement, but rather lift their faces to Christ who comes to pour his healing light upon them and raise them from their suffering, we pray: ◆ That we may be open to the grace to live radical lives of charity and generosity toward our neighbors, family members, and those who are less fortunate than ourselves, we pray: ◆

Our Father . . .

O Radiant Dawn,
all peoples turn their eyes
to see the radiance of your coming.
Come and shine on us,
and fill us with the warmth of your light
   and life
as you reign with the Father
in the unity of the Holy Spirit,
one God, forever and ever.
Amen.

✝ Arise, my beloved, my beautiful one, and come!

✝ My heart exults in the LORD.
(*1 Samuel 2:1*)

Psalm 25 *page 405*

Reading *Luke 1:46–56*

"My soul proclaims the greatness of the Lord; / my spirit rejoices in God my savior, / for he has looked upon his lowly servant. / From this day all generations will call me blessed: / the Almighty has done great things for me, / and holy is his Name. / He has mercy on those who fear him / in every generation. / He has shown the strength of his arm, / and has scattered the proud in their conceit. / He has cast down the mighty from their thrones / and has lifted up the lowly. / He has filled the hungry with good things, / and the rich he has sent away empty. / He has come to the help of his servant Israel / for he remembered his promise of mercy, / the promise he made to our fathers, / to Abraham and his children for ever." /

Mary remained with Elizabeth about three months and then returned to her home.

Reflection

Christmas is quickly approaching, and we are busy with preparations, buying gifts, planning parties, and decorating for the holidays. The weeks of Advent seem to have gone so quickly, yet in these lasts days there is still time to prepare our hearts and think about the mystery of Christ's coming to earth to save us. We can sing with Mary that the Almighty has done great things for us.

Truly, "holy is his Name." Let us take a few moments in prayer to think and remember the real reason why all the preparations, the gifts, and decorations are important for this special day.

Prayers *others may be added*

God, you have done such great things for us. In praise and thanksgiving, let us pray:

◆ **Come, O King of all the Nations.**

For the Church, that, as she looks to the coming of her Savior, all her members may be filled with grace and mercy and joy, we pray: ◆ For all nations, that they may come to know Jesus Christ, the only true desire of man's heart, and that the peace of God's reign may spread throughout all lands, especially places torn apart by division, violence, and war, we pray: ◆ For all the poor, the hungry, the sick and suffering, and for those who have nothing during Christmas Time, we pray: ◆ For all Christians, that they may be generous in sharing their goods with the poor and needy, we pray: ◆ For the grace to praise God for his goodness and mercy in all circumstances, we pray: ◆

Our Father . . .

O Desire of all the Nations,
you are our King and Ruler,
come with your power to banish
the darkness of all evil and to shine
the glory of your radiance upon all
  your faithful.
You live and reign forever.
Amen.

✝ My heart exults in the LORD.

✝ For ever I will sing the goodness of the Lord.

Psalm 85 *page 411*

Reading *Luke 1:39–45*

Mary set out and traveled to the hill country in haste to a town of Judah, where she entered the house of Zechariah and greeted Elizabeth. When Elizabeth heard Mary's greeting, the infant leaped in her womb, and Elizabeth, filled with the Holy Spirit, cried out in a loud voice and said, / "Blessed are you among women, / and blessed is the fruit of your womb. / And how does this happen to me, that the mother of my Lord should come to me? For at the moment the sound of your greeting reached my ears, the infant in my womb leaped for joy. Blessed are you who believed that what was spoken to you by the Lord would be fulfilled."

Reflection

We have been waiting and preparing with the whole Church for the great solemnity of Christmas. There are only a few days left before we celebrate the great mystery of Christ's birth. With Elizabeth we can cry out in wonder, "How does this happen to me?" How can this be that God has come to dwell among us!

Prayers *others may be added*

With Advent joy and expectation, we present our petitions to Christ. Let us pray:

♦ O Emmanuel, come be with us.

For the Holy Father, that he may be blessed with health and strength to guide and lead the Church in wisdom during this grace-filled season, we pray: ♦ For all lands and nations that experience persecution, that faithful Christians and devoted leaders may work for reconciliation and resolution in all areas torn apart by conflict, war, and violence, we pray: ♦ For the sick, the homeless, the hungry, and the poor, that they may receive the help and care they need from the charity and generosity of others, we pray: ♦ For all of those who feel burdened by stress or anxiety during this busy time, that they may place their focus on Jesus Christ, the one thing necessary, we pray: ♦

Our Father . . .

O Emmanuel, God-with-us,
despite our sinfulness,
you come among us to be born
as a little child to illuminate
the world with your radiant light.
Come make your dwelling within us.
You live and reign forever.
Amen.

✝ For ever I will sing the goodness of the Lord.

✝ For ever I will sing the goodness of the Lord.

Psalm 85   *page 411*

Reading   *Luke 1:67, 73–79*

Zechariah his father, filled with the Holy Spirit, prophesied, saying: . . . / "This was the oath he swore to our father Abraham: / to set us free from the hand of our enemies, / free to worship him without fear, / holy and righteous in his sight all the days of our life. / You, my child, shall be called the prophet of the Most High, / for you will go before the Lord to prepare his way, / to give his people knowledge of salvation / by the forgiveness of their sins. / In the tender compassion of our God / the dawn from on high shall break upon us, / to shine on those who dwell in darkness and the shadow of death, / and to guide our feet into the way of peace."

Reflection

The world waits in darkness for the coming of Jesus Christ, our saving light. Let us not be so distracted by the noise, the hustle and bustle of shoppers, the flashing lights, and the bombardment of things to buy that we lose our inner calm and quiet recollection of waiting in vigilance for the dawn of our Savior's coming. God has come among us to set us free. His light of his salvation breaks upon us to illuminate the path of peace and eternal life.

Prayers   *others may be added*

For freedom, Christ has set us free. (cf. Galatians 5:1). Rejoicing in the Lord's coming, let us pray:

◆ Come, Lord Jesus, set us free.

That the Pope, all priests, bishops, and deacons may be given health and strength to perform all their ministerial duties well throughout all the liturgical celebrations of this most holy season, we pray: ◆ That nations torn apart by war and terrorism may cease all acts of violence to establish societies of peace and security for all children and families, we pray: ◆ For all who are ill and suffering, that the darkness of their sufferings may be transformed into the joyous light of new spiritual and physical life for them and for all souls, we pray: ◆ For those considering entering or returning to the Catholic Church, that this Christmas their eyes and hearts may be open to the Christ child who quietly invites all to come and encounter the mystery and fullness of his life in the sacraments, we pray: ◆ For all who have died, and for the comfort of all family and friends who grieve their losses, we pray: ◆

Our Father . . .

Come Lord Jesus,
visit your people who long to see your face.
Banish the darkness of all sin and evil
and bring us into the light of your
    lasting peace.
You live and reign forever.
Amen.

✝ For ever I will sing the goodness of the Lord.

Tuesday, December 25, 2012
Solemnity of the Nativity of the Lord (Christmas)

✝ Glory to God in the highest, / and on earth peace to people of good will.

Psalm 98 *page 413*

Reading *Luke 2:15–19*

When the angels went away from them to heaven, the shepherds said to one another, "Let us go, then, to Bethlehem to see this thing that has taken place, which the Lord has made known to us." So they went in haste and found Mary and Joseph, and the infant lying in the manger. When they saw this, they made known the message that had been told them about this child. All who heard it were amazed by what had been told them by the shepherds. And Mary kept all these things, reflecting on them in her heart.

Reflection

The Lord has made known his great love to us! With the shepherds, let us journey to Bethlehem to see the Christ child who is born among us! God has become man! This is the great mystery we celebrate Christmas Day. Jesus Christ, the Word made flesh, dwells among us! Like his mother, Mary, let us ponder and reflect upon all these things as we are filled with the joy and peace and freedom her Son brings to us this day.

Prayers *others may be added*

Rejoicing with all the heavenly hosts, let us pray:

◆ Glory to you, O Lord!

For the Church, that this Christmas Day, the Pope, the clergy, and all the faithful may be filled with gifts of lasting peace and joy as we celebrate God's presence among us, we pray: ◆ For the end of all terror, violence, and war this day, that the peace of Christ may extend throughout all the world to provide safety and protection for all peoples, we pray: ◆ For all those who are ill and for all who suffer, that in their trials they may never doubt God's presence or His compassionate love for the weak and suffering, we pray: ◆ For all children, that they may be especially blessed this Christmas Day by the love and tenderness of Baby Jesus, we pray: ◆ For all who have died, and all friends and family members who feel their absence this holiday, that they may be forever united with the community of saints of heaven, we pray: ◆

Our Father . . .

Loving Father,
you send your Son Jesus among us
as a little child, born of a woman
in a humble stable in Bethlehem.
This Christmas Day, fill us with
the light and radiance of your Son
who lives and reigns with you
in the unity of the Holy Spirit
one God, forever and ever. Amen.

✝ Glory to God in the highest, / and on earth peace to people of good will.

Wednesday, December 26, 2012
Feast of Saint Stephen, The First Martyr

✝ Into your hands, O Lord, I commend my spirit.

Psalm 98 *page 413*

Reading *Matthew 10:17–22*

Jesus said to his disciples, "Beware of men, for they will hand you over to the courts and scourge you in their synagogues, and you will be led before governors and kings for my sake as a witness before them and the pagans. When they hand you over, do not worry about how you are to speak or what you are to say. You will be given at that moment what you are to say. For it will not be you who speak but the Spirit of your Father speaking through you. Brother will hand over brother to death, and the father his child; children will rise up against parents and have them put to death. You will be hated by all because of my name, but whoever endures to the end will be saved."

Reflection

Today we celebrate the feast of Saint Stephen, the first martyr. As we honor this holy martyr during Christmas Time, we are reminded that as Christians we are called to give witness and testimony to Jesus Christ. We can oftentimes face persecution and difficulties, but the Holy Spirit will give us the words to speak. Let us not be afraid to speak about the truth and joy of this Christmas season: Jesus Christ lives among us!

Prayers *others may be added*

With thankful and joyful hearts we lift our prayers to heaven as we pray:

◆ Strengthen us in faith, O Lord.

For the Church, that she may forever give faithful witness to the birth of Jesus Christ, the Word Incarnate, we pray: ◆ For all who are persecuted for the faith, that through the prayers of Saint Stephen, the first martyr, their testimony may bear fruit in the conversions of many souls to the truth, we pray: ◆ For those who suffer sickness, poverty, hunger, homelessness, and all in crisis situations, we pray: ◆ For our faith community, that we may be united together this Christmas season through our worship of the holy child born in Bethlehem, we pray: ◆

Our Father . . .

All powerful God,
your martyrs gave witness to your glory
    and might.
Grant that you may fill us with the same
    faith and perseverance that you filled
    Saint Stephen,
that after the trials and persecutions of
    this life
we may forever enjoy the glory of heaven
where you live and reign with your Son,
    our Lord Jesus Christ,
in the unity of the Holy Spirit,
one God, forever and ever.
Amen.

✝ Into your hands, O Lord, I commend my spirit.

Thursday, December 27, 2012
Feast of Saint John, Apostle and Evangelist

✝ Rejoice in the Lord, you just!

Psalm 104 *page 416*

Reading *John 20:1–8*

On the first day of the week, Mary of Magdala came to the tomb early in the morning, while it was still dark, and saw the stone removed from the tomb. So she ran and went to Simon Peter and to the other disciple whom Jesus loved, and told them, "They have taken the Lord from the tomb, and we don't know where they put him." So Peter and the other disciple went out and came to the tomb. They both ran, but the other disciple ran faster than Peter and arrived at the tomb first; he bent down and saw the burial cloths there, but did not go in. When Simon Peter arrived after him, he went into the tomb and saw the burial cloths there, and the cloth that had covered his head, not with the burial cloths but rolled up in a separate place. Then the other disciple also went in, the one who had arrived at the tomb first, and he saw and believed.

Reflection

Today we celebrate the feast of Saint John the Evangelist whom tradition identifies as Jesus' Beloved Disciple. Through his writings in the scriptures we encounter Jesus Christ, the Word made flesh and Light of the World. We come to know God's profound love for us as his beloved children and we learn to pray as we rest our head upon Jesus' breast in imitation of John during the Last Supper.

Prayers *others may be added*

Glorifying God for his goodness, we offer our prayers in thanks and praise as we pray:

◆ Incarnate Word, hear our prayer.

That all members of the Church may come to encounter Jesus Christ, the Word of Life through the grace of the holy sacraments, we pray: ◆ That all nations may recognize God in the glory and goodness of his works of creation, we pray: ◆ That all writers, teachers, and those in ministry may testify to Christ, the Word of Life, through their words and actions, we pray: ◆ That the sick and dying may be lifted up and comforted by the prayers and presence of friends and attentive caregivers, we pray: ◆ That all the faithful may be gathered more deeply in the communion of Jesus Christ and the Father through our fellowship with one another, we pray: ◆

Our Father . . .

Loving Father,
open our eyes to see you,
our ears to hear you
and our hearts ready and eager
to testify to the eternal life
you reveal to us in your Son, Jesus Christ
 our Lord,
who lives and reigns with you in the unity
 of the Holy Spirit,
one God, forever and ever.
Amen.

✝ Rejoice in the Lord, you just!

Friday, December 28, 2012
Feast of the Holy Innocents, Martyrs

✝ Our soul has been rescued like a bird from the fowler's snare.

Psalm 116
page 418

Reading
Matthew 2:13–15

When the magi had departed, behold, the angel of the Lord appeared to Joseph in a dream and said, "Rise, take the child and his mother, flee to Egypt, and stay there until I tell you. Herod is going to search for the child to destroy him." Joseph rose and took the child and his mother by night and departed for Egypt. He stayed there until the death of Herod, that what the Lord had said through the prophet might be fulfilled, / *Out of Egypt I called my son.*

Reflection
Graziano Marcheschi

In their earliest days, the Jewish people found refuge in Egypt. God made that great nation a womb-like refuge for Abraham's descendents and they remained there for 400 years until the infant nation was ready to stand on its own and walk toward its destiny. Now, Jesus, too, is sent to Egypt to take refuge there until the time is ripe for his return from exile. In this way, not only is scripture fulfilled as Matthew points out, but Jesus' life reflects the experience of the Chosen People. As they did, Jesus knew the experience of being a stranger in a strange land. In him as in them, the inexorable will of the Father is accomplished.

Prayers
others may be added

Confident in your mercy we lift our hearts to you in prayer.

◆ Lord, hear our cry for mercy.

That the Church throughout the world and all peoples may come to respect and honor the sanctity and dignity of life, we pray: ◆ That all children may be protected from all evil and that they may develop their gifts and strengths for the glory of God and the good of others, we pray: ◆ For all fathers, that they may imitate the obedience and faithfulness of St. Joseph to care for their families with strength and courage, we pray: ◆ For the end of abortion, abuse, war, and violence against children, we pray: ◆ For all who have died, especially for young children and their parents and families who grieve their loss, that the souls of all the departed may enter into the glory and radiance of the Trinity in communion with all the saints and martyrs, we pray: ◆

Our Father . . .

Merciful Father,
through the prayers of the Holy
    Innocents,
hear the cries of all those who suffer,
and bring them comfort and solace.
Illuminate the darkness of sin and evil
with the piercing light of your love
    and mercy.
We ask this through Christ our Lord.
Amen.

✝ Our soul has been rescued like a bird from the fowler's snare.

Saturday, December 29, 2012
The Fifth Day within the Octave of Christmas

✝ Announce his salvation, day after day.

Psalm 62 — page 409

Reading — Luke 2:22–35

Now there was a man in Jerusalem whose name was Simeon. This man was righteous and devout, awaiting the consolation of Israel, and the Holy Spirit was upon him. It had been revealed to him by the Holy Spirit that he should not see death before he had seen the Christ of the Lord. He came in the Spirit into the temple; and when the parents brought in the child Jesus to perform the custom of the law in regard to him, he took him into his arms and blessed God, saying: / "Lord, now you let your servant go in peace; / your word has been fulfilled: / my own eyes have seen the salvation / which you have prepared in the sight of every people, / a light to reveal you to the nations / and the glory of his people Israel."

Reflection

In the secular world, the Christmas music has ceased, people have thrown out their trees, and they are taking down their decorations. However, for us Christians, Christmas has just begun! Christmas extends until the feast of the Baptism of the Lord—the second week of January. Therefore, with great joy, we continue our celebration of this holy solemnity when God, who loved us so much, became man to grant us freedom and new life.

Prayers — *others may be added*

Filled with Christmas joy, we present our prayers and petitions to God as we pray:

◆ Light of the world, hear our prayer.

For all people to recognize the truth of the Christ child, that all may be one in him, we pray: ◆ For all nations suffering destruction from natural disasters, that they may receive the help they need to care for the injured and restore what has been lost, we pray: ◆ For the sick and infirm, those in hospitals and nursing homes, and all who work to serve those in need, we pray: ◆ For the safety of all travelers, we pray: ◆ For all who have died, that they may be brought into the eternal glory of heaven, we pray: ◆

Our Father . . .

Loving God,
you sent your Son among us
to free us from our sins.
Grant that we too may testify to your
    truth and light
with steadfast and unwavering faith.
We ask through Christ our Lord.
Amen.

✝ Announce his salvation, day after day.

Sunday, December 30, 2012
Feast of the Holy Family of Jesus, Mary, and Joseph

✝ A light for revelation to the Gentiles, and glory for your people Israel.
(Luke 2:32)

Psalm 98 *page 413*

Reading *Luke 2:41–43, 46–47*

Each year Jesus' parents went to Jerusalem for the feast of Passover, and when he was twelve years old, they went up according to festival custom. After they had completed its days, as they were returning, the boy Jesus remained behind in Jerusalem, but his parents did not know it. . . . After three days they found him in the temple, sitting in the midst of the teachers, listening to them and asking them questions, and all who heard him were astounded at his understanding and his answers.

Reflection *Graziano Marcheschi*

It was not uncommon for parents to assume their child was in the company of the extended family during a pilgrimage. When finally the parents find him, Jesus insists he was with family, for he was in his Father's house doing his Father's business. It's no stretch to believe that Jesus could converse with the elders as an equal. Jesus didn't one day suddenly become the Son of God. From the beginning, he enjoyed a special communion with the Father that grounded him in prayer and that was manifested in the profound insights he could share, even at this early age. But he had more learning and growing to do, and he did it in Nazareth within the nurturing womb of the Holy Family.

Prayers *others may be added*

With wonder and awe at the beauty of your mystery, Lord, let us pray:

◆ Draw us into your communion, O God.

For the Church, that she may be an open and welcoming family to all people, we pray: ◆ For all civic authorities and those in legislative office, that they may work to protect and defend the sanctity of life and the good of the family, we pray: ◆ For all families torn apart by division, divorce, financial crisis, loss, or difficulty, that through the intercession of the Holy Family, they may receive peace, forgiveness, and healing, we pray: ◆ For all mothers and fathers, that they may learn to be good and holy parents like Mary and Joseph, we pray: ◆ For our faith community, that they may seek to serve each of our spiritual brothers and sisters around us, especially those in need, we pray: ◆

Our Father . . .

Heavenly Father,
in your Son Jesus Christ,
you call us to be your children.
Grant that all families may mirror
the love and communion you share
in the mystery of the Trinity
with your Son who lives and reigns with
    you in the unity of the Holy Spirit,
one God, forever and ever.
Amen.

✝ A light for revelation to the Gentiles, and glory for your people Israel.

Monday, December 31, 2012
The Seventh Day within the Octave of Christmas

✠ The Word became flesh and made his dwelling among us. (*John 1:14*)

Psalm 98 *page 413*

Reading *John 1:10–14*

He was in the world, / and the world came to be through him, / but the world did not know him. / He came to what was his own, / but his own people did not accept him.

But to those who did accept him / he gave power to become children of God, / to those who believe in his name, / who were born not by natural generation / nor by human choice nor by a man's decision / but of God.

And the Word became flesh / and made his dwelling among us, / and we saw his glory, / the glory as of the Father's only-begotten Son, / full of grace and truth.

Reflection

As we look back on this past year, we continue to contemplate the great mystery of the Incarnation that in the fullness of time, God has revealed his mercy and love to us in the person of Jesus Christ, the Word Incarnate. The true light which enlightens everyone has come into the world! May the grace of this holy time continue to grow and increase within us as we testify to the glory of God's grace and truth today and in the new year.

Prayers *others may be added*

With grateful hearts for all the blessings we have received, let us pray:

◆ Renew us with the light of your life, O Lord.

For the Holy Father, that he may be blessed with steadfast faith as he continues to guide the Church into the blessings and trials of a new year, we pray: ◆ For all political leaders that they may work to serve the common good of society in justice and peace, we pray: ◆ For all young people, that with enthusiasm and zeal they may use their gifts and talents to inspire others to experience the blessings, goodness, and richness of life, we pray: ◆ For all the sick and injured, that they may quickly be restored to fullness of health in body, mind, and spirit, we pray: ◆ For all those who have died through accidents and tragedy and for those who grieve their loss, we pray: ◆ For all travelers and those on the road tonight, for their safety and protection, we pray: ◆

Our Father . . .

Gracious and merciful God,
with joyful thanksgiving we praise you
for all the good gifts you have given us.
As we enter into this new year,
bless us with your grace and fill us
with the life of your Spirit,
who lives and reigns with you and your
   Son, Jesus Christ our Lord,
one God, forever and ever.
Amen.

✠ The Word became flesh and made his dwelling among us.

Psalter

Psalm 1:1–2, 3, 4 and 6

Blessed the man who follows not
    the counsel of the wicked
Nor walks in the way of sinners,
    nor sits in the company of the insolent,
But delights in the law of the LORD
    and meditates on his law day and night.

He is like a tree
    planted near running water,
That yields its fruit in due season,
    and whose leaves never fade.
    Whatever he does, prospers.

Not so the wicked, not so;
    they are like chaff, which the wind drives away.
For the LORD watches over the way of the just,
    but the way of the wicked vanishes.

Psalm 8:4–5, 6–7, 8–9

When I behold your heavens, the work of your fingers,
    the moon and the stars which you set in place—
What is man that you should be mindful of him,
    or the son of man that you should care for him?

You have made him little less than the angels,
    and crowned him with glory and honor.
You have given him rule over the works of your hands,
    putting all things under his feet.

All sheep and oxen,
    yes, and the beasts of the field,
The birds of the air, the fishes of the sea,
    and whatever swims the paths of the seas.

Psalm 19:8, 9, 10, 11

The law of the LORD is perfect,
    refreshing the soul,
The decree of the LORD is trustworthy,
    giving wisdom to the simple.

The precepts of the LORD are right,
    rejoicing the heart.
The command of the LORD is clear,
    enlightening the eye.

The fear of the LORD is pure,
    enduring forever.
The ordinances of the LORD are true,
    all of them just.

Psalm 22:26b–27, 28 and 30, 3–32

I will fulfill my vows before those who fear him.
The lowly shall eat their fill;
They who seek the LORD shall praise him;
    "May your hearts be ever merry!"

All the ends of the earth
    shall remember and turn to the LORD;
All the families of the nations
    shall bow down before him.
To him alone shall bow down
    all who sleep in the earth;
Before him shall bend
    all who go down into the dust.

And to him my soul shall live;
    my descendants shall serve him.
Let the coming generation be told of the LORD
    that they may proclaim to a people yet to be born
    the justice he has shown.

Psalm 23:1–3a, 3b–4, 5, 6

The LORD is my shepherd; I shall not want.
In verdant pastures he gives me repose;
Beside restful waters he leads me;
he refreshes my soul.

He guides me in right paths
for his name's sake.
Even though I walk in the dark valley
I fear no evil; for you are at my side
With your rod and your staff
that give me courage.

You spread the table before me
In the sight of my foes;
You anoint my head with oil;
my cup overflows.

Only goodness and kindness follow me
all the days of my life;
And I shall dwell in the house of the LORD
for years to come.

Psalm 25:2-3, 4-5ab, 6 and 7bc

In you I trust; let me not be put to shame,
    let not my enemies exult over me.
No one who waits for you shall be put to shame;
    those shall be put to shame who heedlessly break faith.

Your ways, O LORD, make known to me;
    teach me your paths,
Guide me in your truth and teach me,
    for you are God my savior.

Remember that your compassion, O LORD,
    and your kindness are from of old.
In your kindness remember me,
    because of your goodness, O LORD.

Psalm 27:7-8a, 8b-9abc, 13-14

Hear, O LORD, the sound of my call;
    have pity on me, and answer me.
Of you my heart speaks; you my glance seeks.

Your presence, O LORD, I seek.
Hide not your face from me;
    do not in anger repel your servant.
You are my helper: cast me not off.

I believe that I shall see the bounty of the LORD
    in the land of the living.
Wait for the LORD with courage;
    be stouthearted, and wait for the LORD.

Psalm 33:10–11, 12–13, 14–15

The LORD brings to nought the plans of the nations;
    he foils the designs of peoples.
But the plan of the LORD stands forever;
    the design of his heart, through all generations.

Blessed the nation whose God is the LORD,
    the people he has chosen for his own inheritance.
From heaven the LORD looks down;
    he sees all mankind.

From his fixed throne he beholds
    all who dwell on the earth,
He who fashioned the heart of each,
    he who knows all their works.

Psalm 34:2–3, 4–5, 6–7, 8–9

I will bless the LORD at all times;
    his praise shall be ever in my mouth.
Let my soul glory in the LORD;
    the lowly will hear me and be glad.

Glorify the LORD with me,
    let us together extol his name.
I sought the LORD, and he answered me
    and delivered me from all my fears.

Look to him that you may be radiant with joy,
    and your faces may not blush with shame.
When the poor one called out, the LORD heard,
    and from all his distress he saved him.

The angel of the LORD encamps
    around those who fear him, and delivers them.
Taste and see how good the LORD is;
    blessed the man who takes refuge in him.

Psalm 37:3–4, 5–6, 30–31

Trust in the LORD and do good
  that you may dwell in the land and be fed in security.
Take delight in the LORD,
  and he will grant you your heart's requests.

Commit to the LORD your way;
  trust in him, and he will act.
He will make justice dawn for you like the light;
  bright as the noonday shall be your vindication.

The mouth of the just man tells of wisdom
  and his tongue utters what is right.
The law of his God is in his heart,
  and his steps do not falter.

Psalm 42:2, 3, 5cdef

As the hind longs for the running waters,
  so my soul longs for you, O God.

Athirst is my soul for God, the living God.
  When shall I go and behold the face of God?

I went with the throng
  and led them in procession to the house of God.
Amid loud cries of joy and thanksgiving,
  with the multitude keeping festival.

Psalm 47:2–3, 4–5, 6–7

All you peoples, clap your hands,
    shout to God with cries of gladness,
For the LORD, the Most High, the awesome,
    is the great king over all the earth.

He brings people under us;
    nations under our feet.
He chooses for us our inheritance,
    the glory of Jacob, whom he loves.

God mounts his throne amid shouts of joy;
    the LORD, amid trumpet blasts.
Sing praise to God, sing praise;
    sing praise to our king, sing praise.

Psalm 48:2–3ab, 10–11

Great is the LORD and wholly to be praised
    in the city of our God.
His holy mountain, fairest of heights,
    is the joy of all the earth.

O God, we ponder your mercy
    within your temple.
As your name, O God, so also your praise
    reaches to the ends of the earth.
Of justice your right hand is full.

Psalm 51:3–4, 5–6a, 6bcd–7

Have mercy on me, O God, in your goodness;
    in the greatness of your compassion wipe out my offense.
Thoroughly wash me from my guilt
    and of my sin cleanse me.

For I acknowledge my offense,
    and my sin is before me always:
"Against only you have I sinned,
    and done what is evil in your sight."

I have done such evil in your sight
    that you are just in your sentence,
    blameless when you condemn.
True, I was born guilty,
    a sinner, even as my mother conceived me.

Psalm 62:6–7, 9

Only in God be at rest, my soul,
    for from him comes my hope.
He only is my rock and my salvation,
    my stronghold; I shall not be disturbed.

Trust in him at all times, O my people!
    Pour out your hearts before him;
    God is our refuge!

Psalm 63:2, 3–4, 5–6

O God, you are my God whom I seek;
    for you my flesh pines and my soul thirsts
    like the earth, parched, lifeless and without water.

Thus have I gazed toward you in the sanctuary
    to see your power and your glory,
For your kindness is a greater good than life;
    my lips shall glorify you.

Thus will I bless you while I live;
    lifting up my hands, I will call upon your name.
As with the riches of a banquet shall my soul be satisfied,
    and with exultant lips my mouth shall praise you.

Psalm 66:1–3a, 5 and 8, 16–17

Shout joyfully to God, all the earth;
    sing praise to the glory of his name;
    proclaim his glorious praise.
Say to God: "How tremendous are your deeds!"

Come and see the works of God,
    his tremendous deeds among the children of Adam.
Bless our God, you peoples;
    loudly sound his praise.

Hear now, all you who fear God, while I declare
    what he has done for me.
When I appealed to him in words,
    praise was on the tip of my tongue.

Psalm 72:1–2, 14 and 15bc, 17

O God, with your judgment endow the king,
    and with your justice, the king's son;
He shall govern your people with justice
    and your afflicted ones with judgment.

From fraud and violence he shall redeem them,
    and precious shall their blood be in his sight.
May they be prayed for continually;
    day by day shall they bless him.

May his name be blessed forever;
    as long as the sun his name shall remain.
In him shall all the tribes of the earth be blessed;
    all the nations shall proclaim his happiness.

Psalm 85:8 and 10, 11–12, 13–14

Show us, O LORD, your mercy,
    and grant us your salvation.
Near indeed is his salvation to those who fear him,
    glory dwelling in our land.

Kindness and truth shall meet;
    justice and peace shall kiss.
Truth shall spring out of the earth,
    and justice shall look down from heaven.

The LORD himself will give his benefits;
    our land shall yield its increase.
Justice shall walk before him,
    and salvation, along the way of his steps.

Psalm 86:3–4, 5–6, 9–10

Have mercy on me, O LORD,
    for to you I call all day.
Gladden the soul of your servant,
    for to you, O Lord, I lift up my soul.

For you, O Lord, are good and forgiving,
    abounding in kindness to all who call upon you.
Hearken, O LORD, to my prayer
    and attend to the sound of my pleading.

All the nations you have made shall come
    and worship you, O Lord,
    and glorify your name.
For you are great, and you do wondrous deeds;
    you alone are God.

Psalm 91:1–2, 14–15b, 15c–16

You who dwell in the shelter of the Most High,
    who abide in the shadow of the Almighty,
Say to the LORD, "My refuge and my fortress,
    my God, in whom I trust."

Because he clings to me, I will deliver him;
    I will set him on high because he acknowledges my name.
He shall call upon me, and I will answer him;
    I will be with him in distress.

I will deliver him and glorify him;
    with length of days I will gratify him
    and will show him my salvation.

Psalm 95:1–2, 6–7, 8–9

Come, let us sing joyfully to the LORD;
    let us acclaim the Rock of our salvation.
Let us come into his presence with thanksgiving:
    let us joyfully sing psalms to him.

Come, let us bow down in worship;
    let us kneel before the LORD who made us.
For he is our God,
    and we are the people he shepherds, the flock he guides.

Oh, that today you would hear his voice:
    "Harden not your hearts as at Meribah,
    as in the day of Massah in the desert.
Where your fathers tempted me;
    they tested me though they had seen my works."

Psalm 98:1, 2–3ab, 3cd–4,

Sing to the LORD a new song,
    for he has done wondrous deeds;
His right hand has won victory for him,
    his holy arm.

The LORD has made his salvation known:
    in the sight of the nations he has revealed his justice.
He has remembered his kindness and his faithfulness
    toward the house of Israel.

All the ends of the earth have seen
    the salvation by our God.
Sing joyfully to the LORD, all you lands;
    break into song; sing praise.

Psalm 100:2, 3, 4, 5

Sing joyfully to the LORD, all you lands;
 serve the LORD with gladness;
 come before him with joyful song.

Know that the LORD is God;
 he made us, his we are;
 his people, the flock he tends.

Enter his gates with thanksgiving,
 his courts with praise;
Give thanks to him; bless his name.

The LORD is good,
 whose kindness endures forever,
 and his faithfulness, to all generations.

Psalm 103:1–2, 3–4, 9–10, 11–12

Bless the LORD, O my soul;
    and all my being, bless his holy name.
Bless the LORD, O my soul,
    and forget not all his benefits.

He pardons all your iniquities,
    he heals all your ills.
He redeems your life from destruction,
    he crowns you with kindness and compassion.

He will not always chide,
    nor does he keep his wrath forever.
Not according to our sins does he deal with us,
    nor does he requite us according to our crimes.

For as the heavens are high above the earth,
    so surpassing is his kindness toward those who fear him.
As far as the east is from the west,
    so far has he put our transgressions from us.

Psalm 104:1–2a, 5–6, 10 and 12, 24 and 35c

Bless the LORD, O my soul!
  O LORD, my God, you are great indeed!
You are clothed with majesty and glory,
    robed in light as with a cloak.

You fixed the earth upon its foundation,
    not to be moved forever;
With the ocean, as with a garment, you covered it;
    above the mountain the waters stood.

You send forth springs into the watercourses
    that wind among the mountains.
Beside them the birds of heaven dwell;
    from among the branches they send forth their song.

How manifold are your works, O LORD!
    In wisdom you have wrought them all—
    the earth is full of your creatures;
Bless the LORD, O my soul! Alleluia.

Please omit "Alleluia" during Lent.

Psalm 107:2–3, 4–5, 6–7, 8–9

Let the redeemed of the LORD say,
    those whom he has redeemed from the hand of the foe
And gathered from the lands,
    from the east and the west, from the north and the south.

They went astray in the desert wilderness;
    the way to an inhabited city they did not find.
Hungry and thirsty,
    their life was wasting away within them.

They cried to the LORD their distress;
    from their straits he rescued them.
And he led them by a direct way
    to reach an inhabited city.

Let them give thanks to the LORD for his mercy
    and his wondrous deeds to the children of men,
Because he satisfied the longing soul
    and filled the hungry soul with good things.

Psalm 116:12–13, 17–18

How shall I make a return to the LORD
    for all the good he has done for me?
The cup of salvation I will take up,
    and I will call upon the name of the LORD.

To you will I offer sacrifice of thanksgiving,
    and I will call upon the name of the LORD.
My vows to the LORD I will pay
    in the presence of all his people.

Psalm 117:1bc, 2

Praise the LORD, all you nations;
    glorify him, all you peoples!

For steadfast is his kindness toward us,
    and the fidelity of the LORD endures forever.

Psalm 118:1–2 and 4, 22–24

Give thanks to the LORD, for he is good,
    for his mercy endures forever.
Let the house of Israel say,
    "His mercy endures forever."
Let those who fear the LORD say,
    "His mercy endures forever."

The stone which the builders rejected
    has become the cornerstone.
By the LORD has this been done;
    it is wonderful in our eyes.
This is the day the LORD has made;
    let us be glad and rejoice in it.

Psalm 121:1bc–2, 3–4, 5–6, 7–8

I lift up my eyes toward the mountains;
    whence shall help come to me?
My help is from the LORD,
    who made heaven and earth.

May he not suffer your foot to slip;
    may he slumber not who guards you:
Indeed he neither slumbers nor sleeps,
    the guardian of Israel.

The Lord is your guardian; the LORD is your shade;
    he is beside you at your right hand.
The sun shall not harm you by day,
    nor the moon by night.

The LORD will guard you from all evil;
    he will guard your life.
The LORD will guard your coming and your going,
    both now and forever.

Psalm 122:1–2, 3–4ab, 4cd–5

I rejoiced because they said to me,
    "We will go up to the house of the LORD."
And now we have set foot
    within your gates, O Jerusalem.

Jerusalem, built as a city
    with compact unity.
To it the tribes go up,
    the tribes of the LORD.

According to the decree for Israel,
    to give thanks to the name of the LORD.
In it are set up judgment seats,
    seats for the house of David.

Psalm 130:1–2, 3–4, 5–7a, 7bc

Out of the depths I cry to you, O LORD;
    LORD, hear my voice!
Let your ears be attentive
    to my voice in supplication.

If you, O LORD, mark our iniquities,
    LORD, who can stand?
But with you is forgiveness,
    that you may be revered.

I trust in the LORD;
    my soul trusts in his word.
My soul waits for the LORD
    more than sentiments wait for the dawn.
Let Israel wait for the LORD.

For with the LORD is kindness,
    and with him is plenteous redemption.

Psalm 139:7–8, 9–10, 11–12ab

Where can I go from your spirit?
> From your presence where can I flee?
If I go to the heavens, you are there;
> if I sink to the nether world, you are present there.

If I take the wings of the dawn,
> if I settle at the farthest limits of the sea,
Even there your hand shall guide me,
> and your right hand hold me fast.

If I say, "Surely the darkness shall hide me,
> and the night shall be my light"—
For you darkness itself is not dark,
> and night shines as the day.

Psalm 141:1–2, 3 and 8

O LORD, to you I call; hasten to me;
> hearken to my voice when I call upon you.
Let my prayer come like incense before you;
> the lifting up of my hands, like the evening sacrifice.

O LORD, set a watch before my mouth,
> a guard at the door of my lips.
For toward you, O God, my LORD, my eyes are turned;
> in you I take refuge; strip me not of life.

Psalm 144:1b, 2, 9–10

Blessed be the LORD, my rock,
  who trains my hands for battle, my fingers for war.

My refuge and my fortress,
  my stronghold, my deliverer,
My shield, in whom I trust,
  who subdues my people under me.

O God, I will sing a new song to you;
  with a ten-stringed lyre I will chant your praise,
You who give victory to the kings,
  and deliver David, your servant, from the evil sword.

Psalm 145:2–3, 4–5, 10–11

Every day will I bless you,
  and I will praise your name forever and ever.
Great is the LORD and highly to be praised;
  his greatness is unsearchable.

Generation after generation praises your works
  and proclaims your might.
They speak of the splendor of your glorious majesty
  and tell of your wondrous works.

Let all your works give you thanks, O LORD,
  and let your faithful ones bless you.
Let them discourse of the glory of your Kingdom
  and speak of your might.

Psalm 146:1b–2, 6c–7, 8–9a, 9bc–10

Praise the LORD, O my soul;
  I will praise the Lord all my life;
  I will sing praise to my God while I live.

The LORD keeps faith forever,
  secures justice for the oppressed,
  gives food to the hungry.
The LORD sets captives free.

The LORD gives sight to the blind.
The LORD raises up those who are bowed down;
  the LORD loves the just.
The LORD protects strangers.

The fatherless and the widow he sustains,
  but the way of the wicked he thwarts
The LORD shall reign forever,
  your God, O Zion, through all generations! Alleluia.

Please omit "Alleluia" during Lent.

Psalm 150:1b–2, 3–4, 5–6

Praise the Lord in his sanctuary,
    praise him in the firmament of his strength.
Praise him for his mighty deeds,
    praise him for his sovereign majesty.

Praise him with the blast of the trumpet,
    praise him with lyre and harp,
Praise him with timbrel and dance,
    praise him with strings and pipes.

Praise him with sounding cymbals,
    praise him with clanging cymbals.
Let everything that has breath
    praise the Lord! Alleluia!

Please omit "Alleluia" during Lent.